Muscular Learning

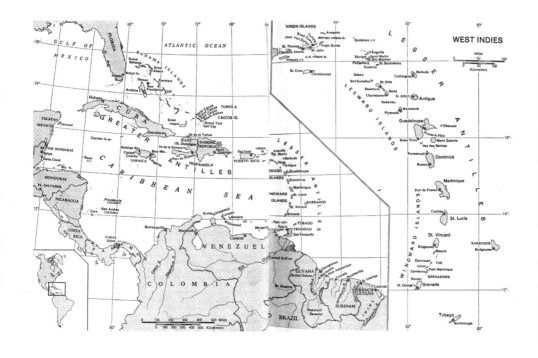

WEST INDIES

Muscular Learning

Cricket and Education in the Making
of the British West Indies at the End
of the 19th Century

Clem Seecharan

For David —
a bit of ourselves —
Love, Clem
8/06/06

Ian Randle Publishers
Kingston • Miami

First published in Jamaica, 2006 by
Ian Randle Publishers
11 Cunningham Avenue
Box 686
Kingston 6
www.ianrandlepublishers.com

National Library of Jamaica Cataloguing in Publication Data

Seecharan, Clem
    Muscular learning : cricket and education in the making of the British
West Indies at the end of the 19th century / Clem Seecharan

    p. ;   cm.

    Bibliography : p.   .- Includes index

    ISBN 976-637-230-6 (pbk)

    1.   Cricket - West Indies - History - 19th century 2. Education - West
Indies, British   3.   Slaves - Social conditions
    I.   Title

796.358   dc 21

Cover: J. 'Float' Woods (standing) and Archie Cumberbatch: the Barbados-
born Trinidadian fast bowlers who conquered Lord Hawke's team in 1897.
Woods toured England in 1900.

Cover and book design by Allison Brown

Printed in the USA

To

Donald Wood (1923–2002)

for his friendship, integrity and pioneering scholarship

Contents

LIST OF ILLUSTRATIONS   ix

ACKNOWLEDGEMENTS   xi

ABBREVIATIONS   xiii

CHAPTER ONE   1

Slave Society and Cricket: A Preliminary Exploration

CHAPTER TWO   20

The Elite Schools and British Imperialism: Cricket,
Christianity and the Classics, the 1860s–90s,
with Special Reference to Barbados

CHAPTER THREE   47

The Making of a West Indian Intelligentsia: The Culture of
Protest in the 1890s

CHAPTER FOUR   95

The First English Cricketers in the West Indies and the Advent
of Black Players: Slade Lucas's Tour, 1895

CHAPTER FIVE   124

Lord Hawke's (and Priestley's) Tours of the West Indies, 1897:
The Political Context

CHAPTER SIX   177

'Going Home': The First West Indies Tour of England, 1900 —
An Intellectual History

CHAPTER SEVEN   **230**
The Shaping of West Indies Cricket: The Pitfalls and Challenge
of Insularity, the Jamaican Case, 1900

CHAPTER EIGHT   **264**
A Temperament for Gradualism in the British West Indies:
The Intellectual and the Cricketer

APPENDIX   **285**
The West Indian Cricket Team.
Full Report of their First Tour in England, June-August, 1900

NOTES   **337**
BIBLIOGRAPHY   **353**
INDEX   **361**

Illustrations

Bahamas-born, Dr Robert Love (1839–1914), radical
intellectual/politician in Jamaica from the 1890s — 53

Joseph Ruhomon (1873–1942): the first Indian intellectual in
the West Indies — 77

Prince Ranjitsinhji (Ranji) (1872–1933): the beacon of
Indo-West Indies cricket; he represented Cambridge University,
Sussex and England — 90

The Barbados team and Lord Hawke's team in 1897 — 125

The British Guiana team and Lord Hawke's team in 1897 — 136

Sir Pelham Warner (Plum) (1873–1963): champion of black
cricketers; Trinidad-born captain of England — 148

The first West Indies team in England, 1900. The team had five
black players: from left to right (standing): W.J. (Tom) Burton
(black), C.A. Ollivierre (black), Hon Aucher Warner, W.H. Mignon,
G.C. Learmond, P.I. Cox, M.W. Kerr, P.A. Goodman; (sitting):
'Float' Woods (black), Fitz Hinds (black) [dubiously identified?];
S.W. Sproston, G.L. Livingston, Lebrun Constantine (black) — 178

C.A. Ollivierre (1876–1949): the first black West Indian to play
county cricket (Derbyshire, 1901–07); toured England in 1900 — 203

Lebrun Constantine (1874–1942): father of the great Learie;
first black first-class cricketer; toured England in 1900 and 1906 — 210

Sir Frank Worrell (1924–67), first black captain of the West Indies
team and Lord Constantine (Learie) (1901–71) in London, 1963 — 227

C.L.R. James (1901–89), the author of *Beyond a Boundary*
(1963): the bible of muscular learning

Acknowledgements

Most of the research was done at the British Library (Newspaper Library), Colindale, the University of the West Indies Library (St. Augustine, Trinidad), the National Archives (Georgetown, Guyana) and the MCC Library (Lord's). I am grateful to the staff of these institutions for their help, especially Cecil Eversley of the Archives in Guyana and Stephen Green, former curator of the MCC Library and Museum. I suppose this study has its roots in the mastery of the great West Indies team of the early 1960s, under Sir Frank Worrell; the magic of my village hero, Bumbry (born 1925), a cricketer with abundant natural gifts that remained untamed; the thwarted genius of my classmate, Errol 'Lul' Bahadur, a batsman of ferocious driving-power, a friend and contemporary of Alvin Kallicharran; and my discovery, around 1965, of C.L.R. James's masterpiece, *Beyond a Boundary*, and Jawaharlal Nehru's *The Discovery of India*. But it is also inspired by the pioneering scholarship in West Indies cricket of Professors Hilary Beckles, Frank Birbalsingh, Keith Sandiford and Brian Stoddart, as well as the perspicacious reflections and elegant writings — over many decades — of Ian McDonald on just about everything.

I am also indebted to several students in my cricket course, 'Cricket and the British West Indies, 1865–1968', for making me rethink, particularly David Blundell, Franklyn Jacobs and Phyllis Knight. Many friends, members of our 'Oval Boys Group', sustain the obsession: Kevin Fitzgerald, Mike Koupland, Tim Marr, Jonathan Moore, Bob Morgan, Royston Seecharran, Sunil Seecharran, John Sparrowhawk, Graham Taylor-Russell and Andrew Wright; so do John Hardial, Denis Judd and Roland Quinault. I am eternally grateful to Mike Koupland whose magnanimity and support over the last 12 years have made my job as a teacher substantially less onerous. The Chancellor of my university, Brian Roper, though not a devotee of the game, has been an avid supporter of my cricket projects; he, too, has fostered the obsession. I am energized by the imperishable belief in me of Andrew Bishop, Mazrul Bacchus, Kassem Baksh, Bridget Brereton, Jack and Esna Balder, Jagdise Chandradatt (Django), David Dabydeen, Gad Heuman, Farook Jahoor, Kampta Karran, Manohar Kaywal (Duck), Brij Lal, Barry Newton, Deodatt Persaud, Yisu Persaud, Sonny Ramphal, Brinsley Samaroo, Yojraj Sarran (Kishan), Roy Sawh, Camille Seecharran, Edward Sohan (Smally), Sheila Sohan (Saba), Mary Turner and Sophie Vaughan, to whom 'Aja is powerful'.

My colleagues, Rita Christian and Jean Stubbs, have helped to create a research environment at the Caribbean Studies Centre that challenges and energizes me continually for the hard labour of writing. Two Canadian friends, Henry Gulabh and John Smoliniec, have endured my monologues on cricket for many years, yet the friendship is inviolable. To Chris, my deepest gratitude for absolving me of most domestic responsibilities so that I can watch cricket all year, often 'ball by ball'. For the evocative pictures I am indebted to Steve Blunt, the photographer at my university. I am grateful to Mr Vijay Kumar, cricket writer of New York, for providing me with a copy of the rare document which forms the appendix. Finally, my thanks to Ian Randle for publishing this book, and Kim Hoo Fatt for her fine work in preparing it for publication.

Clem Seecharan
Professor of Caribbean History
London Metropolitan University

Abbreviations

BCC   Barbados Cricket Committee

BCCA Barbados Challenge Cricket Association

GCC   Georgetown Cricket Club [British Guiana]

MCC   Marylebone Cricket Club [Lord's]

QPCC Queen's Park Cricket Club [Trinidad]

QRC   Queen's Royal College [Trinidad]

Chapter One

Slave Society and Cricket:
A Preliminary Exploration

'What do they know of cricket who only cricket know?' This is the fundamental question posed by C.L.R. James (1901–89) in *Beyond a Boundary*, his classic book of 1963. Shaped by the ethos of imperial Britain propounded in the premier elite school in Trinidad, Queen's Royal College, and proud to proclaim that he was a British intellectual before the age of ten, James argues that the British West Indies were unlike any colonial society in the far-flung British Empire — virtually everybody was of immigrant stock. No ancient indigenous cultures, with their resilient internal reverences, stood in the way of British imperial hegemony and its declared civilizing mission. The diversity of cultures among enslaved Africans, the dominance of the slaveholders with their enormous power to define, the termination of the slave trade in 1807 and the attenuation of links with Africa, and the proselytizing passion of the non-conformist missionaries from the early nineteenth century, rendered African cultures increasingly peripheral to slave societies. It does not mean that many aspects of the African legacy did not influence the creolization of Africans and others in the West Indies; these, however, were anathema to imperial definitions: constructions of Englishness as the medium of civilization. Moreover, the subject peoples (coloureds [mixed race] and blacks), even before the end of slavery in the 1830s, had already begun to internalize the notion that English culture and learning were indispensable instruments of freedom and mobility within British colonial society.

Another peculiarity of the British West Indies was the size and growing significance of the 'coloured' or mixed race group, and the assessment by the white ruling minority that their own numerical inferiority required that this group be designated as discrete and recognized as distinct from the black majority. In fact, unlike the southern United States with white security rooted in numerical preponderance, the coloured group was constructed as a 'buffer' and deemed central to the preservation of white supremacy in the West Indies. Therefore, coloureds had to be tutored to internalize this notion of difference from the black majority, to believe in their intrinsic superiority over Africans.[1] They also had to absorb the concept of comparative lightness, in a delicately constructed scheme of hierarchy — status conferred on the basis of incremental propinquity to whiteness. Lightness of skin was at the core of claims to attributes of civilization in the West Indies. However, once these concessions to gradations of lightness were made on the slippery road of racial differentiation, it was virtually impossible to hold back the potential incremental claims of right to recognition of those progressively darker in complexion. The light coloureds alone could not fill all the junior positions in the civil service, teaching and other professions in civil society, after slavery. The colour line could not be definitive — immutable. Access to colonial space would soon be contested even by the very dark, after Emancipation. Elsa Goveia locates the origin of this process in the British Leeward Islands with reference to the coloureds of St. Kitts:

> When the free coloured protested, in the 1820s, against the practice by which even the white foreigner seeking his fortune in the islands was 'at once clothed with a political superiority over the majority of free inhabitants', and when they demanded 'the correction of this incongruity — which would carry the distinction of caste to such an extent as to declare moral rectitude, and intelligence, the peculiar attributes of one ... order of men', they were attacking the idea of racial inferiority, and proposing a basic change of principle in the political system. By their success in achieving legal and political equality with the whites, they introduced the principle of equality, without regard to race, into the laws of the islands, and claimed their share of the political power which had previously been denied them. Part of the elaborate structure of racial subordination was destroyed, and a fundamental change took place in the legal and political status of free men of colour. As a result, the slaves on their emancipation were able to claim legal equality with all other free men in the population of the islands.... After emancipation the rise of a substantial coloured middle class, possessing political rights, made it necessary for the whites to modify their belief in the inherent racial inferiority of Negroes.[2]

Indeed, the germ of mobility had already been planted on the plantations in slave society. Enslaved black artisans, skilled tradesmen, sugar boilers, blacksmiths, coopers, masons, 'drivers' or field supervisors were given specific rewards and comparatively elevated status, commensurate with their superior skills. Despite the physical and psychological oppression, the dehumanization implicit in slavery, some black or African people had already internalized conceptions of mobility, the notion that one could be trained or 'educated' out of the lowest rungs of the system — that was what mastery of a craft represented in this sugar plantation universe demanding myriad skills. It was a ghastly world, but it was not static. Separating coloureds from blacks, giving some light coloured men and women privileges, the means to rise, spoke to blacks of their own capacity for mobility. Even before the end of slavery, a few free blacks, too, were already well on the road to social elevation and recognition. Like the coloureds, they were projecting themselves in terms of an English frame of reference, distancing themselves from their African antecedents, the resilient badge of inferiority and bondage. This elaboration of indices of civilization was predicated on the assumption of the moral superiority of an overarching English culture. Among these were Christianity, western education and dress, and even before the end of slavery, the game of cricket. But, in the West Indies, an African element was ever present, conducing to the subversion and enrichment of the received hegemonic British culture. It was at no time mere mimicry: never simply a case of black folks being the supine recipient of that which fell from their master's table.

The role of play in the shaping of African peoples in slave societies has eluded exploration in the historiography of the Caribbean. But it is irrefutable that music and dance, so central to African cultures, transcended ethnicity among the enslaved and accelerated the making of a genuine African. Therefore, this activity, like other forms of play, was necessarily dichotomous: infused with the potential for containment, as the plantocracy saw it, as well as subversion, from the standpoint of the enslaved. That explains the ambivalence of the plantocracy towards the use of the slaves' free time in their own space, the slave quarter: the 'nigger' yard. The expression, 'yard', because it was suggestive of communal space that bred solidarity, has survived in the region as a testimony to an ongoing sense of community among the persistently poor. Time that was not supervised, that did not fall within the controlling regime of work — when the iron control was temporarily lifted — engendered fear among the white minority because it kept alive the unquenchable thirst for freedom: the spirit of the yard was potentially subversive. For the enslaved, however, such unsupervised time, however ephemeral, because it constituted reclamation of their time, was highly prized. They appropriated it with a passion, whether to work their provision grounds or to play: to sing, make music and dance — allowing the body to talk. Gordon Rohlehr's analysis of the planters' perception of dance is instructive for the extent to which it demonstrates African people's consciousness of the power of play as an instrument of resistance:

> In the Antilles, as in Africa, song and dance are closely related expressions.... Dances among the enslaved generally took place on Saturdays and Sundays when, in spite of laws which stipulated a 9.00 p.m. ending, they frequently entended long into the night.... Slave dances were viewed by the planters with a mixture of suspicion and tolerance. On the one hand, they provided gatherings of black people with private space and the power of assembly, and had been known to lead to rebellious uprisings throughout the Antilles. On the other hand, they provided therapy for the enslaved, trapped in the tedious ménage of plantation labour.... The connection between song and dance assemblies and rebellion, was early acknowledged in the French Antilles, and in Martinique, in 1654, an Ordinance was passed prohibiting such assemblies. Regulations against dance assemblies were codified in the Code Noir of 1685 and updated in 1758 and 1772. Before 1700 both the British and the French had prohibited the use of certain instruments such as drums and horn-trumpets, whose playing they viewed as an incitement to rebellion. Such rebellions did occur from time to time, and slave masters who neglected to search their slaves' quarters every week for drums, horns and other loud instruments were punishable according to a 1688 law. Among major insurrections believed to have been plotted at dance assemblies were the 1739 South Carolina rebellion and the Easter Sunday uprising in Barbados.[3]

Any play, cricket included, was both potentially containing and subversive. This game was being played by the planters, the mercantile group, colonial administrators, Anglican clergymen, and visiting military personnel as early as the eighteenth century. Even in Demerara, which was under Dutch rule until 1796, the fact that English colonists had been allowed to migrate from Barbados since the early 1770s facilitated the propagation of cricket in that colony: '[A] letter dated 1778, from a local employer of the Dutch West India Company, to one of the company's directors in Holland ... [spoke] of the social life in Demerarie [sic] and the advent of some English settlers who "play a game with a small ball and sticks".... [I]n the early 1770s a few English planters had acted upon the invitation of a previous Dutch Commander, Laurens Storm Van Gravesande, and had migrated from Barbados and the Leeward Islands to seek their fortunes.... [W]e must thank "Little England" [Barbados] for sowing the seeds of cricket enthusiasm and glory among our ranks'.[4]

So the game was probably being played in the British colonies earlier, by the mid-eighteenth century at least. Cricket in the British West Indies was reserved for the white elite and became an epitome of Englishness early, encapsulating all the virtues of that perceived high civilization. But these were societies in which the enslaved African was the sole manual worker: he, therefore, was required to play a crucial role in the preparation of the cricket pitch, the weeding or scything of the ground, retrieving the ball from the ubiquitous cane-field, and performing a range of chores connected with the entertainment of guests — the abundant hospitality for which West Indian planters were legendary. The slave was certainly not centre-stage, but he could, even from beyond the boundary, make a seminal claim on the game as an instrument for asserting his humanity, showing off his embryonic skills and panache in the marginal spaces accessible to him.

This was possible because cricket grounds tended, as in Barbados and the Leeward Islands where land was scarce, to be located in clearings in the canefields. The ball would disappear constantly in the thick undergrowth; it was the recurring task of the slave to retrieve it. To return the ball from beyond the boundary, accurately to the wicket, was a self-imposed challenge. Many of the slaves were robust men with splendid physique, long-limbed, with the ability to throw the ball astounding distances. The simple motion of demonstrating this gift contained a more deep-seated, if submerged, aspiration — releasing the body, symbolically, from the thraldom of bondage and dispossession of self. That was why drumming, dancing and stick-fighting were so important among the enslaved; for, as Maureen Warner-Lewis observes: 'aggressive danced sports diffused across the Atlantic [under slavery] from various locations in Africa'.[5] Every act of uninhibited movement, muscular liberation through play, was tantamount to a small step in releasing mind and body from their fetters. Cricket, the dominant imperial game, was necessarily a site for this therapeutic imagining of freedom. The free coloureds and free blacks were playing the game very early, by the mid-eighteenth century; but there are accounts of planters encouraging slaves, too, to play cricket. As noted above, the game encapsulated Englishness, qualities of refinement, virtues of 'home'; but it could also serve as an instrument of self-assertion.[6] The hurling of the ball a long way, from canepiece to playing area, was an act of freedom: it represented a fleeting presence in the central scene. It was a symbolic, portentous projection of self-generated energy from the canefield, the sphere of bondage, unto the cricket field, an area of freedom. The black slave, though excluded, was never far away from the area of play of whites: centre stage. In this tentative conception of autonomy may be located the germ of the game as an instrument of liberation for black and coloured West Indians. It would become indispensable to claims of belonging for all West Indians, including (East) Indians and Madeiran Portuguese in Guyana (Demerara or British Guiana) and Trinidad.

Michael Manley explains why cricket and fast bowling (education, too) would prove so alluring to young enslaved Africans on the sugar plantations — the genesis of the passion for many generations of black West Indians:

> The inhabitants of the English-speaking islands in the West Indies play cricket because the English brought the game with them.... By the nineteenth century the sugar grown by the black slaves and shipped by the white planters had made profits which, in turn, had contributed substantially to the financing of the emergence and expansion of modern capitalism in England. And as the wealth was moving from the colony to the centre of the Empire, so was cricket moving from the centre of the Empire to the colony.... [The British] built the biggest empire because they had the best navy and the earliest start in the Industrial Revolution. But they lost it

with the least bloodshed because they did more than exploit.... For every buccaneer like Henry Morgan, for every slave-owning plantocrat, there was an earnest missionary or an idealistic pedagogue who revelled in the role of apostle of British values such as Christianity, law or parliamentary democracy; or British culture in the form of Shakespeare, the romantic poets and cricket.[7]

Manley sketches the peculiar context of the emergence of cricket in the British West Indies — as an instrument of resistance for black people, a 'lash' in reverse:

The sight of a great fast bowler gathering speed, attaining his maximum and then arching his back to provide the body whip from which the arm extends like a lash and all ending with a ball that may be travelling at more than 90mph is a sight that can bring terror to the heart of a batsman and levels of appreciative participation which border on the primitive in the case of the spectator.... In the tropics where the temperature in the shade will not often fall below 90°F in the course of the average day, batting is a less arduous pursuit than bowling. In due course, the young sons of the slaves were required to bowl at the young sons of the slave-owners, or to the army officers doing garrison duty, to provide batting practice. Of course, the sons of the slaves practised batting in their spare time. And so in due course, the Caribbean populations learned cricket as an integral part of the cultural practices which they absorbed as each generation grew to manhood.[8]

As in the canefield, a virtual ethnic division of labour was reproduced on the cricket field. It is not possible to ascertain precisely when slaves first bowled at white batsmen, their masters and their sons, or itinerant military personnel. However, the fact that they played informally on the plantations, with crude implements, with evident passion, must have endowed some of them with appreciable cricketing skills. Moreover, because bowling in the tropical heat was not accorded the same halo as batting, the slave who was identified as a competent bowler was assigned to provide the white batsman, 'massa', practice at the nets. Now, the slave had definitely moved within the boundary. This was necessarily a profoundly loaded act — the enslaved black man delivering the ball at menacing pace, impelled to bowl his owner out, unimpeded by the pervasive hegemonic codes of control. He was demonstrating his acquired skill thus underlining his humanity by mastery of a difficult craft — he was not a thing, as the system defined him.

By propelling a cricket ball at his owner or his owner's son, he was symbolically contesting their unbridled power over his person: *their property*. Bowling it at ferocious pace encapsulated the idea of an embryonic countervailing power: a potentially subversive action. This act fed a consuming challenge to the black cricketer, animating his universe of bondage and driving him to mastery of the craft. It also brought material rewards and, possibly, a lightening of routine tasks. In this context, therefore, cricket could not be just a game: it was definitely an instrument of mobility, if not liberation. Blacks, coloureds and whites (Madeiran Portuguese and Indians later) would use bat and ball to shape their own narratives, making their own identities within the Empire. Symbols are intrinsic to the contestation of power and the construction of identities. Cricket was a potent symbol, the site for African imaginings of liberty and the recovery of self. The fact that it was at the core of the imperial mission rendered the game an effective vehicle to carry African yearnings for freedom, and the undermining of imperial hegemony with its ordained hierarchies.

Richard D.E. Burton observes that the notorious Jamaican slaveholder, Thomas Thistlewood, recorded the following terse, casual reference to cricket in his diary entry of June 11, 1778: 'In the evening Mr. Beckford and Mr. John Lewis, etc, played at cricket'. This prompts Burton to ponder: 'Were the slaves watching? And if they were, did they think that here there was something of Buckra's that they could take over and not so much mimic as invest with their own meaning and style?'[9] It is inconceivable that they would not have been involved in retrieving the ball, hurling it back, that they were not already playing cricket on the plantations with crude implements. Burton cites a remarkable corroboration of this, from the 1780s:

> The discovery on the banks of the River Tweed [in Scotland, by Clive Williams] in the 1980s of a belt buckle depicting a black man wearing a slave collar batting in what is clearly a West Indian setting (probably Barbadian) suggests that some slaves did play cricket as early as the 1780s.... That the slave in question seems to

be connected with the Royal Navy is particularly significant given 'the mutual confidence and familiarity' that were said to obtain between slaves and sailors: 'In the presence of a sailor the Negro feels as a man.'[10]

The apparent ease of communication between slaves and naval officers or sailors is not hard to comprehend. The presence of the latter was a constant in British West Indian life, as was their playing cricket with the planters and colonial officials. They were white figures of authority with whom the slaves came into contact as they prepared the pitch, retrieved the ball or later bowled to in practice sessions. But the fact that they were peripatetic, ever on the move, meant that they could accommodate a degree of banter, a longer threshold of familiarity, with slaves. That the belt buckle depicts the slave, unmistakably in bondage, with bat in hand, suggests that the creator of the scene on the buckle must have detected in their cricketing endeavours the germ of the quest for self-expression, if not liberation. Moreover, the slave's possession of a bat, not a ball — a batsman not a bowler — the task that usually propelled him temporarily within the boundary, adumbrates a subversive intent on the part of the shackled African: it speaks of going against the grain. However, there is a suggestion of the novice, of fallibility, in the depiction of the slave's batsmanship: essaying what looks like a leg-glance, he is clean bowled.

It is noteworthy that the batsman 'looks like a well-fed, well-muscled mulatto, probably the offspring of a white overseer and a black slave mother. She was probably a cook [house-slave], which would account for his access to good rations and a better-than-average diet. He appears to be in his late teens. The ring of naval chain around his neck, and apparently bare feet, confirm his slave status'. If the assumption of the slave's ethnicity as 'coloured' or mixed race is correct, this would be totally in character, for it was this discrete, intermediate group — constructed as a distinct entity from blacks or Africans — that were invariably the first to achieve a degree of mobility on the slave plantations. That his mother was probably a cook, a house-slave, would also have aided his access to some recreation, even if he were still encumbered by his badge of bondage. And the fact that the scene, with its windmill and cabbage palm, is evocative of Barbados renders it most credible: it was on this island, under unbroken English occupation since 1627, that the game was probably first introduced in the region. It is very interesting, therefore, that the belt buckle from the bank of the Tweed has been traced to 'a noted naval family' from that area (upstream from where it was found) the Hothams, with links to eighteenth-century Barbados. Marcus Williams elaborates:

> [Their] prowess at cricket while at Westminster School is recorded by the family biographer in the same context as the game's famous 18th century patrons, the Sackvilles (Dukes of Dorset). [Anna-Maria Stirling writes]: 'the Hothams, both on account of their proficiency in the new pastime as well as their successes in after-life, were later described with dual meaning as being "among the *lucky hits* of Westminster".' The best known of the Hothams was Admiral Lord William, the first baron (1736–1813), and in 1779–80, then a Commodore, he was stationed off Barbados. Perhaps he organised cricket matches for his men — and there were many hundreds of marines as well as sailors in the fleet, and local slaves proficient at the game were included. Perhaps again it was Admiral Hotham's nephews, Henry or William, both of whom served in the area, that were involved in cricket in Barbados some years later.[11]

Westminster School and the Hothams: the public school and cricket, the foundation of the education of the English upper class, were transplanted to Barbados. More than any British colony, this 166 square-mile island absorbed that robust tradition, the study of the classics and the pursuit of cricket: muscular learning. This was not restricted to white Barbadians; it percolated to coloureds, then to the sons of slaves who had been artisans or 'drivers' (field foremen) or female cooks in the great house. As I argue later, the construction of a discrete coloured stratum and their selection for preferential treatment by the plantocracy bred invidious comparisons among blacks and it delayed their mobility, but it did not destroy ambition. It ignited a passion among some to follow the coloureds on the road away from the stigma of enslavement: education and cricket were key instruments for this task.

Richard D.E. Burton argues that stick-fighting and other games involving sticks were popular among slaves, and that under slavery and beyond, white masters were perennially apprehensive of sticks and rods in the hands of blacks. Perhaps Africans saw the stick as a potential rod of correction, an instrument for turning the tables:

meeting the slave master's whip with a rod of redemption. It is significant that Joshua's rod would be appropriated in African Caribbean iconography as an instrument of liberation. There is therefore merit in Burton's suggestion that the slaves and their descendants appropriated the cricket bat, also, as an instrument of redemption. With bat and ball, they could begin to reclaim their humanity, their passion to be free. Burton adds that the pedigree and panache of West Indian batsmanship may be traced to the Trinidadian *batonnier* (stick-fighter) and the honing of his skills through the art of 'breaking'. He quotes a contemporary source: 'It consisted in having one or two fellows stand 15 or 20 yards off and hurl stones at you in rapid succession, and it is your business — and, of course, to your interest — to "break" (i.e. parry with stick) these stones successfully. A very proficient "breaker" would often have three men hurling stones at him, and it was seldom, indeed, that he got hit.'[12] He is persuasive on the possible line of continuity between the dexterity and iron concentration of the *batonnier* and the aggressive, conquering modern West Indies batsmen, such as Sir Clyde Walcott, Sir Everton Weekes, Sir Garfield Sobers, Rohan Kanhai, Sir Viv Richards and Brian Lara:

> [W]ith stick-fighting virtually outlawed and driven underground, the ex-kalinda kings [stick-fighters] took over the archetypal game of their colonial master and his local white agents [cricket] (in much the same way that their forebears had taken over carnival and transformed it), injected it with specifically Afro-Creole meanings and values, and gradually turned the game against its inventors.... In this perspective, West Indian cricket becomes the ultimate oppositional practice in which Quashie (with a little help from Sammie [Indians]) takes on Massa at his own game and not only wins but in time establishes himself as the virtually unassailable champion of champions; not surprisingly, it is as a ritual of inversion that ... West Indian cricket has commonly been read.[13]

Maureen Warner-Lewis observes that the skills of the Trinidadian master *kalenda* kings were honed in the context of drum and rhythm, and that the sport carried deep undercurrents of warfare. The fact that stick-fighting was superseded by cricket lends support to Burton's argument that the imperial game was infused with the precision and iron reflex, rhythm and choreography, ferocity and magic of *kalenda*, its African-derived attributes. Warner-Lewis explains its derivation, and remarks that coaching young men the co-ordination of hands, feet and eyes was central to the craft. The transition from stick-fighting to cricket, therefore, is not a far-fetched assumption: '*Kalinda*, or *Kalenda*, is the traditional Trinidadian term for stick-fighting. The word perhaps derives from *lenda* ... to oppose, with *ka-*, a nominal diminutive prefix found in southern Koongo and Mbundu [Angola]. All the same, *ka* was a term for 'drum' because ... it was 'made out of a quarter-barrel or *qart*, pronounced [ka] in French creole. It was usual for Trinidad stick-fighters to call out "give me keg/ka", meaning that the drummers should play in such a way as to give them encouragement and verve'.[14]

She elaborates:

> [It] is clearly related to warfare, except it is more ritualised and involves the choreography of a sport. As aggression, however ... [one informant], recalling stick-fighting in the twentieth century, considered it a sport which was 'necessary to self-defence, and people of all classes regarded it as necessary to know'. *He ... affirm[ed] that boys used to learn it 'just as they learn cricket now'.* Young boys would gather 'in the evening about a teacher, all armed with *chipon* (or cocoa shoot) ... to reach from the ground to the navel. First, drums were beaten and foot works learned according to the beat. The teacher stands in the middle, the drums beat, teacher shouts: "boys, you going to breaks"; he dances and suddenly gives a blow in some unsuspected direction'....[Another informant] stipulated: 'You must have good eyesight, and watch your opponents' feet. You have to be stepping: you must move with the keg [drum]. The drummers must be neutral, but they control the fight by their tempo and beating.... The aim of each player is to deliver a blow that will hit the opponent on the body — any part above the waist — hard enough to fell him to the ground.'[15] (emphasis added)

On the other hand, because cricket was a quintessentially imperial idiom, its rules and codes sanctioned by the hegemonic culture, it was seen as a means of canalizing any potential for insurrection among the enslaved and their descendants. However, as with their music, dance and other forms of play, the subversive strand in the culture of the submerged, though constrained, was not neutralized: it percolated through the medium, reshaped it, and infused it with liberating properties. Hilary Beckles argues that people of African descent appropriated cricket early, as an instrument of resistance; in the process they extended its role and transformed its character, weaving the spontaneous flair and collective exuberance of their ritual tradition — their style: the rhythm and extroversion of the 'yard' — into their play:

> [Blacks] ... had been encouraged from the slavery period to use their 'free time' in full indulgence in the sort of cultural activity that did not in any way appear to whites as informed by a spirit of resistance. Any cultural expression that whites feared or considered rebellious was outlawed. By the end of slavery, then, a complex entertainment system was to be found within the plantation villages — an established tradition that was also characterised by the adoption and adaptation of European forms to their own material and ontological condition. The African-derived performance and celebratory social system absorbed the cricket missile — tamed and domesticated it as part of the culture complex. *With their propensity to collectivise cultural ritual and to blend comic, heroic and tragic drama within the single form, blacks brought spectator theatre and participatory festiveness to bear upon the idealisation of the physical and artistic elements of cricket.* Cricket, then, found a soft resting place within the residual African ontology.[16] (emphasis added)

It is arguable, therefore, that because the game was being grafted on to diverse African or African-derived forms of play, immanent with discrete modes of resistance to slavery, cricket, too, was necessarily infused with the seeds of resistance. But at a purely non-tendentious level of play, also, because of its esteem as a dominant cultural form among whites, it became an attractive medium for the articulation of creole African cultural effervescence, their vocal and physical exuberance. And its juxtaposition with the comparatively staid, less spontaneous play of whites, enlarged its rebellious properties. In the absence of protective gear, as I have written elsewhere, uninhibited style and daring play endowed a boyhood of privation with a heroic dimension. The growing technical competence, in conjunction with the passion, would impregnate the game with power way beyond the boundary, after freedom was won — an authentic instrument of resistance. From the early years, cricket in the West Indies was political. The exclusion of most blacks from politics until the end of the nineteenth century therefore enlarged its role as an instrument for the projection of racial identity and self-assertion.

For white men in the British West Indies, however, playing cricket was an assertion of unbroken identity with home, affirming what was seen, certainly by the 1780s, as a fount of Englishness. It demonstrated that they had not succumbed to the universe of the 'native' — the bush — that their 'northern energy' (Trollope) had not been undermined by the tropical lassitude of the negro; indeed, that they were still grounded in the civilized temper of home, with its energetic pursuit of order and control informed by moral superiority. Cricket enabled white West Indians to seek reassurance from those 'at home' that they had not been weaned from their inherent cultural ascendancy by the coarseness and chaos of the enervating, unrefined Tropics — that they were not contaminated by the barbarism of their slaves, suggestions of which their visiting compatriots were obsessively vigilant to detect, the lavish hospitality notwithstanding.[17]

Jack Williams argues that cricket in Victorian and Edwardian England was impregnated with notions of the cultivated essence of a pastoral Englishness, the sustainer of a moral superiority that validated their imperial mission. But even in West Indian slave societies, this elevated and elevating association fostered similar notions that enabled the plantocracy to create order out of tropical disorder, to domesticate its inherently savage otherness — an aspect of their perennial need to elude the lingering taint of being slaveholders. Cricket facilitated their imagining the tropical slave plantation in terms of the rural idyll that embodied the quintessence of Englishness: continuity, order and moral irreproachability. Cricket brought that order and its moral connotations to the crude plantation and helped to assuage the guilt of the slaveholder. Therefore, what Williams observes of the English at home needs no revision with reference to slave society in the British West Indies in the early nineteenth century:

> They saw cricket as an expression of their moral worth. Cricket was thought to have higher standards of sportsmanship than other sports. Cricket discourse emphasised that playing cricket encouraged moral qualities such as selflessness, putting the interest of the team before one's enjoyment, accepting the decisions of

umpires and captains without complaint, observing the spirit rather than the letter of its laws, all qualities that were seen as resonating with Christian ethics. The interest in cricket of so many clerics reinforced assumptions that the sportsmanship of cricket expressed Christian morality.... Assumptions about the supremely English nature of cricket and of the morality of cricket were linked with perceptions of cricket as essentially a sport of the English countryside.... Even today cricket is often presented as a sport played on a village green fringed with trees and the spire of the Anglican church and the village inn as indispensable features of the scene. Such adulation of cricket can be related to the English pastoral tradition, which idealised the rustic as the repository of traditional English moral values.[18]

Cricket became for many white men in the British West Indies a means of reasserting their Englishness. But in the context of slave society, it had deeper resonance, something therapeutic: it could help to temper the barbarism of the plantation; the smack of ball on bat was infinitely more pleasing, masking the crack of whip on black back and fostering nostalgic imaginings of pastoral Albion. In Barbados, in particular, one of the oldest colonies with a resident white population that saw themselves as belonging to that land, the landscape itself could be made to speak of home. It is interesting, therefore, that on the eve of Barbados's independence, in late 1966, the Jamaican novelist, John Hearne, could still imagine the island as a kind of rural England:

> It is ... the most un-West Indian of the islands, in appearance and in 'atmosphere'. Sugar cane or no sugar cane, when I as a Jamaican drive through the Barbadian countryside I cannot feel the sense of familiarity and similarity that I feel in, say, Grenada. It is a piece of England, much modified to be sure, and 'sunburnt' by the tropics, but still and stubbornly a corner of the English countryside. And we must never underestimate the significance of landscape in our lives and perceptions. Like the first stories of our childhood, it fashions us in a thousand secret ways.[19]

For subordinate groups, too, the power of the game to confer on all its practitioners a halo of Englishness was irresistible. Many of the free coloureds and free blacks could see in the game a means of asserting their own claims to civility, a kind of arrival: worthiness of being differentiated from the masses of enslaved black people. Cricket reinforced their assigned elevated status as the 'buffer'. But because cricket was endowed with civilizing impulses, it could carry the burdens and contradictions of diverse political agendas. Black men, in slavery, were already aware that the game was a potential instrument of liberation; that it had reverberations beyond the boundary; that it could carry the spirit of freedom that resided in them because it was congruent with the highest articulation of the supposed genius, rationality, circumspection and moderation of the ruling race: their gift for compromise and control of the emotions contrasting with the barbarism and primary instincts which supposedly ran copiously, uncanalized, in the lesser races. Cricket conferred on the black man the idea that he could, if given the chance, be as good, if not better, than the white and coloured man. If blacks had been totally excluded from cricket it could not have borne the burdens with which they were saddling it. It was because they were engaged with it from the beginning, on the slave plantations, that it quickly became a site for their struggle to give expression to their humanity and their yearning for freedom: from slavery, through Emancipation to Independence, for civil and political rights. As Hilary Beckles argues:

> In the promotion and legitimisation of cricket as an institution of high culture, and in its integration into the wider system of hegemonic oppression, the colonial elite also succeeded in establishing a cultural sphere within which the anti-systemic resistance of disenfranchised blacks could be assured ... the 'exclusive' activity of the elite was appropriated by subordinate social groups. The downward social mobility of cricket into the villages of blacks was guaranteed as long as the elite ascribed to it the normative values of respectability and honour, since the frantic search for betterment by this 'semi-free' population involved the attainment of these social goals.[20]

Education and cricket were at the core of their endeavours. It is hardly surprising, therefore, that the game would become central to the quest for a kind of British West Indian identity; it would also help to shape the rudiments of a national consciousness, across the racial divide, even in a place as ethnically diverse and uncompromising as

British Guiana (Guyana) or Demerara, as it was called in the nineteenth century. Cricket has been a serious business in the region, evoking prowess, passion and punctiliousness from players and crowd, as the white Guyanese novelist, Christopher Nicole, observed in his cricket book of 1957:

> Cricket is more the national game of the West Indian than it is even of the Englishman. No other sport or pastime has such a hold upon the mind of the average Barbadian, Trinidadian, Jamaican or Guianese, no matter what his age, religion, colour, race or social standing. On the cricket field these differences are merged, and a man stands or falls by his prowess. He is watched by a knowledgeable crowd, never quite as large as the biggest games in England or Australia, but one that knows its men and the finer points of the game.... This keenness sometimes carries enthusiasm beyond the bounds of propriety.... [H]owever, the West Indian spectator becomes so absorbed in the struggle going on on the field that he sometimes loses himself in it, and in this keenness, which is really a splendid thing, we must find our excuses for his exuberance.... [But] we would concentrate on the cricket, not missing a ball, and discuss the finer points with the gravity and learning of professors.[21]

Brian Moore considers cricket and education as vital components in the transmission of British culture in the British West Indies in the latter half of the nineteenth century. In the same way that muscular Christianity was conceived as an instrument to civilize colonials, muscular learning, with cricket at its core, was construed as central to the inculcation of British or English values in these societies where the reversion to 'barbarism' continually threatened — this was how the Morant Bay Rebellion in Jamaica, in 1865, was seen. Cricket, like education and Christianity, was, as Moore argues, crucial to the projection of 'cultural power' at the heart of the Imperial mission:

> [A]fter the codification/standardisation of its rules in the mid-nineteenth century, cricket was seen not just as a sport for amusement and recreation, but as an instrument of socialisation: to train disciplined young men in the virtues of honour, fair play and honesty, decorum and etiquette, loyalty to one's fellows (the team and the club), unquestioned obedience to authority (the

umpire [Empire] and the captain), and hardiness in the face of adversity.... [T]his sport was adopted in the English public schools and elite universities with great enthusiasm in order to provide the future leaders of the nation, and indeed the empire, with those social characteristics which middle class Victorian society held in great esteem. Indeed, cricket became the embodiment of what was good in English Victorian culture, a symbol of excellence. The British residents in the West Indian colonies fully absorbed those ideas, and transformed the cricket culture into a way of life.... Because cricket was endowed with significant social values, it was fully incorporated into the fabric of elite colonial culture designed to control the subordinate ethnic groups, and slowly emerged as one of the dominant elements, alongside education and religion (Christianity), in the cultural thrust to provide value consensus around the idea of the superiority of things British.[22]

But this was never an exercise in mere mimicry on the part of subordinate sections: they would use education and cricket to pursue their own nationalist agenda, however tentative or inchoate. They invested these instruments of mobility with their culture of resistance, with roots in slavery and indentureship. Even the quintessential Imperial game would be creolized, on and off the plantations, as non-white West Indians infused it with the peculiar temper of their cultures, in pursuing incremental political objectives. Moore concludes:

[I]n their adoption of this British culture form, the Creoles were ... determined to play it is a spirit quite different from the genteel manner in which the elites did. Like the working class professionals in Britain, the Creoles played hard with a view to winning rather than promoting camaraderie. Still, when viewed in conjunction with other borrowed aspects of Afro-Creole culture (e.g. Christianity, legal marriage, British education, etc.), it seems clear that the Creole adoption of cricket signified their acceptance of the superiority of things British as a means of attaining social respectability, although that did not preclude them from creolising it and transforming it into an important mechanism of resistance against white domination.... [E]ven though some cultural values of British imperialism were indeed inculcated while learning cricket, the Creoles never seemed to accept the idea of their inferiority on a level playing field. If anything sport, and cricket in particular, gave them the opportunity to excel at the white man's game, and to demonstrate that they were just as good, if not better than, their imperial 'masters'. Cricket, the imperial game *par excellence*, was thus transformed by the Creoles into a ritual of resistance, a medium through which they could express in unrestrained manner their continuous struggle for social equality and psychological liberation.[23]

Cricket was a political instrument in the British West Indies, from the latter days of slavery through Emancipation and Independence. It is entirely appropriate, therefore, that the belt buckle from the bank of the Tweed, 'the oldest known artefact relating to cricket outside of Britain', was depicted on a postage stamp in Barbados in 1988,[24] the sixtieth anniversary of West Indies test cricket.

Chapter Two

The Elite Schools and British Imperialism:
Cricket, Christianity and the Classics,
the 1860s–90s, with Special Reference to Barbados

Reflecting on the seminal influences on his colonial boyhood in Tunapuna, Trinidad, in the first decade of the twentieth century, C.L.R. James recalls: 'Our house was superbly situated, exactly behind the wicket.... By standing on a chair a small boy of six could watch practice every afternoon and matches on Saturdays.... From the chair also he could mount on to the window-sill and so stretch a groping hand for the books on the top of the wardrobe. Thus early the pattern of my life was set'.[1] This was less than 75 years since the abolition of slavery in the British West Indies, but the pattern was already deeply etched in the psyche of a small but increasingly confident African or black lower middle class, the true shapers of their people's destiny in colonies such as Jamaica, Barbados, Trinidad and British Guiana (Demerara). These were the pathfinders, the architects in the making of the British West Indies, one of the most intellectually remarkable products of the colonial encounter. In this process three key factors are discernible: the example set by the coloureds or mixed race people in the latter half of the nineteenth century; the permeation of Victorian values through the elite schools: the classics, Christianity and cricket; and the adoption of this ethos by some black artisans and a few bigger farmers, the base for the emergence of a black middle class by the 1890s.

Although British West Indian societies were deeply sensitive to nuances of race, colour and class, it would be wrong to assume that the consciousness of the coloureds as a distinct ethnic group was totally pernicious. Indeed, it facilitated the development of this group as a buffer between white and black; but in the process, it made a minority of blacks — pathfinders — recognize that the barriers to mobility were not immovable; that the incremental advances of coloureds, in education, including university education in Britain, and their social elevation through the professions of law and medicine, were attainable. The absence of a large white population in the West Indies had opened the way for the admission of a number of light coloureds to the colonial civil service, by the 1850s–60s. If these people had been categorized as 'black', if opportunities for a degree of mobility had been blocked for all non-whites, then notions of possibilities would have been vastly circumscribed and could not have taken root as quickly as they did among darker people. For, as in Africa, the assumption that the 'natives' were unfit for intellectual improvement — not readily responsive to upliftment from the savage state — would have rationalized the importing of British expatriates (birds of passage to do basic administrative work) well towards the end of Empire. But in the British West Indies, with a paucity of whites and the necessity for greater inclusiveness than in the United States, adumbrated in attitudes towards coloureds, valuable experience was already being gained by black people in the administration of civil society. In spite of the tardiness of constitutional change, progress in this sphere was admirable: in the lower echelons of the civil service, local government, journalism and the editing of small newspapers, the church (including black-led ones), the denominational schools, local government and myriad voluntary associations. The rudiments of self-government were being learnt.

It was the descendants of the skilled slaves, the artisans, who were among this ascendant minority in the West Indies — the owners of a few acres of land who had, by the 1860s, already demonstrated a measure of independence, as farmers, by escaping the plantation frame of reference. During the last years of slavery and in the aftermath of Emancipation, this small stratum of successful Africans took the example of the coloureds as a beacon. In Jamaica, for instance, the coloureds had gone into business and had also pioneered alternatives to sugar — bananas and coffee. In the Windward Islands, like Grenada and St. Vincent, too, coloureds had seized upon the demise of the plantocracy to create new agricultural niches. The small black middle class was therefore inspired to emulate their coloured compatriots. They found it difficult to get into urban businesses, but in the rural areas some of them were able to expand their landholdings and create a stable financial base to enable them to educate their sons. Many were able to send them to secondary schools, and by the 1870s a minority were able to gain admission to some of the excellent elite schools which had emerged in the British West Indies since the late seventeenth century: Combermere (1695), Harrison College (1733), Lodge (1745), in Barbados; Queen's College (1844) in British Guiana; Queen's Royal College (1859) and St. Mary's College (1863) in Trinidad; and Kingston College and Wolmer's Boys' School (1729) in Jamaica. There was a tradition of education to look up to.

Indeed, the success of the coloured middle class was established by the 1870s, and the fact that they were determined to distance themselves from their African antecedence tended to exacerbate the snobbish propensities of this elevated stratum. Edgar Mittelholzer (1909–65), the Guyanese novelist, a man from the coloured middle class whose family had deep roots in the colonial church and the civil service, has captured the deep-seated nature of light-coloured superciliousness in colonial Guyana. He is speaking of his boyhood, just after the First World War. This attitude was probably even more virulent in Victorian British West Indies:

> [T]he pure whites were ... a very small minority, and simply could not afford to show open discrimination or practise any unpleasant form of segregation. Indeed, sad to relate, it was my own class — people of coloured admixture but of fair or olive complexion — who dispensed any colour snobbery it was possible to dispense. It was my class which looked down upon the East Indian sugar plantation labourers ('coolies' we called them, whether they were labourers or eventually became doctors or barristers or civil servants). It was my class which considered the [Madeiran] Portuguese social inferiors because of their background of door-to-door peddling, rum-shops, salt-good shops and pawn-shops and their low standard of living. We, too, treated the Chinese sweet-sellers and shopkeepers with condescension because of their poor-immigrant status. We even looked with a certain distinct aloofness upon the young Englishmen who came out to serve as sugar plantation overseers [in fact, usually poor Highland Scots]. We deemed them 'white riff-raff'. *And as for Negroes, it goes without saying that they were serving people; that was an accepted tradition since dating from slavery days.*[2] (emphasis added)

But this arrogance and bedevilling preoccupation with hierarchy of shades did not stifle African initiative in areas they considered crucial to their welfare: religion, education and cricket. It is arguable that the motivation to challenge their putative coloured superiors was stronger at this phase in West Indian social history than their resistance to the British rulers, until the rise of nationalist aspirations from the 1930s. For the small black middle class, education and cricket became the site for the assertion of their rights. As the political terrain was still mined against blacks, these arenas in which coloureds had shown their competence galvanized Africans to contest them with an assiduity and passion that would later find expression in the political sphere. And their numerical advantage would eventually supersede the head-start gained by the coloured middle class through the British penchant to give incremental concessions to them. The Christian denominations and the denominational primary schools were the foundation of the mobility aspirations of black West Indians; but it was the flaunting of the supposed superiority of the light-coloured middle class, who wore that privilege of skin like a badge of aristocratic pretension, which provided the stimulus for the African or black middle class to achieve in the fields to which they accorded prominence.

With the introduction of compulsory education ordinances Africans were able to aspire to and challenge coloureds for an elevated place in colonial space. By the late 1860s and early 1870s they were already immersed in the primary education system, as schoolteachers and headmasters. It is noteworthy that many young black women, also, were able to secure places as primary school teachers. This tended to enhance the perception of education among all black people; it became central to their mobility aspirations. The interest in and commitment to education was sustained because of demonstrable social and economic benefits, as well as its link to the Christian church, the non-conformist Baptists, Congregationalists and Methodists; Anglicans and Roman Catholics, as well. Primary education was at the heart of the whole ideology of redemption and moral elevation in post-Emancipation British West Indies. It could never be seen just in secular terms. Proximity of church and church-school, and the English pastor's vigilance over his flock, gave to the process of elementary education, for boys and girls, associations with a religious calling. From the late nineteenth century many young women became schoolteachers through the pupil teachers' system. This tended to reinforce educational endeavours with something of a moral imperative in the black community. Brian Moore elaborates:

The principal avenue of advancement chosen by the Creoles [coloureds and Africans] was education. A tremendous premium was placed on it for socio-economic mobility. This was so from the moment they won their freedom, and many ex-slaves and their children attended schools and chapels set up by the missionaries to acquire literacy skills. Education was considered the passport to better jobs, higher income, an improved way of life, elevated social status and respectability. It enabled the Creoles to move out of unskilled low-paying agricultural work into skilled crafts and white-collar jobs. Many parents longed for the day when their sons might become proud messengers or clerks in lawyers' offices, or cash boys in dry-goods stores; even better if they could be admitted to junior positions in the colonial civil service. If they could accumulate the money, they tried to send their brightest sons to Britain to study for one of the 'liberal professions': law or medicine. *While this did bring about social mobility, it also signifies that the ex-slaves were locked into the colonial system and were prepared to play by its rules in order to advance within it rather than overthrow it — they sought equality within the existing order. It also demonstrates that they shared the same values as the white residents as to what conferred honour, status and respectability.*[3] (emphasis added)

It is noteworthy that at the end of the nineteenth century, in Kingston, Jamaica, there were several girls' schools which were rated highly: they gave to the 'young womanhood of the community quite as good an education as can be had in the best and most advanced schools in the mother country'. And on the occasion of the prize-giving day in 1900 of one such imaginative establishment, Miss Harris's School, the *Jamaica Daily Telegraph* expressed pride in its part in shaping 'generations of cultured, accomplished' women: 'We make special reference to this school because it is one of those private schools that have been in existence for upwards of half a century, and which, in unbroken continuity have imparted to the successive generations an education quickened by the progressive spirit of the passing years and in touch with the improved methods and exacting requirements of the most modern education system.' The paper was impressed with its innovative approach to the education of girls: 'In the excellent drama in which the pupils acquitted so well, there was a combination of singing, dancing, drill exercises, etc. This reminds us that physical training is now an important feature in the education of girls as well as boys. That is as it should be.'[4] It is true that this was an elite school, but as with the boys' schools, they were not racially exclusive and were characterized by a trickle of coloured and black middle-class girls from the early years. This would have planted among even very dark girls the idea of possibilities, which fed ambition.

This was what gave many black people (not only the middle class) confidence, early, in aspects of English culture: the Bible, the hymns, English literature, classical music and dance, public speaking and oratory, journalism, dress, table manners and other forms of social etiquette. These achievements are sometimes condescendingly deemed 'Afro-Saxonism', but this pejorative characterization ignores the fact that African competence in these areas hastened their intellectual development and equipped them to assert their rights in Victorian West Indies. The process was accelerated by the fact that a few black boys, following the example of coloureds, were able to gain admission to the elite schools. They embraced, mastered and themselves started to propagate the central ideas of the Victorian public schools: the classics, Christianity and cricket. The muscular Christianity of the Victorians found good soil among West Indians, blacks and coloureds, because they had faith in the ethos of English education, its utilitarian and moral dimensions. Hilary Beckles explains the context in which this African fascination with education developed in Barbados; its roots ran deep; it was central to their conception of freedom:

> Education for slaves ... was generally conceived as religious instruction. The many schools and academies which developed in Barbados between 1733 when the Harrison Free School was established, and 1826 when the Central School of Bridgetown for girls opened its doors, did not accept blacks, slave or free though the children of some free coloured planters and merchants obtained, on occasions, rather controversial entry. The free coloureds generally provided for their own children, and sometimes blacks were accepted. When the Colonial Charity School was opened in 1818 as a public institution, financed by free coloureds and free blacks, it provided lessons for more than fifty free coloured and thirty slave children. The Methodists, however, pioneered the policy of teaching slave children to read and write, while the Anglican clergy supported the planters' view that slave literacy was socially dangerous. In October 1823, Methodist minister

William Shrewsbury, who had published a pamphlet critical of the pro-slavery mentality of the white community, had his chapel destroyed by angry whites, and in 1827, St Lucy parishioners [whites] publicly abused their unorthodox Anglican minister, W.M. Harte, for 'inculcating doctrines' of racial equality in the blacks which were 'inconsistent with their obedience to their masters and the policy of the island'. Harte was taken to court, found guilty of misdemeanour and fined one shilling, but was pardoned by George IV after making a royal appeal.[5]

This is the soil that triggered and nourished the quest for education of Fitzherbert Adams, a black man, the father of Sir Grantley Adams, the first Prime Minister of Barbados. He became the headteacher of one of the largest primary schools on the island and went on to marry Rosa Frances Turney in the late 1890s. She was 'a woman of very fair complexion ... [and] this counted for a great deal in the stratified society of the island. The fact that she could claim two white sisters, though they were only half sisters and "poor whites", also tended to raise her social status in the eyes of nineteenth century Barbadians'.[6] Marrying light was one of the potential privileges educated men could achieve. Cricket and education were deeply rooted in the curriculum of the elite schools. For the black minority who drank from this fountain, much could be gained: material comfort and social status. West Indian societies were hierarchical, narrow, deeply rooted in associations of lightness of skin with status, but they were not immutable, caste-ridden social constructs. One could aspire to mobility: education and cricket could lift some, even the very dark, out of the poverty and despair of plantation labour and the retarding hierarchical constructions of colour. Already, by the late nineteenth century, as Brereton and Yelvington argue, Africans and coloureds were erecting their own bases for the construction of identities; deeply influenced, it is true, by European intellectual codes, but gradually salvaging aspects of their African heritage. The idea of an imagined ancestral homeland had seeped into their conceptions of belonging to the Caribbean:

One of the most important social developments after the end of slavery was the gradual emergence and growth of a black and mixed-race [coloured] middle stratum in the Caribbean colonies, led by men and women who had been exposed to formal education and were familiar with European culture. They, too, began to develop their own cultural institutions and to develop their world-view. For instance, most of the colonies in the nineteenth century had one or two newspapers owned or edited by black or mixed-race men, and these journals (even if their lives were often short and their circulation painfully small), provided an important forum for them to formulate a sense of identity. Many of them began to develop a sense of racial pride and to construct an identity with which to confront white racism. Intellectuals and writers such as Edward Wilmot Blyden ... of the Danish West Indies, Samuel Prescod of Barbados, Robert Love of the Bahamas and Jamaica, J.J. Thomas of Trinidad, and Hegesippe Legitimus of Guadeloupe were important precursors of the better-known twentieth century ideologues of race awareness and *negritude*.[7]

Many of these ideologues and politicians were educated in the elite schools of the West Indies. The Barbadian educational experience, rooted in the muscular Christianity of the Victorian public school, typified the curricula of all these schools. The authority on the subject, Keith Sandiford, has explained what this meant in terms of the orientation of the curriculum in Barbados: cricket and the classics dominated it, as the exponents of the doctrine could see no merit in adapting their Oxbridge learning to the peculiarities of the West Indian environment. What he observes of Barbados needs no revision with regard to C.L.R. James's Queen's Royal College, just before the First World War, or for that matter, Queen's College in British Guiana:

[T]he three leading secondary schools [Combermere, Harrison College and Lodge] made by far the most significant contribution to the development of the cricket cult in Barbados. In spreading the gospel of athleticism, they studiously copied the approach and methods of the leading public schools of Victorian Britain. The majority of the latter had put enormous store on physical education. In an age dominated by muscular Christianity and social Darwinism, British teachers and parents had stressed the importance of games in the development of character. Hence playing-fields, gymnasia and swimming pools had gradually become more important than class rooms and curricula. The Victorians had seen games not only as a means of strengthening the body but also of teaching moral and spiritual values. They had consequently glorified play and turned it into work largely because their Puritan ethics had devalued relaxation. To the Victorians recreation never meant fun and games. It meant the constructive regeneration of mind and body. As a result, such sports such as cricket, soccer and rowing became vital features of the public school curriculum. The universities [Oxbridge] also became involved in perpetuating the games ethic, and their graduates disseminated muscular Christian ideas all over the [E]mpire.[8]

Two such products, Horace Deighton and Arthur Somers-Cocks (1870–1923), would become the principal disseminators of the muscular learning that shaped several headmasters and teachers who then settled throughout the British West Indies — the foundation of the solid educational tradition of these islands. Deighton, a mathematics graduate from Oxford and the headmaster of Harrison College between 1872 and 1905, is the father of muscular learning in these colonies, for he was unwavering in his propagation of the Etonian and Harrovian ethos of the supremacy of cricket and the classics in building character in youths. As Sandiford sees him: '[H]e exalted ... [cricket] as a prime medium for the inculcation of all the requisite civic virtues. Convinced that there was a strong link between mental acuity and physical fitness, Deighton firmly believed that there was no possibility of a strong mind being accompanied by a feeble body.'[9] His 33 years at Harrison produced a remarkable crop of Barbadian cricketers/scholars, the first generation who laid the foundation for West Indies cricket. Most were white, but a few, even in the 1890s, were coloured and black. Prominent among the Harrison graduates were H.B.G. Austin (later Sir Harold) (1877–1943), considered the father of West Indies cricket; George Challenor (1888–1947), the first great West Indies batsman, a white Barbadian who toured England in 1906, 1923 and 1928, of whom *Wisden* wrote: 'He had everything — style, hitting power and strength of defence.' There was also the legendary Sir Pelham (Plum) Warner (1873–1963), who captained England in Australia in 1903–4, played first-class cricket in England from 1894 to 1929, scoring 29,028 runs, and became a pillar of the M.C.C, including manager of the England team during the infamous bodyline series in Australia in 1932–33.

Plum attended Harrison College from 1884 to 1887, before moving to England, to Rugby. He recalls the impact of Horace Deighton's muscular learning, and considers Harrison the nursery of his cricket, in sketching its West Indian origin:

Early in 1884 I was sent [from Trinidad] to Harrison College, Barbados, under the headmastership of Mr. H. Deighton, an old Cantab [sic], a man of most imposing, and rather frightening, presence, with fine eyes and a long beard — a very keen cricketer, who ... believed in the rod. His instrument of correction was a bamboo cane, which was most unpleasant I was told by those who suffered at his hands.... Mr. Deighton made Harrison College, and it remains to this day a famous school. Cricket was indeed the only game.... There was a lawn-tennis court — but cricket was *the* game. I got into the Third Eleven — there were about two hundred boys in the school — at a very early age, and we used to play the Second Eleven of The Lodge [another elite school], at the other end of the island.... We played on pretty good wickets, and I do not recall being coached in any special way. One developed one's natural style, and I think the marble gallery at the Hall [the Warner's home in Trinidad] helped considerably in my acquiring a fairly straight bat. Both Harrison and The Lodge have produced a large number of good cricketers, and I doubt very much whether any school of its size has turned out so many in so short a time as Harrison. They made us work hard, too, and behind our thirst for knowledge was the spectre of that bamboo cane![10]

Cricket and education were Plum's provenance. He visited his alma mater in 1948, over 60 years since he had sailed for England; but it was the cricketing memories that flooded his imagination, such was the power of the cult inculcated by the indomitable Horace Deighton. He himself, as well as other masters, played with the boys in their games against adult teams, the foundation of a bold tradition of introducing students to first division cricket in Barbados. Young men were thus thrown early into a context of a high standard of play, demanding skill and discipline, while evoking pride in the school. This was etched indelibly on the mind of Plum Warner:

As I stood on a platform in the College hall memories came chasing back across the long years, from the day I arrived in a sailor-suit to the day on which, early in 1887, at the age of thirteen, I made 31 against the Garrison [British troops stationed on the island], and

was for a short while something of a small hero, and there was a
lump in my throat when I spoke. I owe much to Harrison College,
for it was there that the foundations of any skill I may have acquired
at cricket were built, and where many friendships began which
continue to this day.... Well indeed do I recall the Challenors, the
Piles, the Howells, the Skeetes, the Spencers, the Sealys, the
Evelyns, George Hickson, who gave me my First Eleven colours,
and others. They were all good and kind to me, and occasionally I
was allowed to spend a week-end at one or other of their comfortable
country houses.[11]

These are all white Barbadian families, deeply shaped by the
Harrison–Lodge ethos of muscular learning; but such was the size of
the island that however prejudiced they were, this small colonial world
was already being penetrated by coloured and black Barbadians: first,
through Combermere, but by the 1890s, Harrison, too; the Lodge,
later. By the late nineteenth century this muscular learning was
definitely not the monopoly of white Barbadians. The process was
marked by a diffusion of Deighton's graduates or Oxbridge colleagues/
disciples to Lodge, Combermere and the rest of the British West Indies.
One such was William Burslem, C.L.R. James's headmaster at Queen's
Royal College, Trinidad, during the First World War. A key teacher in
Deighton's muscular learning mission was Arthur Somers-Cocks, whom
he appointed in 1892. An Oxford graduate, he was a classical scholar
and fine cricketer. The son-in-law of Deighton, Somers-Cocks, too, is
synonymous with Harrison: he stayed for 31 years and became
headmaster in 1922, having succeeded Dr Herbert Dalton, another
Oxford man, who had pursued Deighton's work with the same ardour
since 1905.[12]

Somers-Cocks, who played first-class cricket for Barbados —
including against Lord Hawke's team in 1897, was a great inspiration
to students at Harrison College. Sandiford assesses the impact of the
muscular learning fostered by Deighton, Dalton and Somers-Cocks. It
was a long-term project, encompassing 50 years of Barbadian social
history. It would have ramifications throughout the British West Indies,
shaping an intellectual temperament that would be receptive to liberal
democracy and the politics of gradualism. Sandiford observes thus of
one of Deighton's finest graduates, G[ustavus] B[lagrove] Y[oung]

(Gussie) Cox (1870–1958), a white Barbadian headmaster and cricketer of unassailable stature and integrity:

> Gussie Cox ... was a Harrison College pupil in Deighton's time. He returned to teach at his alma mater after graduating with a classics degree from Codrington College [a theological college in Barbados] in the early 1890s. After an association with Harrison that amounted to more than 30 years, he took his classical and cricketing skills to Combermere, where he served as headmaster from 1926 to 1934. Gussie remains one of the most celebrated scholar-athletes in Barbadian legend and history. He left a huge imprint on both Harrison College and Combermere, contributing enormously to the development of cricket at those institutions.[13]

A similar product with the Deighton pedigree was Oliver DeCourcey 'Bill' Emtage, the eminent headmaster of the Lodge for the first three decades of the twentieth century, when he made the school a distinguished exponent of muscular learning. In January 1900, for instance, the Lodge was advertising in the *Argosy* of British Guiana as a boarding school situated 'in an open, healthy and cool position on the windward side of the island, 700 feet above the sea [in the eastern parish of St. John]'. Its headmaster, Bill Emtage, and two of the three assistant masters were Oxford graduates, while the third was a Cambridge man. The curriculum was stated as the equivalent of a first grade grammar school, embracing the following subjects: divinity, classics, mathematics, English, elementary science and chemistry.[14] The advertisement was strangely silent on the permeation of the curriculum by the muscular learning of Emtage, a white Barbadian, a graduate of Worcester College, Oxford. But in their estimate of this indefatigable headmaster's legacy, Sandiford and Stoddart do not miss this key ingredient:

> From 1831 until 1931 ... [Bill Emtage] consciously set out to produce a replica of an English public school, introducing the prefect system and setting up a model boarding establishment. By far the most important headmaster of Lodge, he made it one of the most famous boarding schools in the British Empire, himself making vital contributions towards improving the school buildings and playing fields. He supervised games personally and encouraged

senior boys to sit on the important Games Committee which he established.... Born in Barbados in 1867, he studied under Deighton at Harrison college between 1879 and 1886, and won the blue ribbon Barbados scholarship that took him to ... Oxford, where he performed well in mathematics and athletics. Returning to Barbados, he served as a Harrison College master under Deighton for eight years before his relocation to The Lodge. He never lost his interest in cricket or his belief in its character-building powers.[15]

They elaborate on Emtage's modus operandi, which did not deviate from the tradition established by his mentor, Horace Deighton:

For many years Emtage addressed the school through his 'Headmaster's Letter' which appeared in the *Lodge School Record*. On almost every occasion he alluded to the value of games, remarking in 1924, for instance, that a schoolboy 'is receiving by the practice of these arts very valuable training in obedience of muscles to the eye, promptness in deciding and foresight in judging the motives of his opponents'. In 1926, after lamenting some mediocre academic results, he consoled himself and his boys that 'our lack of success in school is, however, to some extent made up for by a fairly successful year as far as games are concerned'. In 1927 his 'Letter' appealed for more assiduous practice at cricket, and in 1928 bemoaned the alarming frequency of unnecessary run-outs. For Emtage, through games such as cricket came responsibility, teamwork and a set of moral precepts of both the Victorian system of faith in games and its quite consciously adopted colonial derivative.[16]

What is remarkable about the concept of muscular learning was not the commitment of the white colonial elite to its supposed elevating properties, but the assiduity with which the colonized elite would embrace it as an instrument of mobility. Some idealists probably emphasized the muscular development at the expense of the intellectual; but as suggested by the advertisement of the Lodge School cited above, most West Indians would have given priority to the latter component. Blacks and coloureds seemed to have struck a balance between the overly 'muscular' ideal, the classics/cricket focus of Harrison College and The Lodge and a vocational orientation. This was manifested in the curricular development of the Combermere

School under the headmasterships of two white Barbadians: Rev T. Lyall Speed (1879–96) and G.B.R. Burton (1897–1925). Both were steeped in the muscular education absorbed from their respective schools, the Lodge and Harrison. Where they departed, however, was their recognition that an increasing number of their students were coloureds and blacks, whose parents were very aware that spaces were being opened up in the lower rungs of the commercial and administrative spheres, and, therefore, while adhering to the muscular learning code of the elite schools, the curriculum must accommodate a more practical core. Speed was astute in this respect. Keith Sandiford, himself a Combermere man, has reflected on the legacy of Lyall Speed (1843–96):

> Speed brought Combermere into line with the grammar schools that were then sprouting up all over Britain [in the 1880s] and, like his counterparts at Harrison College and the Lodge School, tried to copy as many of the British models as he could. He thus played a notable role in the anglicisation of Barbadian education at the end of the Victorian age. It may well be true that some of the British disciplines and techniques were inappropriate in a Caribbean setting, but they were the only ones which Speed and his Barbadian contemporaries knew. The process of anglicisation, in any case, had begun before the age of Speed.... In one significant respect, however, Speed's institution differed from its British counterparts. Whereas the latter focused narrowly on the classics and humanities, then considered the prerequisites for gentility, Combermere broadened its curriculum to cater to the needs of the commercial elements within the society. Combermere was deliberately intended ... to train its boys for lower middle-income positions, while the vast majority of secondary schools in the [E]mpire were geared towards supplying the needs of the aristocracy and the upper middle classes. This was the case ... with Harrison College and the Lodge ... as well as the few grammar schools that began to appear in other colonies within the Caribbean area. In Speed's time, several West Indian parents seeking a practical secondary education for their sons found Combermere a very attractive option.[17]

Thus, from the late nineteenth century, a coloured and black lower middle class was being created in Barbados, people equipped with a range of skills to play a part in civil society: accountants, clerks, managers, civil servants and elementary school teachers. This explains why, as I argue later, here as well as in other islands, they were able to take advantage of the incremental advances in representative government as they slowly emerged in the twentieth century. But at the level of muscular learning, too, several headmasters and teachers, products of the Deighton stable, would find themselves in other parts of the British West Indies towards the end of the nineteenth century. This was the age of high imperialism and the ethos of the Victorian public school was more easily transplanted to these older colonies, quintessential immigrant societies, unencumbered by ancient indigenous values. Deighton, Dalton, Somers-Cocks and William Burslem, for instance, were rigorously tutored for their imperial mission in English public schools and at Oxbridge. J.A. Mangan has explained the ideological context in which the public school stimulated a passion for colonial adventure, while being simultaneously animated by images of heroism from the imperial mission:

> It was the new imperialism of late-Victorian Britain which produced the precarious fusion of Christian gentility and social Darwinism. Three sets of values became enmeshed: imperial Darwinism — the God-granted right of the white man to rule, civilise and baptise the inferior coloured races; institutional Darwinism — the cultivation of physical and psychological stamina at school in preparation for the rigours of imperial duty; the gentleman's education — the nurture of leadership qualities for military conquest abroad and political dominance at home.... [Consequently] the need to prepare for imperial service was incessantly preached in the late-nineteenth century public schools.... Headmasters were intoxicated with the grandeur and nobility of the gubernatorial exercise. Welldon [headmaster of Harrow, 1881–95] gloried in the solemnity of the responsibility of the British Empire to elevate inferior races.... [T]he exciting world of empire was systematically and frequently publicised in the school magazines by means of contributions from former pupils.... To a considerable extent it was the games field that prepared boys for these imperial adventures.... [T]he rise of imperialism put a premium on authority, discipline and team spirit allegedly learnt in these arenas.[18]

In 1893, in a population of 180,000 in Barbados, whites comprised 15,000 or a little over 8 per cent, but their power to define in this colonial space was immense. This small dominant creole white minority still saw itself as an extension of 'home'; therefore, the imperial ethos and its inculcation through the elite schools had powerful resonance. Most white Barbadians, apart from the menial, marginalized 'redlegs', constructed themselves in terms of representations of Englishness that were not readily accessible to whites in other colonies. Their claim to being among the earliest English settlers in the New World, in this colony of sole English colonization, enhanced their conception of self, as if they were entitled to first claim on the hierarchy of English authenticity overseas. They would sedulously cultivate that image which, as I argue earlier, sought to construct their Barbadian plantation in terms of an imagined homeland — a kind of rural Albion: England in the Tropics. This is how one English observer saw the creole whites in Barbados in the early 1890s:

> [They] are, of course, chiefly the descendants of the English settlers [in the seventeenth century].... The higher class of whites pride themselves on their blood, and even the mean whites ['redlegs'] have as a rule married with one another and have seldom formed legal or other unions with the coloured [black] people.... The Barbadian English are more like born Englishmen than are some others of our colonial peoples; there is a quiet and old-fashioned air about them. The small size and propinquity of the estates to one another have enabled them to keep up the civilities of social intercourse, which are apt to be forgotten in newly settled and sparsely populated countries. There is consequently an absence of the rough unpolished colonial type that is frequent in some of the later settled colonies in other parts of the world.... Barbadians still speak of and look upon England as 'home', and all who can afford it send their children to be educated in England, and, to give a final touch, Germany. Among their ancestors were some of the oldest English families, who emigrated or were banished during the troublous times of the 17th century.[19]

Aspects of this construction by creole whites were inevitably internalized by Africans within this colonial space, so that although blacks responded to their own internal reverences, they, too, would subscribe to the superiority of facets of this construct of Englishness. Education in the elite schools throughout the British West Indies, obsession with its muscular learning, its received codes and other perceived indices of civilization, would make a massive contribution to the making of many great black West Indians, such as Grantley Adams, Norman Washington Manley, C.L.R. James, Eric Eustace Williams, W. Arthur Lewis and others, who emerged from the elite schools in the first two or three decades of the twentieth century. However alien the public school code might have seemed to many in the colonies, it provided a framework for order and it inculcated a discipline that enabled black and coloured students to demolish a fundamental assumption of European imperial rule: the intellectual limitations of the native mind, its natural incapacity for resolve and continuity of focus, its vulnerability to impulse — infantile. Muscular learning made it possible for young black scholars to demonstrate their mental and physical equality with the ruling race, while establishing that they were no less endowed with rationality, perseverance and self-control. The concentration and collective endeavour required of the game of cricket, therefore, had much more than leisure appeal to many black and coloured boys in the West Indies. What Richard Holt suggests the game demanded of public school boys in England and contributed in terms of 'character training' requires no revision with regard to non-whites in the elite schools of Barbados, Trinidad or British Guiana:

> The resolute schoolboy, who plays out a difficult innings in fading light with the same resolve that he later takes command of a desperate situation with 'the Gatling jammed and the Colonel dead', sums up the heroic ideals of generations of schoolboys brought up on tales of imperial adventure and the thriving new genre of schoolboy fiction. The importance of sport from the point of view of the educationalist and the soldier lay not simply in acquiring fitness or in being competitive, but in the sense of solidarity, duty and service it inculcated.[20]

Keith Sandiford has reflected on the power of Victorian Anglo-Saxonism to inspire English public school graduates, teachers and missionaries, to propagate its ideal within the imperial mission. In the British West Indies where, as I have argued, there was no resilient indigenous culture, unlike Africa and India, to deflect, resist and neutralize the hegemonic culture of the ruling race, the black and coloured elite pursued the received culture with a consistency and resolve that has attracted the opprobrious characterization 'mimic men' or 'Afro-Saxons'. But for black West Indian boys like C.L.R. James, the codes of the elite schools were not a trivial matter, although nationalists and white liberals, such as Aneurin Bevan, were inclined to sneer at them.[21] James became a communist of varying denominations from the 1930s, and remained so for the rest of his life, but he was unflagging in his respect for the muscular learning ethos inculcated at Queen's Royal College (QRC) in Trinidad, under William Burslem, his headmaster during the 1910s. Burslem had been the headmaster of the Lodge, in Barbados, from 1893 to 1895, and had previously worked as an assistant master with the legendary Horace Deighton, at Harrison College. He was a good cricketer and classical scholar. His impact on James, therefore, encapsulated all the virtues of scholarship and physical training that the latter would later deploy to intellectually assert the mastery of black men beyond the boundaries set for them, in the context of slavery and the protracted racist limitations of its aftermath. Muscular learning in the British West Indies was a challenge to the black boy to show that he had the strength of character to compete with his white contemporary at the highest level of this tradition. Like his Trinidadian friend, the great Learie Constantine, at the heart of James's intellectual endeavour shaped by the codes of QRC was the renascent assertion: 'They are no better than we.'[22] Failure to comprehend this fundamental prompting behind a basic exercise in self-reclamation, to be condemnatory of the codes as alien and supercilious, is a common response. But it is flawed, and James was most contemptuous of it. He sought to define what the public school code meant to him:

> Later, as I grew older and won my place in the cricket and soccer elevens, I took my part in the election of the captains, the secretaries and the committees. A master presided but that was all he did.... We managed our own affairs from the fifth eleven to the first.... We chose our own teams, awarded colours ourselves, obeyed our captains implicitly. For me it was life and education. I began to study Latin and French, then Greek, and much else. But particularly we learnt, I learnt and obeyed and taught a code, the

English public-school code. Britain and her colonies and her colonial peoples. What do the British people know of what they have done there? The colonial peoples, particularly West Indians, scarcely know themselves as yet. It has taken me a long time to begin to understand.... It came doctrinally from the masters, who for two generations, from the foundation of the school [QRC], had been Oxford and Cambridge men. The striking thing was that inside the class rooms the code had little success.... But as soon as we stepped on to the cricket or football field, more particularly the cricket field all changed.[23]

James explains how this code was honoured at this elite school, in colonial Trinidad in the 1910s, with its congeries of ethnic groups. It partially explains a postcolonial phenomenon — why liberal democracy would take root in these puny colonial backwaters, former slave societies, as if it were an indigenous plant:

We were a motley crew.... Yet rapidly we learned to obey the umpire's decision without question, however irrational it was. We learned to play with the team, which meant subordinating your personal inclinations, and even interests, to the good of the whole. We kept a stiff upper lip in that we did not complain about ill-fortune. We did not denounce failures, but 'Well tried' or 'Hard luck' came easily to our lips. We were generous to opponents and congratulated them on victories, even when we knew they did not deserve it. We lived in two worlds. Inside the classrooms the heterogeneous jumble of Trinidad was battered and jostled and shaken down into some sort of order. On the playing field we did what ought to be done. Every individual did not observe every rule. But the majority of the boys did. The best and most-respected boys were precisely the ones who always kept them. When a boy broke them he knew what he had done and, with the cruelty and intolerance of youth, from all sides our denunciations poured in on him. *Eton or Harrow had nothing on us.*[24] (emphasis added)

Blacks and coloureds in the British West Indies, especially the former, were seen in post-Emancipation society as being in a potentially recidivist state — vulnerable to relapse into barbarism. It was therefore necessary to guide them through a gradual process of civilization. This attitude had permeated the reaction of *The Times* to the Morant Bay Rebellion by black peasants and labourers in Jamaica in 1865: the savage state was not amenable to speedy extirpation:

> It seems ... impossible to eradicate the original savageness of the African blood. As long as the black man has a strong white Government and a numerous white population to control him he is capable of living as a respectable member of society. He can be made quiet and even industrious by the fear of the supreme power, and by the example of those to whom he necessarily looks up. But whenever he attains to a certain degree of independence there is the fear that he will resume the barbarous life and fierce habits of his African ancestors.[25]

Paradoxically, the sugar plantation, *the* real site of barbarism under slavery, was still identified as the principal institution wherein the 'Negro' could be civilized, through the discipline of its work routine. But this idea of an imagined haven did not lend itself to popular absorption. Africans, since the late 1830s, had sought to counter this tired imperial doctrine: wherever possible, they bought land and tried to liberate themselves from the plantation frame of reference. Many of the non-conformist missionaries had concurred with this idea that land-ownership was the foundation of black people's future; and that education and English culture and manners — muscular learning — must be at the core of the freed people's construction of their new world. However, in Barbados, because 85 per cent of the land was in the hands of the plantocracy as late as 1896–97, black people had few opportunities to advance through agriculture. Only 166 square miles, it had 'one of the highest population densities in the British Empire'. As the Norman Commission observed in 1897, Barbados was 'markedly different from that of any other colony of the West Indies ... very thickly populated ... no crown lands, no forest, no uncultivated areas'.[26] Education, therefore, was identified as the principal instrument of mobility, so the creolization process would be accelerated on the island. For blacks and coloureds, there was no credible alternative to mastering and adapting elements of the imperial culture, to build their self-esteem, erase the legacy of slavery and establish their intellectual equality with white people. As Sandiford argues: 'If the Barbadian whites played cricket to signify their gentility, the blacks did so to demonstrate their equality with their social superiors.'[27] They took to education, too, as many have remarked, like duck to water, for the same reason. Therefore, one could comprehend why the black and coloured middle class appropriated the manners and codes of their putative white superiors so passionately: to eliminate the perennial threat of allegations of their reversion to savagery. The following is a contemporary account of black middle class behaviour in Bridgetown, Barbados from the early 1890s. They were asserting their arrival; there was no other index of superiority to appropriate:

> Many, if not most, of the shopkeepers in Bridgetown, and nearly all the clerks and assistants, are coloured [black and mixed race] people. The more prosperous of them have their little villas on the outskirts of the town, keep their horse and buggy, dress well, and appear in gorgeous array on a Sunday, the men in black suits resplendent with a watch chain and seals of the Georgian style, and flashy rings — the ladies in silk dress, more or less tastefully adorned, but always adorned in some fashion. These people are fairly educated; they speak good English and interest themselves in all current affairs.[28]

This was the world of the black middle class of the British West Indies: they had no parallel anywhere in the British Empire, anywhere in the world, as C.L.R. James would remark over and over. They took what they had learnt seriously, and would brook no attempt to ridicule their own claims to a kind of Englishness. On the eve of Barbadian independence in late 1966, John Hearne, the Jamaican novelist who knew the island well, reflected on the peculiar Englishness of a place where the English had encountered no indigenous people, where English rule had been unbroken since 1627, and where the plantocracy was a resident one — authentically Barbadian in a way unparalleled in the British West Indies. This gave the black Barbadian a discernibly different persona:

> [H]e is English in a way that the rest of us are not. History Englished him by giving him an exclusive association with that potent and wonderful country just at the time when it was in one of its most creative phases. More Englishmen, from a wider range of social classes came to Barbados — and became Barbadians — earlier than any of the other islands.... The range of classes represented

among the first Englishmen is, I believe, important. It meant that some values, some concept of manners other than the purely materialistic ones of looting and exploitation had time to take some sort of root. The simple code of grab, and cent per cent which was, to a large extent, the legacy left to Jamaica by an 'overseer'class [and absentee proprietorship], had certain refinements added to it in Barbados that would seem to have had a permanent influence. In Jamaica, for example, towards the end of the eighteenth century, education at anything above the basics of reading, writing and arithmetic was at such a low level as to be written off with contempt by most perceptive travellers. Barbados, which was not as large as some Jamaican parishes, had a well-established foundation that taught the classics.... There were more whites ... speaking proportionately, in Barbados than in any other of the British Caribbean territories. And more important of all, more white women: this meant more home life and a further gentling influence on domestic and public manners. Barbados did not, of course, altogether escape the brutalising, coarsening effects of a slave-based plantation system.... It was a greedy, cruel place, like any other West Indian sugar island, but certain proprieties, a certain sense of style were observed by a larger sector of its population.[29]

Many black Barbadians could sit comfortably with their 'little England' assumptions. Like C.L.R. James, Sir Grantley Herbert Adams (1898–1971), the only prime minister of the short-lived West Indies Federation and the founder of the Barbados Labour Party, the father of modern Barbadian politics, was also shaped by the muscular learning of Victorian public schools, transplanted unadulterated to the elite schools of the British West Indies. He played cricket, was immersed in the classics, won the Barbados Scholarship and entered Oxford in 1919. His education at Harrison College would have been essentially that offered at Eton, Harrow, Rugby, Uppingham or Winchester. Most of his masters at Harrison College were graduates of a public school in England, trained at Oxford or Cambridge, steeped in the classics and cricket; so were most of the teachers, as I have shown, of the other elite schools in the British West Indies: Lodge and Combermere (Barbados); Queen's College (British Guiana); Kingston College and Wolmer's Boys' School (Jamaica); and Queen's Royal College (Trinidad). F.A. Hoyos traces Adams's path to Oxford; but even for those black boys who did not make it to Oxbridge, the experience would have been identical, for all the public schools of the British West Indies were rooted in the same code:

> From Fitzherbert Adams [his father], Grantley derived his love of books and his passion for cricket. From an early age he began to read voraciously.... [But] nothing would please him better than when his father took him to see a cricket match or gave him a bat to reward some minor triumph in the game. The great hero he worshipped in those days was A.E. Stoddard, who visited Barbados in 1896 [1897] with an English cricket team [Priestley's] and whose legendary deeds on the field had been communicated to him by his father. It must have been gratifying to Fitzherbert Adams to see his son practising assiduously to emulate the skill of the famous English player.[30]

Hoyos, who knew Grantley Adams very well, elaborates on the other dimension of his muscular learning, his immersion in the classics:

> Before going up to Oxford [in September 1919], Grantley Adams had read widely of the Greek and Latin Classics. His sixth form master at Harrison College, Arthur Somers-Cocks [an Englishman, an Oxford graduate, who played cricket for Barbados], had once advised him to read a hundred lines of Homer before beginning the day. This practice he adopted and in due course read all the books of the *Iliad* and the *Odyssey*. He pursued his private reading avidly and, while still in the sixth form, he devoured all the writings of the Greek tragedians, Aeschylus, Sophocles and Euripides, all of Horace and most of Catullus. In addition, he read all the complete works of Thucydides and Herodotus, except the last chapter, and substantial portions of Demosthenes, Cicero, Tacitus, Livy, Juvenal, Lucretius and Pindar. Then to improve his translations from the Classics, he began to range widely through the treasures of English prose and poetry.[31]

C.L.R. James corroborates this while linking himself to the classical pedigree of their colonial learning: 'When I was talking to ... [Grantley Adams] a few years ago, he told me that before he left Harrison College he had read Homer, Hesiod, Euripides, Sophocles and Aristophanes, and he was a great master of Aeschylus; he could read Greek almost as well as he could read English. That is the way he was educated.... That was the way that generation was brought up. That's how we became what we are, and if Grantley is a man about whose [political] career one has reservations, he still has very much to his credit'.[32] It was typical of James, his Marxism notwithstanding, that he was unwavering in his celebration of his muscular learning, including the classical and literary strands in his European intellectual provenance.

The year after Adams graduated from Oxford and returned to Barbados, he met Grace Thorne, the daughter of an upper class white Barbadian whom he married in spite of the objection of her family. Education and cricket often brought that cherished crowning of one's achievement — a light or white wife. This, too, runs deep in the West Indian tradition. However, fortified by intellectual excellence and proficiency at cricket at the elite schools, a minority of middle class blacks could challenge the supercilious assumptions of coloureds. Moreover, they began to see themselves as being in no way inferior, intellectually or physically, to the great imperial race. In the process, they were clearing the way for their people as a whole to redefine themselves. Such was the ramification of the training of the mind in this unique colonial environment.

Sandiford observes that no cricketer, black, brown or white, who had not been to an elite school, represented Barbados before the Second World War: they had played their first match, against British Guiana, in February 1865. Yet the game developed everywhere in the West Indies, on the plantations and in the villages and towns, at the lowest level, among all groups, including the Indian and Madeiran Portuguese indentured labourers in Trinidad and British Guiana. By the last decade of the nineteenth century, to belong to the British West Indies such latecomers had to demonstrate some proficiency at cricket. The game, more than any other medium, became a mirror of the society. All the social divisions in West Indian societies were reflected in it; it tended to minimize potential ethnic conflict, but did not transcend it: social interaction tended *not* to go beyond the boundary. Cricket shaped a tenuous West Indian consciousness but this was refracted through clearly discernible ethnic prisms: white, black, coloured, Portuguese and Indian. I have written elsewhere thus of cricket in British Guiana in the late nineteenth century:

[It] represented the highest popular manifestation of English culture, and the working classes of all races claimed it because it was accessible. It cost nothing — bats and wickets were contrived out of tree trunks, twigs, the branches of the coconut palm, wooden crates, pieces of wood 'liberated' from a neighbour's fence; at times a ball made from balata was procured. Often, as Ignatius Scholes observed, [in New Amsterdam, Berbice] in the mid-1880s, young blacks were even more ingenious: '[A]n old paraffin tin, all bruised, battered and just managing to stand, does excellent duty as both bails and wickets. The red leather ball resigns the honour to some old rags tightly twisted and fairly rounded, or at a great push, an oblong mango stone supplies its place'.[33]

I elaborate on the reshaping of the game by the spirit of the masses, thus infusing it with a proletarian flair:

Pads or other forms of protection for more vulnerable areas were unknown, thus heightening the element of danger; this made the game infinitely more alluring. A cocky ostentation flourished even at this rudimentary level. Cricket thus played endowed a boyhood of severe privation with fantasies of heroism. Cricket in British Guiana, as in the West Indian islands, became a medium for the release of pent-up feelings of hurt in this ex-slave environment, and the white ruling class did not suppress it. In fact, many planters and businessmen promoted it: it was probably identified as a ... means by which notions of oppression and injustice among the lower classes, with their potential for feeding 'subversion', could be canalized and dissipated. By the last quarter of the 19th century, several cricket clubs were founded in Georgetown and many gifted black and coloured cricketers could demonstrate their superiority over white players in this fairly open environment. This enhanced the popularity of the game and broadened its appeal.[34]

But it was Barbados that set the example to coloureds and middle class blacks of their own potential, to challenge the white ruling class at the highest level of the game. Mastery of this complex game enabled them to assert their right to be taken seriously — as thinkers, not merely as the long-suffering hewers of wood and drawers of water. The Barbadian plantocracy and mercantile elite, most of them graduates of the Lodge and Harrison College, had founded the Wanderers Cricket Club in 1877. On class grounds, however, whites from the civil service or lower ranks were excluded. This was the context in which the celebrated cricketing family, the Goodmans, founded Pickwick in 1882. But on class grounds, too, poor whites, the so-called 'redlegs' of rural Barbados, could not dream of admission to Pickwick, nor could coloureds or mixed race people, however respectable. Consequently, in 1893, largely through the initiative of Sir Conrad Reeves, the coloured Chief Justice of Barbados, Spartan was founded for coloured middle class cricketers, with a sprinkling of black middle-class men. A few were graduates of Harrison College; most were from Combermere. Thus the coloured and black elite, as early as the 1890s, could compete with whites in the Barbados Challenge Cricket Cup (later BCCA), the symbol of cricket supremacy on the island.[35] But the black plebeians, although they played with as much passion as their counterparts in British Guiana, could not gain admission to Spartan: they were deemed 'professionals' and summarily excluded. It was this discrimination on the basis of class that led gifted fast bowlers — Woods, Cumberbatch and Burton — to migrate to Trinidad and Demerara in the latter half of the 1890s, and Herman Griffith and others to form Empire in 1914. As for the rural black folk, plantation workers and small farmers, these, too, played avidly but had to await the formation of the Barbados Cricket League, in 1936, by Mitchie Hewitt, before they could play first division cricket. The history of education and cricket in Barbados is necessarily a study in attitudes to race, colour and class, as well as incremental access, as the cases of Spartan and Empire demonstrate. Gradualism was central to the process, and it established a pattern of responses rooted in a fundamentally moderate ethos.

Cricket reflected with amazing fidelity the race, colour and class divisions within West Indian societies. The small white minority in Barbados, about eight per cent, still exerted extraordinary influence politically and economically: most businesses and plantations were white-owned; very few blacks had the vote. Yet although this was a highly stratified society, marked by old, resilient prejudice, it was not totally closed: some mobility was possible, and coloureds and blacks pushed back the barriers wherever they could, with the help of English missionaries in the non-conformist churches and progressive headmasters, especially at Combermere School, which became a predominantly black and coloured institution from the 1880s and 90s. Indeed, many black Barbadians already had good educational qualifications by the 1880s, and several migrated to Trinidad and

British Guiana to teach in primary and secondary schools. Barbadians were crucial to the permeation of education among black and Indian people in both colonies.

Moreover, although black and coloured Barbadians could not represent the island at cricket until the turn of the century, by creating Spartan, which competed with exclusively white Wanderers and Pickwick, they had already pushed the racial barrier back in a most emphatic manner. The fact that they were competing against whites, in domestic first division cricket, since 1893, sharpened their game and impelled them to master the craft. As noted above, few black Barbadians had the vote; hardly any owned businesses: education and cricket, therefore, were the instruments for fighting for their social and political rights. Cricket was more than a game: from the inception, under slavery, as I have argued, like their religious zeal that fed the rebellious spirit, the game was a weapon of liberation. Hilary Beckles concurs:

> Whether it was during the period of the Amerindian–European encounter, or the subsequent slavery epoch, the majority of West Indian inhabitants have sought to define their own existence in terms of an appropriation of space that could be autonomously manipulated in the building of discrete realities of freedom. Cricket, then, became enmeshed in all these considerations, and represented an ideological and cultural terrain on which these battles were fought. This is precisely why James was able to argue that the cricket history of the region is but a mirror within which its modern social undertakings can be examined and assessed. It is also expressive of the manner in which black West Indians took the ploughshare of Empire and turned it into a sword which they later placed at the throats of the imperial order. As far as the late nineteenth-century English sponsor of cricket in the Empire was concerned, 'cricket was an essential and symbolic part of the imperial order and manners'. Could they have envisioned that West Indian recipients in the late twentieth century would promote cricket as an agent in the dismantlement of the imperial order and a symbol of liberation?[36]

What do they know of cricket who only cricket know?

Chapter Three

The Making of a West Indian Intelligentsia:
The Culture of Protest in the 1890s

Cricket, C.L.R. James argues, could carry the struggle of the colonized, their intricate constructions and mercurial assertions of identity — the quest for self-belief — because it is a game of high skills and complexity: excellence was an affirmation, therefore, not only of the nimbleness of body but also dexterity of mind. Moreover, it was at the core of the imperial mission, the very essence of English civilization; more than purely intellectual pursuits, it embodied the quintessential values of the ruling race. As early as the 1890s, Africans in the British West Indies (Madeiran Portuguese, too) were excelling at both cricket and education, thus planting the seed of their assertion of rights to greater representation in government. Because the political arena was still monopolized by the white elite, other instruments had to be found to ventilate their growing democratic impulses. Classical education and cricket, because they were central to the colonial project — the foundation of the imperial civilizing mission — were endowed with those constituents which were coterminous with the English vision of civilization, and, therefore, recognized by all ethnic groups in the British West Indies as the key to mobility. This was the way forward in undermining the persistent threat of being tarred with the brush of savagery. The young Indo-Guyanese intellectual, Joseph Ruhomon (1873–1942), observed in 1894 that if Indians wished to be taken seriously in the region they had to pursue western education; but as I have argued, to be accepted as being of the place — to really belong — competence at, if not mastery of, cricket was imperative.[1]

Coloured and African West Indians had laid a sturdy foundation for this. By the 1880s and 90s, many were beneficiaries of English education as developed in the Victorian public schools and transplanted virtually as a 'hot house plant', as James puts it, into institutions such as Harrison College, Queen's Royal College and

Queen's College. But at the popular level, too, elementary education had already had a discernible impact by the 1880s, as Raymond Smith, the anthropologist, observes with regard to the shaping of rural post-Emancipation West Indian societies:

> The system of elementary education was aimed at the lower class of ex-slaves, but it found its principal support among the more prosperous small and medium-sized farmers engaged in the production of 'minor', that is to say non-plantation crops. Its existence also led to the creation of a lower middle class of primary school teachers who became a reservoir of black leaders. Whatever its shortcomings elementary school teaching was almost the only means by which poor blacks [men and women] could escape manual labour.... However, in the rural communities where church and school were most effective, particularly among the middle farmers who could make enough money to maintain a respectable style of life, the school teachers were the local elite.[2]

Teaching brought status although the financial rewards were not impressive. As early as 1884, the Association of Schoolmasters in Jamaica had sent a memorandum to the Colonial Office advocating compulsory education, so that the 'peasantry could be thoroughly civilised and enlightened'. What is noteworthy about this initiative was the discernible forthrightness, tact and confidence of the small middle class: 'Your memorialists who are all black men and coloured men are natives of different parts of the Island, are the best judges in this matter; and we assert, that should the system of education which we are advocating be introduced here, for the civilisation and enlightenment of our people, it will greatly add to their love for our Most Gracious Queen and their loyalty to her throne'. They countered the notion that 'universal education would lead to discontent among Negroes', peddled by 'strangers' (an allusion to the planters and their allies), who had 'no real interest in the welfare and prosperity of our country and in the progress of its people'.[3] They were already saying that the future of Jamaica was in their hands.

Throughout the British West Indies, by the middle of the nineteenth century, coloured or mixed race men had created a tradition of radical journalism while pledging unswerving loyalty to the Empire. Their early access to education, going back to the late eighteenth century, a privilege that came later to blacks, enabled them to compensate for the restricted franchise by ventilating the grievances of their people in small newspapers, as they started to challenge the supremacy of the plantocracy. The democratic impulse was certainly fostered and quickened by this initiative from coloured journalists. As Peter Roberts argues, as early as the 1820s and 30s their perspectives had gained recognition even in England:

> Increasingly the coloured population saw the newspaper as an avenue for having their voice heard. For example, in the early 1820s a coloured man was the editor of the main newspaper in Antigua…. Samuel Prescott had a newspaper (*New Times*) in Barbados in the 1830s; and a protégé of Prescott, Charles Falconer, took over *The Dominican* from three coloured creoles who had founded it in 1839. By the middle of the nineteenth century, therefore, Charles Day [author of *Five Years' Residence in the West Indies*, (1852)] was moved to say … 'Coloured men are very fond of being editors of newspapers, as it increases their importance in the eyes of their own race'. What is more important as far as the influence of these newspapers is concerned is that, as Day goes on to say, 'it is from these papers that extracts are usually printed in England'. In other words … news and analysis of the situation in the West Indies was seen in England through the eyes of the local press, which in some cases mirrored the views of the aspiring coloured population.[4]

By the 1870s and 80s, the black middle class as well were claiming their right to reshape the colonial space, to determine the contours of a freer society. Bridget Brereton discusses the process in late nineteenth-century Trinidad:

> In Trinidad they established literary and debating societies intended to prepare young persons for leadership, to encourage self-education, to help develop political agendas and to 'prove' their equality with (if not superiority to) local whites in all matters pertaining to culture. A good example is the Trinidadian Athenaeum, formed in the 1870s by J.J. Thomas, the self-educated linguist, educator and writer who wrote *Creole Grammar* (1869) and *Froudacity* (1889) and was a source of great pride to the coloured and black intelligentsia in the late nineteenth century…. From at least the middle of the nineteenth century brown or black men owned or edited one or two papers, even if the lives of their publications were often short and their circulation painfully small.

Among the Trinidad papers which articulated the views of the
middle stratum in this period were *New Era*, the *Trinidad Press*,
the *Trinidad Colonist*, the *Telegraph*, *Public Opinion*, *Truth*, *The
Mirror*, and several more ephemeral publications. Proprietors,
editors and contributors like Joseph Lewis, Samuel Carter, J.J.
Thomas, William Hibbert and Edgar Maresse-Smith used these
papers to air the grievances of the group, to develop political
agendas, and to move towards an ideology with which to confront
the pervasive racism of colonial society.[5]

In Jamaica and British Guiana, too, small radical newspapers were
instruments to counter the political marginalization of non-white
peoples. But they did more than that: these papers sustained and
extended their conception of freedom, fed notions of a greater role in
civil society, and exposed them to imaginative, often unorthodox,
thinking that enabled them to begin to revise the received construct
of Africa as history-less — a savage place — exacerbated in the
aftermath of the European 'scramble'. These were vital constituents in
the retrieval of self-belief and the shaping of a democratic temper —
a long apprenticeship in self-government. A democratic political
culture, inspired by the Gladstonian liberal political tradition, was
slowly being absorbed, while its lengthy gestation in British West Indian
soil bequeathed it sturdy roots in a way that it did not, possibly could
not, in most other tropical colonies with their resilient atavistic
promptings and cultivated resurgent primordial essences, the tenuous
base of their construction of imagined nations.

The tradition of newspaper publishing among coloured and black
West Indians also facilitated another embryonic democratic practice
among many literate black people: writing letters to the press to expose
one injustice or another. Chronic depression throughout the 1890s
threatened the very economic base that was supposedly indispensable
to the cultivation of civilization in these former slave colonies: the
sugar industry. Ironically, however, it was the threat of extinction of
sugar that opened the way for the subordinate groups to really assert
those rights which they had continually sought since Emancipation:
land reform; alternative industries; educational reform; constitutional
change; broader political representation; and the pursuit and
reaffirmation of their Africanness or Indianness — the redefinition of
ancestral cultures away from stubborn assumptions of savagery. The
latter, in the case of blacks, was stimulated by the yearning for an

imagined homeland to compensate for the deracination of slavery, and the imperative to locate ancestral validation against the void of dispossession and self-contempt, in the largely involuntary African diaspora. It had little or nothing to do with the needs or yearnings of those in Africa. But that did not invalidate the effort.

A principal architect in this project of black affirmation was Dr Robert Love (1839–1914), a Bahamian doctor who had studied and worked in America and Haiti, and settled in Jamaica at the start of the crucial decade of the 1890s. In terms of the elevation of black people, the 1890s were like the 1830s: in both decades they made major strides in their consuming fight for freedom and the expansion of possibilities. Dr Love was, in 1880, apparently the first black graduate at the University of Buffalo, in New York State. In December 1894 he founded a newspaper, the *Jamaica Advocate*, which superseded another black paper, *People's Paper*. In the first issue, on December 15, he sketched his political philosophy and observed that the paper would be the organ of black opinion, the advocate of their social and political rights:

> In politics we are decidedly DEMOCRATIC. Our ideal is a government which is defined by the formula: 'Everything for the people; everything by the people; and nothing without the people'.... We endorse the general platform of the Liberal-Unionists [in Ireland], by which we understand the largest measure of Home rule consistent with a conservation of the integrity of the Empire.... We will not fail to express our views on all questions which affect the interests of the masses; and which tend either to advance or to retard the development of the social and political condition of the common people, of whom we are one.[6]

The Secretary of State for the Colonies, Joseph Chamberlain, argued in 1895 against demands by non-whites for greater representative government in the Empire, countering that concessions could not be made on the same premise as 'a wholly white and British population'. In April 1896 he elaborated on his thesis with reference to the British West Indies: 'In many islands it means only the rule of a local oligarchy of whites and half-breeds — always incapable and frequently corrupt. *In other cases it is the rule of the Negroes — totally unfit for representative institutions and the dupes of unscrupulous adventurers.*'[7] (emphasis added) For Chamberlain, then, black people were a long way from any experiment in self-government.

Dr Love rejected his constipated construction of representative government, the corollary of which was the perpetuation of the glacial pace of constitutional change. As early as December 1895, he had observed that on 'the extended representation' issue — a broader franchise — only the white or light elite's views were being ventilated; and he exhorted ordinary Jamaicans, black people, to utilize the columns of the *Advocate* to articulate theirs. His own stance on the matter was a distinctly advanced one that would have drawn opprobrium from the local elite as well as the Colonial Office. He argued:

> The necessary elements of self-government exist among us and exist in maturity. The desire of the people is a reasonable and lawful one, and when that desire shall have been put before the Crown by the PEOPLE — and not by a few eminent public men only ... a denial of it would be nothing less than an act of unnecessary tyranny. Let the people, therefore, make themselves heard.... Our present condition is a transition[al] one. We are marching slowly toward self-government, which ... must come as the normal condition of free people.... We are radical enough to demand nothing less than what belongs to Englishmen. Self-government is the right of loyal Englishmen, and such are we. Our mistake is that we did not request autonomous government instead of Extended Representation.[8]

Joy Lumsden observes that 'this attitude of claiming rights accorded to Englishmen was to be a continuing theme throughout Love's political career'. It is ironic but astute of Robert Love that he often asserted that Jamaicans, black and coloured, were Englishmen loyal to the Empire, while advancing the case for self-government and re-engagement with their African antecedence. Moreover, he was scrupulous in rejecting 'unconstitutional means to obtain their rights':

> [T]he NEGRO, born under the Union Jack, is none the less an Englishman, although his antecedents take him back to the Western coast of Africa. We use the term 'Negro' not in the narrow sense which confines it to the pure black man; but in the wide generic sense which comprehends all persons of African descent. It is in this sense we say 'our people' and being given that each representative of a race, though cherishing a strong national sentiment, feels an instinctive sympathy for, and a peculiar interest in, the people with whom he is identified by blood, the same conditions are to be expected in the Negro.[9]

*Bahamas-born, Dr Robert Love (1839–1914), radical intellectual/
politician in Jamaica from the 1890s*

Love's intellectually robust and fearless advocacy of his people's case for greater representation in colonial politics earned him the calumny of the white establishment. He was deemed a 'dangerous man', stirring up racial animosity and fomenting 'restlessness and discontent' among the lower orders. Love, however, was not intimidated by such allegations of 'sedition'. On the contrary, he saw these as a vindication of his work, and implored his people to be brave, to mobilize, in order to gain political recognition. As late as May 1895 no black man (as opposed to coloured) had been elected to the Jamaican legislature. This was the context in which Love shed his customary tact and circumspection, and became vitriolic in his resolve to force the pace of constitutional change:

> Our people shrink from a clash which gives promise of unpleasant accompaniments. They bear about with them the terrible weight of a consciousness that they are in the face of those who are opposed to their political advancement, and would meet their efforts with resistance, and perhaps, persecution.... *Hence they give way to the pale face who comes from God knows not where, and as God knows how, to assert an imaginary superiority over them in their own land....* *[B]lack men* [potential leaders] *can no longer hide themselves without being guilty of treason to the best interests of their race and to the hopes which that race have a right to entertain of them. The hour has come: its duty is plain....* Some are whispering that we (of the *Advocate*) are dangerous. We don't care if we are. If to speak our thought freely and fearlessly — if to denounce oppression and wrong — if to teach the class [race] to which we belong their rights and privileges, as well as their duties and responsibilities — if to do these is to be dangerous, then we wish to be dangerous as we can be, and no power can arrest our action in this direction.[10] (emphasis added)

The *Advocate* was unremitting in its ventilation of the grievances, aspirations and achievements of a broad cross section of African Jamaicans. A prolific black correspondent was Walter Whitfinch from Old Harbour (St. Catherine), who had apparently been politically active since the 1860s. He, too, was an avid advocate of self-government, as is evident from his letter to the paper in January 1895: 'It is said by some that the people do not require self-government, [that] they do not wish it. Those who say so are those who do not wish to see the natives becoming their own rulers. Why are not meetings held to know from the people what is their desire on the question of self-government? I am quite sure the result of each meeting would give the denial to such statements'. Another correspondent, self-styled ironically, 'Pro rege et patria', was even more robust in his repudiation of the common official stance on the issue: '[I]n order to occupy a place of respect among the peoples of the earth, it is absolutely necessary that we be entrusted with that which is our birthright. Self-government. *We do not ask a favour. No! We ask for the restoration to us of STOLEN PROPERTY.*'[11] (emphasis added)

Dr Love was committed to black participation in the politics of Jamaica, therefore he was never enamoured of Crown Colony Government, which since the Morant Bay Rebellion of 1865 had been the principal device for stemming any possibility of black or coloured control of the legislature. Although the 1866 constitution was revised in 1886 and an elected majority of two was conceded (nine electives as opposed to the Governor, four ex-officio and two nominated members), that did not alter the fact that executive control was still firmly vested in the Governor in the Executive Council, the real instrument of government. Although any six of the electives could veto financial proposals, this potential for unanimity was purely obstructionist, as they exerted no executive responsibility. In a despatch of August 22, 1899 the Secretary of State for the Colonies, Joseph Chamberlain, recommended that the nominated element, presumably more tractable, be increased by four in order to neutralize the potential of the electives to obstruct financial legislation. The pretext was the urgent necessity for greater financial control and fiscal responsibility by the government, to tide the island over the chronic depression of the late 1890s.[12]

Chamberlain's proposal evoked an energetic, frequently inflamed, campaign by Dr Love to stall what he deemed a draconian measure to abridge constitutional advance. In 1886, for instance, there were only 7,443 electors in a population of 500,000: 3,766 blacks out of 444,186 African Jamaicans; 2,578 coloureds out of a mixed population of 109,946; 1,001 whites out of a white population of 15,000; and 98 Indians out of 11,016 on the island.[13] This was not a massive electorate, but the notion of representative government was already firmly planted, and Dr Love, an elected member of the Kingston City Council, was scrupulous in his resolve to defend that principle, its embryonic state in the British West Indies notwithstanding. In the latter half of 1899 opposition to its further erosion galvanized a broad cross section of Jamaican society. Dr Love was pivotal to the mobilization. According to Patrick Bryan, the doctor believed that the political progress of black people depended ultimately on the quality of their education:

> Black involvement in Crown Colony politics was limited by the strictures imposed by the colonial state on black participation.... Black leaders operated within the confines of the colonial state apparatus, and through the voices of Robert Love and others mounted a moral crusade, seeking to use the conscience of empire to correct its social injustices.... Robert Love, therefore, viewed access to political decision-making as a crucial variable in black progress.... [But] black influence on political decision-making was reduced by their lack of education (and by their poverty) but there was never enough education because the colonial system did not view education as a priority.[14]

Education and political mobility were inseparable. In October 1899 Dr Love moved a resolution in the City Council that a committee be appointed to 'draft a protest against the invasion and destruction of the rights and privileges now enjoyed by the people of Jamaica', as recommended in Chamberlain's despatch. He was not averse to straight talking, and he categorically blamed the Governor of Jamaica, Sir Augustus Hemming, for the impending subtraction from their limited constitutional rights: 'The great executioner ... was the Governor himself for whom he had not the slightest charity. He had been the cause — because of his cowardice — of the whole trouble which had fallen upon the country. He had given Mr Chamberlain the opportunity he wanted to ... take away from them their liberty.... He had assisted in this infernal plot against the people of Jamaica.'[15] Moreover, he interpreted Chamberlain's suggestion that the education vote be reduced as inimical to their education for citizenship and access to representation in the Empire; it was 'in accord only with a policy of establishing permanent Crown [Colony] government'. Love deemed the Secretary of State's despatch 'unjust and oppressive' and 'destructive of the legitimate hopes and aspirations of the people'. However, he hoped the Jamaican people's voices would 'roll ... in thunders of protest', in conjunction with the petition they were sending from the Kingston City Council to Queen Victoria, against the retrograde constitutional measure.[16]

Speaking to the Jamaica Association, of which he was a prominent member, with regard to a memorial to the Queen, Dr Love advocated 'constitutional resistance' against the government's 'infringement of popular rights and privileges'. The memorial, bearing the imprint of his draftsmanship, noted that the articulation of popular protest was orderly, wholly constitutional, and actuated by unswerving loyalty to Her Majesty the Queen.[17] Speaking at a public meeting in Kingston, on the evening of

October 11, 1899, under the auspices of the Jamaica Association, he again pledged loyalty to the Queen ('God Save the Queen' was sung), but was reportedly very agitated in his denunciation of Chamberlain's constitutional proposal because their 'liberties were menaced':

> [N]ot one word of sedition had been spoken at that or any other meeting. All they desired to do was to protect their rights as loyal British subjects. They must make one great terrible howl that would be heard across the Atlantic and make the ears of the British lion tingle (laughter and cheers). A conspiracy had been hatched against their liberties, aided by the complicity of Sir Augustus Hemming [the Governor].... Mr. Chamberlain, the despot of the Empire, was the most insolent man England possessed, and they should repay his insult by striking him right in the solar plexus; he was a man with whom they should have no patience whatsoever.... If they were to be slaves let them be sullen, unhappy, dangerous slaves; if they were kept in bondage let them at least let their masters feel they were not in safety.[18]

The *Gleaner* remarked that Dr Love's speech included a good proportion of 'very strong abuse of Mr. Chamberlain'. The doctor retorted that this was calculated to create the impression that 'everything' he said was 'vulgar abuse' of the Secretary of State. That was 'grossly erroneous'. But he was not apologetic: 'It is not that I care whether I abused Mr. Chamberlain or not, since, in my judgment, no abuse flung at him could equal either his deserts or his own abuse of power; but I object to having attributed to me, in this, or in any other case, any words or acts which are not mine.'[19] On the same day that they published his letter, the paper, which was generally supportive of the constitutional protest, carried a leader in which they attributed to Dr Love's speech in Kingston on October 11, manifestations of 'disloyalty to the British Throne':

> If what [Dr Love] said was not sedition it came pretty near it, and it was, to say the least, most inflammatory in its tendency. In some countries, in Germany, France, Russia, or even the United States, he would have been promptly clapped into prison for the exhibition, and it can only be his lack of judgment which makes him abuse the liberty he enjoys under the British flag.... He had previously remarked that he should not like Mr. Chamberlain to be present in the Theatre. It was, indeed, as well. But Mr.

Chamberlain, or rather the Colonial Office, will know all about it, and they will conclude that if Dr. Love's sentiments and loyalty are the sentiments and loyalty of the majority of the people of Jamaica the sooner the colony is under Crown Government or military rule the better for the safety and peace of the country.... [W]e have very little hope for public agitation of this kind.[20]

The Jamaica Association had taken exception to the *Gleaner's* rebuke of Dr Love, a member of their executive council, and its President was requested to reject the charge of 'seditious utterances and disloyalty to the Throne'.[21] Nothing came of this, but the Archbishop of the West Indies intervened quickly, making the classic argument for imperial trusteeship: the necessity for gradualism in constitutional development. He was obviously not impressed with Dr Love's speech, for he cautioned leaders of public opinion to guard against the imputation of evil motives on the part of imperial leaders. He felt that much of the current agitation was driven by wrong assumptions: 'there is no need to import into the debate any question as to our needing to struggle for the present retention of any political liberties and rights we possess, because of the fear that what may be yielded now, in a period of difficulty, will not be recovered again when circumstances justify it'. The Archbishop was sanguine that colonials did not have to wage a struggle for change, as the paramount goal of the British Empire — 'the greatest, freest empire which has ever existed' — was the expansion of 'justice, liberty and self-government' in each colony. To 'struggle' was superfluous; to those who know how to wait, all shall be given:

The more quickly and the more completely any colony can reach the stage of being capable of efficiently managing its own affairs, with the lowest minimum of interference from home, the better pleased are the home authorities. Whatever be the greater or smaller political changes which may take place in any colony in view of varying circumstances, they are all controlled by this universal, though unwritten, law of the Empire, that each colony must have its own responsible government as soon as it is fit for it. There is no need to contend for these rights and privileges: the only thing necessary is for the colony to fit itself for the beneficial use of them.[22]

The *Gleaner*, though highly critical of the immoderate rhetoric of Dr Love, was not impressed either with the Archbishop's pontificating on the merits of trusteeship and the assumption of balance and supreme wisdom at the heart of the Imperial order. It is arguable, therefore, that by dramatizing the issue, infusing the debate with his passion and rich imagery, however abrasive, Love had captured the public imagination. Indeed, it was a reflection of the depth of that popular response against Chamberlain's constitutional imposition, that a generally conservative paper could now adopt a progressive stand on a matter in which 'the passions of men have been mastering their judgment and common sense'. The *Gleaner* rejected categorically the Archbishop's unquestioning *raison d'être* of Imperial rule:

> We find now that a step backward is to be taken in the political progress of Jamaica and, therefore, the Imperial Government considers that we are not yet fully able to discharge the responsibility that has been laid upon us.... The Government is to be in a permanent majority with the complete power of such a position, and the opposition is to be in a permanent minority with no power save that of criticism. The franchise would only have a fictitious value and it would be better not to go to the trouble of having elected members at all. If it be said that the system is necessary for a time in order to get the finances into a better position, then this should be made perfectly clear.... Our own belief is that the Colonial Office could manage to rehabilitate the colony and keep a firmer grip on the finances without in the slightest degree interfering with the present valuable educative system.[23]

The *Gleaner* was consistent, for it had earlier reproduced and endorsed a leader from the *Times* on the demerits of Crown Colony government in the British West Indies. The paper had argued cogently that the cure for irresponsible opposition by elected members in colonial politics was 'responsible self-government':

> The true remedy for obstructive criticism is to call upon the obstructionists to take responsibility of alternative measures. Representative institutions, under which an elective Opposition can never be subjected to this test, put a premium upon obstruction. Their value as a constitutional instrument is simply to secure Government control ... over the early acts of communities unused to the exercise of independent power. To attempt to maintain such control permanently when financial independence has been conceded is a negation of all the goals upon which the principle of

representation itself is based.... The question arises why representative institutions in the West Indies should not lead, as in the case of other British colonies, to the enjoyment of responsible self-government.[24]

Chamberlain, under the pretext of facilitating urgent, tighter financial management, had stripped the electives of their veto power on financial matters, and was in the process of augmenting the nominated element to give Government decisive legislative control. The *Gleaner* was not persuaded that this was a condign initiative to alleviate an economic crisis largely not of the Jamaican people's making:

> The country will not object to the Imperial Government exercising stricter supervision over the finances, and even giving it certain additional power in this direction if only the local measure of representation now enjoyed is left untouched, and the people feel that they still have a real hand in directing the affairs of the colony. But the appointment of four extra members on the Government side will destroy this position and induce a sense of wrong in the minds of the people which will lead sooner or later to a disturbing agitation. Mr. Chamberlain should be advised to leave well alone.[25]

But the robust combativeness, sustained largely because of the unremitting militancy of Dr Love, had kindled 'a sense of wrong' among black people, even evoking an idealistic response in some, fed by a messianic vision of illimitable possibilities for progress in the imagined African homeland. Fact and fantasy run deep in West Indian peoples' constructions of their identities. In October 1899, for instance, the *Gleaner* cited the case of 'A Negro of Jamaica', a correspondent who argued that 'the people of the country are chiefly ruled for the benefit of their rulers. If ... the Negro is not judged worthy of real representative government, the sooner the British people restore him to his birthright by sending him back to the native land of his race the better'.[26] As will be seen later, this messianic strand was at the core of the mission of the Barbados-born visionary, Dr Albert Thorne.

But the spirited, pragmatic advocacy of representative government and the necessity for black participation, advanced untiringly by Dr Love, was a substantially more persuasive element in the political awakening of African Jamaicans at the end of the nineteenth century. One such correspondent, in November 1899, W. Provost, was emphasizing the importance of educating 'men', black leaders, capable of assuming responsibility for their own future — tutoring them in the art of self-government. He posed several questions:

> [W]ill Crown Colony Government ever produce such men? Has it ever done so? Where on all the globe will we see this form of government producing self-reliant, manly, righteous men? Can you expect it should, when you take from them the one great subject upon which the mind of men should be exercised, viz ... how to govern. From this standpoint alone Crown Government has failed, absolutely failed. It can make slaves — never men. It can make beasts of burden, never thinking, reliable men and women. Never yet has prosperity moved in the midst of slaves nor has progress come from beasts of burden.... This is the work of Representative Government.[27]

Lord Olivier, the Colonial Secretary (1900–04) and Governor of Jamaica (1907–13), observed thus of the response to Crown Colony government in Jamaica: 'The Island politicians were sobered by the experiences of the [Morant Bay] rebellion [of 1865], and were content to acquiesce for a period in the suppression of their ancient self-governing liberties.'[28] This was no longer the case by the end of the nineteenth century, with the emergence of a black middle class determined to assert their rights. Robert Love was the black people's principal champion of representative government in the 1890s and the first decade of the twentieth century; he was *the* Jamaican advocate.

Dr Love was an intrepid thinker far advanced of his time. Not only was he punctilious in ascertaining the thoughts of black workers and peasants, he was, as early as April 1895, resolved that the education of black women must be treated as a matter of urgent priority. Black people could not advance if their women folk were kept in darkness. He argued:

> We have concentrated on the elevation of our men — clergymen, lawyers, etc. — but not on our daughters. The race must rise by families not by individuals. Men are still despised in spite of their achievements. The race rises as its women rise. They are the true standard of its elevation. We are trying to produce cultured men without asking ourselves where they are to find cultured wives. We forget that cultured families constitute a cultured race and that a cultured race is an equal race. The elevation of women to equality with [their] white counterparts is the condition *sine qua non* of the elevation of the Negro race.... Every pound spent to

educate the black boy tends to elevate a class only, but every pound spent to educate a black girl, tends to elevate the whole race. Fathers and mothers, bear these facts in mind, and send as many of your black daughters to England as you can. Some tell you that your girls can be just as well educated here. Ask them: why then do they send theirs to England?[29]

I have argued that the emergence of an educated elite, by the 1890s, gave black people a voice, but the economic depression of that decade and the precarious state of the sugar industry, endowed this voice with a passion and tenacity of purpose that was to shape the political culture of the British West Indies profoundly. However tentatively or spasmodically, the foundation of its democratic tradition, patterned after their colonial masters, was being laid, a temperament for its cultivation was in the making. Dr Robert Love was its principal architect at the end of the nineteenth century, so too were the Jamaican doctor and medical missionary in Africa, Dr Theophilus E.S. Scholes, an Edinburgh graduate, and the young Indian intellectual in British Guiana, Joseph Ruhomon (1873–1942), an autodidact. Although they all continually professed loyalty to the Queen, they were great admirers of their respective ancestral homelands, Africa and India. They saw no contradiction in celebrating the ancient and contemporary achievements of Africans and Indians ('at home and abroad'), while being committed to the advancement of the British West Indies. In fact, they believed that to achieve the latter, it was imperative to build self-belief, and this could not be attained without knowledge of, and the cultivation of pride in, one's ancestral heritage. There was no substitute for racial pride — as opposed to racism, which spoke of racial chauvinism: bigotry — in countering self-deprecation and inferiority complex, the inevitable legacy of a history of subjugation under slavery and indentureship.

Dr Scholes was born in St. Ann, Jamaica in 1856 and studied medicine and theology at Edinburgh and Brussels respectively. He was a medical missionary in Central Africa (Congo) for five years (1886–91) and New Calabar, Nigeria, for two (1891–93), travelled widely in the continent, observed diverse societies with empathy and discernment, writing later with great conviction of Africa's role in the 'civilization' of Europe, as well as on manifestations of human ingenuity and achievement in contemporary Africa. These are developed in *The British Empire and Alliances*, published in London in 1899, and his two-volume *Glimpses of the Ages, or the 'Superior' and 'Inferior' Races so-called, Discussed in the Light of Science and History*, published in 1905 and 1907 in London as well. As a contemporary observed:

> The life of this excellent gentleman and accomplished scholar supplies a happy instance of the harmonious union of religion with learning, of ardent piety with the pursuit of literature. Dr. Theo. E. Samuel Scholes, the distinguished author of *Glimpses of the* Ages, and whom the *New York Times* and a few other leading journals suppose is a white man, is a native of Jamaica.... Besides the double qualifications of the Royal College of Surgeons, Edinburgh, which Dr. Scholes holds and which he took in 1884, he also took the M.D. Degree of the University of Brussels in 1893.... Dr. Scholes is a huge Negro and is proud of his African blood.... [He] has rendered the race a valuable service in giving to Negro literature such a book as *Glimpses of the* Ages. He has proved the truth of the axiom that 'the Negro was born to scholarship'. Every Negro who thinks should read *Glimpses of the* Ages.[30]

Patrick Bryan assesses Dr Scholes's contribution thus: '[He was] to a significant extent a pioneer of black history ... relentless in his determination to establish that blacks had a history of distinction. But he went further, to establish that that history was the root, if not the branch, of all that was assumed to be civilised in 1900'. Bryan adds that Scholes's debunking of the myth of white supremacy, with 'irony and intellectual aggression', was indicative of his deep pride in his African antecedence. This is encapsulated in the following excerpt on the Nile Valley civilization from his book of 1899: '[U]nless it can be proved that when these Egyptians were the greatest civilised power in the world they were white, and when the white races of today were barbarians they were black or brown, the theory that the white skin only is associated with progress and greatness cannot be sustained; neither can the obverse, that the dark skin is associated with littleness, be maintained.'[31]

Dr Scholes was unequivocal in whatever claims he made for African civilizations. He argued that the ancient Egyptians, people of a high civilization, were 'Negroes'; moreover, that Europeans had systematically distorted this fact in order to deny agency to Africans — their proven intellectual acuity, creative energy and scientific pedigree, so as to sustain the myth of their savagery and perpetuate their exploitation.

But he contended that it was the 'Negro Egyptians' whose intellectual legacy had been appropriated by the Greeks; they, therefore, were 'the educators of modern Europe'. Black Africa, paradoxically, had helped to shape the instruments for European subjugation of 'Ethiopians':

> The Egyptians having from the various fields of nature gleaned and systematised knowledge called the sciences, and having further skilfully adapted that knowledge, or the sciences, to practical ends called the arts, the adoption by the Greeks of these sciences and arts has directly and indirectly made the Egyptians the educators of modern Europe.... The truth ... is, that the white race having formed the idea that it is with itself that civilisation should have originated, has not only refused to have that idea modified by the facts that reveal its groundless assumption ... but in antagonism to the spirit of honest research ... it has, in conformity with the methods of Procrustes, proceeded to cut and to carve, to set and to reset, to cast and to recast these facts, until they seem to sanction its idea that it was with itself that civilisation began.[32]

But it was not only through the episodic — manifestations of ancient grandeur — that Scholes sought to establish the intellectual legacy, the civilized credentials, of Africans. His life in Africa, in conjunction with his wide travels on the continent, enabled him to identify and celebrate small, but admirable, examples of ingenuity, mental alertness and achievement in contemporary Africa. To West Indians, enmeshed in unflattering Eurocentric constructions of the homeland, exacerbated by the 'scramble' for the 'dark continent', this illumination from one of their own — he had gone 'home' — must have stimulated immeasurable pride in their African provenance. In the 1790s, Bryan Edwards, the Jamaican planter/historian, had remarked on the literacy of a few of his Mandingo slaves: 'I had ... [a] Mandingo servant who could write, with great beauty and exactness, the Arabic alphabet, and some passages from the Alcoran [Koran]. Whether his learning extended any further I had no opportunity of being informed, as he died soon after he came into my possession.... The advantage possessed by a few of these people, of being able to read and write, is a circumstance on which the Mandingo people of the West Indies pride themselves greatly among the rest of the slaves, over whom they consider that they possess a marked superiority.'[33]

Some of the descendants of the enslaved in the West Indies were of Mandingo or other Muslim stock, such as the Fulas, and they were, indeed, so proud of this that it stayed with them long after Emancipation. Therefore, they would have readily identified with Scholes's fine appreciation of their people's physical and cultural attributes. But he was complimentary of some other groups as well:

> The Mandingoes inhabit a tract of country situated to the north of Sierra Leone, which derives its name, Senegambia, from two important streams, the Senegal and the Gambia, by which it is drained.... [They] are tall in stature, with slender, athletic forms, and purely black complexion.... [T]hey are a progressive people. I am now speaking more particularly of the Mohammedan Mandingoes. Their industrial enterprise for example, agriculture, the tanning and dressing of leather, the weaving of cloth, the smelting of iron, the melting and drawing out of gold into wire, their work in pottery and wood-carving, their schools, the size and arrangement of their dwellings, their value of chastity, their refinement in social intercourse, the freedom of speech in their assemblies — all certify to their progress.... But we pass on to compare the Mandingoes, who are admittedly among the most progressive of the peoples of Africa, with other African nations and tribes.... It may be generally stated that all African peoples work in iron.... But besides the working in iron throughout Africa, and the working in gold by several African peoples, there are such handicrafts as pottery-making, weaving, wood-carving, as well as the building of permanent settlements.... Hence, as far as the spontaneous progress of the Mandingoes is concerned, other African nations and tribes may generally be said to be on a level with them.[34]

Like Edward Blyden (1832–1912), the scholar and statesman from the Danish West Indies who had settled in Liberia in 1851, Scholes was an intellectual and indomitable champion of African peoples. He argued perceptively that the best way to ascertain the intellectual capacity of diverse peoples was to compare their respective achievement in areas where they lived and worked under more or less similar conditions. By this measure, Africa had much to celebrate: from the ancient Egyptians to contemporary times. But he was equally proud of African achievement in the diaspora. He conceded that many in the New World still laboured under severe handicaps: racial discrimination was still rampant, especially in the southern United States. Yet, as he observed of a banquet given by African-Americans in Atlanta in 1899 in honour of their hero, Booker T. Washington, the 'refinement' and cultural mastery demonstrated on that occasion was astounding. It was an eloquent defiance of the chronic racial discrimination; and it gave Dr Scholes evident pride to quote a white guest, a Colonel John Temple Graves, who had written magnanimously and graciously of the event:

> The master of ceremonies was Rev. H.H. Proctor, and no better presiding officer has come under observation in Atlanta. From first to last he was the graceful master of the occasion; dignity, impressiveness, felicity of manner, accuracy of speech, and the keenest and most tactful statement of the meaning of the occasion and of the appropriateness of each speaker to the programme. We have no presiding officer of either race in Atlanta who could have bettered the performance last night. He was a dark mulatto. In the speech of Dr. J.M. Henderson, an even darker man, the public in attendance was treated to as fine a specimen of fiery and impassioned eloquence as I have ever heard in Atlanta. I say it deliberately, that we have no orator of either race in this city that could surpass in force, in magnetism, in delivery, and in vigorous diction the really magnificent burst of this Negro educator.

Graves concluded his appreciation thus:

> Booker Washington presented his case with a tact, a courtesy, a plausibility, and a power which no publicist in Georgia has surpassed.... [T]he exercises of this notable reception were closed by a baritone solo from Lawrence Steel, an extremely black man, whose voice has no natural equal among the vocalists in the capital of Georgia. Now these four Negroes represent the highest development and the highest attainment of their race. They had 'what the white man wanted'. If he wanted eloquence, they had it to burn. If he wanted wit, it was there. If he wanted wisdom, it was on hand. If he wanted common-sense, it was plentiful. If he wanted music, it rolled in waves of melody from the throat of the singer. No white had a greater stock of these qualities.[35]

The African people of the Americas, by the 1890s, were already on the move. It was only half a century since Emancipation in the British West Indies, in the case of the United States, a mere 34 years. That was why this commendation from a white man would have made such a profound impression on Scholes. Indeed, all black people could claim such manifestations of excellence as a reflection of themselves; the credit was magnified when it came from the pen of a white man in the American South. With this kind of leadership, therefore, Scholes was more than optimistic for the future of black people in the diaspora. He argued thus: '[A] correct estimate of the position of a race ... presupposes some knowledge of its ability or its inability to produce great leaders.'[36] And he proceeded to elaborate on the gifts of Toussaint L'Ouverture, Frederick Douglass, Booker T. Washington and Edward Blyden, '[the first] three of whom had been slaves', he quickly pointed out.[37] Like most 'Ethiopians' (Africans) in the New World, he believed that they were demonstrating their capacity, when given a fair chance, to compete successfully with the white man. Unlike Blyden, however, Dr Scholes was not an advocate of 'return' to the homeland, but he wished that the people in Africa would soon emulate the example of their successful American compatriots:

[W]hen the progress of the white section of the United States is composed, we discover that there is not an element in that highly organised system that has not been reproduced by the Ethiopian. Thus education, theology, manufacture, invention, agriculture, commerce, finance, politics, military prowess, journalism, music, painting, poetry, oratory, literature, political economy, philosophy, and refinement of feeling and of manner, are among the objects that have excited his interest; that have enlisted his talents and activities. In relation to Western civilisation, therefore, the position of the Afro-American may be fittingly described as that of complete identification and of complete assimilation. And as the Afro-American adumbrates the African race, that race must also be said to possess the ability to identify itself with, and to assimilate Western civilisation.[38]

For Dr Scholes, the diverse progress of Africans in America and the West Indies was heightened immeasurably by the fact that it was accomplished despite the unimaginable savagery of supposed Christians. A devout Christian himself, a medical missionary, he considered the European–African encounter in the New World a most reprehensible experience, the antithesis of Christian precepts and assumptions. As the Jamaica *Daily Gleaner* remarked in 1899, shortly after the publication of Scholes's *The British Empire and Alliances*, he was so appalled by this that even Turkey's infamy with regards to her treatment of subject peoples paled by comparison:

> One of his [Scholes's] aims is to prove the inconsistency of the United States, a professedly Christian nation, in connection with its treatment of the Negroes. Here he scores heavily as he could not fail to do. America he contrasts with Turkey to the former's disadvantage. The religion of the Turks [Islam] sanctions or commands his atrocities; the religion of the Americans forbids his barbarities and yet he commits deeds which surpass those of the Turk in cruelty. Some of these are detailed in the book and they are horrible enough in all conscience. This chapter on the relation of the white and dark races is of the nature of an indictment, bald, grim and scathing.[39]

The *Gleaner* notes that his perception of this relationship in the West Indies was also marred by its prejudicial character, to the detriment of the welfare of non-whites: 'the author treats of the West Indies and the sugar question, arguing that the sugar industry has never been carried on properly according to natural economic conditions, but has always been artificially bolstered up with the object of maintaining the position and prestige of the white, and the continuation of class government. This class government, he states, is the result of race prejudice'. The paper was less supportive of his verdict on the black West Indian condition, for they considered the black–white encounter in the United States markedly less open. This was supposedly corroborated, in December 1899, by B.P. Wynter, a black Jamaican correspondent to the *Gleaner* resident in America, who wrote: '[O]ur condition is far in advance of the American negro. We have the rights of citizenship; we have rights of the franchise. Already a member of our race has found a seat in the Legislative Council [of Jamaica]. We have the advantage of a modern education in the same school as the white man's children. We are learning to respect each other's rights.'[40] None-the-less the *Gleaner* saw Dr Scholes's book as an achievement, informative and provocative: 'though somewhat laboured and heavy, [it] is an interesting one, supplying much information on the subjects of which it treats, and provocative of reflection. When a book compels one to think it has achieved a useful purpose and justified its publication'.[41]

Scholes and the African elite in the diaspora had no reservations about the pedigree of their progress, that what they were 'mastering' was 'the highest type of civilisation'. But they had acquired sufficient self-confidence to argue that their role was not simply imitative; they were not just mimic men. He felt that they had the 'genius' to 'enlarge or extend it'. They were, indeed, bringing something of their African personality, their tradition, to the process, thus enriching western civilization immeasurably. Dr Scholes concluded, on the eve of the twentieth century, with the following reaffirmation of African peoples' history, thus enhancing the case, as he saw it, for the antiquity of Africa's contribution to the refinement of Europe:

> [T]he ancient Egyptian discloses the brain of the Negro as being the fountain-head, whence the great river system, Western civilisation, has had its origin.... Africa, heathen, with a culture purely native...in quality [was] higher than Europe, heathen, at the time of the Roman Conquest. From the Mohammedan states, stretching along the great Soudan belt of the continent ... the Ethiopian has been able to adjust himself to the higher culture of the Arab. And this ability of the Ethiopian to assimilate a culture higher than his own, finds its most striking confirmation ... under Christian culture.... Therefore, in virtue of these facts, there exists no evidence in support of the assertion, that between the Negro and the Caucasian there are mental differences of a racial character. And since the alleged superiority of the colourless race, and the alleged inferiority of the coloured races, are professed to be founded on these differences, I conclude that no ground exists for the assertion that the Caucasian is superior to the Ethiopian or superior to the coloured races.[42]

Inherent in Scholes's reading of African history is the notion of 'cycles of civilisation', that the high point of his people's achievement was the Egyptian civilization of the lower Nile Valley — the cultural sophistication and technological superiority of a black people. As with all great civilizations, however, its decay was inevitable; the decline into barbarism could not be arrested. But the inherent greatness of Africans and their gift for recuperation were also reflected, later, in the way they assimilated and creatively advanced received Islamic and Christian cultures, deemed 'higher than their own'. It was this perception that the African in the New World, having mastered Western civilisation, could accelerate the 'civilising' process in 'fallen' Africa, that had driven the West Indian scholar, statesman and visionary, Edward Blyden, in the latter half of the nineteenth century, to devote his intellect and abundant energies to promoting the settlement of

Africans in the diaspora, in West Africa — Liberia. By the late 1890s, a Barbadian who had settled in Jamaica, Dr J. Albert Thorne, also, was advocating a back-to-Africa movement.

There was always a missionary/messianic component to the New World Africans' conceptions of 'return'. There was also a romantic strand that, as Patrick Bryan observes, permeated Rev Robert Dingwall's vision of the new Africa. He anticipated the construction of a rejuvenated political Africa of 'internal righteousness' and 'moral regeneration'. This would, in turn, produce a new African: 'noble, majestic, princely'.[43] In the case of Dr Thorne's African Colonization Enterprise or African Colonial Enterprise, enunciated in December 1899, a discernibly more pragmatic scheme was advanced, but it also was permeated by an element of the messianic, coupled with the assumption of the moral and intellectual superiority of most blacks in the diaspora. He did not even countenance the logical region of potential 'colonization', West Africa, as in Blyden's Liberian mission, or the resettlement of 'creoles' in Sierra Leone. Moreover, Dr Thorne's scheme was predicated on the common assumption of 'darkness' and 'superstition' in Africa and the rightness of the European missionary's zeal to uproot such iniquities. His scheme embraced the following:

1. To assist enterprising members of the African race now resident in the Western Hemisphere to return and settle down in their fatherland, Nyasaland [contemporary Malawi], British Central Africa, being the site selected.
2. To develop agricultural, commercial and other available resources of the country.
3. To give the natives a suitable and profitable education.
4. To extend the Kingdom of God in those vast regions, by leading such as are in darkness and error or superstition to Jesus Christ.
5. To improve the status of the African race.
6. To foster and cement the bonds of friendship and brotherhood between all races of mankind, without respect of colour or creed.[44]

Dr Thorne had, as early as March 1897, attracted severe censure from the *Daily Gleaner* in Jamaica, which had imputed to him selfish motives in his promulgating of the colonization scheme. The paper recalled that he was a native of Barbados, a schoolteacher, who had studied medicine at the University of Edinburgh, having graduated in

1893. They claimed that he had raised at least £350 by November 1896, and had augmented that in the United States whence 'subscriptions have flowed in more or less regularly since'. In 1899, when Dr Thorne arrived in Jamaica, the *Gleaner* was still not persuaded of the bona fides of his scheme:

> The African Colonial Enterprise is no nearer realisation than it was when Dr. Thorne first conceived it in his student days in Edinburgh. It seems that practically the whole of the funds have been expended on Dr. Thorne's maintenance and travelling expenses ... [while] the preparations towards the colony are confined to a few bags of seeds and a few cases of medicines presented by philanthropic firms. There does not seem to be the faintest prospect of any West Indian or American Negroes ever settling in Nyasaland under the aegis of the African Colonial Enterprise.[45]

The *Gleaner* interviewed Dr Thorne at the end of October 1899, in Kingston; he remained sanguine that he could raise the funds he needed to go to Africa to start the colony: his friends in England and America, he was sure, would support the initiative. And he rejected the paper's claims that he had done well off a fictitious venture: 'He ... [countered that he] had ... sacrificed much for the benefit of his race. He had lived on very little when he might have made a handsome income by medical practice. The undertaking had not been financially profitable by any means'. This did not lessen the paper's obduracy in rejecting the scheme, apparently first adumbrated in July 1895:

DG: Have you been to Nyasaland yet to see the colony?

JAT: No, but I hope to do so soon. Sir Harry Johnston, Her Majesty's Commissioner, has promised grants of land for each settler.

DG: Have you got your first lot of emigrants to promise to go yet?

JAT: No, but I shall get them together in due course. You see the preliminary arrangements take some time.[46]

The paper deemed the Nyasaland colony a 'castle in Spain', and recalled that they had first encountered Dr Thorne in 1896 when, in papers received from Scotland, he had argued that the decline of the sugar industry in the West Indies had exacerbated the poverty of its black population. Those islands were detrimental to the mobility of 'educated and enterprising' Africans. It was to expand their possibilities and quicken the civilizing of the 'natives' of Africa that he had launched the African Colonial Enterprise. The *Gleaner* sought to sketch the key features of the scheme, but their incredulity persisted:

> The idea was to acquire a tract of land in British Central Africa, the descendants of the race here [the West Indies] being utilised to develop its resources. At first 100 suitable families were to be selected. They were to be placed on allotments of 100 acres each near a civilised centre. During three years each head of family was to receive sufficient food and clothing for his household, and from the fourth to the tenth year he would receive an annual allowance of £30. At the close of the tenth year the land was to become his property. Any profits during the ten years were to be devoted to spreading civilisation among the surrounding natives, and to assist other enterprising West Indians to settle.[47]

Dr Thorne had responded to the *Gleaner's* interview with him, declaring that he was not surprised by its antagonistic 'tone', as the paper was predictable in its instinct for calumniating all African endeavours. He declared: 'It is a well-known fact that the editor of the *Gleaner* is one of the most bitter enemies of my race in these West Indian islands'. However, a substantially more favourable report is rendered by the same paper in early December 1899, when Dr Thorne addressed a public meeting on his colonization scheme, at Porus Baptist Chapel, in the parish of Manchester. The audience was estimated at about 600, and the reporter noted:

> After a few short statements of his native place [Barbados], parentage, early training and the help that he received in England and Scotland in preparing himself for his life's work, the Doctor, with much simplicity and great earnestness, put the whole of his admirable and comprehensive scheme, together with his resources and ultimate intentions, before the audience in about an hour and fifty minutes. He made a good impression on the people who listened to him most attentively. At the close the pastor of the church had a collection taken up for the purpose of encouraging the Doctor in his lecturing tour on this side of the island.[48]

And as a correspondent wrote to the *Gleaner*, if Dr Thorne wished he could have made a good living because of his 'ability and attainments' as a doctor. There was really no need for him to eke out an uncertain existence, unless he was actuated by a sincerity of purpose.[49]

In mid-December 1899 Dr Thorne wrote to the editor of the *Gleaner*, whom he accused of trying to 'rob him of ... [his] reputation'. He said that he was owed an apology. The paper responded by reproducing a piece from the *Argosy* of British Guiana, which also sought to challenge the integrity of the organizer of the African Colonial Enterprise, even suggesting his usurpation of the title of medical practitioner, in his duping of white liberals — it commenced by citing him thus: 'Dr. Thorne'. The correspondent alleged:

> Dr. Thorne was a student at Edinburgh University, and having the good fortune to be a black man, his scheme to extend the Kingdom of God to the natives of Africa, and assist black men in the Western Hemisphere to return and settle in their fatherland, was received by goody-goody 'naturals' in Scotland with enthusiasm, albeit certain of the hard-headed Scots would have none of him. Since then, on the strength of the names of the Committee which he succeeded in forming in Scotland, he has collected money in various parts for the furtherance of the scheme, but otherwise there has been no progress and there is no money left.[50]

Nothing did come of Dr Thorne's scheme, but he settled in Jamaica, practising as a doctor in St. Elizabeth and Manchester.[51] His visionary conception of Africa must have had some impact on young Marcus Garvey growing up in the parish of St. Ann at the turn of the century: it was the precursor of the 'back-to-Africa' strand in his own vision of redemption for Africans in the Western Hemisphere. Moreover, it illustrates the extent to which Africans in the diaspora, in the aftermath of 'the scramble for Africa' and the continual denigration of the continent and its peoples, were impelled, at the end of the nineteenth century, to seek to re-engage with and redefine notions of Africa — to construct imaginary homelands congruent with their pursuit of intimations of ancestral greatness and the antiquity of such achievements. As I have argued, these imagined homelands had everything to do with the need to create their own heroes and a yearning for engagement with a constructed past of initiative, enterprise and high civilization, essential to their rehabilitation from the deracination of slavery and its legacy of self-contempt. Africas of the imagination, therefore, were an essential ingredient in the making of black British West Indian identity; but it was easier for them to foster inclusive constructions of homeland, to think in pan-African terms, than for Africans at home, rooted in their discrete ancestral spaces with autonomous cultures, and immersed in the peculiarities and rivalries of diverse societies. But it does not make the West Indian's interminable quest for 'return' — largely metaphorical — invalid.

Dr Love's *Jamaica Advocate* constantly addressed issues relating to Africa and colonialism. For instance, in July 1904, as Rupert Lewis observes, Love challenged the following thesis by Joseph Chamberlain: 'as the dominant race, if we [the British] admitted equality with inferior races, we would lose the power which gave us our dominance'. He countered, prophetically, that the bigotry and arrogance at the heart of the assertion would eventuate in the abrogation of imperial rule:

> It is with this principle that they vex the Africans with 'punitive expeditions', and destroy the Indians with famine and oppression. It is thus minded that their Governors and officials and under-strappers come to these isles [the West Indies]. But Englishmen will wake up some day to find they are making a great mistake.... The subject races will not always be governed by that spirit. They were not always thus governed. The Indian will some day repel the assumption, the African will do the same thing, the Egyptian, the Burmese, etc., will vindicate their individuality, and will prove that temporary dominance is not evidence of constitutional superiority.[52]

Several West Indians had gone to Africa to work as teachers, missionaries and skilled craftsmen in the late nineteenth century. They were driven by their own assumptions of superiority — 'to assist in the enlightenment of neglected Africa'. Most, though, had no contact whatsoever with the homeland, but the *Jamaica Advocate* kept Africa alive in the minds of its readers. Dr Love reproduced excerpts from various West African newspapers continually, and in 1897 he carried a series of articles by Dr Scholes on European rule in Africa. The paper also carried the elegant, scholarly writings of the greatest black intellectual of the nineteenth century, the author of *Christianity, Islam and the Negro Race* (1887), Edward Wilmot Blyden of the Danish West Indies (later the US Virgin Islands) and Liberia.[53]

These were the intellectual foundation of Garveyism and the race pride movement of the 1920s. In it the radical ideas for political representation and social reform, advocated by Dr Robert Love, the revisionist theories of Dr T.E.S. Scholes and Edward Blyden on African history, and the notion of physical return to the homeland of Rev Dingwall and Dr Thorne to accelerate the civilizing process, met and energized black people universally to fight for their rights. But African self-assertion was an inspiration, too, for people of Indian descent in the British West Indies, as early as the 1890s. A little over half a million had been taken from India to the Caribbean between 1838 and 1917, primarily to British Guiana and Trinidad, as indentured labourers on the sugar plantations. Their first intellectual, Joseph Ruhomon (1873–1942), was born in British Guiana. In 1894 he exhorted his compatriots to emulate the African people in their quest for belonging, in the British West Indies. The key constituent of the African example, as I have been arguing, was a commitment to Western education and cricket — the essence of the public school code — interwoven with a resurgent pride in an imagined homeland. By the end of the nineteenth century, the African example was percolating to children of those indentured labourers from India, disparagingly called 'coolies'.

By the 1890s, as some Indians in the West Indies acquired financial security from land-ownership, rice, cattle, cocoa, sugar and commerce, a small middle class was taking shape. A minority of Christian Indians, such as the Ruhomons and their cousins, the Luckhoos, in British Guiana, embarked on the arduous task of erasing the resilient 'coolie' image — the badge of indentureship and the instinct to see all Indians as menial labourers or jobbers. The first person to locate this endeavour within an intellectual framework was Joseph Ruhomon, a self-educated young man, a virtual disciple of the Anglo-Indian missionary in British Guiana, Rev H.V.P. Bronkhurst (1826–1895), who was chronicling some of the magnificent achievements of ancient India.[54] Like their African counterparts in the 1890s, the Indian middle class hankered after intimations of ancestral greatness — real or imagined — to lift the dark legacy of slavery and indentureship and lessen the humiliation engendered by European domination of Africa and India.

In this context, therefore, Ruhomon was able to call both on ancient India and the progress of Africans in the diaspora, in offering his Indian compatriots a compass away from the 'coolie' persona, the retrieval of their self-respect. Like Africans who had started on that road earlier, western education and cricket, too, would be key instruments to chart the journey. It is noteworthy, though, that it took the emergence of a middle class in both communities before the narratives of rehabilitation and self-pride could be constructed. It required some self-belief to do this, indigenous and exogenous promptings. The location of their antecedents in a remote past of acknowledged supremacy and high achievement: civilized Egypt and India — imagined homelands — was crucial.

In a lecture on October 4, 1894 (published in December of that year, with an introduction by his mentor, Rev Bronkhurst), Joseph Ruhomon celebrated ancient and contemporary accomplishments of both Africans and Indians. Moreover, he implored Indians in the colony to emulate Africans in the field of education:

> Two of the greatest nations in the world that have been noted for gross moral and intellectual darkness were Africans and East Indians. Both were renowned many, many centuries ago. Both have had an interrupted career, both have had a break in the course of their progress ... and both today are climbing up the ladder of progress.... The Negroes are a great people; they have been so from the earliest times, and though there have been many impediments to their progress, they are rising and making their influence felt far and wide.... Africans have been famous since the earliest times.... Here [British Guiana], intellectually, morally, religiously and socially, they are wonderfully improving ... nothing can now contort or cripple the giant might of [their] nature and hinder [them] in [their] march of progress.[55]

Ruhomon then articulated his own pride in his Indian antecedents before challenging Indians in British Guiana to cultivate the intellect. Here again, the imagined homeland, the fount of ancient grandeur, was the foundation stone for the pursuit of contemporary goals: 'East Indians are an inherently great people, and I feel supremely proud of the fact as one who has the pure, genuine East Indian blood flowing in his veins. In their own literature, science and art, Indians have held their own'. He amplifies this with a quote from Bronkhurst, whose voluminous writings on British Guiana were published in the 1880s and early 1890s: '[Indians] have very largely contributed towards extending our knowledge of nature, in mathematics, astronomy, mechanics and other sciences, arithmetic, geography, algebra, etc ... [they] have produced poets, philosophers, mathematicians ... whose original lofty genius is now universally admitted by those who have deeply studied them to be by no means inferior to that of Shakespeare, Lock and Newton, making due allowance, however, for the remote age in which they flourished.'[56]

Joseph Ruhomon (1873–1942): the first Indian intellectual in the West Indies

This was Ruhomon's perception of India's ancient heritage. From this vantage point of pride and optimism, he challenged his Indo-Guyanese compatriots in 1894 to follow the example of the people of their motherland. Like Dr Love, he foresaw the end of the British Empire; but this would be accomplished, he argued, only if they mastered the western idiom:

> I am not only convinced ... of the greatness of India as a country ... but I am joyfully and confidently anticipating the time when in intelligence, in culture, in morals and intellectual attainments, the great East Indian Race [sic] shall be second to none in the world.... They have indeed drunk deep drafts at the fountain of European thought and learning, and there is no question about their being beaten in competition with Europeans. *The time is fast coming when the Indians will be able to live independently of British rule*, will have the powers of Government thrust into their own hands, will know how to look after their own affairs and take care of themselves.[57] (emphasis added)

Like Dr Love, he advocated the cultivation of the mind, identifying the education of women as an urgent task, if the community were to genuinely lift themselves beyond the stigma of indentureship and the sugar plantation — the 'coolie' universe — and earn the respect of others. Ruhomon concluded:

> You have the glorious gift of intellect — cultivate it by the numerous means that are at your disposal and you shall enjoy a pleasure that is genuine and lasting and true.... Books are one of the greatest blessings in life, and the educated mind that dives into literature, enjoys a pleasure of which the rude uncultured mind knows nothing. In association with our young women — and woman, you know, is one of the most important factors in society, and one of the most powerful of forces at work in this 19th century, not only for the emancipation of her sex but in the common cause of humanity — in association with them, I say, you will obtain far better results in seeking to advance your own interests and the interests of our people than you can by working alone.... Work together.... Cast aside pride of intellect and pride of soul which militates against anything that is noble and good, and march on ... [with] the noble object of promoting the interests of our race in British Guiana.[58]

Ruhomon's message to the Indo-Caribbean people replicated that enunciated by Dr Robert Love and Dr Theophilus Scholes. It spoke of the imperative of self-discovery through 'submerged histories', giving shape to notions of homeland — sustaining ancestral visions — to stimulate their own creative engagement within their colonial space, however limited and limiting. But to liberalize that environment they also had to master many of the idioms of their imperial rulers. There was no other way for Indians to progress. The African people in the British West Indies had set the pattern: education and cricket were necessarily central to all creole agendas.

It is noteworthy that Indian competence at cricket in the West Indies seemed to have attracted seminal recognition in the 1890s, precisely the decade of important political stirrings among middle-class Africans. Indians in Guyana were not oblivious of the latter's example in various spheres of colonial life, but they had now acquired a small middle class of their own, in the capital, Georgetown: these people were at a stage where they craved recognition in creole society. To achieve this, as I have argued elsewhere, Indians had to demonstrate that they could play the game with the passion and panache of other West Indians, including the Madeiran Portuguese, who were already established in the commercial and professional spheres in British Guiana.[59]

In the rural areas, in villages and on plantations, Indians were now playing cricket with flair and passion. At Plantation Port Mourant, on the less malarial Corentyne Coast, in the county of Berbice, the passion seemed to have reached fanatical proportions. D.W.D. Comins, sent by the Government of India to report on the condition of Indians in the West Indies, visited this estate on August 15, 1891 and was told of a memorable cricketing episode from the previous month. He noted:

Fifteen or sixteen colony-born cooly [coolie] youths asked for a three days' pass to plant rice on their own lands. Instead of doing so they went to cricket matches for three days, and then were absent for three more days on their own ground. Mr Murray [the Manager] summoned them, and they were fined $3 or seven days in jail, which latter alternative they all preferred. These were some of his best shovelmen, born on the estate, and in receipt of high wages, and all took money to pay their fines, but when they heard their stay in jail was to be so short, they all decided to go to jail.[60]

This was the plantation — and the foundation — that would yield, 60 years later, a stream of West Indian Test crickets, Africans and Indians: John Trim (4 Tests), the great Rohan Kanhai (79 Tests), Ivan Madray (2 Tests), Basil Butcher (44 Tests), Joe Solomon (27 Tests) and Alvin Kallicharran (66 Tests). Three other Berbice plantations also produced Test cricketers: Roy Fredericks (59 Tests), Len Baichan (3 Tests) and Sew Shivnarine (8 Tests).

The sugar planters were keen to promote the game on the plantations. They probably saw it as an instrument to blunt resistance that had culminated frequently, since the 1870s, in the shooting and killing of several of their predominantly Indian workers. Young Indians certainly saw the game as a means of gaining a measure of respect from other groups in colonial society. Proficiency at cricket gave 'immigrant' groups ('coolies' were still seen as aliens well into the twentieth century) the self-confidence to assert their right to belong in the West Indies. It also enabled Indian and African boys, as was the case in British Guiana, to achieve a delicate tolerance, as Comins observed in 1891: 'Many of the sons of East Indians born in the colony play cricket regularly. On Saturday afternoon on most estates a game can be seen going on, the players being partly Creole cooly [sic] boys and partly black, and the game is played with great spirit. Many managers encourage them to play, and some even get up rival matches with neighbouring estates.'[61]

In the year 1895, the first English team, under Slade Lucas, toured the West Indies; this was the occasion of the formation of the first organized Indo-Guyanese cricket club, the Asiatic Cricket Club, in Georgetown. On December 26, 1895 they defeated a Portuguese team, the Lusitana Cricket Club, by 38 runs. The captain, F.E. Jaundoo, a civil servant, was praised for 'the able manner in which he conducted the game throughout'. I have sketched elsewhere the context of this path-breaking event:

> This seemingly minor victory ... was an historic achievement; it was gained against the [Madeiran] Portuguese, the ascendant group in 1890s British Guiana, with an equally avid commitment to the game; the team comprised Hindu, Muslim and Christian Indians of North Indian as well as Tamil ancestry [Jaundoo was of Tamil stock].... To play cricket in the British West Indies was to begin to stake an emphatic claim for recognition in Creole society; to possess something of the spirit of the place; to be of it. It is

noteworthy that this elevation ... of Indo-Guyanese cricket coincided with the meteoric rise in England of the great Indian cricketer, Prince Ranjitsinhji [Ranji] (1872–1933). From the mid-1890s ... his elegant stroke-play, his 'lightning quickness of conception and execution', enthralled all: those who saw him; those who read of him; even those, like many illiterate Indo-Guyanese 'coolies', who could only imagine the mastery.[62]

The newspapers in British Guiana and the West Indies, from the early 1890s, gave copious coverage to Ranji's ascendancy — that master batsman with the inimitable, deft leg-glance, an exotic touch which every summer decorated the English county grounds. Readers were continually treated to biographical sketches that spoke of his magisterial rise: from Rajkumar College, a public school in India, to Cambridge, where he played cricket in the early 1890s, to Sussex, and finally into the England team, scoring a century in his debut Test, at Manchester, in 1896. As early as 1893, the *Barbados Globe* carried the following accolade from the London *Times* (of June 16):

An Indian prince on the cricket field earning the applause of the most critical of crowds by his brilliant batting, is a spectacle sufficiently novel to awaken the sympathy of all who have the spark of either the vast empire from which the player comes, or in the great national game which is so characteristic of England. Kumar Shri Ranjitsinhji, whose excellent achievements in the Cambridge University Eleven have led to his obtaining the coveted honour of a place in the annual inter-University match [v. Oxford at Lord's], is a Rajput prince of Jareja descent and a relative of the reigning prince of Jamnagar. After study at Rajkumar College in Rajkot he came to England in 1888 and two years later he entered Trinity College, Cambridge. In 1891 he had, by his cricketing prowess, won his college colours, and at the end of the season his average was 54. In addition, he is an excellent player at tennis and racquets and a good shot. Mr. Ranjitsinhji has, this season, had remarkable success with the bat, scoring 58 and 37 (not out) in the match v. Australia on 10 June.[63]

Indians in the West Indies would have been buoyed by his acclamation, in England; and the fact that Ranji was a prince — their prince — conferred on his magnificent achievement an element of the divine: a heroic act that could have been imagined as belonging to the great text, the *Ramayana*. It was a narrative tailor-made for their project of self-affirmation; it was also an illuminating example of muscular learning in the service of the 'motherland': the accomplishment of this Indian prince was a credit to all India, and was claimed by many Indians, whatever their station. It is arguable that Indian nationalism had at least some of its roots in Ranji's mastery and acclamation in England, at the heart of Empire. With book and bat (Oxford and Cambridge had magical associations of high learning even among the unlettered), this regal son of the homeland was a beacon also for Indians in the West Indies, who were now embracing education and cricket in seeking to belong to the West Indies. The Ranji narrative was sententious, indeed.

This fledgling self-confidence, as in the case of Bechu, the amazingly erudite indentured labourer, found an outlet in letters to the press, in verse and in the occasional article. In August 1894, for instance, a would-be 'creole coolie' poet from Georgetown, George C. Rampaul, penned a sharply ironic riposte to a white man who apparently had doubted his capacity to compose, alleging that one of his poems was 'too good', it must have been plagiarized:

> Gape mighty censors! Comprehend the change!
> A manuscript rejected as too good!
>
> And why pronounce 'too good', too good for what?
> Only too good because it comes from me [a 'coolie']?
> Were it a nobler person's idle thought
> 'Twould all consistent and appropriate be....
>
> The Anglo-Saxon waxeth great in pride,
> And well he may for great have been his gains.
> But granting this and what you will beside,
> Has he monopoly of wit and brains?[64]

With bat and ball, book and pen, Indians in the British West Indies, like their African and coloured counterparts, were unwittingly, imperceptibly, reshaping the British West Indies. In Guyana (Demerara) and Trinidad, where the Indian presence was strongest, the 'cricket cult' had deep roots. In the former, as Sandiford observes, the association of cricketing competence with belonging was firmly entrenched:

When the cricket cult spread like wildfire across the Caribbean during the 19th century, one of its earliest victims was Guyana, then known as Demerara. The game prospered there largely because of the support it found from the local aristocracy [white plantocracy and commercial elite]. The Georgetown Cricket Club, established to serve the interests of the elite, came into being in 1852 and has played a major role in West Indian cricket ever since. It soon established its headquarters at Bourda.... It was, in fact, the Demerarians who led the way in promoting intercolonial cricket in the Caribbean during the last third of the 19th century. They undertook the first visit to Barbados ([February]1865), became Trinidad's first opponents (1869) and hosted the very first Barbados touring team (1871) [in fact, September 1865]. It was [a] Demerarian, E.F. Wright, who recorded the first century ever made in first-class cricket in the West Indies — v. Trinidad (Georgetown 1882). Four years later, it was another Demerarian, George N. Wyatt, who did most to facilitate the first tour of a composite West Indian team. In that year [1886], three Barbadians and six Jamaicans joined four Demerarians in an invasion of Canada and the United States. They played 13 matches, won 6, lost 5 and drew 2.[65]

It was from Demerara, too, that the first initiative to send a composite West Indies team to England seemed to have originated. The aim was to send four Demerarians and three cricketers each from Barbados, Jamaica and Trinidad, in the summer of 1893. The prospectus emanating from Georgetown defined the aim of the projected tour clearly: 'to see and to get some good cricket, and to obtain return visits from cricketers in the UK with a view to the ultimate improvement of the game in the West Indies.' The *Barbados Globe* had endorsed it, for they envisaged substantial gains from the seminal effort: 'We want to learn more day by day; this is a rare chance offered.'[66] Nothing came of the project, and the first West Indies team did not tour England until 1900; but the idea was reflective of the commitment and imagination that Demerarians brought to the game as early as the late 1880s and early 1890s; and, as will be seen later, English teams did tour the West Indies in 1895 and 1897.

It is true that these Demerarian pioneers were all white; that British Guiana was, substantially more than Trinidad, a quintessential plantation colony dominated by the sugar plantocracy. This had enlarged the white elite's capacity to control this polyglot society.

And Indians, largely confined to the plantations and adjacent villages, whether indentured or free, generally succumbed to their massive power to define. Therefore, though latecomers, they soon imbibed the assumption of the centrality of western education and cricket as instruments of mobility. However, because of the Indians' numerical importance in Guyana and Trinidad, they were a force of latent consequence in both societies. Already, by the 1890s, their rehabilitative narratives were being constructed from the overarching imperial text, though interwoven with strands from their own resurgent internal reverences: sub-texts inspired by Hinduism and Indian Islam and the discovery of their ancient Indian legacy unearthed largely by western scholarship: Indology.

British Guiana in the 1890s represents the creation of an Indian cultural site on which a more confident Indian middle-class persona could be constructed: marginal, elitist perhaps, but with ramifications for all Indians. An imagined Indian master text would become a cardinal reference point for even the most creolized of Indian scripts. This is evident in the founding of an Indian organization in British Guiana, in 1892, and the beacons by which the small middle class structured its responses. This Indian organization had a short life, but much can be discerned about the Indians' quest to belong in the British West Indies from a survey of its limited activities. The founder of the East Indian Institute, William Hewley Wharton, was the son of indentured labourers. The Institute had sent a letter of congratulations, in October 1892, to the first Indian M.P. elected to the House of Commons in Britain, Dadabhai Naoroji, a Parsee from Bombay, the Liberal member for Finsbury Central. On July 28, the *Daily Chronicle* carried the following terse note on the historic event: 'An interesting figure in the next Parliament will be the Parsee, Naoroji, whom Lord Salisbury (the Tory leader), held up to mistaken ridicule as a "black man". His return in Central Finsbury, by three votes, was challenged by the Conservatives, but a recount confirmed Naoroji's poll.'

The East Indian Institute of British Guiana quickly read Naoroji's victory in terms of its own colonial project, the erasure of the gnawing 'coolie' image engendered by the extant indentureship system (it was not abolished until 1917). This lingering stigma was especially haunting for the Indian middle class. They saw the emergence of an Indian M.P. as a triumph for the 'East Indian nation'. No such nation existed; this was a construct, an imagined community. But the exile Naoroji answered the ambiguity, the psychic void: the angst of separation and the yearning to 'return' (some were still doing so), on one hand, and the growing longing to belong in the new space, on the other. Naoroji's elevation by the ruling race constituted an eminent addition to the imagined master text of Indian identity, crucial to the shaping of Indo-West Indian identity. Like Africans in the region, they, too, were constructing validating indices, intimations of progress from the imagined homeland. This was immanent in the Institute's letter to Naoroji, composed in Georgetown and sent to him, in London, on October 1, 1892:

> We ... deem it not only an honour but a duty of our race in this remote part of Her Majesty's dominions, to tender you our unanimous and most hearty congratulations for the distinguished position you have achieved. We are fully conscious of the multifarious difficulties you must necessarily have had to surmount in order to secure your success in this, to our nation, memorable election, and that fact alone impels us to doubly prize the honour which the *East Indian nation* has, through your meritorious instrumentality, attained — an event unparalleled in the History of India. We need hardly say that although we are thousands of miles separated from you, it will be our foremost interest to read of your career, and earnestly trust that success will attend your undertakings both politically and otherwise, and we further venture to hope that the example which you have so nobly set will be fruitful in actuating others of *our ancient race* to follow; and thereby rid themselves and countrymen of the political oblivion [into] which they have been presumed hitherto to be sunk....We fervently hope that Almighty God will direct your every movement in your elevated sphere, and thereby ensure a brilliant and happy career for one *in whose veins courses our kindred blood.*[67] (emphasis added)

Although Naoroji was a Parsee and socially and ethnically far removed from the impoverished universe of eastern UP and western Bihar, whence came most of the indentured 'coolies', creole Indians like Joseph Ruhomon and William Hewley Wharton were punctilious in claiming him (and Ranji) for the imagined 'East Indian nation', a construct which would have had no resonance with Naoroji or most members of 'our ancient race'. Indeed, it is doubtful whether the M.P. would have acknowledged a 'kindred blood' relationship with Indians in the West Indies: he was very light — almost white — they were generally dark; he belonged to a group that saw itself as more 'Persian' than Indian. But that was immaterial to the representation of Indianness being constructed in the British West Indies at the end of the nineteenth century; indeed, his light colour would have enhanced the perception. It was essentially an exercise in expunging the 'coolie' stain, with its encapsulation of the savage 'other'. Therefore, when a perceived member of 'the East Indian nation' received the recognition of the ruling race, in England, as was the case with Ranji and Naoroji, he was quickly claimed and acclaimed by Indians 'at home and abroad'. The imagined homeland was central to the shaping of an Indo-West Indian identity — it had nothing to do with the 'motherland' or Mr Dadabhai Naoroji and his endorsement of it. But it was not an invalid exercise.

In June 1900 the *Port of Spain Gazette*, in Trinidad, reported that it was the practice of 'young roughs' on the waterfront, presumably non-Indians, to stone 'any unfortunate East Indian whom they may happen to see coming along'. However, it is a measure of the unfathomable 'otherness' of the 'coolie' in West Indian societies that it was he, the victim, who was often penalized for the reprehensible practice of the youths. The paper felt impelled, therefore, to subtly reprimand the conduct of the police in the matter: 'The invariable result [of the stoning] is a volley of the most fearful curses and obscene language from the coolies, for which he generally gets "run in" and fined by the magistrate. It is, of course, a very difficult matter to catch these young ruffians; but it could easily be done by means of a little determination on the part of the police; and perhaps a few good examples made of the worst offenders would act as a deterrent on the rest.'[68] The crudity of the outbursts by 'coolies', a reflection of their impotent rage, was obviously deemed more offensive than the stoning, in Trinidad. The same assumption of singular culpability often characterized official and popular responses to 'coolies' in British Guiana as well. The taint of barbarism was still strong.

Is it surprising, then, that educated Indians were desperate to escape that universe of the 'coolie'? That some would, indeed, seek a space in a version of the current imperial script that sought, through supposed linguistic affinity, to establish an ancient 'kindred blood' relationship between the British and the Indian peoples — their supposed common Aryan antecedents exemplified in the ideas of the eminent German-born Oxford Indologist, Friedrich Max Muller (1823–1900)? Young Joseph Ruhomon, in his seminal lecture of October 4, 1894, for instance, had expressed his pride both in his Indian antecedents, and in the imagined common ancestry of all 'Aryan' peoples, British and Indian:

> Today I am not only convinced ... of the greatness of India as a country, and the greatness of her sons and daughters as a people, but I am joyfully and confidently anticipating the time when in intelligence, in culture, in morals and intellectual attainments, the great East Indian Race [sic] shall be second to none in the world.... I may add ... that we also in British Guiana and all our ancestors in India are closely allied by blood relationship to the British nation, as the following poem by Ben Elvry [an Englishman] entitled 'To India' ... will show:-
>> Brave brothers of the sun-kissed face
>> Heirs of the ancient Aryan name;
>> Like heritage with you we claim,
>> Our tongue betrays our kindred race.[69]

A similar imagining to serve the contemporary project — the construction of an Indo-West Indian identity against the grain of the stubborn taint of the 'coolie' — was manifested by William Hewley Wharton, the founder of the East Indian Institute, in 1899, the year before he graduated in medicine from the University of Edinburgh (the alma mater of Dr Scholes and Dr Thorne). He, too, was very proud of his Indian ancestry, and was honoured by his Indian colleagues with the presidency of the Edinburgh Indian Association in 1898–99. On January 7, 1899 he chaired the annual dinner of the Association. The guest speaker was Professor Sir Thomas Grainger Stewart, Physician-in-Ordinary to Queen Victoria, who had also taught medicine at Edinburgh. The commendation Dr Wharton received from their eminent guest made such an enduring impression on him that, nearly 50 years later, he included it in his biographical entry in *Who is Who in British Guiana, 1945–48*. Those few precious words, from a dark, wintry evening at the end of the century must really have illuminated his life thereafter:

> Here is a young gentleman who was born in British Guiana, possesses an English name, fills the chair at this banquet with much dignity and grace, and still insists on calling himself an Indian. I may as well call myself an Indian, as we both belong to the same common stock — the Aryan family.

The claim of an ancient lineage with the ruling race — with its assumption of a shared superiority — was congruent with the current imagining of a 'golden age' of high indigenous civilizations by educated Indians. The validation of the antiquity, artistic opulence and intellectual attainments of several pre-Islamic Indian civilizations, by western scholarship, was conducive to this constructed rehabilitative rendering. Most Indians in the West Indies could call up an amnesia with regard to the recent India of caste degradation, child marriage and child widows, chronic destitution, disease and early death, whence they or their parents had fled; locate their privation on the plantation of the West Indies as a moment in their conception of time as vast cyclical ages; and imagine the heroism and grandeur of ancient India in terms of the golden age of Ram Raj, the benevolent rule of Lord Rama in the *Ramayana* — as if it were the real history of India. They could invest disparate contemporary India, obsessed with its differences, with magnificent powers of redemption, as if it were about to be returned to its ancient reverences and glory. Within these constructs of redemption, the supposed Aryan antecedents of ancient India, also, could be readily slotted in. Fantasy was central to the construction of notions of the Indian homeland, as it was to the conception of 'many Africas' by black West Indians. In the late 1880s, Rev H.V.P. Bronkhurst, Ruhomon's Anglo-Indian mentor, would even seek poetic corroboration in his claims for India's ancient glory:

> Ours the glory of giving the world
> Its science, religion, its poetry and art;
> We were the first of the men who unfurled
> The banner of freedom on earth's every part,
> Brought tidings of peace and of love to each heart.[70]

Ranji, 'the Prince of Cricketers', therefore, could also be imagined within this construct of glory, and invested with all the rehabilitative powers of the divine and regal: another plank in the shaping of Indo-West Indian identity. The images of Ranji crafted in articles reproduced in the local press, in British Guiana and Trinidad, because they were permeated by an element of eastern mystery, could be easily read within the constructs of the Indo-West Indian identity project. Cricket belonged to the aggregate of strands of self-affirmation deemed crucial to that endeavour, infused with imperial as well as ancestral indices of progress. Ranji had negotiated the ambiguities of both of those wellsprings of identity. His play, therefore, was just as crucial to the Indian in the homeland, as it was to the Indo-West Indian in the 1890s. On October 28, 1896 the *Daily Chronicle* of British Guiana reproduced an article from the *Daily Telegraph* (London). It was inspired by a banquet at Cambridge University to honour Prince Ranjitsinhji, following his triumphal entry of the Test arena, for England against Australia, in the summer of 1896. It contained all the elements for a reading within the parameters of the 'East Indian' national project: affirmation by sources at the heart of Empire, in a context of bat (and learning) — cricket and education, at the end of the nineteenth century:

> If happily poor Chester Macnaghten, himself an old Cambridge cricketer, had lived long enough to be present in the Guildhall of the great University town tonight, he would have been no true son of *Alma Mater* if he had not been prouder of the fact that he gave the first lessons on the great pan-Anglican game to Kumar Shri ... Prince Ranjitsinhji, than of all the other elements of knowledge instilled by him into the mind of his distinguished pupil when a boy student in Kathiawar [at Rajkumar College, India]. The love of our national pastime thus begotten, has held its sway so strongly against all rivals that the young Indian prince who celebrated his twenty-fourth birthday in our midst on the 10th of this month [September 1896], is acknowledged without any disparagement of the great Gloucestershire veteran [Dr W.G. Grace] and others, to be both the finest exponent of the game and the most popular cricketer of the day.... Although he learnt to play cricket in India when only eleven or twelve years of age, the desire to become a great cricketer only seized him when, in the year 1888, he was taken by his tutor to see the match between Surrey and the Australians at the Oval. In the summer of 1892 [at Cambridge], by an accident, as he puts it, 'he was pressed into service as a substitute in one of the Trinity matches', for which he got his college cap, to be followed, in the succeeding year, by his 'Blue'. It is a matter of history now how, after being left out of the first test match against Australia during the past season [1896], he was unanimously chosen to play in the other two encounters, especially distinguishing himself at Manchester by scoring 62 and 154 not out, when such well-tried men as Grace and Stoddart were comparative failures.[71]

Prince Ranjitsinhji (Ranji) (1872–1933): the beacon of Indo-West Indies cricket; he represented Cambridge University, Sussex and England

At the base of Indo-West Indian cricket is the Prince, but his presence transcends the game, for in the West Indies, more than anywhere else, cricket goes beyond the boundary. As I have written elsewhere: 'Ranjitsinhji was, to the Indians in British Guiana, not some remote, cricketing prince; he was claimed as a hero whose mastery could be appreciated in creole society [in the British West Indies] — another expression of Indian excellence to challenge the "coolie" image.' But, as the following grand remark from the Jamaica *Daily Gleaner* of October 13, 1899 suggests, his power to enthral was universal. Ranji was captaining a team on a tour of the United States, and the best team there had succumbed to him: 'The Philadelphians go down before Prince Ranjitsinhji as the Philistines did before Sampson.'

In the early 1960s I grew up with an image of Ranji as almost a mythical figure from the great Hindu classic, the *Ramayana*. I had seen pictures of him executing that delicate, but imperious, leg glance. I had also seen a picture, in a 'library book', of him in his regal attire; and my volatile, impressionable mind had lodged him among the Hindu deities whose framed pictures, garlanded each day by my mother, hang on the wall of our house. He was no mere cricketer: he had brought something of the divine to this game that we played passionately with our primitive gear — he had transported us from the canefield to the heart of England: Lord's. So I was prepared to believe and keep the most stupendous tales about Ranji. My father was not very knowledgeable about the game: he could not bowl; a bat looked very alien in his hands a couple of times I fleetingly bowled to him when I was little, having cajoled him into the incongruous act. But when, occasionally, he ventured into cricket's rich narratives I took his pronouncements as unimpeachable. I grew up with his yellow cutting from the *Daily Argosy* of British Guiana, impaled on a wire hook — 'the file' to the household. It was inviolable, this piece on Hanif Mohammad's marathon innings of 337 for Pakistan, following on against West Indies in Barbados in January 1958. He memorized — so did I — all the records scaled by Hanif in his innings of 16 hours 10 minutes [970 minutes], still the longest played in first class cricket, an 'epic feat of concentration ... [when] Hanif proceeded to immortality', as Michael Manley recalls it.[72] My father had made it 999 minutes: it was conducive to memory, and added a touch of magic to Hanif's vigil. Even more memorable, though, was his unassailable tale of how the 'racialist' Australians had refused to allow Ranji to enter their country, when he toured with England in what seemed like ancient times. Our secular narratives were dateless; like the Hindu stories that instructed and entertained, this timelessness enhanced their power to awe. He would relate, with an authority that betrayed no fallibility, that Queen Victoria was so appalled by the humiliation meted out to 'her Prince' that she ordered the ship to return to England if Ranji could not land. Shamed by the Queen, the Australians quickly relented, while the Prince proceeded to score a century in the first Test. It was years before I discovered that Ranji did tour Australia with Stoddart's English team in 1897–98 and that he scored 175 in the first Test at Sydney; however, I was really upset that I failed to unearth any evidence to support dad's tale. But I could never bring myself to tell him that, and in a strange way, I continued to wallow in the fiction. It was inviolable, for many Indians in colonial Guyana had learnt to relate a version of the tale. In their eyes, the genius of their Prince now had the blessing of the great Queen in England, the Viceroy of India.

I have pondered much on this, but only in recent years have I been able to dissect this imagined bit of sententious 'history' — the manner of its telling; peeling back its many layers, slowly comprehending its part in the shaping of Indo-West Indian identity. But there was enough history or 'more-or-less history', to use Nehru's evocative expression, to give solidity to the Ranji persona, so crucial to the task assigned to it by Indians in the British West Indies: not just the 'Prince of cricket' but also something of a mythical figure, like Lord Rama of the *Ramayana*. Fact and fiction are often inseparable in our universe. Fantasy exerts great power in our construction of self. It also animated our cricket and enhanced its role in making us West Indians.

But it was Ranji's inexhaustible capacity to enthral, to make even sober, circumspect observes wallow in fantasy, throughout England during the 'golden age' of cricket, that continues to fascinate me. And it is images such as the following evocation by A.A. Thomson that will stay with me, an enduring tribute to Prince Ranjitsinhji, who had something to do with the construct I am:

> The image conjured up by the name showed a prince from a Far Eastern fairy-tale, and not only a prince, but an oriental magician. If Ranji had arrived at the crease in a golden turban and carried a jewelled scimitar instead of a bat, it would have caused less astonishment ... than you might suppose.... [T]he legend of his

magic that had preceded him would have prepared the waiting crowd for something rich and strange, some excursion into the realms of fantasy.... [H]is personal charm was so compelling that he could with a smile have persuaded M.C.C. to agree to such a change of implements. In any event, whether he held a bat or any other weapon in his hand, he would undoubtedly have wielded it like a flashing scimitar.[73]

Imagining the Indian Prince in this manner was magnified by the primitive standard of recorded moving images before the First World War. However, it was fed primarily by Ranji's delicate, but magisterial, execution of his craft, coupled with his perceived exoticism — even his most celebrated stroke gave itself to a kind of fantasy. Thomson's boyhood imagination has left us a compelling image:

His best-remembered stroke, the leg-glance, has come down to us almost as though it had been an illusion.... The immense progress in the development of camera-lenses which has taken place in the intervening half-century might have shown it as it really happened. We who watched it can only say what we think we saw, and I only saw it comparatively late in his career, when he was probably much slower in his reactions than when he was in his prime. It seemed, if you sat near the sight-screen behind the bowler's arm, that the batsman, poised nonchalantly in front of his wicket, would execute an almost imperceptible flick of the wrists and the ball, very fast, of apparently perfect length, and pitched dead on the middle stump, would fly low to the finest of fine-leg boundaries. Ranji then appeared to be standing, still lightly poised, bat held high and right heel lightly raised, ready for the next ball. This *sight, or illusion,* was frequently seen by me during my first youthful visits to Headingley ... and my first sojourn in London. I would wriggle into position to see it 'just so' and the magic of it remains in my mind to this day. When people told him he would be out, plumb leg-before-wicket, if he missed the ball, he replied politely, almost apologetically: 'Yes'. And went on playing just as he had been playing before.[74] (emphasis added)

Is it not possible, then, that this great, compelling spirit of Ranji, a quality of extravagance and delicacy, which inspired a decisive seminal devotion to the game among Indo-West Indians, also shaped their greatest cricketer, Rohan Kanhai, born in British Guiana in 1935?

Trevor Bailey's appreciation of that master batsman, 'one of the finest
... one of the most exhilarating cricketers of his generation', certainly
suggests lineage with the creative impulse of the Prince; and like the
latter he had a peculiar stroke for which he was 'especially famous' —
'a cross between a pull and a sweep which he attempts to lash so fiercely
that he ends up flat on his back'— what Sir Neville Cardus once
imperiously titled 'the triumphant fall':

> Rohan Kanhai is not the greatest batsman I have bowled against but
> few, if any, have had the power to fascinate and satisfy me more.
> Just as the sauces can transform a good meal into a feast, it is the
> stroke execution that garnishes a Kanhai innings which would make
> it unforgettable even when his score is not particularly large. Rohan
> Kanhai is a Guyanan [Guyanese] of Indian extraction and like the
> most exciting cricketers of Asian origin there is more of a touch of
> eastern magic about his batting. For, though slightly and almost
> delicately built, he has overcome this by a combination of timing,
> eye and the use of his wrists. He has the ability to flick, almost caress
> the ball to the boundary, which is especially attractive. On one
> occasion I fractionally overpitched a ball on his off stump. He drove
> it and at the very last moment impacted an extra touch of right
> hand, slightly angled the bat so that it streaked between mid-wicket
> and mid-on before either could move.... Rohan is essentially an
> extravagant and colourful performer. He is always liable to embark
> upon strokes which others would not consider, let alone attempt to
> execute. This flamboyant approach to batting has on many occasions
> brought about his downfall, but is the reason why I find him so
> satisfying. When he is at his best there is more than a touch of
> genius about his play which has an aesthetic appeal. He reminds
> me of a great athletic conjurer whose tricks sometimes fail — not
> because of inability, but because he attempts so much, sometimes
> even the impossible — he is seldom mundane. If I could choose how
> I would like to be able to bat, I would select Kanhai as my model.[75]

Is it not possible that the culture of protest of the 1890s, also, was
an ingredient in the making of this great Indo-West Indian batsman?
Hybridity is at the core of belonging in the West Indies.

Chapter Four

The First English Cricketers in the West Indies and the Advent of Black Players:
Slade Lucas's Tour, 1895

The late 1880s and 1890s were marked by chronic depression in the sugar industry. So prolonged was it and injurious to workers and farmers, that many authorities had, at last, started to question the wisdom of relying so comprehensively on one major industry to sustain these islands, since Emancipation at the end of the 1830s. This was the context, as I have argued, in which coloured, black and Indian West Indians had sought to gain greater space for themselves in the affairs of their colonial societies. The fight for greater constitutional change had begun; they were editing small newspapers in order to articulate their rights; they had started to earn respect by their own professional achievement in law and medicine; they had entered the lower echelons of the colonial civil service; and had already dominated the ranks of primary school teachers and the clergy of the non-conformist churches. A few middle-class men, more deeply shaped by the British tradition than any other colonials, were demanding political rights in the British West Indies. Cricket, at the core of the colonial mission, would play a major part in building their self-esteem and self-confidence.

Bridget Brereton has documented this process for post-Emancipation Trinidad; it needs no major revision for the British West Indies as a whole. However, as I will show later, Trinidad did have some peculiarities that made it a substantially more open environment conducing to greater options for non-white peoples. Brereton assesses black and coloured advances by the late nineteenth century — the making of the middle class:

> [T]he middle stratum had its origins in the free coloured/black 'second tier' of slave society. By the 1830s this stratum was led in Trinidad (as elsewhere) by a small group of educated men,

generally though not exclusively light-complexioned, relatively well-off and European in their cultural orientation. But this middle stratum, predominantly urban, grew significantly in the century after emancipation. The growth in the size and importance of Trinidad's towns, especially Port of Spain [the capital] and San Fernando, opened up new employment opportunities for educated coloureds and blacks as clerks, store assistants, civil servants and minor professionals, teachers, pharmacists, nurses and journalists. The towns were the base for coloured and small business people and a growing intelligentsia which would eventually challenge white supremacy.[1]

She traces the process meticulously: some mobility was always attainable and mastery of European cultural norms was indispensable in exploiting whatever niches were accessible:

After the end of slavery there was considerable movement from the black masses into the middle stratum. First, through independent farming or the skilled trades, ex-slaves might accumulate some capital and/or land which would give them a social and economic position above that of the mass of labourers and poor peasants. Second, exposure to elementary education in church or government schools might lead to white colour jobs and enhanced status ... these two paths were interrelated: the child of a relatively secure peasant farmer or artisan was far more likely to be chosen as a pupil teacher or to get a place in a secondary school. Third, the churches played a role in social mobility for blacks and coloureds. The church-oriented 'respectable' labourer or peasant families were again more likely to secure access to the schools for their children and to occupy leadership positions in the community.... [T]he middle stratum was itself stratified along lines of economic position, colour (shade), educational levels and occupation. At the top were persons who enjoyed all or most of these advantages: fairly high incomes, prestigious occupations such as law, medicine, clergy, secondary school teaching, a secondary or tertiary education, and light complexion. At the bottom were persons with lower incomes, less prestigious jobs as minor clerks and civil servants, store assistants, nurses, rural elementary school teachers, with no secondary education and with darker skins. However, all members of this stratum were distinguished from the masses by their white-collar jobs, their literacy, their command (in varying degrees) of 'good' English and their adherence to European cultural norms.[2]

What is significant about the British West Indies was the inculcation of a philosophy of gradualism among non-white aspirants to power. The free coloureds and free blacks were socialized into a culture of incremental advances, economic and educational mobility in stages. In post-Emancipation society, this shaped an essentially gradualist temperament in the wider society, as educational opportunities expanded and more black people acquired non-manual jobs in colonial society. In cricket, too, black people were prepared to pay their dues in their protracted climb up the representative game. The English tours under Slade Lucas (1895) and Lord Hawke and Priestley (both in 1897) constitute a fascinating site for the exploration of the gradualist orientation of British West Indian societies. The cricket culture was central to the universe of the middle class. Because it was also at the core of the imperial mission, and because blacks and coloureds were still excluded from the highest levels of the game, in spite of their demonstrated competence in many aspects of it, the gifted black cricketer was already perceived as a kind of liberator among African people. Like the black doctor or lawyer, he belonged to all blacks whatever their social position: a pathfinder — the bearer of the rod of redemption. But here, too, their gradualist outlook would be evident, as they chiselled steps for themselves on the slippery slope of a fledgling West Indies cricket.

The visits of Slade Lucas's team to the West Indies in early 1895 enhanced the stature of the game, planted a foundation for England–West Indies cricket that would provide an arena for challenging imperial assumptions, as well as the contestation of power by and between subordinate groups. These contests started unspectacularly but, as I will demonstrate, enabled black and coloured cricketers to enter the main space, actors in their own right, not just observers beyond the boundary. It was also central to their tenuous constructions of a West Indian identity, however circumscribed by the region's deep-seated insularity. Moreover, to play cricket was to belong to the place, despite the tendency for an ethnic dimension to determine the social construction of belonging. In the late nineteenth century, as Hilary Beckles observes, cricket was already crucial for the advancement of black people's rights. He explains the process:

Cricket had found its way into the West Indies at the end of the eighteenth century as a cultural import of the white colonial elite — soldiers, administrators, planters and merchants. The paramountcy of race ideology in slave society, and its implications for class relations, meant that cricket functioned initially as an instrument of ethnic social exclusion as well as a force of class cohesion for those with managerial responsibility for the colonising mission. By the mid-nineteenth century, however, an increasingly determined political struggle by the emancipated to remove social privilege and ethnic apartheid from public institutions could not be contained by the boundaries of the elite game; barriers were lowered and some walls breached. What was true of cricket also obtained for politics, commerce and the respected professions. By the end of the century, middle class coloured [mixed race] men, who brought with them some privileges from slave society, played for white clubs or formed their own. In turn, they would engage black teams in 'friendly' games — but these teams were not generally invited to the clubhouses. It was within this socially segregated environment that the institutional and ideological formation of cricket developed.[3]

The mere fact that coloureds and blacks could breach some walls onto the arena of play made the game an ideal site for the assault on racial privilege in the wider society while expanding notions of possibilities. If they had been excluded totally, the game could not have played this role. From slavery through Emancipation and beyond, as Beckles argues, cricket could carry the burdens of an ethnically diverse West Indian agenda, their pursuit of civil and political rights:

[D]ifferent groups of colonial West Indians made enormous social investments in traditional English cricket culture for widely different reasons — and with diverse effects. The returns on these expenditures, however, have been the collective infusion of the colonial game with a new democratising identity, a radical philosophical mandate, and a revitalised sense of cultural purpose. Freshly emerged from the scaffold of a slave-based dispensation, and frantically searching for cultural renewal and ontological recognition, the majority of West Indians confronted the ideologically backward Victorian activity with a demand for social inclusion and equity. In so doing, more so than other colonials, they provided cricket culture with an opportunity and an ability to realise in concrete terms the game's highest moral vision.[4]

The tours of English cricketers to the West Indies accelerated the process and validated cricket as a site for the embryonic contestation of power in these colonial societies. Moreover, not only did they infuse their own cultural peculiarities on the game, they also expanded its moral ascendancy beyond its Victorian postulates. The incremental inclusion of blacks and coloureds in the representative game, from the 1890s, would have reverberations beyond the boundary. R. Slade Lucas's tour of the West Indies in 1895 was announced in December 1894, the principal architect being a Lincolnshire man, Dr R.B. Anderson, former captain and secretary of the Plymouth Cricket Club, who had lived in Tobago (the sister island of Trinidad) since 1872. It was noted that the team comprised English amateurs and that the social side of the tour was of no less importance than the cricket. This was an indication that white West Indians exclusively were at the core of local cricket, as the social side would not have been emphasized if black people were involved, with the potential for embarrassing social repercussions. *Cricket* reported: 'The principal cricket clubs in the West Indies have taken up the matter with great warmth, and Mr. Lucas and his party therefore are assured not only of a trip interesting in itself but in addition of a most enjoyable time socially.'[5] The team left Southampton on January 6, 1895 and arrived in Barbados on January 28. It was anticipated that Lord Hawke, the Yorkshire captain, would have captained the team, but he was unavailable. On their arrival in Barbados, *Cricket* again underlined the social dimension of the tour, alluding to the scenic and climatic virtues of these somewhat forgotten islands. The paper made a distinction between Lucas's tour and the established Ashes contest between England and Australia, which was inaugurated in 1882, with all matches between the two countries since 1877 granted retrospective 'Test' status. The English tour of the West Indies was clearly envisaged as a substantially less demanding interlude:

> From the outset the social side of the trip has received full consideration. While cricket is necessarily the primary purpose in the selection of the team, regard has also been had to proficiency in other sports.... A proficient himself in other sports besides cricket, Mr. Lucas also had an eye in the choice of his team to those who had

also proved their skill in other games. Hockey, for instance, will, in addition to the captain, have capable exponents in Messrs Sewell and Barker. In billiards, and lawn tennis, too, the team should be able to hold their own. As far as cricket is concerned they can be classed as a moderate side. *Still, as the cricket is not to be taken too seriously, the team will no doubt fulfil one of the many purposes of the visit in making a personal acquaintance with the natural attractions of the West Indies as well as the many advantages they offer in respect of climate as health resorts.* In any case, whatever the success of the team as cricketers, the value of the tour if only from an educational standpoint should not be underrated. Of one thing Mr. Lucas and his men are thoroughly assured, the heartiest welcome wherever they go.[6] (emphasis added)

As the captain recorded, while still on board the ship to the West Indies, several players, himself included, were demonstrating their versatility in activities other than cricket: they played various musical instruments, sang, danced, acted and participated in conjuring and 'amusing athletic sports': potato, egg and spoon (the men having to hold the spoon in mouth), turtle and thread-the-needle races.[7] *Cricket,* towards the conclusion of the tour, in April 1895, reported that 'irrespective of the cricket' the tourists were impressed with the 'warmth of the reception ... everywhere'. Whatever the implications for the future of West Indies cricket, they added that the tour would have given the islands 'a bold advertisement' with regard to their natural advantages. They were appreciative of Dr R.B. Anderson for his imagination and enterprise which made the first English tour of the West Indies a reality.[8]

After noting that cricket had been flourishing in Trinidad, Barbados, Demerara (British Guiana) and Jamaica since the late seventeenth century, *Cricket* sought to ascertain the state of the game in the West Indies at the end of the nineteenth century. They were able to interview Dr Anderson in England. Although he had been the main architect of the 1895 tour, he was not there to see the 'highly successful tour'; but his immersion in local cricket during the 23 years he had lived in Tobago, made him a most knowledgeable informant on the subject. The interviewer was 'spellbound by his eloquence on all that pertained to the country of his adoption'. There is so much of relevance to early West Indies cricket in the interview — none of which has been published before — that I reproduce it almost in its entirety.

Moreover, for West Indians of all races the English tour of 1895 was a major event in their social history, as Dr Anderson expected:

Dr. Anderson: I consider that the visit of the cricketers under the captaincy of Mr. Lucas is one of national importance, not merely as regards the West Indies but also in relation to this country. It will certainly mark an epoch in the history of the game out there, and it will not be without its educational effect on both countries from a social and, probably, an economic point of view. The fact is that the ignorance of stay-at-home Englishmen about the West Indies is something appalling. Instead of regarding it as a great health resort, which it undoubtedly is in winter, people in this country seem to regard it as a special manufactory for ague and malarial fevers. I only wish I had some of the letters Lucas has sent over. Why, he and his men are delighted with the climate, charmed with the people, and enthusiastic about the sport.

Cricket: Tell me something about cricket on the islands — its class, by whom it is played, and how it is likely to develop.

Dr. Anderson: Ah, that would be a long story ... but if I tell you a little about Tobago you may take it as indicative of most of the more important islands. First, I must tell you that *the natives take to the game like duck to water.*

Cricket: Then, the coloured men play, too?

Dr. Anderson: I should just think they do. Coloured men [mixed race] and black men, too, for there is a difference, you know.

Cricket: And all classes? Labouring men and merchants?

Dr. Anderson: Why, certainly. Just as in England, it is the national game. Everybody plays it, and many of the best players are coloured [mixed race and black] men.

Cricket: Had you any difficulty in teaching the men of Tobago at first?

Dr. Anderson: Very little. *They are so intelligent — even the poorer classes — and so enthusiastic that they soon overcame the initiative* [sic] *difficulties, and after a short time the joy of the game grew upon them that the difficulty was to leave off.* Two points required a good deal of teaching. One was to get work on the ball, and the other to judge distance in running for a catch. So far as 'pitch' was concerned, I adopted Routledge's plan in putting down a piece of white paper and asking them to aim at it in bowling. As regards catching, I found that if a ball went up in the long field the fieldsman, instead of starting to run in the direction of the ball, would stand gazing at it till it almost reached the ground, instead of going for it at once. Of course, we soon got over those elementary difficulties, and *in a short time we numbered natives amongst our best bowlers and fielders.*

Cricket: Would you name a couple of your best bowlers in the early days of the Tobago Club?

Dr. Anderson: There was Bain — a coloured, and Stanley, a black man. The first was round arm with a fast delivery and a splendid wrist action. In business he was a dispenser. Stanley also was a good bowler, and was only a field labourer. *One of the best effects of cricket was that it brought all classes together in a common love of sport, and I never wish to see a better feeling exist than obtained amongst cricketers of high and low degree.*

Cricket: Did you ever receive visits from big teams?

Dr. Anderson: Perhaps the best match we played was against a team from the British Fleet. The Duke of York and the Duke of Clarence were present. We were defeated by eight wickets, but they had a very strong side. In our team were The Rev. Canon Turpin, Mr. Trestrail (of Epsom College), Dr. Tulloch (of Edinburgh), Dr. Witz and myself.

Cricket: Is there any inter-island competition out there?

Dr. Anderson: Oh, Yes! There is a Challenge Cup competed for by Trinidad, Barbados and British Guiana [since 1893].

Cricket: And how would representative elevens [West Indies XI] be made up?

Dr. Anderson: I tried on this occasion to get Barbados, British Guiana, Trinidad and Jamaica to arrange representative West Indies teams consisting in each place of five men selected from the home team and two from each of the other places. *The eleven to be chosen quite irrespective of colour, and entirely on the merits of the men.*

Cricket: Of what strength would you say a good representative team of the West Indies would be?

Dr. Anderson: I should say about second-class county form in England. Our matches against Mr. Lucas's give a fair indication of our strength. Trinidad, for instance, had a fine victory over the Englishmen.

Cricket: And do you anticipate that a West Indian eleven will visit England in the near future?

Dr. Anderson: A good deal depends on whether Lord Hawke [captain of Yorkshire and a key figure in English cricket] will be able to bring out a team in a couple of seasons or so. He may perhaps visit the season after next [1897], and we may be able perhaps next year to organise a tour in England. In any case, *the impetus which Mr. Lucas and his men have given to the game is certain to make our men anxious to visit England in the near future.*

Cricket: And how about your turf? Is it as good as in England?

Dr. Anderson: The turf is lovely. The leaf is low and broad, and makes an admirable batting surface. Of course, it does not get the care and nursing of your best English wickets, otherwise, I should say it would be quite as good. In the summer it gets pretty well frizzled up, but in the winter, say from December to March, which is our cricket season proper, we get splendid wickets.

Cricket: And now Doctor, tell me whether you had any difficulty in getting together the team now touring under the captaincy of Mr. Lucas?

Dr. Anderson: It took a long time to get over initial difficulties; for the idea of cricket in the West Indies was very novel, and the West Indians themselves were doubtful of success. But I had the valuable co-operation of Lord Hawke, Lord Stamford and Mr. Neville Lubbock [of the West India Committee]. Those three gentlemen, with myself, approached the Royal Mail Packet Co., who made a most liberal concession for the round trip. I had a most kindly reception and valued advice and suggestions from the committee and secretaries of the M.C.C. and Surrey County C[ricket] C[lub]; but it was not till Lord Hawke's return from America and a short visit to Jamaica that he succeeded in getting Mr. Lucas to captain and get up the team, when all difficulties were overcome. The team pay their own expenses. There are only one or two places where 'gates' are taken. The Englishmen were, however, the guests of the islanders wherever they happen to be. It will not be an expensive trip, and from what I hear, they are all delighted with their experiences out there, whilst West Indians are eager for a revival of the visit, perhaps the year after next [1897]. The English team was a very happy selection, being just strong enough to win a majority of their matches, and not strong enough to discourage the men they met.[9]

This is a seminal tale of the Herculean struggle to shape West Indies cricket, to inculcate a broader sense of loyalty beyond the parochial ignorance that fed its chronic insularity. Lucas's tour was a tentative, but crucial, step on the road to recognition outside the region. It is tempting to ridicule this embryonic effort, but *Cricket* saw the import of what Dr Anderson had achieved in 1895. They observed that he was determined to enhance the game in the West Indies, which he felt for 'too long ... [had been] treated as poor relations in this country [England]'. The paper also noted that all the main cricket associations in the West Indies had passed resolutions in appreciation of Dr Anderson's imagination and resolve in organising Lucas's tour.[10]

The tour of 1895 was, in fact, of greater significance than has ever been accorded it. As I have argued cricket and education were already identified as avenues for mobility by the submerged groups in British West Indian societies. The tour was noteworthy because it demonstrated that non-white West Indians were prepared to pay their dues, to follow the path of gradualism, incremental advance, in their social evolution in these British colonies. Hilary Beckles has commented on the popular enthusiasm that was generated by Lucas's tour, and the sense of inadequacy evident among a people with low self-esteem: 'Reports in the West Indies indicate that colonials, in spite of receiving a sound thrashing by the English team, were overcome with excitement by the experience. References suggest that colonial sport writers expressed in no uncertain terms the sense of low self-esteem seemingly evident among West Indians with respect to the English.'[11] I prefer to see West Indian popular reaction as a reflection of the underdogs' recognition of their limitations, while maximizing the benefits of their limited apprenticeship: to appreciate the greater competence of the English — their mastery of the finer points of a complex game — and learn from it. This helped to establish a pattern of responses beyond the boundary, in the social and political spheres, that invariably built on incremental steps, on merit: no precipitate granting of Independence here, with the slide towards chronic political instability and economic chaos, as was to happen in many ex-colonies with supposedly more sturdy cultural underpinnings. As with cricket, so in politics, British West Indians were learning the ropes. They would continually profess loyalty to the Empire, but were no less committed to constitutional change, however gradual.

Lucas's team won 10 of their 16 games, lost four and drew two. One of the matches they lost was against an All Trinidad XI, which included five black cricketers. This was especially significant because Trinidad was the only one of the main colonies prepared to include black and coloured men in their team, whereas Barbados and Demerara were adamant that so-called professionals, black cricketers, could not be selected. This was a ruse with foundations in class snobbery in England and reinforced by narrow race, colour and class susceptibilities in the West Indies. Therefore, without the visit of an English team prepared to play against black men, the Trinidadians' emerging liberal attitude with regard to colour in cricket would have remained theoretical. Trinidad was setting the foundations for selection in West Indies cricket based on merit, as Dr Anderson had demanded with reference to a composite West Indies team. The democratic process was taking shape; its roots were being planted through West Indies cricket, and the black masses, most of whom were already exposed to formal education in the denominational schools, knew it. They saw more in the first English tour than met the eye.

When Lucas's team reached Barbados on January 28, 1895, the entertainment committee went on board the ship, 'to the accompaniment of an enthusiastic welcome from all classes [whites and blacks].... The reception was of the heartiest'. Indeed, a picture of the landing shows a predominance of black men, but there were many women at the quayside as well. Although no black men were selected for Barbados in their two games against the English touring team, black people attended in vast numbers. It was clear, though, that the official functions for the tourists were all-white events. For example, on their first evening in Barbados, the team 'attended a ball at Queen's House, the residence of Major-General Read'.[12] Yet the attendance of the black masses at the first game against Barbados, on January 29–30, 1895, was excellent, although they knew that no black or coloured man would have been considered for selection for the island whatever his gifts. *Cricket* records the event thus:

> A public holiday had been granted for each day of the match ... and special trains were run for the occasion. The various members of the team were heartily cheered as they drove to the ground, and their reception in the field was most enthusiastic. The ground had been enclosed by a high fence, and the covered stands which had been erected were in every place. Altogether not less than 6,000 persons must have paid for admission. The ground is situated at Kensington [Pickwick Cricket Club], about a mile out of the town.[13]

The attendance was impressive for such a small island, and the fact that most of the spectators were black, although none of the Barbadian cricketers were, underlined my point that their passion for the game was not dimmed by the racial exclusivity of the team. Indeed, as noted earlier, middle-class coloureds and a few socially advance blacks were, since 1893, playing first division cricket for Spartan against the top white teams, such as Wanderers (founded 1877), Pickwick (founded 1882) and those from the elite schools, Harrison College and the Lodge. Barbados won their first game against the Englishmen by 5 wickets. Lucas's team scored a paltry 48 in their first innings, on a difficult, copiously watered pitch, which the Pickwick paceman, Clifford Goodman (1869–1911), and the Wanderers medium pacer, Arthur Somers-Cocks (1870–1923), a master at Harrison College, exploited prodigiously. Goodman got 6 for 14; Somers-Cocks 4 for 31. Barbados replied with 100, while Lucas's team reached 168 in their second innings. Goodman was again difficult to negotiate, claiming 8 for 71: 14 for 85 in the match. Requiring 117 to win, Barbados did so for the loss of 5 wickets. Goodman's brilliance was attributed to: '[his] right hand medium pace, with a high delivery, [which] was especially difficult'.[14]

The cricket tour had captured the Barbadian imagination: 'There is little chance of being heard or read on any other subject.... Meetings, commissions, committees and entertainments, all but those connected with cricket and the English cricketers, are declared to be suspended *sine die*'. The *Barbados Globe*, though impressed with the island's victory in their first game, tempered their jubilation with the observation that they had not seen the best of the tourists, who were still acclimatizing. In fact, they were extremely modest, almost apologetic, in victory, seeing it as an aspect of their apprenticeship: '[W]e will learn from them all they may be able to teach us on the cricket field.... We feel proud of our victory, but at the same time cannot forget that our visitors had a hard time of it; they did excellent work fraught with many difficulties.' However, the black spectators were unrestrained in their acclamation of their all-white cricket team, as the *Globe* remarked after Barbados had won:

> Before the team could get themselves into the pavilion the crowd had entered on the grounds, surrounded the Grand Stand, and was shouting out their gladness at the unexpected results. Cheers were given on all sides for the teams while the Police Band, which

had been present during both days discoursing sweet music, played 'Rule Britannia'. It is thought that the crowd today was larger than yesterday, the stands being packed. All classes of Barbadian society were present during the match which was much added to by officers of the Army and Navy.[15]

The *Globe* was justified in cautioning against triumphalism, as the second match against Barbados brought a remarkable reversal: 1,373 runs were made in this five-day match, played between February 5–9, 1895. Barbados made 517 in their first innings, the highest score ever recorded in the West Indies, yet no one made a century: Gussie (G.B.Y.) Cox 68; George Learmond 86; Hallam Cole 67; Harold (H.B.G.) Austin 37; C. Browne 74; while W. Alleyne and A. Somers-Cocks, batting at 9 and 10, scored 82 and 62 not out respectively. Lucas's team replied with 303: F.W. Bush scored 101 and R. Berens 87. Clifford Goodman got 6 for 108. Barbados enforced the follow-on, but the Englishmen responded with an impressive 396: 138 from J.M. Dawson and 91 from H.R. Bromley-Davenport. Somers-Cox's bowling was outstanding: 48.3 overs, 8 maidens, 99 runs, 8 wickets. Although Goodman only got one wicket in the second innings, he bowled economically: 62 overs for 121. Barbados were therefore required to make 185 to win. Amazingly, they lost by 25 runs, Bromley-Davenport having taken five wickets and three catches.[16]

How deeply the game had already lodged in the West Indian imagination is reflected in the following report from St. Kitts, in the Leeward Islands, dated February 17, 1895. Some of the English cricketers had gone to visit a leper asylum and were surprised by the inmates' request for bats and balls. They were informed by one of the warders that 'they were all keen cricketers', so a supply was despatched to the institution. The reporter was also able to convey the popular appeal of the sport. Even if many Kittitian spectators were less precocious than those in the larger islands, with regard to the subtleties of the difficult game, they compensated with their passion and irrepressible humour. He noted: 'There were two public holidays given for the occasion; the whole island turned out *en fête* to see the match and there must have been about 4,000 present in the afternoon. The blacks here are a keen enough crowd, but naturally they are not so well versed in the intricacies of the game. A black man caused some amusement by accompanying each batsman on his way to and from the wicket with musical honours of the weirdest description, produced by a sort of clarinet. *There were really three blacks included in the St Kitts eleven.*'[17] (emphasis added)

Trinidad's path-breaking example of selecting black and coloured cricketers to represent the island was even more exemplary. Later, in August 1895, the *San Fernando Gazette* would criticize the premier cricket club in the colony, Queen's Park, for selecting all-white teams; this, they contended, had frequently been responsible for their defeat.[18] Their assertion was based on knowledge of the generally high standard of play among a number of non-white clubs in the island. They were probably also responding to the celebrated recent example of the multiracial All Trinidad team, which had defeated Lucas's by 8 wickets in March 1895, while all-white Queen's Park had lost to the same team. It is significant that All Trinidad had five black players. Bridget Brereton explains the context of this innovative practice of selecting black players for Trinidad. Having already admitted a few coloureds (mixed race) as members of Queen's Park, the foundation for a more inclusive selection policy was in the making:

> The Queen's Park Cricket Club controlled cricket in the colony. Its membership was not exclusively white, but included members of the coloured [mixed race] professional group. For instance, in 1883 the four Trustees of the club included C.H. Phillips and Vincent Brown, who were both coloured. But most [all] of the teams fielded in this period were all-white, and the cricketers were definitely 'gentlemen players' from the 'respected' white families. In 1895, however, the All Trinidad team fielded to play a visiting English side had five non-white members; this apparently was unusual, for the English captain [R. Slade Lucas] telegraphed Reuters that they played 'All Trinidad whereof five were black'. One of the five was Lebrun Constantine, father of Learie.[19]

This underlines my argument that once concessions were made to coloureds, it was only a matter of time before space had to be made for blacks. The latter knew how to wait but they also knew how to accelerate the process: they practised assiduously in order to scale the racial barrier by merit. It could not be just cricket, passionate though their commitment to mastery of the skills.

In their game against the English tourists, Queen's Park had made a meagre 71 in their first innings (12 players per side); Bush took 9 wickets for 22. His bowling was 'absolutely unplayable ... none of the home men could learn to understand [it]'. Lucas's team won the match, played on Thursday 28 and Friday February 29, 1895, by three wickets. The stores in Port of Spain were closed at midday and the attendance was estimated at 5,000 on the first day; as in Barbados, they were drawn from 'all grades of society, including the Governor'. Queen's Park was captained by Aucher Warner, brother of Pelham (Plum), from a distinguished white family with deep roots in Victorian Trinidad. Their eminent status, virtually the first family of the island, bred a security and a discernible liberalism to rival the paternalistic reputation of the somewhat aristocratic French Creole families. As Brereton observes, the Warners were pivotal to the anglicization of Trinidad in the nineteenth century:

> The French Creoles were the leading sector within the white Creole elite, but the English Creoles, if less numerous, were also an influential group. These were people of English descent born in the island, and usually of the Anglican Church. Perhaps religion, rather than national descent, was the main dividing line between the French Creoles ... and the English Creoles. The Warners were the 'first family' of the English Creoles.... Charles Warner [father of Aucher and Plum], the son of a wealthy English planter who settled in Trinidad early in the nineteenth century, was Attorney General between 1842 and 1870, the most powerful influence behind the policy of Anglicisation carried out in the 1840s and 1850s. By common consent Warner was the 'real ruler' of Trinidad during these years, the *bete noir* of the 'foreign' Creoles and the Catholics. His cousin, Frederick Warner, was a prominent barrister who was appointed an unofficial member of the [Legislative] Council in 1861 and was for many years its senior unofficial. Many other members of this large and influential West Indian family occupied important posts in Trinidad in the second half of the century.[20]

The ethos of the elite schools shaped the philosophical outlook of the Warner family: Aucher and his brothers attended Queen's Royal College, the alma mater of C.L.R. James, Eric Williams and V.S. Naipaul; Plum was at the same school briefly, before moving to Harrison College in Barbados and, finally, Rugby and Oxford. Cricket was at the core of this elite education. But because there was an ongoing rivalry between the English and the French Creoles, the latter rooted in Catholicism and economically, from the 1870s, the new cocoa industry, the subordinate groups — coloureds, Africans, Portuguese, Chinese and, later, Indians — were better able to identify and exploit niches, conducive to their mobility, within the interstices of the system. Thus, as seen above, although the Queen's Park cricketers were white, there were already, in the 1880s, some light coloured members who had seized the little space created.

The French Creoles had acquired a reputation for fairly good relations, however paternalistic, with their black slaves and workers. But Trinidad hardly had a slave regime: certainly nothing to compare with Jamaica or Haiti at their peak in the latter half of the eighteenth century; nothing as old as Barbados and the Leeward Islands or reputedly as brutal as that of Guyana (Demerara-Essequibo and Berbice) under the Dutch slave regime. It was a Spanish colony until 1797; they did not establish a slave colony there; the sugar plantation culture only really took off in the 1790s, after the Revolution in Haiti, when white and coloured French slaveholders migrated to virgin Trinidad with their slaves. It became British in 1797, but in 1807 the British slave trade was abolished, and, in 1838, the slaves were freed. It did not have the time to become a big slave colony. At Emancipation Trinidad's short-lived regime had a mere 20,000 slaves, compared to Haiti's 400,000 or Jamaica's 350,000.

The consequence was that the old racial attitudes that poisoned black–coloured–white relations in older colonies did not have the same resonance here: attitudes to race have been discernibly more civilized; it is no idyll but prejudices do not have the painful historical associations to sustain them, as in Guyana, with a hazardous natural environment and two major slave rebellions and brutal suppression, to feed the resilient narratives of humiliation and anger, the source of self-contempt that breeds aggression.[21] Indeed, Trinidadians take great pride in the fact that they have never manifested the same ferocity of responses to other groups as in Guyana; that they are richly nourished by a carnival/calypso culture, with its cleansing powers of sarcasm and satire; indeed, that a comprehensively lighter touch, a gift for humour (*picong*) and self-mockery — not self-contempt — conducive to tolerant attitudes generally, characterizes all its peoples. Much is missed if the peculiarities of these islands are not recognized, as I argue above with regard to Barbados.

It is significant that the English–French Creole rivalry persisted well into the twentieth century, thus keeping the society relatively open, never under monolithic English control. This, in conjunction with good natural conditions for the cultivation of sugar and cocoa — and the discovery of oil, later — shaped discernibly more cosmopolitan, inclusive attitudes compared to Barbados or British Guiana, where the environmental hazards (white monopoly of the best lands and chronic land hunger in the former; malaria and necessity for a complex hydraulic system in the latter) bred a deeper incomprehension among their peoples. Under-populated, virgin Trinidad, therefore, provided a more congenial economic and social climate for submerged groups. This was reflected in the progress of the black and coloured middle class in the latter half of the nineteenth century. Bridget Brereton, the social historian of late nineteenth-century Trinidad, has charted this process:

> It was naturally in Port of Spain and the towns that schools and other social and religious amenities were most available. The pronounced urban orientation of many of the more ambitious and mobile ex-slaves and their children was an important factor in the emergence of a black and coloured middle class after 1838.... [T]hey had acquired their middle class status mainly through their command of British culture and their white-collar jobs.... Most middle class blacks and coloureds ... were involved neither in agriculture nor in commerce. They were teachers, journalists and editors, lawyers, doctors, civil servants and clerks ... a few were planters: even fewer were in business. Joseph Brown, a coloured immigrant from St. Vincent, was a merchant. His three sons were all professional men: Vincent was a successful barrister who rose to be Attorney General; Leopold was a surveyor; and Lionel was also a barrister. H.B. Phillips, a coloured native of Barbados, was a partner in a Port of Spain merchant firm.... He served as Mayor of Port of Spain and was a leader of the campaign for constitutional reform in 1892–5.[22]

So that when Lucas's team visited Trinidad in 1895, a few coloureds and blacks already held some of the highest positions in colonial society. In this environment the authorities at Queen's Park were therefore more inclined to select black Trinidadians to represent the island's cricket team. Moreover, the Warners,[23] 'the first English family', at the pinnacle of cricket in the colony, had both the authority and the will to select cricketers on their merit, irrespective of colour or class.

It was Hon Aucher Warner, as captain of Queen's Park and the All Trinidad team, who was instrumental in choosing five black men to represent the island against the Englishmen, on March 4–5, 1895. These were the opening batsmen, C. Attale and Lebrun Constantine, G. Wilson, C.A. Ollivierre (from St. Vincent; he toured England in 1900), and the gifted fast bowler, J. 'Float' Woods (a Barbadian).

Although the destroyer of the Queen's Park batting, F.W. Bush, did not play in this game because he was 'injured in Saturday's races [athletics]', the margin of victory of the All Trinidad team was very impressive: 8 wickets. The Englishmen made only 94 in their first innings. 'Float' Woods, the black fast bowler, was devastating: 23 overs, 8 maidens, 39 runs, 6 wickets — five were clean bowled.[24] All Trinidad replied with 180, Aucher Warner scoring 77; Lebrun Constantine 22. Woods was obviously a great hero of the black spectators, for although he was the last batsman in and made zero not out, 'his advent was greeted with cheers'; every ball bowled to him by Sewell was 'heralded with applause'. When Woods was bowling, he stirred even greater emotions, his 'every play was popular'. He was injured and unable to take the field in the second innings, so Lucas's team reached 162, thus leaving All Trinidad 77 for victory. They lost only two wickets in getting the score. The victory might have been even more emphatic if 'Float' Woods was able to bowl; but two of the black players, Ollivierre and Constantine, took five of the wickets, the latter getting 3 for 12. A plebeian migrant from Barbados, 'Float' was a source of immense pride to the black masses in Trinidad and the rest of the West Indies.[25] His fast bowling was of such quality that he had already transcended the insular proclivities of the region's fledgling game.

The pattern was being set: the democratic evolution was already in motion; it would be a protracted process, in cricket and in politics, but the temper was being shaped on the long road to liberal democracy. In their evolution towards self-government, the British West Indian colonies offer a unique study in colonial constitutional history: an exercise in tutored, incremental change — gradualism. This spirit also permeated the outlook of the *Port of Spain Gazette*, before the Queen's Park match against Lucas's team. They were novices determined to advance their game, but they were also proud of their educational attainments within the British intellectual tradition, their source of self-confidence:

We hope to beat them and are at the same time quite resigned to defeat at their hands. In either case the gain will be ours. If we win we shall be proud — if we are beaten it will be no shame to us and we shall have learnt much. Their visit, no matter what the result on the cricket field, must be a clear gain for the colony.... [I]n these distant and even now but little known islands there is a deeply rooted love of the Old Country, a genial hospitality, and *a degree of refinement and education* which enables them to compare favourably with far larger and wealthier places.'[26] (emphasis added)

All Trinidad won. But elsewhere in the West Indies, the black spectators were not cowed by defeat, as there was maturity and style in the novices' approach to the game, and a resolve to learn from the Englishmen. Cricket and education in the British West Indies are inseparable: both were at the heart of the imperial mission and these quintessential colonials had a passion for both. As A.F. Somerset reported during Lucas's tour of 1895, the black spectators were demonstrably knowledgeable about the finer points of the game. They brought a subtlety of perception to their cricket; they also took their exuberance, musical passion and gift for humour, ridicule and laughter to the grounds — a sense of theatre: 'A good ball dealt with brings a shout of "played!" all around the ground, and to stop a "yorker" [a delivery pitched virtually at the toes of the batsman at good pace and, therefore, difficult to negotiate] evokes a yell that would not be given for a hit out of the ground in England. When that comes off a large part of the crowd spring on to the ground, throw their hats and umbrella in the air, perform fantastic dances, and some of them are occasionally arrested by the police.'[27]

Even under slavery, black people were irrepressible in their spontaneous projection of themselves: as in their religious functions, they could not be staid supplicants. In late nineteenth-century cricket, too, such as in Barbados where they were still denied a place within the boundary, they could still dance their way unto the stage of play. All the Barbadian players were white, either masters or graduates of one of the elite schools: Harrison College or the Lodge School. Gussie Cox and Somers-Cocks, Oxford graduates, were Englishmen who taught at Harrison. Several of the players would go on to build the foundation of West Indies cricket: Clifford Goodman and young Harold (H.B.G.) Austin (1877–1943), in particular. Of the Goodman family, C.L.R. James has observed: 'Clifford Goodman was a white man, member of a cricketing family which has done an immense amount for Barbadian cricket, his brother being Percy Goodman, one of the finest of Barbados batsmen and a first-class slip.'[28] H.B.G. Austin (later Sir Harold) captained the West Indies in England in 1906 and 1923, before they were conferred Test status in 1928. James considered him 'the father of West Indian cricket'.[29] Keith Sandiford concurs; he sees Austin as 'one of the greatest names in the history of Caribbean cricket'. He adds:

> He became a long-serving captain of Wanderers, Barbados and the West Indies. When his playing days were over, Harold Austin continued to serve as the leading cricket administrator in the region. In 1927, he was the driving spirit behind the establishment of the West Indies Cricket Board of Control and served as its first president. He captained the West Indies team in England in 1906 and 1923.... For Barbados, he appeared over 30 times between 1894 and 1926, scoring over 1,300 runs and averaging more than 32.... [T]his remained a record until it was broken by John Goddard in 1958 [Goddard captained the West Indies in 1950 during their first victorious series in England; and less auspiciously against Australia in 1951–52 and England in 1957.] An energetic public servant in later years, Sir Harold Austin was the first native Barbadian cricketer to be honoured with a knighthood.[30]

Learie Constantine deplored the persistence of the race factor in selecting only whites as captains of the West Indies, until the 1950s, but he conceded that 'In the cases of [Aucher] Warner [to England, 1900] and Austin [to England, 1906, 1923] no comment is necessary. Austin, in particular, would have got his position before all others, white or black.'[31] Yet, as noted earlier, the colour bar notwithstanding, the Barbadian crowds were effusive in their support for their all-white teams. In January 1895, for instance, Slade Lucas recorded the response of black Barbadians to that first match played against his team, in Bridgetown, which Barbados won. He was struck by their verve and ingenuity:

> The Governor had granted today and tomorrow as public holidays throughout the island, and the influx of the country people was enormous, special trains being run for the occasion on probably the most primitive of railways, which has never paid any dividend

since it was opened. The individual members of the team were loudly cheered when recognised as they drove to the ground, clapping of hands and shouts of 'success!' 'good luck!' greeting them. Substantial stands had been erected to accommodate about 2,000 spectators with a charge of £2 per head for those in the best positions, and the tickets for the lot were sold in less than two hours from the time the lists were opened. The whole of the ground had been enclosed by a high wooden fence, and every coign of vantage point (even to high palm trees) was crowded with black humanity. One of them fell, though no one seemed to be hurt. In another part, outside the ground, on some private property, the police actually cut the tree down as being the only means of causing the occupants to descend! Quite 6,000 people paid for admission ... (it being the first time that Sambo had ever been asked to put his hand in his pocket ... to witness a cricket match) ... while there was a large crowd outside, who were looking through the cracks in the fence, and on the second day, not being satisfied with this limited vision, they improved the situation by cutting holes to peer through.[32]

When Lucas's team landed at Bridgetown on January 21, 1895, he was impressed with the popular manifestation of the welcome, as he was by the display of passion by black people when Barbados won their first game. They were not merely partisans; they had acquired a sense of discernment that spoke of knowledge of the finer points, as well as the importance of the game as a vehicle for the articulation of high social impulses. The following excerpts are indicative of the extent to which cricket had permeated the soul of the Barbadian by the end of the nineteenth century. Slade Lucas recalled:

Five minutes steaming brought us near to the quay, and none of us were prepared for the reception. Every coign of vantage even to telegraph poles had been seized upon by a struggling mass of black humanity. It seemed as if every man, woman and child, of the Negro race had turned out to welcome us, and loud were the shouts of 'success' and 'good luck boys', which greeted us. A large 'posse' of dusky policemen, with thick sticks which they used feely on the skins of their compatriots soon cleared the way for us to get to the carriages which had been provided. We drove off, amid enthusiastic shouts of the populace, to our quarters at the Marine Hotel, Hastings, about two miles from Bridgetown.... At the close of the [first] match [against Barbados], thousands of Negroes assembled in front of the Pavilion and shouted themselves hoarse, and sang 'God save the Queen!' being wild with delight at the result [Barbados won by 5 wickets], although they probably would have been just as pleased had we won, for they are thoroughly good sportsmen, and very keen and appreciative cricketers, and it is really extraordinary to see the large amount of interest they all take in the game. One of the papers remarked that nothing had stirred the 'nation' more, and it really would be difficult to conceive wilder enthusiasm.[33]

Another source, *The Agricultural Reporter*, documented the peculiarly West Indian character of the black spectators' celebration of the victory over the Englishmen: 'Men grew wild with excitement, and the dense crowd which lined the enclosure made a rush for the Pavilion, waving their hats and brandishing their sticks and cheering vociferously. This act was not surprising, for, having regard to the high character of the opposing team, Barbados had won a great victory.'[34]

This magnanimity towards their all-white teams enabled black and coloured West Indians to tolerate discrimination in the selection of representative cricket teams for several decades, but it also gave them the humility to learn from their white counterparts with the privilege of earlier entry into organized cricket, while nurturing a fierce ambition, tantamount to a religious fervour, to infuse the game with their own style and, eventually, to conquer. However, Brian Stoddart has sought to establish that cricket tended to make most black Barbadians acquiesce in the hierarchical social system that survived Emancipation. He argues:

Through cricket most Barbadians pledged their faith in a social system predicated upon British cultural value, British concepts of social progress, British morality codes, British behavioural standards and British attitudes towards social rankings. In so doing, Barbadians at large accepted the framework of social power elaborated by the dominant culture to replace that lost in 1838. The transformation from slave-master to contract-master was acquiesced to by the former slaves become labour servants as were the social systems, cricket chief among them, which reproduced the patterns of inequality.[35]

This is only partially correct. Their response to the retention of white dominance was not radical; it spoke of the seemingly long apprenticeship of British West Indians as a whole, being tutored for responsibility. As with cricket, so in education and politics, advances were incremental and the finer skills were learnt in a measured manner; but the competence and the temperament would become deeply ingrained in the British West Indian psyche. This facilitated their adding something of their own personality — their passion, sense of theatre, rhythm and athleticism — in the making of West Indies cricket.[36] Once the competence was earned, their self-belief grew, allowing them to experiment, to give expression to their Afro-Creole cultural peculiarities shaped in the colonial context. It bore the marks of solidity that today sustain largely free, democratic societies in the post-colonial Anglophone Caribbean. This is not a small achievement in puny countries, several with virtually no natural resources. It is tempting to depreciate the gradualist temper of many West Indians, the so-called 'Afro-Saxonism' of the black middle class. This must be tempered: the small middle class were laying the foundation for the stability which obtains in most Anglophone Caribbean societies today, over four decades after the British left Jamaica and Trinidad, and 39 years since they left Barbados. By the late 1890s, as the sugar depression bit, this small middle class was already extending its wings, within and beyond the boundary.

Lucas's tour of 1895 helped to enhance the self-perception of all West Indians, whatever their colour. Yet even white West Indians still harboured inferiority complexes, especially with regard to what was seen as the civilized values of the 'Mother Country'. Moreover, as late as the 1890s, the legacy of slavery still cast a long shadow, a past of humiliation resistant to psychic rehabilitation. Hon H.A. Bovell, the Attorney General of Barbados, at the luncheon to mark the departure of Lucas's team for England, on April 20, 1895, expressed those fears and the part he thought the tour and cricket in general would play in changing perceptions of the West Indies 'at home'. Vindication of their progress in the great imperial game was an affirmation of all British West Indians, a testimony to the acquisition of the civilizing properties inherent in its mastery:

[A]part from the pleasure which it has given us to receive a body of gentlemen representative of the great national game of England, it is difficult to over-estimate the value, to us, of their visit. An impetus has been given to cricket on this island which will leave lasting effects, and do much to promote excellence in the game. We look to the Mother Country to give us the key to a better understanding of a game which has come almost to be an art, and the matches played between the contending teams have undoubtedly afforded local cricketers instruction which they could not otherwise have hoped to acquire. So great is the stimulus given to cricket since the arrival of Mr. Lucas's team, that wherever we turn, in every field ... in every alley and lane, there are to be met lads and men playing cricket, with a wicket that is in many cases wonderously constructed (cheers).[37]

The Attorney General then reflected on the wider implications of the tour of 1895:

The ideas entertained about these colonies, by the great majority of Englishmen, are very erroneous. There seems to be often an impression that these colonies are uncivilised places, not far from barbarism, and there is a general vagueness as to where and what they are. A considerable uncertainty exists as to whether they are a province, a part of the mainland, an island, or a continent. Very few, indeed, of the British public know anything of the West Indies, and we can readily understand the hesitation and doubts which might have arisen to prevent English cricketers visiting places and regions unknown to them, and about which so little is known at home.... That these difficulties have been successfully combated by Mr. Lucas's team, is a matter of congratulation to all of us, and each member of the team will become a centre of information to let the public of Great Britain know that there are some lights as well as shadows in the West Indies (cheers). Great men are brothers everywhere, and the complement of bravery is generosity; and, what is applicable to great struggles is also true in the case of amicable contests like those we have recently witnessed. Mr. Lucas has exhibited that generosity which is a fitting appendage to the noble game of which he is a representative. This is proved by the fact that when a telegram was sent to record the result of the first match, a match which was unfavourable to the visitors, he generously inserted the words that the victory had been won by the Barbadians by 'good cricket' (loud cheers).[38]

The local whites craved whatever morsel of reassurance emanated from English sources; it was, as I argued earlier, tantamount to recognition that they were still English; that they had not been claimed by the untamed tropics; and in the case of the West Indies, that they had essentially eluded the barbarism of these former slave societies which, in anti-slavery iconography, had assumed bleak associations of a kind of savagery that was not readily amenable to refinement. This was why the Solicitor General of Barbados (Hon W.H. Greaves) was scrupulous to underline, at the farewell banquet for the English cricketers, that white Barbadians had lost none of the virtues of unadulterated English blood:

> We feel that we are more brothers than friends (Hear, hear). This strong filial feeling is only the natural outcome of the relationship that exists between us and the Mother Country. *We are sons of old England (cheers). Barbados was the first colony planted by England in the West Indies, and we have kept our English blood intact. The feeling which we have for our Mother Country is as strong today as two hundred and seventy five years ago, when our forefathers left England and settled here. We still look upon her as our mother in spite of all the buffets and blows which we have received (loud cheers).*[39] (emphasis added)

This was what made the racism in Barbadian cricket so resistant to broader liberal suasion, rendering it vastly more pernicious than in Trinidad. There was little unadulterated English blood in the latter: Spanish, French, African, Portuguese, Chinese and Indian were all intermingling to create a substantially more polyglot Trinidad than even British Guiana, also marked by its ethnic diversity.

C.P. Bowen observed, in complimenting the Earl of Stanmore and Dr R.B. Anderson for their 'indomitable perseverance' in arranging the tour, that people in the West Indies were, virtually to the end, convinced that it would not materialize because of resilient notions abroad of the danger of these tropical colonies, the antithesis of the safe, controlled, predictable environment of the mother country. The West Indies, however, were still enmeshed in constructions of 'otherness', defying possibilities of ordered apprehension and resistant to civilized imaginings. Bowen, too, underlined the 'otherness' of these islands in the sun:

To the English gentleman, these colonies are far-distant, uncivilised places, to which a visit would be fraught with risk and danger; danger from the treacherous tropics and the much-dreaded hurricanes, which are supposed to sweep without warning from some mysterious region, like terrible monsters carrying death and destruction in their wake; and risk from the onslaught of the 'yellow Jack' which is said to have a partiality for the 'blood of an Englishman'. It would naturally take some time to disabuse the minds of the average Englishman of these legends, and, therefore, it was known that the Earl of Stanmore and Dr. Anderson had both set their minds on sending out to the West Indies a party of gentlemen to have a friendly contest with the colonists, and also to let them see that these islands are comfortable little places to live and settle in, and by no means the plague-stricken spots they have often been represented to be, [but] we must say we had not much hope of the success of the undertaking. It was consequently with much pleasure, albeit with surprise, that we learned of the undoubted fact that Lord Hawke and Mr. R. S[lade] Lucas had been successful in organising a cricketing tour around these islands.[40]

As I have argued, cricket with its bucolic associations and virtues that epitomized the idealized spirit of 'home' — cultured rusticity, order, respect for constituted authority, control of the passions — was constructed as an instrument of civilization in savage spaces. The English players deemed the tour a great achievement; and it was left to Slade Lucas to convey that much-needed affirmation, the ultimate seal of approval, to proclaim the credentials of civilization of white Barbadians. He did not disappoint his lavishly generous hosts:

This is the first English Team that has visited your shores, and I assure you it won't be the last. We have done the West Indies thoroughly, and are taking back the recollection of your hospitality, of your kindness, and of your courtesy and attention, which we will never forget (cheers). We wish to thank you for all you have done for us.... So far as cricket is concerned we shall always back Barbados on your own ground; you played admirable cricket, and made the record score [517 in their second game; but still lost by 25 runs], which will go down to posterity. If you meet Trinidad, Demerara or Jamaica, Barbados would come out first; you have a far larger number of good batsmen (cheers). Demerara has some very fine bats but no bowlers; and Jamaica has some very good bowlers but few good bats — but as far as your bowlers are concerned C[lifford] Goodman will soon be by far and away the best bowler in the West Indies.... [I]n the season of 1896 we will come to you again if you will have us, and last mail Lord Hawke wrote to say that he would come with a team in 1896 (enthusiastic cheers). You will appreciate Lord Hawke when he comes; cricket in the West Indies will be sure to improve and receive a stimulus, for you will be sure to like him.[41]

Lucas concluded with the gist of the telegram he had sent to the various colonies at the end of the tour, in which he expressed 'full appreciation of [the] merit of your cricket, the excellence of your grounds, the perfection of your climate, and the warmth of your hospitality'.[42] He had said precisely what he thought his hosts wanted to hear. It is interesting that Lucas did not mention that Trinidad had defeated them, primarily because they found their black fast bowler, Woods, a very difficult bowler; neither did he comment on the revolutionary example of Trinidad in selecting five black players, on merit, at a time when this could not be countenanced in Barbados, Demerara (British Guiana) and Jamaica. He did not speculate either, in extolling the virtues of the white Barbadian batsmen, on how they might have fared against Woods, a black Barbadian exile. To do so would have upset his Barbadian hosts, who used their so-called amateur selection criteria to keep talented black players, so-called professionals, out of the team, until after the first West Indies tour of England in 1900, when five black players were chosen, one of whom was Barbadian, a most controversial selection.

It is to the credit of the Trinidadians, especially Aucher Warner and his brother, Plum, as well as the indomitable Lord Hawke that they were prepared to contest the underlying racism in early West Indies cricket. They were, consciously or unconsciously, responding to popular impulses for democratic change in British West Indian societies in the 1890s. By daring to go against the grain, they enhanced the reforming trajectory of the embryonic political culture. Black people themselves, as evident in their mammoth attendance and symbolic encroachment on the grounds, during the tour of 1895, recognized that the cricketing arena was already a key site for the democratic project in the region. They would, of course, take to it their own creative and imaginative vigour, animated by their Afro-Creole culture. But, as C.P. Bowen, a member of the entertainment committee in Barbados for the English tour of 1895, observed, the black spectators — men and women — were no raucous novices beyond the boundary:

> From the hour of 10 o'clock [on Tuesday, January 29] the people began to flock in numbers from all parts of the country, and about 11.30 it was a sight to witness the large crowd which had assembled to see the match. All the stands were filled to over-crowding.... The multi-coloured dresses of the ladies formed a bright and cheerful scene.... [W]e have no means of ascertaining precisely the number of persons who assembled on the ground, but we do not think there could have been less than seven or eight thousand.... The enthusiasm expressed by the clapping of hands, and the shouts which rent the air at a good hit, or a steady 'block', or at a smart piece of fielding, was especially noticed by some of the visitors who expressed themselves as struck with the keen interest taken by the crowd in the game, and the evident impartiality exhibited by them in their applause.[43]

Black Barbadians saw the game as central to their claim to a space in West Indian society, nearly 60 years after the end of slavery. The fact that they were still excluded from representing the colony in inter-colonial games in the 1890s did not deter them: it shaped a resolve to strive for greater proficiency. The game was a vehicle for the struggle for civil and political rights, as well as the means of forging the rudiments of a West Indian identity. More than in any other colonial environment it was necessarily at the core of the political endeavour. This was the foundation on which Barbadian cricket was built; but what Bruce Hamilton wrote some years later about the unquenchable passion for the game and the unpretentious context of its mastery on that island of 166 square miles, could be readily applied to the rest of the British West Indies at the end of the nineteenth century:

> If, as is often asserted, the game as played on the village green is the backbone of English cricket, an at least equally valuable contribution to West Indian cricket has been made by the contests fought out on a few square yards of pasture, on a quite well-prepared pitch on the only piece of level ground, but only one half-split ball and two old bats to go round, square leg out of sight in a gully, silly point standing on an outcrop of rock, and natural boundaries in the form of grazing goats and sheep. In Barbados at least the poorest

black man certainly has no less love of the game that his white brother of rustic England, with a far deeper understanding of it and skill in playing it. Everyone who has practised cricket in the island is aware that any bare-foot boy hanging about the ground is likely, if he is tossed a ball, to bowl reasonably well with it. And the present writer who has watched hundreds of matches at the big English grounds, and heard a great deal of nonsense talked at them, can testify to the superior knowledge of a Barbadian cricket crowd, whose comments and advice, though sometimes 'wuthless' [mischievous], are often extremely witty, and nearly always to the point. It is not a question of intelligence, it simply is that a love of cricket ... is confined to a small section of Englishmen, whereas *in the West Indies it is implanted in the hearts of the entire people.*[44] (emphasis added)

But at a technical level as well, exposure to English touring teams, even if the players were almost exclusively white, induced rapid, incremental progression in technique and competence in the finer points, a general polish that led to a discernibly higher quality of play. H.B.G. Austin, the white Barbadian batsman, the virtual father of West Indies cricket, has recorded the debt of cricket in the region to those early teams from England — Lucas's in 1895; Lord Hawke's in 1897 and Priestley's the same year. Bruce Hamilton has done the same:

So long as West Indian cricket remained in a backwater, the improvement of form beyond a quite moderate standard was an impossibility. According to the late Sir Harold Austin, local cricket in his early days was a pretty crude affair, aptitude for the game, strength of arm, quickness of eye, were all present; but there was little of the polish and perfection of method which were essential for getting the best out of these qualities, and which could only develop out of the example given by wider contacts. That is why the first English tours to the West Indies, from the English point of view all rather small beer, were of such importance to the cricket in these parts.[45]

In terms of the apprenticeship of West Indies cricket, 1897 would be an even more fruitful year than 1895: the tour by Lord Hawke in particular would have repercussions beyond the boundary, and pave the way for the first West Indies tour of England in 1900.

Chapter Five

Lord Hawke's (and Priestley's) Tours of the West Indies, 1897:
The Political Context

The tour of an English team under Lord Hawke (1860–1938) to the West Indies in early 1897 represented an advance over that of Slade Lucas's in 1895. Apart from the pedigree and prestige of the man himself, captain of Cambridge in 1885, the legendary captain of Yorkshire (1883–1910), when they won the County Championship eight times, and an influential figure at the heart of the MCC, the team included a number of county players, among them the 24-year-old white West Indian, Pelham Francis (Plum) Warner (1873–1963) of Trinidad, graduate of Harrison College (Barbados), Rugby and Oxford, who was already playing for Middlesex. For most West Indians, whatever their race or class, the visit of Lord Hawke's team, two years after Lucas's path-breaking tour, seemed like a vindication of their embryonic cricketing endeavours, recognition by the Mother Country of their enhanced status as a people worthy of her premier game and its attributes. It is noteworthy, too, that through some misunderstanding and the arrogance of Lord Hawke, another team from England, led by Arthur Priestley (he had toured with Lucas in 1895), visited the West Indies simultaneously. The latter is memorable possibly solely for the fact that for the first time, in February 1897, to mark the centenary of British rule in Trinidad, a composite West Indies team, comprising several black cricketers, played against Priestley's team. It was entirely appropriate, therefore, that the West Indies captain was a Trinidadian, Hon Aucher Warner, a brother of Plum.

Three black men, all from Trinidad, the most racially tolerant colony in the region, played for the West Indies and were largely responsible for their victory over Priestley's team: Lebrun Constantine, the batsman, and the two fast bowlers, 'Float' Woods and Archie Cumberbatch, as noted above, Barbadians who had migrated to Trinidad because of the racist selection policies of their homeland. It

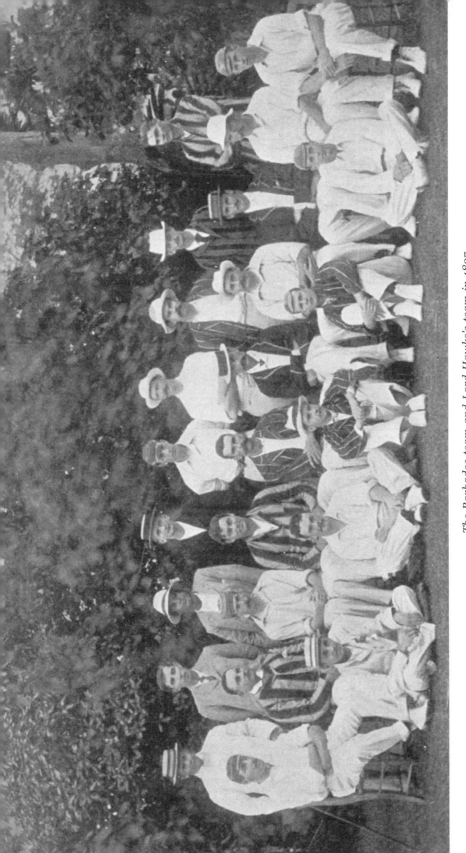

The Barbados team and Lord Hawke's team in 1897

is also significant that while both Priestley's and Hawke's teams encountered minimal opposition from most of the islands, they lost all four games against Trinidad: Woods and Cumberbatch were peerless in their supremacy. The tradition of West Indian pace bowling that would take them to the pinnacle in the last quarter of the twentieth century, was germinating. The magnificence of these two black bowlers in 1897 mirrored, within the boundary, an emerging pattern of incremental self-confidence of non-whites beyond the boundary, in education and early constitutional politics, however circumscribed by old prejudice. The seminal achievements of black cricketers against their English competitors gave credence to their claims in the 1890s to a greater stake in the political evolution of these British islands. With a solid educational base and competence in manipulating many of the cardinal indices of Englishness, black and coloured West Indians were quietly, but effectively, asserting their right to shape their own lives — within the Empire. The anti-colonial agenda would not really emerge until the late 1930s.

In assessing Lord Hawke's, and to a lesser extent Priestley's, tour of 1897, it is necessary to look beyond the boundary. It is not possible to grasp its full import if it is isolated from the socio-political context of the British West Indies. The 1890s witnessed a great depression in the sugar industry, the premier economic activity in most colonies, yet, as I have argued, the spaces opened up by the grave undermining of this so-called agent of civilization, eased the hegemony of the plantocracy and gave a modicum of credibility to the notion that non-white peoples, through education and the mastery of British colonial codes, could play a greater role in the making of the British West Indies. Even latecomers, the Indians, were able to develop their rice and cattle industries in their endeavour to minimize dependency on the plantations. Meanwhile, coloureds and blacks, already dexterous in appropriating and manipulating diverse imperial symbols, felt competent and sufficiently confident to challenge the plantocracy's dominance of colonial politics.

I will elaborate on the character of creole (African and coloured) responses to this dominance, with special reference to British Guiana. It is arguable that the advances made here were generally representative of the rest of the British West Indies, as I have already documented for the educational achievements of black and coloured Jamaicans. The scale of the depression at the time of Lord Hawke's tour was palpable in the following retrospect of the year 1896 in British Guiana:

[C]ommercially the past twelve months constitute a very dark chapter in our annals. A year ago we had to record the fact that the commercial outlook was sombre in the extreme, but it was probably not anticipated at the time that the year had so much misfortune in store for us. The staple industry of the colony has so long been in a distressful condition, that at the present time it seems veritably to be tottering to its foundation. The planters still hold out against the tremendous pressure of the Continental bounties [subsidies to European beet sugar], but it is impossible to say how long they will be able to maintain the struggle.[1]

While the sugar planters were bemoaning the decline of the sugar industry, Indian cultivators sought to reduce their dependence on the plantations by developing the rice industry. This was possible because the African, coloured and Portuguese middle class had agitated for change in the draconian Crown Land regulations, which, between the 1840s and early 1890s, had restricted the granting of such lands primarily to the big planters. Mobilized within the People's Association, the advocates of change secured partial reform of these regulations, while gaining mild constitutional change in 1891 to enfranchise middle-class black and coloured people.[2] The temper of the colonial polity was being altered — gradually — but in the process the shapers of reform were gaining vital political experience in constitutional politics. But they could not afford to become complacent, for the plantocracy were unremitting in their resistance to the democratizing of the political culture, the incremental trajectory of change notwithstanding. The latter's attitude is encapsulated in the following excerpt from a confidential correspondence sent to the Colonial Office in November 1897. The author is Henry K. Davson, the head of one of the more progressive sugar planting families in British Guiana:

I mentioned [in a letter to the Norman Commission] the desirability of encouraging the peasantry to cultivate rice, and as I had for some time previously held that policy, I had given instructions to my attorney to act on it on the Blairmont Estate [in Berbice]. The result has been very successful as far as the coolies [Indians] are concerned, but has certainly not been to the advantage of the Estate, as their reaping time has clashed with our own, and we have suffered greatly for want of our usual supply of time-expired immigrants, thus confirming my very strong conviction of the absolute necessity of continuing immigration to replace those labourers drawn away by their own operations [rice and cattle] [Indian indentureship was not abolished until 1917].

Henry Davson appreciated the relevance of the constitutional issue to this and other matters, and though comparatively progressive with regard to his worker's health and housing, he was not enamoured of political reform:

> May I also refer to the present constitution of British Guiana. You are aware that I was adverse [averse] to any change in the late Constitution [in 1891] under which we were virtually a Crown Colony.... The result of this is that the suffrage is now entirely in the hands of the black population whose votes are filling the Legislature with native barristers [blacks and coloureds], who have no stake whatever in the colony.... I would respectfully suggest a comparatively small place like British Guiana does not admit of the same extensive change as the larger colonies like Canada and Australia.... I regard the abolition of the present Constitution and the substitution in its place of a Crown Colony as well as the continuation of immigration, even on a limited scale, as only second in importance to the abolition of the bounties.[3]

Being a pillar of the plantocracy, Davson understood very well the relationship between politics, on one hand, and land reform, the development of alternatives to sugar and the continuation of Indian indentureship, on the other. His principal concern was the retention of what he thought was best for the sugar industry; that did not encompass the expansion of the democratic potential of the people of British Guiana. The subordinate groups, conversely, had no doubts of the merits of the latter and its importance in challenging the plantocracy's strategy for a return to the status quo. Education and cricket were key instruments in building the platform for the democratic evolution of the British West Indies; it is hardly surprising, therefore, that the planters would seek to retard the educational development of their predominantly Indian workforce, and that they advocated a conservative approach to constitutional change.

This was exemplified in the fight of Arthur Barrington Brown (A.B.) to secure election to the Court of Policy (the Legislature) in 1897. Two coloured men (mixed race) had already been elected to the Court some years before: Patrick Dargan and D.M. Hutson, both of them barristers with formidable reputations. The *Argosy*, a paper unapologetically prejudiced in favour of the plantocracy, had come to terms with that, but A.B. Brown's case was of a different complexion. He, too, was a barrister, but he was a very black man (in the parlance of the age, 'coal-black'); moreover, he was challenging a white planter, B. Howell Jones, the incumbent in the West Demerara district. The paper acknowledged Brown's suitability for electoral honours, but cautioned him to know his place — to show gratitude to his white benefactors by deferring to his natural superior:

> Mr. Brown, in our opinion is as well qualified as some who are in [the Legislature]. But we would ask that gentleman whether he has considered the position from the standpoint of ... the member whom he now wishes to supersede. Does he not know that the present member [Jones] is the representative of a long race of [white] colonials — men whose courage, enterprise and intelligence have helped to save the colony from utter ruin; and that they have always been the friends of working people [blacks]; and the advocates of measures for the people's elevation? It is to the votes of men like the present member's ancestors [whites] that the glorious fact of the present education and elevation of the Black people is mainly due. To oppose a colonist who, quite irrespective of his own services in the Court, has such a strong claim on the gratitude and goodwill of the people is an ungracious and invidious position to assume, and we hope Mr. Brown's good nature will induce him to profit by our not unfriendly observations.[4]

In 1896 the Progressive Association had been founded to articulate the interests of the newly enfranchised non-white lower middle class. As the comparatively liberal *Daily Chronicle* observed: 'the proletariat of the colony are awakening to an interest — more or less intelligent — in public affairs.' But they were apprehensive that this element might abuse their franchise: '[L]et there be no disposition to utilise the sacred privilege of the vote for the gratification of class [racial] hatred or the supposed furtherance of class [racial] interests.'[5] The paper rejected 'the element of class [racial] feeling which has already crept into the political arena', and attributed it to the new political organization:

We are aware that the Progressive Association resents the least imputation of class [racial] prejudice, but the fact cannot be denied that, whether the responsibility belongs to that body or not, an element of class [racial] feeling has been introduced into the electoral campaign, and more than one candidate has attempted to win the smile of the voters by general abuse of the Planters and the Planting interest [whites].... We do not say that the Planter in the past had not taken advantage of the dominant position which they enjoyed, but what the electors should consider now is whether this is the time to punish the Planters for his shortcomings, and whether anything is to be gained by depriving our staple industry [sugar] of that position in the counsels of the colony which rightly belongs to it.[6]

However, the *Daily Chronicle* did recognize the merit of having an element of opposition in the legislature, but felt that party politics belonged to the 'very distant future'. Like the *Argosy* they, too, were not enamoured of some candidates of the People's Association, who, allegedly, did not 'possess any experience of public life' nor had any demonstrable compensatory qualities. This was an unmistakable reference to A.B. Brown, as they were effusive in their commendation of the pragmatism of the President of the Association, Hon Patrick Dargan, the coloured legislator, who was able 'to modify theoretical principles to meet practical necessities'.[7] Brown won his seat in the Court of Policy — the first black man to be elected. It is clear that through his elevation, African people in colonial Guyana at the end of the nineteenth century, whether they had the vote or not, experienced a psychological boost. They identified each success in education, politics or cricket as an achievement of all blacks. The spread of popular education, and the emergence of a few lawyers and doctors by the 1890s (Dr John Rohlehr, for example, who was unsuccessful in his bid for the Legislature), did much to enhance African self-esteem. This engendered a heightened racial consciousness in British Guiana, productive of a degree of rancour. The situation was exacerbated by the lack of magnanimity on the part of the local white elite who, conversely, were inclined to interpret such advances as a threat to the colonial order. The absence of generosity was only marginally rectified with the victory of Brown, as seen in the following self-serving excerpt from the *Argosy* that could not leave well alone:

For the first time in the history of the colony a Black man will take his seat in the Court, and the occasion is worthy of a thought. His appearance there, he being a son of the soil, born and educated in the colony, and enabled by money earned therein to go to England and in due course to get called to the bar, is a credit, not only to his own people [blacks], but to the Legislators who have preceded him [whites]; whose legislative measures provided most generously, by school and church grants, for the education and moral education of all classes of the people.[8]

It is clear that both the *Argosy* and the *Chronicle* still saw the sugar industry as the key to the colony's future, the chronic depression of the sugar market and the stagnation of the colony in the late 1880s and 90s notwithstanding. Therefore, there was still something sacrosanct about the place of the plantocracy in British Guiana: the election of the white planter to the Legislature was being posed as an economic imperative. So that even when a successful coloured (mixed race) man from the commercial elite challenged the incumbent white planter candidate for the East Demerara seat, the contest was readily defined within an economic frame of reference — supposedly transcending politics — although the motive for supporting the planter was racial. The stance of the *Argosy* on this issue underlines the manner in which assumptions of white supremacy were now being constructed: itself a reflex of greater non-white assertiveness. The coloured candidate was D. Ouckama, a businessman whose credentials, the paper admitted, were unimpeachable: 'a citizen of Georgetown whom we have known for years ... we have no hesitation in saying that if a reputation amongst his fellow businessmen, for industry, steadiness and intelligence is any recommendation to the voters, Mr. Ouckama need not hesitate to present himself.' Yet, while conceding that he was a 'good man for the Court', they could not be sympathetic to his opposing a white sugar planter, Hon E.C. Luard. The paper conceded that he was not 'the embodiment of legislative wisdom', but argued that he deserved the suffrage of his constituents because he was a big employer of labour and 'one of the foremost supporters of the main industry' of British Guiana. All colonists, therefore, were beneficiaries of his investments.[9]

The *Argosy* then alleged that Ouckama's supporters in the Progressive Association were exploiting gullible, recently enfranchised blacks and coloureds. He was 'compromising his intelligence as a shrewd man of business' by not repudiating his canvassers who were fostering 'class [race] prejudice' in their zeal to defeat Luard: 'We are surprised at a man of Mr. Ouckama's intelligence and independent spirit continuing to stand after the kind of advocacy that has been used publicly in his cause. He has been warmly commended to the electorate. Why? *Because he has the good fortune not to be a white man.* This is insulting and degrading, and Mr. Ouckama ought to have denounced it. What would be thought of a candidate claiming to be returned because he was a white man?'[10] (emphasis added)

Ouckama defeated Luard and the *Argosy* quickly sought to establish that the result was attained through 'discreditable tactics' because, allegedly, 'the villagers were appealed to on the score of colour [race], and were harangued by wily demagogues to vote for their own colour'. It is ironic that the paper was so sanctimonious on this issue, as only a few weeks before, it will be recalled, they had opposed the candidacy of A.B. Brown unabashedly on grounds of race: indeed, on the premise that his opponent's ancestors belonged to a 'long race' of colonials endowed with 'courage, enterprise and intelligence'. They were naturally endowed with the gift of leadership. Yet the paper deplored the allegedly sordid campaign by blacks and coloureds to gain political rights through racial mobilization:

> We have a respect for Mr. Ouckama, based upon his business career, but we regret very much to think that he owes his election to the Court of Policy to the deplorable propagation of animosity betwixt two sections of the community [blacks and whites], neither of which can do without each other.... It is a frightfully dangerous expedient that has been resorted to, and we are by no means sure that the danger is over with the declaration of the poll. We are old enough to have seen the result in very disagreeable form of the fomenting of class [racial] antipathy and hatred [a reference to the anti-Portuguese riots in 1856 and 1889], and are able to estimate the guilt of those who go about deliberately to preach class [racial] antagonism as a virtue.... A great deal is allowable in electioneering; but he must regard the honour of a seat in the Court as very high, indeed, who would accept it, no matter how the honour has been obtained.[11]

The *Argosy* were convinced that race and politics were already fatally interlocked in this colonial polity. They had inserted the following apprehensively suggestive verse, captioned 'The New Desideratum', during the elections of December 1897:

> It seems that now, we no more care
> To find a statesman who *is able.*
> It's not a question who is *fair*
> In politics, but who is *sable.*[12]

In the same way that the black skin of A.B. Brown was seen as a taint, ill-equipping him for leadership, the blackness of cricketers in Barbados and British Guiana was seen as a defect militating against their playing the game at the highest level. That explains why no blacks or coloureds could play for Queen's Park in Trinidad or Wanderers and Pickwick in Barbados or the Georgetown Cricket Club (GCC) in British Guiana, founded in 1852. The difference in Trinidad, as I have shown, was that black or coloured cricketers could play for the all-island team against touring teams from England, although they could not represent the island in inter-colonial tournaments against Barbados and British Guiana. But coloureds had already entered the Legislature, and black men were now seeking to do so, on merit: in cricket, also, they were engaged in the same battle — to be selected on merit. It bears repeating that cricket was necessarily a political endeavour. But coloured (mixed race) men were becoming members of Queen's Park and GCC: as in education, now in politics, this example would encourage blacks of talent to challenge the racial foundations of West Indies cricket — peacefully and gradually, from the impregnable vantage point of merit. The coloured candidate, Ouckama, was elected not only to the Legislature; he was also now vice-president of the Georgetown Cricket Club. The Spartan spirit — the permeation of white cricket, first by coloureds, then blacks — was not restricted to Barbados.

Every small step mattered: gradualism was already deeply imbedded in the ethos of the black and coloured middle class. It is ironic that after the 1897 elections in British Guiana, the *Argosy*, which had covered it copiously and with unremitting gravitas becoming of a fundamental process, promptly pronounced on the powerlessness of the electives:

> The fact remains that the members [of the Court of Policy] are the chosen of the voters, and that in them is vested such legislative powers as may be exercised under *our so-called representative*

government.... The responsibility of office is not very great, and for that reason we regard the introduction of the ... ballot-box with not the slightest apprehension of serious trouble, being convinced that any attempt to imperil the interests of the colony by destructive innovations, would be vetoed without mercy [by the all-powerful chief executive, the Colonial Office-appointed Governor and his built-in majority].[13]

This was not just a case of sour grapes: power resided with the Governor, in the totally unelected Executive Council of officials and nominated members — not the Legislature. No black or coloured elective would be nominated to the council for some time yet. But the *Argosy* had missed the point. This was only 60 years since the end of slavery. Blacks and coloureds (Indians, too) were very aware of these constitutional limitations, but each minor success by one of their own, because the options for political mobility were so sparse, represented an achievement for all. That was why, as I have argued, even when racism kept non-white cricketers out of territorial cricket teams, popular enthusiasm was not diminished, as the process of learning was appreciated in the context of its constraints and longer potential ramifications. What went on beyond the boundary, in education and politics, had reverberations within the boundary. Non-whites were an overwhelming majority in the British West Indies, and they recognized that each accomplishment in education, politics and cricket enhanced the foundation on which to build in future. They would have harboured no conception then of Independence, but they were conscious that they had embarked on the long road — however winding and tortuous — away from the legacy of slavery and the sugar plantation. Patience was a great virtue in colonial affairs: the elite education codes, cricket and the politics of West Indies cricket helped to shape and inculcate that quality in West Indian politics.

In November 1896 the Governor of British Guiana, Sir Augustus Hemming, wrote the Colonial Office requesting that the West India Royal Commission, under the chairmanship of Sir Henry Norman (former Governor of Jamaica), should visit British Guiana first. Their terms of reference were to examine the grave depression facing the British West Indies and to make recommendations for its alleviation and the future development of these colonies. The problem, though, was that their impending visit would have clashed with the visit of the English cricket team under Lord Hawke scheduled to be in the colony in March 1897. Governor Hemming was apprehensive that obsession with the tour would undermine the quality of local contribution to the Commission. Hemming himself would not have been focused; his own attraction to the game bordered on the obsessive. The Colonial Office acceded: the Norman Commission went to British Guiana earlier, in January–February 1897.

It is noteworthy that whites and non-whites shared this obsession with Lord Hawke's impending tour. In January 1897 the *Argosy* carried a cartoon captioned: 'VERY IMPORTANT'. It depicts a white planter and his wife both formally dressed; he is reading a newspaper, she a book. Beneath was this brief exchange between husband and wife, reflecting the wife's sarcastic response to her husband's real thoughts, the English cricket tour:

> HUSBAND: I see the Royal Commission will be here in a fortnight's time, and we must do what we can to put our circumstances clearly before them, for the future of the colony will depend a great deal upon the nature of the Report.
> WIFE: Yes, dear, it is very important. We must give them a ball. But has the 'Georgetown' [GCC] selected a team to play them?[14]

The preoccupation had percolated to all levels of Guyanese society, as was the case throughout the British West Indies. In March 1897, at the start of Lord Hawke's visit to British Guiana, the *Argosy* observed that since the arrival of the team in the region local people of 'all classes' had shown the 'greatest interest' in the cricket played. The paper observed: 'Day after day during the tour of the team through the islands, the telegraph board at the West Indies and Panama Telegraph Company's Office has been besieged by cricket enthusiasts anxious to see how the various matches had resulted, and the unfortunate delay in the arrival of the mail only served to intensify the excitement already worked up to a high pitch.'[15] By the time Lord Hawke's team arrived in British Guiana, they had drawn with the Queen's Park team in Trinidad; and had defeated St. George's Club, Grenada by 8 wickets; All-Grenada by an innings; St. Vincent by 138 runs; drew one of their matches with Barbados and won the other by 4 wickets; defeated Antigua by 250 runs; and St. Kitts in their two matches by an innings and 38 runs and 278 runs respectively. Their only defeats, significantly, were in the two matches against multiracial All-Trinidad: by 137 runs and by 5 wickets respectively. This reinforced Guyanese preoccupation with the tour.

The British Guiana team and Lord Hawke's team in 1897

Even when Lord Hawke's men were practising at Bourda, the GCC ground in Georgetown, the passion was palpable. A reporter observed: 'At 3 o'clock on Thursday afternoon the English team went up to the Bourda ground for net practice. The enormous crowd of people present testified in the most crowning way to the keen interest that is felt in the game.' The *Daily Chronicle* captured the contagious spirit that possessed the capital city at the end of March 1897, during the first match against the English cricketers, and deemed it 'wholesome':

> [O]n Friday [March 26] almost the whole population of Georgetown, together with a large contingent from the country, was congregated on the Bourda ground or its environs. On the street, in the store, and in those places where naught but business is transacted, the matches, their probable final outcome, and the merits of the respective players have been the absorbing topic of conversation. *It is doubtful whether there is any other city outside this quarter of the globe, which could afford the spectacle of a whole people giving itself so unreservedly to the enjoyment of the game; and there are some, perhaps, who may be disposed to question whether the custom which prevails here of interrupting business so readily as we do is altogether a commendable or desirable one.* But however opinions may vary in reference to this point, it is unquestionably a wholesome symptom when we see so general a desire to take such a keen and vigorous interest in a game which ranks as the most popular amongst English sports and pastimes.[16] (emphasis added)

Although all the British Guiana players were white, a few members of the Georgetown Cricket Club (GCC), such as Ouckama, were coloured. This was not insignificant. I have argued that in education, politics and the lower and middle echelons of the civil service, West Indians were schooled in incremental access. Gradualism, therefore, was an acquired constituent of their mental universe. This was the case with cricket as well. As noted earlier, most Guyanese (most West Indians) were claimed by the magic of this imperial game. It is probable that the great depression had magnified the interest, a form of escape; but it is also possible that the expanding liberalism of the 1890s, the educational strides and the embryonic political advances, enhanced the perception that cricket, too, was now within the purview of blacks, coloureds and Indians — another area of potential access and accomplishment. The fact that English cricketers under Lucas, Priestley and Lord Hawke, within two years, 1895–97, were touring the West

Indies enlarged the already commanding stature of the game, rendering it another instrument with which non-whites in the region could measure their progress. Not only ancestral references, but English indices of mobility, also, were central to their construction of identities within the British Empire. The two English teams were, indeed, drawn largely from those in the County Championship, with some outstanding players included: A.E. Stoddart, S.M.J. Woods, R.C.N. Palairet (Priestley's team); H. Leveson-Gower, H.R. Bromley-Davenport, P.F. Warner (Lord Hawke's team). Priestley's team visited Jamaica, but did not go to British Guiana (Demerara); Lord Hawke's team played three matches in the latter but did not go to Jamaica.

Cricket historians in the West Indies have tended to overlook the contribution of English cricketers in the making of West Indies cricket. Plum Warner had remarked on the impact of the two English touring teams of 1897: 'Both English elevens met to all intents and purposes exactly the same opponents, except that.... Lord Hawke did not visit Jamaica, and Mr. Priestley did not go to British Guiana.... Both teams had a most enjoyable time, and there can be little question that cricket in the West Indies was considerably improved. It was, perhaps, taxing the hospitality of the inhabitants somewhat severely to have to entertain both teams, but on the other hand, two or three of the islands made money over the gate receipts at the different matches.' The latter point is especially interesting, as the cricket was being played, as noted earlier, in the context of one of the worst depressions in the history of the region's staple industry: sugar.[17]

It is important, therefore, to record the names of some of these pioneers in the shaping of the region's game, at the end of the nineteenth century, Priestley's team and Lord Hawke's respectively:

A. Priestley (MCC), captain; A.E. Stoddart, W. Williams (Middlesex); S.M.J. Woods, R.C.N. Palairet, H.T. Stanley (Somerset); R.P. Lewis (Oxford University); F.W. Bush, C.A. Beldam (Surrey); Dr. G. Elliott, J. Leigh (Uppingham Rovers); C.C. Stone (Leicestershire); R. Leigh-Barratt (Norfolk); and G. McLean [not stated]

Lord Hawke (Yorkshire) captain; H. Leveson-Gower (Surrey); G.R. Bardswell (Oxford University and Lancashire); H.R. Bromley-Davenport, P.F. [Plum] Warner (Middlesex); R. Berens (Oxford Authentics); W.H Wakefield (Liverpool CC); C. Heseltine (Hampshire); R.W. Wickham (Yorkshire Gentlemen); A.E. Leatham (Gloucestershire); J.M. Dawson and A.D. Whatman (Eton Ramblers).

Lucas's tour had been a stimulus to the expansion of the cricket culture, as was Priestley's, but the prestige of Lord Hawke, a pillar of English cricket and the most avid promoter of the game in the Empire, conferred on his tour a special aura. Therefore, All-Trinidad's two victories against the Englishmen, their only defeats (of the 14 matches played nine were won and three drawn), constitute a foundation stone of West Indies cricket, and I will explore their significance. Lord Hawke's first game in the West Indies was against the all white Queen's Park Cricket Club in Trinidad, the club of which Aucher Warner was captain. The match ended in a draw, with his brother, Plum Warner, scoring 119 of 428 in Lord Hawke's team's first innings. In their completed innings of 217, no Queen's Park player made 50. Their bowling, too, was not very impressive, although C. Gittens had fine figures: 51 overs, 9 maidens, 164 runs, 7 wickets. *Cricket* thought it necessary to qualify this performance: 'The home team was weak in bowling, and relied mainly on C. Gittens to take the wickets, although he was not considered good enough to go on first.'[18]

The first All-Trinidad game against the tourists, therefore, was profoundly significant for non-white West Indians as a whole. As with Lucas's tour in 1895, unlike Barbados and British Guiana, Trinidad selected some of their best black players to represent the island's team. Five were chosen for the first match on February 1–3, 1897: C. Attale, an opening batsman; Lebrun Constantine, a middle order batsman, wicket-keeper and occasional bowler, who had played against the English in 1895; and three fast bowlers, J. Woods ('Float'), the black Barbadian, who had bowled well against Lucas's team in 1895; A. Cumberbatch, also a black Barbadian, and S. Rudder, a bowler, another Barbadian exile. The latter three had all left their island because of racism in cricket. It is noteworthy that the white Queen's Park bowler, C. Gittens, played in the match; but he did not bowl a single over: he was not needed; and Stephen Rudder, the other black fast bowler, bowled only five overs in the first innings and none in the second. The fast bowling of Woods and Cumberbatch was virtually unplayable. All-Trinidad made 168 in their first innings: Leveson-Gower 4 for 45; Lord Hawke's team replied with 165, Plum Warner made 74, the highest score in the match. Woods's figures were: 22 overs, 4 maidens, 74 runs, 4 wickets; Cumberbatch's 27 overs, 7 maidens, 65 runs, 5 wickets. In their seconds innings All-Trinidad made 192, D'Ade 55; Constantine 32: Bromley-Davenport 5 for 36. Hawke's team required 196 for victory. They fell for a meagre 58; once more, the two black fast bowlers were unconquerable: Woods's figures were 14 overs, 4 maidens, 25 runs, 5 wickets; Cumberbatch's 13.2 overs, 4 maidens, 29 runs, 5 wickets. Woods had taken 9 for 99 in the match, Cumberbatch 10 for 94. All but six overs in the match (all in the first innings), were bowled by them. Of their 19 wickets (the other one was run out), 15 were bowled. It was an astounding performance, with profound social significance for the British West Indies as a whole. Trinidad won by 187 runs.[19]

The following are the details of this match: Lord Hawke's Team v. All Trinidad [February 1–3, 1897], Port of Spain:

TRINIDAD

L.S D'Ade c Heseltine b Bromley-Davenport	17	— c and b Bromley-Davenport	55
C. Attale b Leveson-Gower	22	— c Heseltine b Bromley-Davenport	14
J.L. Agostini b Leveson-Gower	12	— c Bardswell b Heseltine	4
M. Smith c Bradswell b Leveson-Gower	20	— c Hawke b Heseltine	7
A. Warner [capt.] c Bromley-Davenport b Heseltine	10	— b Davenport	32
L. Constantine c Bardswell b Leatham	20	— c Bradswell b Leatham	7
H. Hutton c Wakefield b Leveson-Gower	10	— c Heseltine b Bromley-Davenport	12
A. Cumberbatch c Bardswell b Leatham	5	— b Heseltine	7
C. Gittens b Leatham	4	— b Bromley-Davenport	26
S. Rudder lbw Wickham	23	— c Hawke b Heseltine	0
J. Woods [Float] not out	21	— not out	4
Extras	4	—	24
Total	168	—	192

LORD HAWKE'S TEAM

P.F. Warner b Cumberbatch	74	— c and b Cumberbatch	1
G.B. Bardswell b Woods	8	— b Woods	1
A.D. Whatman b Woods	6	— b Woods	5
Lord Hawke [capt.] c Constantine b Cumberbatch	6	— b Cumberbatch	0
H.R. Bromley-Davenport b Cumberbatch	12	— b Cumberbatch	1
H. Berens run out	22	— b Woods	15
H.D.G Leveson-Gower b Cumberbatch	8	— b Woods	0
R.W. Wickham b Woods	1	— b Cumberbatch	7
C. Heseltine b Woods	18	— c and b Woods	10
A.E. Leatham b Cumberbatch	0	— b Cumberbatch	13
W.H. Wakefield not out	0	— not out	1
Extras	10	—	4
Total	165	—	58

LORD HAWKE'S TEAM BOWLING

	Overs	Mdns.	Runs	Wkts.		Overs	Mdns	Runs	Wkts.
Leatham	20	4	37	3	....	6	1	27	1
Heseltine	14	5	34	1	....	12	3	38	4
Wickham	9	1	28	1	....	7	3	19	0
Bromley-Davenport	8	2	19	0	....	17	9	36	5
Leveson-Gower	15	2	45	4	....	9	1	26	0
Bardswell		10	4	20	....	10	4	20	0

TRINIDAD BOWLING

	Overs	Mdns.	Runs	Wkts.		Overs	Mdns	Runs	Wkts.
Woods	22	4	74	4	....	14	4	25	5
Cumberbatch	27	7	65	5	....	13	4	29	5
Rudder	5	1	15	0	....				
Smith	1	0	2	0	....				

[The black cricketers are listed in bold]

The second match against All-Trinidad, on February 5 and 6, 1897, was virtually a repeat of the first: the same five black players were selected; Woods and Cumberbatch were equally insuperable. Lord Hawke's Team batted first and made 130; he top scored with 26; Plum Warner, opening the batting again, made 10. Woods's analysis was: 28 overs, 9 maidens, 46 runs, 7 wickets; Cumberbatch's 29 overs, 11 maidens, 65 runs, 3 wickets; the only other bowler used, Rudder, bowled one over. All-Trinidad replied with 123; Aucher Warner made 38; Lebrun Constantine 35: Leveson-Gower got six wickets for 49. Although the Englishmen had a slender lead of 7, they again succumbed to the mastery of Woods (13 overs, 8 maidens, 21 runs, 3 wickets) and Cumberbatch (16 overs, 4 maidens, 26 runs, 5 wickets): 63 all out, with Plum's 25 the best score. Set 71 for victory, All-Trinidad won by 5 wickets. Aucher Warner top scored with 32. Woods got 10 for 67; Cumberbatch 8 for 91; Rudder got one; the other was run out. Plum felt that the Trinidadian batting was not at the same level of competence as the bowling, although he did identify a couple cases of admirable batting prowess: 'D'Ade batted excellently, while every man on the side seemed capable of making a few runs, though the batting, without doubt, is the weak point of the team. In fact, all over the West Indies, with perhaps the exception of Barbados, the bowling is superior to the batting.... D'Ade and [Lebrun] Constantine are excellent batsmen; their fielding is A1 and they are well captained [by Aucher Warner].'[20]

The following are the results of the second match against Trinidad, played on February 5 and 6, 1897: Trinidad won by five wickets:

LORD HAWKE'S TEAM

P.F Warner c Plummer b Cumberbatch	10	—	c D'Ade b Rudder	25
R. Berens c Constantine b Woods	23	—	c Rudder b Cumberbatch	1
H.D.G Leverson-Gower c and b Woods	4	—	Cumberbatch	4
H.R. Bromley-Davenport b Woods	6	—	c and b Cumberbatch	0
J.M. Dawson b Woods	0	—	c Smith b Cumberbatch	10
Lord Hawke[capt.] c Woods b Cumberbatch	26	—	c Constantine b Woods	11
C. Heseltine c and b Cumberbatch	6	—	Constantine b Woods	6
A.D. Whatman c Harragin b Woods	0	—	Attale b Woods	0
A.E. Leatham lbw Woods	4	—	Plummer b Cumberbatch	1
R.W. Wickham not out	20	—	run out	0
W.H. Wakefield b Woods	12	—	not out	0
Extras	19	—		5
Total	130	—		63

TRINIDAD

A. Warner [capt.] lbw Leveson-Gower	38	—	lbw b Bromley-Davenport	32
M. Smith b Leveson-Gower	27	—	c Leatham b Bromley-Davenport	3
H. Hutton c B-Davenport b Leveson-Gower	0	—	b Bromley-Davenport	1
L.S. D'Ade st Wakefield b Leveson-Gower	3	—	not out	15
A.E. Harragin b Leveson-Gower	4	—	b Bromley-Davenport	6
L. Constantine lbw Leveson-Gower	35	—	b Bromley-Davenport	1
C. Attale b Heseltine	1	—		
A. Cumberbatch c and b Heseltine	0	—	not out	10
E. A. Plummer b Bromley-Davenport	5	—		
J. Woods c Wakefield b Bromley-Davenport	4	—		
S. Rudder not out	0	—		
Extras	6	—		3
Total	123	—	(for 5 wickets)	71

TRINIDAD BOWLING

	Overs	Mdns.	Runs	Wkts.		Overs	Mdns	Runs	Wkts.
Woods	28	9	46	7	....	13	8	21	3
Cumberbatch	29	11	65	3	....	16	4	26	5
Rudder	1	1	0	0	....	4	1	11	1

LORD HAWKE'S TEAM BOWLING

	Overs	Mdns.	Runs	Wkts.		Overs	Mdns	Runs	Wkts.
Bromley-Davenport	8	1	29	2	....	11	3	25	5
Heseltine	10	1	28	2	....				
Leveson-Gower	22	3	49	6	....	6	0	24	0
Wickham	12	5	11	0	....	5	0	19	0

[The black players cited in bold]

As noted above, Lord Hawke's team's defeats in the two games against Trinidad were their only losses in the West Indies. The two black fast bowlers had been largely responsible for the victory of Trinidad, and Plum Warner was generous in his recognition of the gifts of his countrymen. In his column for *The Sportsman* of London he observed:

> In Cumberbatch and Woods we had met two really good bowlers, especially the former, who bowls fast right and changes his pace well.... *The winners [Trinidad] thoroughly deserved their victory, as they played good cricket right through the match, while in Woods and Cumberbatch, who are both black men, they possess two really first class bowlers.* Woods takes a very short run but bowls at a tremendous pace. His delivery is rather low, but every now and then he brings the ball back considerably. Cumberbatch ... bowled splendidly and is perhaps the best bowler of the team. [He dismissed Plum three of the four times they met].[21] (emphasis added)

Plum Warner's magnanimity was again evident in his piece for the 1898 *Wisden*. He was very pleased with the standard of the game in the island of his birth, but was especially proud of the progress of the black 'Trinidadian' cricketers, particularly Woods and Cumberbatch:

Here three matches were played. The first against the [all-white] Queen's Park Cricket Club [captained by Aucher Warner; Plum made 119] ended in a draw considerably in our favour, but in the next two encounters, which were against the combined Island team, we were decisively beaten: the first time by 137 runs, and in the second by five wickets. The chief credit of the victory rested with the two black [fast] bowlers, Woods and Cumberbatch, who between them took 39 wickets in the two matches [in fact 37: Rudder got one and two were run out]. Woods bowls very fast, with a somewhat low and swinging action. He is very straight and every now and then breaks back considerably. Cumberbatch, who is perhaps the better bowler of the two, is a medium pace right-hander. He breaks a little both ways, and varies his pace with much judgment. The fielding of the Trinidad team was splendid. The black men were especially fine fielders; they throw very well, and seldom miss a catch.[22]

In the two matches against Lord Hawke's team, 'Float' Woods's bowling analysis was: 77 overs, 25 maidens, 166 runs, 19 wickets, for an average of 8.73; Cumberbatch's was equally impressive: 85.2 overs, 26 maidens, 184 runs, 18 wickets, for an average of 10.22. It is important to note that although these two, along with Clifford Goodman (the white Pickwick and Barbados fast bowler), were probably the three best bowlers in the West Indies, they could not represent their native Barbados because of the whites-only policy in late nineteenth-century inter-colonial cricket. The visits of the English teams, in the latter half of the 1890s, gave Trinidad an opening to break the racial mould. Ironically, now that Cumberbatch was a rising star, the *Barbados Globe* had the temerity to remind Trinidadians that he was Barbadian (surprisingly, Woods was not claimed): 'We see that Mr. Connell Gittens [the white bowler for Queen's Park and All-Trinidad] has been claimed by Trinidadians as a native, as well as the groundsman [at Queen's Park], Cumberbatch. We would like to learn the truth of this claim as we feel sure that they are both Barbadians born and bred.'[23] After Cumberbatch had taken 9 wickets in the victory of the first ever West Indies team to be constituted, against Priestley's XI, in February 1897 in Trinidad, the *Globe* was proud to count this black fast bowler among the five Barbadians (the other four were white) who had contributed amply to West Indies victory by 3 wickets: H.B.G. Austin, Clifford Goodman, D.M. McAuley (Barbados), A.B. Clarke (representing British Guiana). In a display of island chauvinism that would become chronic in West Indies cricket, the *Globe* offered the following calculation: 'We are thus accountable for 178 runs — just half the score, and had the honour of capturing every wicket. Of the 11 catches taken against the Englishmen, six fell into Barbadian palms. To crown it all the Centenary Gold Medal for batting has been won by Mr H.B.G. Austin, he having made 75 not out, in a manner that was "almost faultless".'[24]

The Barbadian paper could not summon the generosity to note that Lebrun Constantine, the black Trinidadian batsman, was second top scorer after Austin, with 38 in West Indies first innings; neither did it record that a Mr J. McCarthy had presented a bat to Constantine, which he had promised him if he made over 30 runs. Big scores were a rarity on Trinidad's matting wickets: centuries were a phenomenon suggestive of divine intervention. Priestley's XI batted first and made 179; West Indies replied with 215, a lead of 36, Austin's 75 not out the top score. The tourists made 176 in their second innings. West Indies therefore needed 141 to win. They got this for the loss of 7 wickets, with Constantine's 45 the highest score. This is the context in which the black Trinidadian's two scores, 38 and 45, must be viewed: a crucial contribution, indeed.[25]

It is noteworthy that Clifford Goodman, the white Barbadian fast bowler got 9 wickets in the match, so did Cumberbatch. Goodman's match analysis was: 60 overs, 18 maidens, 125 runs, 9 wickets; Cumberbatch's was 60 overs, 20 maidens, 133 runs, 9 wickets. Trinidad deserved the credit for the latter's achievement. If he had stayed in Barbados, he would not have had the opportunity of playing for his island, neither would he ever have represented the West Indies. When he migrated to Trinidad, Cumberbatch played club cricket for Pickwick, a 'leading team' in the cup competition. His figures were incredible: 124 overs, 45 maidens, 113 runs, 61 wickets, and an astounding average of 1.8 runs per wicket. From this solid foundation, Cumberbatch had earned a place as a 'ground boy' at the Queen's Park Club; he was a so-called professional, which in his homeland would have been the spurious premise for excluding him from the island's team. By ignoring this travesty, Trinidad had short-circuited the racist underpinnings of Barbadian and Demerarian cricket.[26]

Trinidad, therefore, had a greater claim to celebrate this first West Indies victory; the match had 'created great excitement ... the attendances large'. When the winning run was scored, there was a 'tremendous outburst of enthusiasm'.[27] It was entirely appropriate that this first composite team should have been assembled to play in Trinidad, on February 15–18, 1897, on the centenary of her accession to British rule. In those 100 years Trinidad had emerged as the most tolerant of the British West Indian colonies, and had taken a bold step by selecting black men to represent it whether, like Constantine, they were born there, or, like Cumberbatch and Woods, they had escaped the racism in Barbadian cricket. By being a key force in selecting this first West Indies team, Aucher Warner set the pattern of assessing people on the basis of merit: from the inception, therefore, a composite regional team discarded the racist principles of Barbados and Demerara by selecting black men of talent. Both Woods and Cumberbatch had been selected for this match, but the former did not play for some unknown reason. However, as observed above, Lebrun Constantine, the black Trinidadian batsman, did play. All the others were white: **Trinidad:** Aucher Warner (captain), L.S. D'Ade (Queen's Park); **Barbados:** H.B.G. Austin, D.M. McAuley (Wanderers), Clifford Goodman (Pickwick); **British Guiana (Demerara):** A.B. Clarke, S.W. Sproston, O.Weber (Georgetown Cricket Club).[28]

Trinidad was the pathfinder, and Aucher Warner had a central role in this. Their progressive policy on blacks and cricket probably would have encountered much local white resistance if it did not have the authority and unimpeachable credentials of Aucher Warner: the unimpeachable stamp of the 'first family' of Trinidad. And it was entirely appropriate that he should captain the first West Indies team, and that he would also do so in England in 1900. As he said after the victory against Priestley's team, and after commending the notable performances of Goodman, Austin, Clarke, Constantine and Cumberbatch: 'A great many of us played a very secondary role — I among them; but it gives me very great pleasure to think that I should happen to be the captain of the first all-West Indian team ever got together. And I hope it is the beginning of greater things for cricket in the West Indies, and that the combined colonies may again meet teams such as this which Mr. Priestly has brought out.'[29]

Without Aucher Warner, it was very likely that Lebrun Constantine, 'Float' Woods and Cumberbatch — the first black pillars of West Indies cricket — in the common phrase of despair spawned by the region's game, would have 'died on the vine'. And it is to the eternal credit of those early black cricketers that they did not let their few white sponsors down. At the bottom of their endeavours they knew that cricket went beyond the boundary: they spoke for many who had, indeed, died on the vine. Woods and Cumberbatch, in particular, were remorseless in their dominance — they were the founders of West Indies fast bowling tradition; and those who had the privilege of seeing them were very proud of their mastery of the craft.

Like Lord Hawke's team, Priestley's was defeated by Trinidad in both of their matches. As the correspondent for *The Sportsman* observed, after the ignominious defeat by the Trinidadians in their first game against Priestley's XI: 'The less said of our display the better: it was one of those rapid processions to and from the wickets. Only an hour was occupied in the procession, Cumberbatch and Woods working the execution.... Beldam's 8 was the top score'. In the match played on February 19–22, 1897, Priestley's team made 33; Trinidad responded with 174, Constantine scoring 46. Priestley's team replied with 141. Trinidad required one run to win: they won by 10 wickets. As usual Woods and Cumberbatch dominated the bowling, securing 17 of the 20 wickets: Rudder, the other black bowler, got two wickets. The bowling analysis of Woods for the match was: 37 overs, 10 maidens, 70 runs, 6 wickets; Cumberbatch's was: 42 overs, 19 maidens, 59 runs, 11 wickets. It is noteworthy that the best batsman in Priestley's team, A.E. Stoddart, the English Test cricketer, fell to Woods in both innings for 4 and 3.[30]

In their second match against Trinidad, on February 25–27, 1897, Priestley's team suffered another ignominious defeat, by 8 wickets. The bowling of Woods and Cumberbatch was again awesome: they accounted for 18 of the 20 wickets, Rudder again got only two. Trinidad batted first and made an impressive 284, with L.S. D'Ade scoring 140 not out; S. Rudder made 53; the two had an extraordinary last wicket partnership of 103. Priestley's XI replied with 164; the follow-on was enforced and they scored 212. Trinidad won the game for the loss of only two wickets. Woods's figures for the match were: 59 overs, 18 maidens, 115 runs, 11 wickets; Cumberbatch's were: 42.1 overs, 9 maidens, 152 runs, 7 wickets. It would be difficult to find a parallel of such mastery as displayed by Woods and Cumberbatch for Trinidad, in their games against Lucas's team in 1895 and Hawke's and Priestley's teams in 1897.[31]

What this meant for the self-esteem of black people can only be imagined; and Trinidad was at the heart of this achievement. In 1900, on the eve of the first West Indies tour of England, Plum Warner published

Sir Pelham Warner (Plum) (1873–1963): champion of black cricketers; Trinidad-born captain of England

his first cricket book, *Cricket in Many Climes*. His tour to the West Indies had made such a profound impact on him, especially the recent inclusion of black men in the Trinidad team that played against Hawke's and Priestley's, that he thought it necessary to underline his impressions of 1897. He had no doubt that black players were indispensable to the future of West Indies cricket, indeed, that they were at the core of the shaping of its future, within and beyond the boundary. He was obviously moved by the spontaneous affection he, personally, and Lord Hawke's team had received in all the islands, as he was impressed with the black people's unbridled enthusiasm for and knowledge of the game. Plum recalled the context of their arrival in Barbados, on January 25, 1897, on the heels of Priestley's sojourn there:

> Mr. A. Priestley, having arrived at Barbados a fortnight before us, had played and been defeated in two of his first three matches. Our first news of his doings was received from a grinning nigger [sic], who screwed his head in through a port-hole and, shouted at the top of his voice, 'Stoddard, he only make six, sah!' [The great batsman made 6 and 5 in the second innings of the second and third games, both times bowled by Clifford Goodman. He was dismissed five out of six times by him: clean bowled thrice.] The whole population was mad on cricket; and when we appeared on the deck we were surrounded by an excited little crowd, who thrust papers containing the scores of the matches into our hands, declaring ... that Barbados had beaten England; and I verily believe that many of them think to this day that Lord Hawke's and Priestley's elevens represented the pick of England's cricketing talent.

Warner adds:

> After breakfast we went on shore, where a huge swarm of black men awaited us on the wharf. 'Bromer' [Bromley-Davenport], who had visited the West Indies with R.S. Lucas's team [in 1895], and had been very successful as a bowler [113 wickets at 8.61], was at once recognised, and was greeted with cries of 'De bowler, De bowler', 'Look at the bowler'. Martin Hawke [Lord], too, was an object of real interest as a real live Lord.... After a thoroughly good practice at the Pickwick ground at Kensington, where we found that more than one of the black men bowled uncommonly well, we adjourned to the Bridgetown Club, and there met 'Sammy' Woods, Stoddart, and

several members of Priestley's eleven. They one and all were loud in praise of C[lifford] Goodman, the crack island bowler, who had done more than anyone else to bring about their defeat, and they assured us with ominous looks that we should find him a hard nut to crack.[32]

A white Barbadian fast bowler from a distinguished cricketing family, a graduate of the Lodge and a member of Pickwick, Clifford Goodman was a very fine fast medium bowler in the 1890s. He was brilliant against Priestley's team (36 wickets at 8.33), but was much less impressive against Lord Hawke's team. This did not diminish Plum's respect for him, as reflected in his assessment of Goodman in *Wisden* of 1898: 'Clifford Goodman is a remarkably fine bowler.... He is right hand medium pace, and breaks principally from the off, but at times he sends down a faster one which comes with his arm. He is undoubtedly one of the three finest bowlers in the West Indies.' The other two, he had observed, were the redoubtable Woods and Cumberbatch.

Though not centre stage yet, black people brought their energy, flair and imagination to spaces they considered crucial: observing, learning, slowly cultivating the basic skills, but never cramped into a dull mimicry or an impotent rage over the slow pace of change. Indeed, as I have argued, although black cricketers could not represent the island, black Barbadians identified with the victory of their white team: their own construction of a Barbadian identity embraced aspects of that Englishness which their white countrymen sought so assiduously to cultivate. So that while they were probably peeved by their marginal status, their acquired gradualist temperament could easily accommodate and appreciate the victory of local whites over the imperial 'motherland': an adumbration of themselves was contained in the achievement. They would learn and gradually establish their competence and merit, as they sought to create a niche for themselves in colonial society, at the end of the century. This was possible because, as in the latter stages of slavery, though peripheral, they were never totally excluded from the game.

It is noteworthy that black groundsmen, so-called professionals, who could not be selected for their various islands, bowled with venom and commitment at white batsmen, at the elite cricket clubs for whites, such as Wanderers and Pickwick (Barbados), Queen's Park (Trinidad) and the Georgetown Cricket Club (British Guiana). These black men carried the submerged hopes of all black people. Although still excluded from competitive cricket, they were within the boundary, however tenuously, sharpening their skills. Their inbetweenity sustained the gradualist temper and was conducive to effort: marginality fed a challenge to excel, to bowl faster at the white batsman, to field sharply, to strive for mastery, in practice sessions. Many visiting English cricketers, such as Plum, were greatly impressed with the black 'ground' bowlers. The game could not have carried the social burdens of all ethnic groups, implicit in the shaping of West Indian identities, if the subordinate groups had been completely excluded from it.

The potential of the underdogs was transparent, as were their energy and their commitment to cricket that already suggested a calling; but it was the English tours at the end of the century that really released some of this potential and enhanced its stature. Behind this endeavour were the progressive ideas of Dr Anderson, Lord Hawke and Plum Warner: these were the godfathers of West Indies cricket, the architects who transported local, marginalized talent to a higher plain of respectability. But this was not mere altruism: Woods, Cumberbatch and Lebrun Constantine, by their energy, skills and panache, had made this possible. They were beginning to earn white recognition, in England, thus expanding notions of possibilities for all black people in the region, within and beyond the boundary. When Lebrun died in Trinidad in January 1942, his obituary spoke of 'his dynamic cricket energy'; and it was observed that this spirit, his uninhibited style, had given his play a contagious effervescence: 'He was one of the most attractive figures on the cricket field, a devastating batsman with an effective, if unorthodox, style, a wonderful fieldsman in his later years.... His famous hook stroke, though pronounced unorthodox, has been copied by many Trinidadian batsmen. Lebrun Constantine was a terror to bowlers and scored at a rapid rate. His unerring sight enabled him to drive with great power and he was also a fine exponent of the cut stroke, taking balls from the off stump when set.'[33]

One of the people who absorbed his 'dynamic energy' was his eldest son. Three decades later, in the early 1930s, the great English cricket writer and correspondent of the *Manchester Guardian*, Neville Cardus, wrote a preface to the first book on cricket by a black West Indian, *Cricket and I*. The author, the Trinidadian all-rounder, Learie Constantine (1902–71), Lebrun's son, had achieved even greater recognition, in England, than his father. But what Cardus saw in Learie's style could be located only in the temperament of the West Indian people; it has as its source the same basic promptings that drove Woods, Cumberbatch and Learie's dad: the endeavour of West Indians of African descent to shape an identity subversive of the worse legacy of slavery — self-contempt. Their cricket spoke for their people:

> [Learie] Constantine is a representative man: he is West Indian cricket, just as W.G. Grace was English cricket. When we see Constantine bat or bowl or field, we know he is not an English player, not an Australian player, not a South African player. We know that his cuts and drives, his whirling fast balls, his leapings and clutchings and dartings — we know they are the consequences of impulses born in the blood, a blood heated by the sun and influenced by an environment and a way of life much more natural than ours; impulses not common to the psychology of the over-civilised places of the earth. *His cricket is racial.* Professionalism with Constantine has not expelled nature. When he hits a ball for six, he laughs hugely, and seems to say, 'Oh golly. I like it: let me do it again'. Cricket is his element; to say that he plays cricket, or takes part in it, is to say that a fish goes swimming. His movements in the field are almost primitive in their pouncing voracity and unconscious beauty. There are no bones in his body, only great charges and flows of energy. A genius, and, as I say, a representative man. *He has made a contribution to the style and technique of cricket; at the same time he has told the tale of his people.* At Lord's last year while Constantine played a wonderful innings a number of his compatriots wept for joy and shook hands in brotherly union. Constantine was their prophet; they saw in his vivid activity some power belonging to their own blood, a power ageless, never to be put down, free and splendid.[34] (emphasis added)

There was gradualism in the shaping of this mastery, but the energy of the play, the spontaneity and dramatic impulse in its execution, 'the voracity', spoke of its antithesis: rebellion against the inhibiting constraints of the colonial order and the persistence of racial criteria as the yardstick of merit. It was this spirit (irrespective of the promptings) that Plum Warner had seen in the black pioneers of West Indies cricket at the end of the nineteenth century, which impelled him to advance what Hilary Beckles calls the 'Plum Warner Project'. He argues: 'Plum's social understanding was that white and black cricketers in the West Indies, and those in England for whom he was a conduit, were held together by ideological bonds symbolised in the social and cultural practice of cricket'. But Beckles notes that Warner recognized the pitfalls in the realization of this ideal thrown up by white racial attitudes in the Empire: cricket had to transcend the limitations of its environments: 'According to [Keith] Sandiford, Plum sought to identify a high moral ground for empire, but was sensitive to the contradictions evident within the concept as it related to the politics of race hatred and colonial exploitation.... Cricket, Warner believed, should symbolise social progress and justice, and not ... endemic racial oppression and class alienation.... He spoke of the fairness of the game's value system and believed that it was an important vehicle on which West Indians of all ethnicity could travel into a more democratic future.'[35]

Plum would play a crucial role in the introduction of black and white West Indian cricketers to the discipline and rigour of the English game at the end of the nineteenth century. The family's West Indian pedigree was certainly at the core of the ardour with which he pursued the 'project' (in fact, his earliest ancestor, Sir Thomas Warner goes back to the dawn of English colonization in the region, to St. Kitts of the 1620s), but it is arguable that the generosity of spirit of several ordinary black people from his childhood, and their pride in him so abundantly demonstrated during Lord Hawke's tour in early 1897, kindled a special empathy for black cricketers. He recalled the impact of that sojourn, over half a century later, in his memoirs published in 1951:

> I naturally looked forward to a visit to the scenes of my childhood, and when, on landing in Trinidad, a cab nearly ran over me the driver was rated soundly. 'Good God, man, what you do? Nearly run over Mr. Pelham. Can't you see it's Mr. Pelham grown big? Take your d[amn] jackass away!' In the opening match of the tour in Trinidad I made 119, and several men broke on to the Queen's Park ground, shouting out, 'I taught you, Mr. Pelham. You play well, sir. I am proud of you', while one said. 'This is a great day for me, sir. I see my little boy make a hundred. I go home and tell my wife, sir, and she die of joy, sir'. And my old nurse, Kitsey, embraced me in front of the hotel, to the huge delight and amusement of the rest of the team: 'Oh, Puggie darling, I am glad to see you! Let me look at you well. You not so pretty as you were — you pretty little boy. Still, you not bad'. Kitsey lived to a great age, and when I was in Australia in 1903-4 [as captain of England] she wrote me a most affectionate letter in which she said, 'I hear my little boy become a big cricketer.'[36]

Implicit in the primary responses of Plum's black compatriots to him was something of the spirit of the great house: black domestics often harboured genuine love for the white children to whom they were surrogate mothers and fathers. The white children, too, could not wipe out those many seminal creole influences that profoundly shaped their lives. Within the interstices of these complex relationships across the racial chasm sprouted the ambivalences so crucial in the making of a peculiar West Indian hybridity. C.L.R. James was right: the West Indian personality has no parallel in the history of the colonial encounter in terms of the internalizing of the attitudes of the 'other'. That explains why education and cricket could take such sturdy roots in the British West Indies, why, too, Plum Warner could feel genuinely attached to the aspirations of many black West Indians.

It is hardly surprising, therefore, that he would, shortly after the tour, in his article for *Wisden* of 1898, immediately seek to demonstrate the merits of black cricketers by underlining the superiority of Trinidad, captained by his brother, Aucher Warner, who had the courage, possibly with Plum's prompting, to select talented black men in their matches against Lucas's, Lord Hawke's and Priestley's teams and in the composite West Indies team against the latter, in 1897. That was the watershed in West Indies cricket, and Plum was emphatic that this initiative could not really reach its optimum if black men of merit were excluded from colonial teams. He observed:

> In estimating the respective merits of Trinidad, Barbados and Demerara, it must not be forgotten that Trinidad played black professional bowlers, while Barbados and Demerara did not. For the Inter-Colonial Cup which is played for every other year between these teams, black men are excluded; and Trinidad, thus deprived of its bowling, is by no means so good as either of its opponents. In the smaller islands, such as Grenada, St. Vincent, Antigua, St. Kitts and St.Lucia, black men are always played, (and as a matter of fact, it would be impossible in these islands to raise a side without them [they did not play in the all-white Inter-colonial Cup], but Barbados and Demerara have strenuously set themselves against this policy. *With the attitude taken up by Barbados and Demerara I cannot altogether agree. These black men add considerably to the strength of a side, while their inclusion makes the game more popular locally, and tends to instil a great and universal enthusiasm amongst all classes of the population.*[37] (emphasis added)

Lord Hawke, too, recognized the dominant role of the black fast bowlers in Trinidad's two victories against his team in 1897. He wrote thus of Woods and Cumberbatch in his memoirs of 1924:

> Meeting All-Trinidad was a very different affair. Aucher Warner ... had under him *a couple of native [black] bowlers, very fine ones, who were altogether too good for us*. Woods, taking a decidedly short run, was very fast with a low action.... Cumberbatch, pretty quick medium, possessed a lot of variety, and I thought him the better of the two. He always tucked his trousers into his boots before going on to bowl.... The Attorney-General of Trinidad had promised Cumberbatch a couple of dollars if he bowled me out. I knew this and was particularly careful when I faced him. To see my middle stump prone on the turf before I had scored made me sadder and Cumberbatch more wealthy.... As it turned out, *we did not lose another match on the tour, though it may be mentioned that neither Barbados nor Demerara played natives [blacks] against us*.[38] (emphasis added)

The Lord was acknowledging the superior skills of the 'natives' in some aspects of the game — a generosity of spirit with which most native whites were not richly endowed. And Plum would continue to press their case for selection — purely on merit: he asked for no concession to black novices simply for them to learn the ropes. As bowlers, he was saying, they had already demonstrably superseded their white counterparts. Moreover, as he made clear in his article in *Wisden*, any West Indies team touring England must include the top black players or the venture would be futile. Plum was challenging the white authorities in West Indies cricket, at the end of the nineteenth century, to make merit the only criterion for selection:

> The visit of a West Indian team to England is by no means improbable, and there can be little doubt that a capital side could be got together from the different islands and British Guiana, if the black men were included. Without them it would be absurd to play the first-class counties, and a West Indian combination would derive no benefit whatever from playing the second-class.... The team would compose nine or ten gentlemen [whites], and four or five black men, who would of course play as professionals. To expect the team to play Surrey or Lancashire would be too much, but I am confident that a good fight would be made against the other

counties.... I think the bowling and fielding of the West Indians superior to that of the Philadelphians [who toured in 1898]. A West Indian XI should not arrive in England until the middle of June, so as to avoid the cold winds of early summer, which the black men of the team would naturally feel keenly. In expressing these views on the merits of the West Indian cricketers, it must be borne in mind that I am judging them on the form they showed on their own grounds, and under conditions quite different from those of the old country. Light, different wickets and surroundings must be taken into consideration. But still I am of the opinion that the experiment would be well worth trying.[39]

On the eve of the visit of the first West Indies team to England in 1900, Warner underlined the proficiency of black West Indian cricketers — as fast bowlers and fielders, precisely the spheres in which they had had a prolonged apprenticeship in the context of the white-dominated imperial game. Plum had succeeded in his 'project': black cricketers would be included in the team:

The batting will be the weak point of the team, but that may be expected to improve rapidly as the tour advances.... The bowling and fielding will be the strong points, and I am confident that Woods, Cumberbatch [he was not selected although Plum and Lord Hawke considered him the best bowler in the West Indies] and the rest, if they keep fit, will bowl out many a good batsman.... Cumberbatch and Woods I shall expect to be successful on all wickets, while Mignon [a white Grenadian] is a capital medium pace bowler, and gets a good deal of spin on the ball. The great difficulty will be the selection of a captain, for the post is rendered even harder than usual by the inclusion of the black men, some of whom will want a great deal of looking after.[40]

An element of paternalism characteristic of the age notwithstanding, Plum was evidently optimistic that now that black cricketers had a chance to prove their worth, they would not squander the day:

The fielding will certainly be of a high class. The black men will, I fear, suffer from the weather if the summer turns out cold and damp, as their strength lies in the fact that their muscles are extremely loose, owing to the warm weather to which they are accustomed. Woods takes only two steps and bowls as fast as Mold! Englishmen will be very much struck with the throwing powers of these black men, nearly all of them being able to throw well over a hundred yards. On the whole, I feel pretty confident that the team will attract favourable attention all round.[41]

Plum concluded: 'The visit of any new team to England is always an experiment, attended with more or less possibilities of failure; but that they will be a failure I do not for a moment think, and in any case West Indian cricket will be greatly improved.'[42] This inaugural tour of 1900, as Plum noted, 'originated' with his friend, Lord Hawke, who had the 'active support' of Sir Neville Lubbock, the President of the West Indian Club in London, an arm of the old organization representing British companies in the region, the West India Committee, which was founded during slavery, in the eighteenth century.[43] But it was Warner primarily who, with the authority conferred by his creole West Indian pedigree, was able to go against the grain — to stake a claim for black cricketers to represent the West Indies in teams drawn hitherto exclusively from white amateurs. This was, in the context of the colonial assumptions of the 1890s, a revolutionary step: it is difficult to conceive of any other person advocating the 'Warner project'; harder, still, of imagining such rapid erosion of entrenched racist attitudes hidden behind the imperial distinction between 'amateur' and 'professional' and its hierarchical pretensions. It is arguable that at the base of Plum's lofty principles was a genuine belief that cricket should project a different kind of Englishness in the Empire — an epitome of the sublime — from the narrow, supercilious variety he was familiar with from his boyhood in Trinidad and Barbados. A.A. Thomson's tribute to him, shortly after his death in 1963, aged 90, captures the unimpeachable values of the man who helped to make West Indies cricket, and in the process contributed immeasurably to the shaping of the democratic temper of British West Indian societies:

Cricket ... embraces the English country scene, English individuality and English laughter; and it embodies that ideal of honour and the rule of law which we call fair play. These are delicate, almost private, matters and are best not paraded, but once in a while comes a man in whom all these traits are nobly blended. There have been greater performers ... but no one has in his person more truly symbolised cricket; its pageantry, its dignity and decency, its sense of 'civilisation under the sun' than ... Pelham Francis Warner.[44]

The radicalism permeating Plum's campaign is better appreciated when viewed against the racial and class assumptions of the white elite in British Guiana in 1897, during Warner's and Hawke's visit. The colony lost both games: by seven wickets and nine wickets. A number of people, presumably non-whites, had argued that if the local team that played the tourists was representative of all clubs, rather than the perceptibly white elite Georgetown Cricket Club exclusively, the results could have been substantially more flattering. The *Argosy*, which spoke for the commercial and plantocratic elite, countered in a manner that underlined the urgency for reform of the narrow colonial order: 'Much has been said and written about the wonders that would have been accomplished if the visitors had been pitted against a colonial team, that is a team chosen from all the clubs in the colony; but the suggestion is impracticable. The visitors did not come here to play the colony; they came as the guests of the Georgetown Club, by whom they were entertained, and if they had waited to be invited by all the clubs of the colony they never would have come at all. They are not professionals, but amateurs, all gentlemen of birth and station, and we are not democratic enough yet as a nation to ignore social distinctions even in sport, as long as the sport is confined to amateurs.'[45]

The paper did not mention that in neighbouring Trinidad the visitors were 'entertained' by the all-white Queen's Park Cricket Club, but had had no objections whatsoever to playing an All-Trinidad XI that included five black players, and which vanquished them twice — their only defeats on the tour. The *Argosy* could learn nothing from the Trinidad example; instead, it sought to minimize the ignominy of the Demerara defeat, while slipping into a mire of inanities. Unwittingly, however, by admitting that those representing the colony had hitherto been 'measuring themselves by themselves', they gave credence to those who were demanding space in Guyanese cricket for non-whites:

[W]e think our men have done by no means badly, neither of the completed matches having been a one-innings victory. That Lord Hawke's men, including the best of English cricketers, should require a second innings to dispose of us is something to be able to say.... [But] we have certainly seen our men do very much better and we have seldom seen them do very much worse. But the reverse is a grand moral tonic, not pleasant to the taste, but calculated to do good for allaying that feeling of self-complacency or sufficiency which is apt to attack men who through force of circumstances acquire the practice of measuring themselves by themselves.[46]

The Demerarians would continue to exclude black players from the team for some time: 'measuring themselves by themselves'. And the *Argosy* would continue to validate old assumptions of hegemony rooted in plantocratic foundations of status, at variance with the democratic temper that was already animating subordinate groups in the British West Indies in the 1890s. Both Trinidad and Barbados had played against Hawke's as well as Priestley's team. As noted earlier, it was the latter that had played against the first composite West Indies team, comprising black players, in Trinidad. Demerara, however, obdurately refused to invite Priestley's team; but the *Argosy* was still reactionary in their defence of the colony's isolated stance:

> Priestley thinks he had been badly treated, in his invitation to Georgetown being cancelled, and lots of people here think so too; but Hawke is Hawke, and therefore Priestley has no ground of complaint.... Of course, Mr. Priestley is very much to blame in the matter ... especially with regard to Demerara. When we asked him to give way to Lord Hawke, the influence which led up to the request was based upon one of our grandest national characteristics, the recognition of Order. If Priestley is a true-born Englishman, he will see the propriety of his stepping one side to allow a Lord to be received and entertained. If he himself had been Lord Wicket or Baron Stumps, there would have been no occasion for the tears; and we must ask him to give us credit for being as truly national in our snobbery as if we lived at Home.[47]

The white elite in British Guiana and Barbados, much more than in Trinidad, found it extremely difficult to throw off the old assumptions, to accommodate anything that mildly vitiated their imperial frame of reference. In the same way that they could see no merits in non-white Guyanese seeking to construct a more inclusive Guyanese identity, using cricket as an instrument to democratize their society, similarly they could not read the hidden script implicit in black achievement, however small, within and beyond the boundary. On the dismissal by

Lord Hawke at a practice session at the Bourda ground in Georgetown — bowled by 'a black boy [man]', a so-called professional — the *Argosy* interpreted the incident as a manifestation of imperial unity: cricket as the catalyst for deeper imperial promptings among all peoples of the Empire. That this incident could have augmented the resurgent racial pride among blacks, prompting the call for a more inclusive Guyanese team, missed the paper completely. It is likely that the exclusion of non-whites from the Demerara team had so antagonized many Guyanese that, as Plum Warner remarked, they expressed jubilation after the colony's second defeat by Hawke's team. The paper's interpretation of the 'black boy's' victory over the Lord, therefore, might not have drawn the same responses from their black readers as the imperial rendering suggested. For them cricket was more than an instrument for neutralizing subversive instincts and fostering respect by the 'native races' for the 'mother country'; it was already a means of self-affirmation:

> How far England's immunity from the revolutionary upheavals which have shaken Continental countries as moral earthquakes is due to the catholicity of cricket is a subject worth the investigation of the social historian. What is of even more interest to colonists, however, is cricket as an imperial factor. Even more than the tie of language the tie of cricket helps to hold together the units which compose the vast British Empire. A striking instance of cricket in both the aspects of which we have been speaking occurred on the ... [Bourda] ground on the 29 ... [March 1897], when Lord Hawke was cleaned bowled by a black boy in the employ of the ... [Georgetown Cricket] Club, and the significance of the incident was not lost upon the crowd. Here was a practical example of cricket both as a social and imperial factor, and in that small event the philosopher might read a large part of the secret of the loyalty and affection of what are known as the native races to the Mother country.[48]

To locate the probable response of 'the native races' to the 'black boy's' achievement, we have to go beyond the boundary, to the changing political and intellectual temper in the British West Indies of the 1890s, to the 'texts' of the black and coloured educated elite. In this respect 1897 was a watershed for black and coloured men, within and beyond the boundary. While Woods, Cumberbatch and Lebrun Constantine were claiming equality for all black people on the cricket field, coloured and black men, like Patrick Dargan and Dr John Rohlehr in British Guiana and Dr T.E.S. Scholes of Jamaica, were asserting similar rights beyond the boundary. And, in the midst of the great depression and catastrophic decline of the sugar industry, against the backdrop of the visit of the Norman Commission, every achievement of the non-white groups had reverberations for the society as a whole. Reform was, indeed, in the air: within the interstices of the decline, new attitudes were taking shape.

By January 1897, for instance, the popular coloured member of the Court of Policy in British Guiana, Hon Patrick Dargan, had been conducting his virtual single-handed campaign for constitutional reform, in a planter-dominated legislature, with such skill and resolve that the *Daily Chronicle* adopted a similar stance, for a greater measure of constitutional change in order to dilute the power of the plantocracy. Many of the people who supported Dargan and the Progressive Association were black, coloured and Madeiran Portuguese (not seen as white). They, therefore, would have empathized with the paper's generally progressive attitude with regard to reform, in spite of its apprehensions of the enfranchisement of 'undesirable elements' and its strictures on party politics:

> It is true that Mr. Dargan is the President of an association which threatens to introduce somewhat undesirable elements into public life, and that he represents a policy which in its entirety does not engage the whole of our sympathies nor yet those of the most intelligent and responsible section of the community. At the same time Mr. Dargan has proved himself a valuable member of the Court, and shown himself capable of modifying theoretical principles to meet practical necessities. His legal knowledge has more than once proved of great use in Committee, and, though he suffers somewhat from the not uncommon habit of speaking long and speaking often, he usually has some important contribution to make to the discussion, and the Court has learnt to listen to him with respect. Apart, however, from Mr. Dargan's personal merits, the question must be considered whether it is not better in the public interest that there should be some sort of Opposition in the colonial Legislature. We do not plead for a fully developed system of party government as obtains in Great Britain and other great democratic countries. The time when such a state of things would be desirable for this colony belongs to the very distant future. But

it is not all well that the Legislature should be all of one mind or that one interest should entirely monopolise it.[49]

Because of the agitation of Dargan, Dr John Rohlehr and others in the Progressive Association, the question of constitutional reform had percolated to the wider society, thus giving a 'populist' feel to the exercise. This probably exaggerated the scale of reform achievable, but it was another step in the cultivation and inculcation of the democratic spirit in the British West Indies. This is the context in which the *Chronicle* could argue for an element of popular representation:

We should tremble for the welfare of the colony were the Court of Policy and the Combined Court [to be] wholly composed of nominees of the Progressive Association, and in a less degree it is not in the best interests of the community that the Courts should consist exclusively of planters. Therefore, if it be advisable to have a certain amount of opposition in the Legislature, it is important that that element should be represented by able men, and since Mr. Dargan has shown himself worthy of his responsibilities as a member of the Court of Policy, we think it would be regrettable were he to lose his seat [in the 1897 elections]. It is impossible to speak so favourably of some of the other 'Progressive' candidates, who are being put forward, or who have put themselves forward for election.... With one or two exceptions they do not even possess any experience. [50]

The paper did not ponder on the fact that one could not gain experience of public life if the constitution deliberately precluded the acquisition of such experience, but the foundation for a democratic tradition was being laid. Central to this was the emergence of a black and coloured middle class with firm roots in the British education system, a temperament for gradualism and a predilection for parliamentary democracy engendered by a range of British institutions, including the elite schools and their faith in muscular learning. The franchise was expanded slightly after the reforms of 1891: the black, coloured and Portuguese middle class were enfranchised. But the plantocracy would seek to resist change, even try to turn the clock back, as is evident in the assertions of Edward Davson, the head of a comparatively progressive planting family with interests in British Guiana. As late as March 1908, in an address to the Royal Colonial Institute in London, although power still resided principally in the hands of the Governor and the plantocracy still exerted inordinate influence in politics, Davson would argue that 'the major part of this power is in the hands of the black and coloured community'. He added: 'This section has banded together in more or less open association to further its interests and constitute a hindrance, if not danger, to the state, especially when it can always command a majority at the polls.'[51] Edward Davson claimed that he preferred a constitution that would facilitate a more equitable distribution of the franchise, but the real basis for his opposition to the broadening of the democratic culture was racial, as Harold Lutchman observes:

> [Edward Davson] ... did not believe that in any colony of the Empire 'the white element should be subject to the coloured, whether it be black, brown or yellow — African, Indian or Mongolian'.... He was also closer to what he really wanted when he stated that, in his view, 'the officials, the representatives of imperial rule, should have a permanent majority in the Court, which may be guaranteed to take a broader and more impartial view on matters than those whose knowledge of economics, finance or commerce has oft-times not a very deep foundation'.... The sugar and commercial interests, alarmed at what they considered a threat to their position and existence, looked to the Government for their protection, and it is true to say that the Government and these interests were generally at one in these matters. For example, most officials shared the view that the large sugar and commercial interests were 'special interests', in need of special protection and representation, moreso than the bulk of the population. They believed that economic worth was more important than numbers, and therefore saw an important part of their role as being the protection of these 'special interests'.[52]

Thus plantocratic assumptions tended to predominate, but the black and coloured middle class were not detracted from their belief in representative institutions, in the shaping of a more inclusive, tolerant civil society, rooted in their muscular learning in the elite schools and often reinforced by university education in Britain. It was a long apprenticeship, epitomized, for instance, by the achievements of two distinguished coloured (mixed race) Barbadians, Colin Jackman Prescod (1806–71), a legislator, and Sir Conrad Reeves, the Chief Justice of Barbados, 1882–1901. Hilary Beckles has located these men in the context of the Barbadian struggle for democratic rights after Emancipation. Prescod, the son of a free-coloured woman and a white planter, had become a fervent anti-slavery advocate by the mid-1830s. By 1838, Beckles observes, 'he had emerged as the most popular and astute spokesman for the emancipated people and represented a major figure around which criticisms of planter policy were rallied.'[53] Prescod also made a major contribution to the establishment of the democratic tradition among non-white West Indians: he became editor of a radical newspaper, the *Liberal*, in the late 1830s. The paper 'expressed the grievances of the disadvantaged propertied coloured community ... [but it also] gave expression to many of the grievances of the black working class'. Beckles assesses Colin Jackman Prescod's contribution to the shaping of the liberal democratic tradition in Barbados, but it has resonance for the British West Indies as a whole. It is therefore appropriate to quote him at length:

> On 6 June 1843, black, coloured and white voters in Bridgetown elected ... [Prescod] to the Assembly as their representative — the first man of known black ancestry to sit in the House.... By the time of his death on 26 September 1871, Prescod had agitated on behalf of the less privileged classes on a wide range of issues. The nature of his political role suggests that he was undoubtedly the greatest leader of popular opinions in the colony during the post-slavery era.[54]

Beckles explores the making of his radical temperament from as early as 1838:

> On 11 August 1838, a comment in *The Liberal* which echoed Prescod's sentiments, stated: 'Gentlemen, you cannot require me to inform you, that it is not, not by declaring people free, that they are made free in reality — but that it is by conferring on them such privileges as put some proportion of the power which you now exclusively enjoy into their hands.' It was the objective of winning some measure of political power for the freed people, by strictly constitutional means, that shaped the political activities of Prescod over the next twenty years. The social forces behind Prescod's agitation emerged from the protest action of ex-slaves.... [His] contribution, therefore, was not in the initiation of protest or formulation of radical thought, but in the expression and leadership of such opinions at the highest

levels of society.... Governor MacGregor was ... accused by Prescod of plotting with planters to reduce the civil rights of blacks by means of repressive legislation, and Prescod suggested that workers should withdraw their labour until ... the Colonial Office offered a clear opinion on matters concerning labour laws.... [Earlier] when Prescod and other non-whites [had] attempted to form a Barbados chapter of the Anti-Slavery Society, Governor MacGregor referred to them as 'unhappy imitators' seeking 'outlets in the colonies for the diffusion of their revolutionary poison'. Prescod was also accused by officials within the Colonial Office of attempting to orchestrate the triumph of coloureds and blacks over whites in Barbados. But he rarely referred to racial struggle within his campaign but spoke endlessly of the privileges of the propertied class, and the misery of the landless, within the context of Christian theological precepts. As leader of the 'Popular Party' ... he had also attempted to win over the support of middle class whites, especially the more liberal mercantile community.[55]

Beckles sees the contribution of Prescod as the fight for civil rights for blacks and the planting of the liberal democratic tradition in Barbados:

The manifesto of [his] Party called for the protection of blacks' civil rights, the reduction of race/colour prejudice within institutions of government and elsewhere, and the extension of the franchise. Determined to ensure that the 'labouring classes' be given 'all the civil rights and immunities of free men', Prescod agitated for the extension of the franchise. On June 6, 1840 the legislature finally agreed to a Franchise Bill.... The new constituency of Bridgetown was created, but the juggling of reduced property qualifications made minimal difference in terms of the extension of the franchise to blacks. Prescod referred to it in this regard as only the 'postponement of the question'.[56]

This reforming temper was being shaped in the shadow of Emancipation, with many of the assumptions of slave society still intact. Yet the election of Prescod to the Legislature as early as 1843 was a quiet revolutionary step: the first coloured man had penetrated the hallowed chambers of white power, only five years after the end of slavery. Another coloured Barbadian, an eminent legal personality,

Sir Conrad Reeves, would take up the struggle to broaden the franchise
— like his predecessor, from within the system. As noted earlier, as a
founder of the first cricket club for the coloured and black middle class
(Spartan), in 1893, Reeves was predisposed to fighting discrimination
with the tools of liberal democracy, thus imbedding in the Barbadian
psyche their celebrated moderation, perceived evenness of temperament
and partiality for constitutional means to redress wrongs, however
blatant or resilient.

The Chief Justice of Barbados from 1882 to 1901, Reeves was able to
keep the society animated by the notion of incremental constitutional
reform as the means to greater inclusiveness in governance. The pace
of change in his time, at the end of the nineteenth century, was still
protracted. But, as I have argued, this must be assessed in terms of its
long-term legacy: the domestication of the democratic impulse in the
colony. To do otherwise, to see people like Reeves as Afro-Saxons, as
some contemporary commentators are inclined to, is to completely
depreciate the invaluable political education, their long apprenticeship
in liberal democracy, in these former British colonies. The virtues of
that tradition were absorbed, not imposed: freedom is sacrosanct;
power must be constitutionally circumscribed however frustrating
the attendant limitations; indeed, power is sovereign: it resides in the
people and must be relinquished if they so determine. As Beckles
observes, in the 1880s Sir Conrad Reeves helped to nurture the tender
plant left by Samuel Jackman Prescod:

> [T]o consolidate ... the representative system ... [he] began his
> agitation for franchise reforms — picking up where Prescod had
> left off — so as to increase the size of black political participation.
> Unlike Prescod, Reeves was not a radical. He shared the conservative
> ideology of the more liberal minded among the elite. For this reason,
> he was able to assert more influence on the legislative process. In
> 1884 he succeeded in persuading the legislature to pass a Franchise
> Act which reduced the property qualification.... [But] the number
> of voters was only slightly increased, and in 1900 there were less
> than 2,000 registered. In this regard, the legislature had succeeded
> in defeating Reeves as it had done Prescod earlier, by allowing only
> marginal increases in the number of blacks who could exercise the
> franchise.[57]

Small changes, certainly, but they were crucial in sustaining popular belief in the possibilities of representative government. Like the incremental reforms that fed ambition among coloured and black cricketers in the 1890s — the people as a whole — the merits of the representative principle as embedded in British parliamentary democracy, were not vitiated, although the incorporation of the popular will was frustratingly measured. Because possibilities for legislative honours were marked by such parsimony, popular acclamation of the election of non-white representatives was magnified. The disenfranchised as well as the enfranchised minority could vicariously share in their elevation, appropriating it as a site to build their self-esteem, and so enhance their own competence, whatever their work. This was the context in which the class factor would be neutralized among many non-whites, predisposing them to radical rather than revolutionary suasion. An educational, cricketing and political tradition — perceived as crucial to the mobility of subordinate groups — was emerging at the end of the nineteenth century in the British West Indies.

This is the source of the liberal democratic impulses immanent in the political culture of most of the former British colonies. Though limited and hedged in by caveats designed to restrict participation of non-whites, the concession of the franchise to a few coloureds and blacks and the consequential trickle of such men into the legislature, established a pattern that would not only facilitate incremental constitutional advance, it also planted the seeds of parliamentary democracy in these colonies. This was not a scramble to create some semblance of indigenous political maturity — that well-known contrivance forlornly accelerated as the Empire got rid of itself. Each concession to representative government in the West Indies had to be struggled for originally, in a vibrant imperial context. This enabled its roots to take hold, so that it became a genuine indigenous plant: creole. The radical component was not expunged by the constitutionalist challenge to imperial tardiness; but extremism became anathema to the British West Indian gradualist temperament.

This radical, democratic orientation was embodied in the writings of the black Jamaican intellectual, the Edinburgh-educated, Dr T.E.S. Scholes. When the Norman Commission was visiting the British West Indies in 1897, he published a pamphlet, a critical response to the colonial condition, based on informed scepticism. His aim was political:

in ventilating his views on the poverty of the small farmer in Jamaica, Dr Scholes was craftily seeking to influence the Norman Commission. Both the chairman (a former Governor of Jamaica) and the secretary, Sydney Olivier, were Fabian socialists, perceived locally as potentially more amenable to radical promptings from leaders of black opinion.

Scholes dramatized the parlous state of the working class during the depression, citing cases of chronic deprivation among rural Jamaican workers, men and women. He had been away from Jamaica for 12 years, studying, working and writing in Europe and Africa, so he brought to local problems his powers of observation and a fine discernment:

> Able-bodied men receive per day as wages,1s.; and this after walking sometimes in search of work six or twelve miles, or even longer distances. But in some kinds of labour, such as road-making, the wages paid a man is only 9d. per day; and its smallness is further aggravated by the fact that many of these labourers are not permitted, from the narrowness of the labour market, to work more than three days in the week; whilst others are unable at all to find any kind of employment. Women, too, experience difficulty in getting work. One form of outdoor labour that attracts female workers is the breaking of stones for macadamising public roads ... a woman has first of all to collect the stones, which may be found in sufficient quantities on the hill-sides or hill-tops of varying height; and when found they are rolled down to the level, where in the broiling sun, and with a hammer of two pounds weight they are broken. The broken stones are then measured in flour-barrels, and for each barrel the woman receives three pence. Four to six barrels are the amount that one woman in a day can break, it being not only dependent on the skill of the worker, but on the prevalence or scarcity of stones in the region; but here, too, the weekly limit of this occupation is three days.

Scholes continues on the plight of Jamaican workers:

> Another kind of employment for which the services of women are in demand is cane-cutting. The canes are put up in bundles of thirty pieces each; and for six such bundles, the worker is paid 9d.; some only manage to cut to the value of 6d. per day; yet even under conditions so disadvantageous, these cutters again are not allowed to work more than three days in the week. We think it will

be seen that persons in the situation we have been describing, though possessing a few fruit trees, giving a yearly crop, or having an acre or two of coffee which also yields yearly, or whether cultivators of average provision fields, after clothing themselves and families, supplementing the products of their fields by purchases, settle their taxes, and discharging incidental claims they will either be loaded with debts or practically starve.[58]

Scholes then addressed what he thought was the crux of the problem for the Jamaican peasantry: land hunger. It was his contention that the plantocracy, big planters in league with colonial government, were, since Emancipation, implacably tethered to a policy of stultification of the small farmer, in order to control the supply of labour. This, he observed, was manifested in their attitude to land acquisition, taxation and the subsidies granted to planters for the importation of indentured labourers from India. He elaborated on the land problem:

One of the great difficulties the Jamaican peasantry encounter arises from the lack of suitable land for cultivation. From the sugar estates and [cattle] pens, where only, practically speaking, land can be got to rent, the proprietors preferring to keep the best of those lands, situated in the plains and in the valleys, for grazing purposes, rent those in the mountains — miles away from the cultivator's home.... From the rocky nature of the country, lands either in the mountain districts or on the hill-tops are extremely difficult to bring under tillage, thereby defying the plough. With axe and matchet [machete], after hewing and then burning the trees, the cultivator proceeds with pick, crow-bar, and sledge-hammer to dig, break and heap up the less formidable stones and rocks that are deeply imbedded in or almost completely hide the surface of the soil. By this means he succeeds in obtaining patches of earth sufficient to sow his crop. But, of course, such a clearing occupies weeks, and is done in the scorching heat of the tropical sun.[59]

He attributed the pervasive poverty to the prolonged dominance of the sugar industry and the concomitant land hunger engendered by plantation agriculture, in conjunction with government's discrimination against the small farmer, in a quintessentially agricultural colony. Scholes thought it incomprehensible that in spite of the 'privileges' enjoyed by the sugar industry in Jamaica — a differential land tax and an immigration subsidy, for instance — it was languishing in despair. He quoted Adam Smith to establish the benchmark for taxation: that contributions to government be assessed 'in proportion to the revenue which they respectively enjoy under the protection of the state'. The reverse was obtained locally: 'Jamaica, in its method of taxation, seems to have deliberately reversed this maxim, saying instead, those who have more property shall pay less taxes, and those who have less property shall pay more taxes.' Dr Scholes computed the inequality of land taxation, to underline the disadvantages encountered by peasants:

> According to what is known as the Holding tax — ... [that] paid on a holding not exceeding five acres is 2s.... [T]aking this as our standard ... then according to the law of 'respective ability' [Adam Smith] ... we should expect a man possessing 10 acres to pay 4s ... the man with 20 acres would pay 8s, a hundred acres 40s, a thousand acres £20, 1,500 acres £30; but according to the law of inverse ability prevailing in Jamaica, whilst the owner of five acres, one acre, half acre, or a quarter acre has to pay a tax of 2s, he who owns 10 pays 3s. 4d or 4d an acre; 100 acres pays 6s. 8d or 2¾ d an acre; 1,000 acres, 36s. 8d or ¼d an acre, 1,500 acres, 53s. 4d or ¼ d an acre; and lands exceeding 1,500, which is the limit of taxation, pay the same ¼ d per acre. So that the poor man, with 5, 1, ½ , or ¼ acre, pays 2s., and the rich, with 1,000, 1,500, and exceeding 1,500, pays only ¼ d per acre. Again, as 1,500 acres is the limit of taxation, and there are at least 19 sugar estates, with 3,000 acres each, then there must be at least 28,000 acres of taxable land for which no taxes are paid.[60]

He then pointed to significant steps towards a broader economic base accomplished during the depression. In this context, he was advocating greater economic and political spaces for black Jamaican, indeed, all West Indians. It was a call for the final rejection of the resilient, paradoxical imperial idea that the plantation was the institution for the pursuit of civilization in these former slave colonies. Dr Scholes was arguing that in the interest of the majority, Jamaican agriculture had to reject the procrustean mould of the plantocracy:

> The record of West Indian sugar is failure only, two great failures: failure under protection, failure under free trade; thus it has forfeited

its right to recognition as the chief industry of Jamaica and the other islands. For the antiquity of an industry cannot give that industry priority over its utility. Fortunately for Jamaica, a certain section of the community ... have received the truth that the sugar industry is dead, and acting on that conviction, they are proceeding to remove the dead steed from the course and to find another to take its place.... The new era that is being inaugurated in the economic life of Jamaica, is through the increase of coffee cultivation, and the development of the fruit industry.... For future contingencies in agriculture in Jamaica what we believe to be a great and pressing need is a well-equipped agricultural school.... It should be under Government control, as such control ought to be a sufficient safeguard against unjust discriminations.... Entrance to it should be by competitive examination, and opened to all the schools of the islands.... Besides furnishing the means for useful and profitable husbandry, such an institution would popularise one of the most ennobling of human pursuits; and in so doing obliterate the notion of degradation, slavery unhappily attached to it, and that is entertained respecting it by every class in Jamaica.[61]

He concluded on a note that the Norman Commission would shortly endorse: the necessity to invigorate agriculture and educate black Jamaicans to participate in it on a scientific basis: 'Jamaica's wealth is in its soil, and agriculture is deputed to find it; but restricted on the one hand to scattered fragments of the land, and on the other by imperfect knowledge, its operations are feeble, their results small, and the island languishes in the mill of grinding poverty. Unlock the land, then, and train agriculture.'[62]

Dr Scholes's paper was timed well, as the Norman Commission were in the process of preparing their report. Sir Henry Norman, who considered himself a radical, was Governor of Jamaica from 1883 to 1887, and was receptive to ideas to develop the peasantry, such as those articulated by Scholes. The Secretary of the Commission, the young Fabian socialist, Sydney Olivier, already had experience of the West Indies, in the early 1890s, in British Honduras and the Leeward Islands. They did not support the imposition of countervailing duties on bounty-fed beet-sugar as advocated by the plantocracy, but recommended, as Scholes had argued, agricultural diversification and support for the establishment of a peasantry. They did not see sugar as the saviour of these colonies; therefore, they wanted Indian indentureship suspended 'until there is some prospect of the revival of sugar'.

The Report bore the imprint of Olivier's Fabian socialist vision; and it reinforced in the British West Indies a radical trajectory, congruent with the philosophical orientation of many coloured and black thinkers: Samuel Jackson Prescod, Dr Scholes and Dr Love. Indeed, it is a foundation of the social democratic political culture that would take root in the British West Indies during the depression of the 1930s, and the liberal democracy that prevails in the English-speaking Caribbean today. Two excerpts from the Norman Commission Report will suffice to illustrate its congruence with the radical temper being shaped in these islands at the close of the nineteenth century:

> The existence of a class of small proprietors among the population is a source of both economic and political strength. The settlement of the labourer on the land has not, as a rule, been viewed with favour in the past by the persons interested in sugar estates. What suited them best was a large supply of labourers, entirely dependent on being able to find work on the estates, and, consequently, subject to their control and willing to work at low rates of wages. But *it seems to us that no reform affords so good a prospect for the permanent welfare in the future of the West Indies as the settlement of the labouring population on the land as small peasant proprietors*; and in many places this is the only means by which the population can in future be supported. (emphasis added)

> It must be recollected that the chief outside influence with which the governments of certain colonies have to reckon are the representatives of the sugar estates, that these persons are sometimes not interested in anything but sugar, that the establishment of any other industry is often detrimental to their interests, and that under such conditions it is the special duty of Your Majesty's Government to see that the welfare of the general public is not sacrificed to the interests, or supposed interests, of a small but influential minority which has special means of enforcing its wishes and bringing its claims to notice.[63]

Sydney Olivier became the Colonial Secretary of Jamaica between 1900 and 1904; he was the Governor of that island from 1907 to 1913. More than any other colonial authority, he helped to shape the political instincts of British West Indians. His Fabian socialism, especially with regard to the land question, struck a chord in Jamaica and beyond:

> The maintenance of efficient large-scale cultivation is highly important and much efficient and valuable work is being done by large planters and penkeepers. But it is unquestionable that there are many thousands of acres on the larger estates of which far more economical use could be made by small settlers than is being made, or than practically could be made by their proprietors or lessees.... The most unsatisfactory feature of the land system of Jamaica is still the considerable class of decayed proprietors the owners (or lessees) of which make no use of their land except to let grounds to tenants. They are worse than unprofitable to the island. They are a discredit to the ownership which neglects their proper management, and they are a school of bad husbandry, slackness and dishonesty among people that occupy them.... Personal ownership and cultivation of smallholdings of land, with co-operative organisations for common requirements and marketing ... is destined, for so long as it is possible to foresee, to be the most widely prevalent basis of agricultural work in Jamaica. That fundamental economy is most congenial to instinctive and rational prudence ... which demands as the first most important vital necessity, security for the feeding of the individual and his dependents. All African civilisations provide the first place for that and sensibility to that requirement is paramount.[64]

Francis Lee, Olivier's biographer, has assessed his governorship of Jamaica, underlining the extent to which his philosophy of gradualism permeated the minds of the educated elite in Jamaica. He could have added that because the philosophy of the elite schools had already predisposed its British West Indian products, whatever their race or colour, to empathize with the moderate strand in the British intellectual tradition, they were temperamentally at ease with Olivier's non-revolutionary brand of socialism:

> Olivier's predisposition in favour of a smallholding system of peasant proprietorship was undoubtedly, and in the first instance, prompted by purely pragmatic considerations. Yet one cannot help thinking that his highly favourable attitude toward such a system was prompted by the rather romantic, Morrisite [William Morris's], strain in his socialism.... Not only did Olivier sell Crown lands for this purpose, he also put aside some public funds for the compulsory

purchase of derelict estates which was also to be earmarked for sale to smallholders.... [The] Fabian view held that it was neither necessary nor desirable to liquidate the rentier class; they could and should be gently tamed and shackled and would eventually disappear by persuading the general, or more particularly the educated public, that they were largely otiose in modern society. Fabianism, or government by the enlightened, could be carried off by those with such powers of persuasion. This was Olivier's achievement: he managed to persuade many Jamaicans of the necessity for socialistic (if not necessarily socialist) measures; and more importantly, the efficacy of those measures were [*sic*] obvious to all but the most ideologically hidebound. And those he did not persuade were effectively silenced by the success of his reforms.[65]

The radical perspectives of black thinkers like Dr Scholes and Dr Love were enriched by the Fabian socialism that informed the Norman Commission Report, as well as by Sydney Olivier's stewardship in Jamaica. As the *Daily Gleaner* observed of Olivier at the end of September 1900, while he was acting Governor, he was 'a man of marked artistic proclivities' and he brought with him a formidable intellect but a lightness of touch, a truly civilized man who epitomized the best in the English radical tradition. Olivier had style and substance mingled with 'a considerate regard for the sensibilities of others'; many Jamaicans, rich and poor, respected him:

A little graceful sarcasm and delicate irony, not the pitiless and savage kind, form part of his gubernatorial equipment, and he knows just how, when, and to what extent to use them.... [Mr Olivier is recognized] by many as a man of extensive culture, a scientist, a clever financier who yet finds time to be, in a broad sense, spiritually-inclined.... [I]t is a compliment to Jamaica to have a man of intellectual and social eminence, well-known in thoughtful circles in London, appointed here.... It is not a small matter for any man to honestly achieve literary, political and social fame; and these were all achieved by Mr. Olivier before he touched Jamaican soil.... We are ... fortunate in having a man of this calibre, and of pleasing and dignified presence ... appointed to rule ... our lovely, but in some ways, tormenting little island.[66]

Olivier's vision in Jamaica came out of a life of the radical mind and the ebullient spirit and idealism of the 1890s, that innovative ideas could really inspire purpose in government for the benefit of the less privileged: that life could be made better and enjoyed. The time spoke of possibilities. In this outlook, too, may be located the emerging radical, democratic tradition in the British West Indies at the end of the nineteenth century. The embryonic achievements of the black middle class, in education, politics and cricket, gave an intellectual base (in the broadest sense), to the increasingly popular endeavour to gain the right to shape their own societies. The English tours of 1895 and 1897 gave them limited but crucial space to demonstrate their skills and assert their rights to equality and greater representation, within and beyond the boundary. The first West Indies tour of England, in 1900, took them to the heart of the Empire; it would also have wide reverberations.

Having been moulded by the spirit of 1890s England (suggestive of the 1930s and 1960s), Holbrook Jackson, in his classic work of 1913, reflected:

> The intellectual, imaginative and spiritual activities of the 1890s are concerned mainly with the idea of social life or, if you will, of culture.... For that reason alone the period is interesting apart from any achievements in art or science or statecraft. It is interesting because it was a time when people went about frankly and cheerfully endeavouring to solve the question 'How to Live'. From one point of view such an employment suggests the bewilderment of a degenerate world ... but those who lived through the Nineties as young men and women will remember that this search for a new mode of life was anything but melancholy or diseased. The very pursuit was a mode of life sufficiently joyful to make life worth living. But in addition there was the feeling of expectancy, born not alone of mere toying with novel ideas, but born equally of a determination to taste new sensation, even at some personal risk, for the sake of life and growth.[67]

There is a danger in extrapolating from the periphery to the centre — from the radicalism of the small intellectual elite of the British West Indies and their Fabian socialist sources of inspiration, on one hand, to the imagination and inquisitiveness of the young British intellectual elite, on the other. However, within the interstices of the received metropolitan cultural fluidity of the 1890s, the emerging 'elite' in these old colonies could begin to dream. This was the backdrop to the emergence of Scholes, Love, Ruhomon, Woods, Cumberbatch, Lebrun

Constantine, Patrick Dargan and A.B. Brown; Plum Warner of Harrison College and Rugby and Sydney Olivier, too. It is, therefore, not fortuitous that West Indian education and cricket were already yielding rewards for the submerged groups in the decade of the 1890s. What made the period vastly exciting for many British West Indians was the fact that they had, at last, reached the point where they felt confident that they could really begin to shape their world: no longer mere hewers of wood and drawers of water. Demonstrated merit in education and cricket were at the heart of this vision.

I have argued that within the colonial framework, mastery of primary idioms of the imperial mission was not mimicry; it was imperative to the transcendental exercise in self-affirmation, combating the legacy of slavery and indentureship. But it also carried with it the seeds of resistance and regeneration. For the educated minority, such as the young Indian intellectual in British Guiana, in 1894, Joseph Ruhomon, it was a time of 'expectancy', 'to taste new sensation' — to dream; to question; but it was also a time of challenge, self-discovery and possibilities. Optimism bred magnanimity:

> Some fifty-odd years ago, the black man was the white man's slave in this colony. He was not counted as a human being, and was treated as a beast of burden by his tyrannical master. He had not the same advantages and privileges that his white brother had. He had no opportunities for raising and improving himself. But the short period of half a century has worked a great change in the patient, plodding, ambitious and resolute black man. Today, he is free and untrammelled from the gyves of moral, intellectual and political serfdom. Nothing can now contort and cripple the might of his nature and hinder him in his march of progress. In the pulpit, our coloured [black] brothers can hold their own; at the bar they are astute debaters and sound commonsense practitioners; as 'medicos' they seem to be masters of their profession, and in many other departments of work in this colony they are acquitting themselves in a manner creditable to themselves, and the pushing aggressive race from which they have sprung.[68]

This, indeed, was the context of the first English tours of the West Indies in 1895 and 1897, and the West Indies tour of England in 1900.

Chapter Six

'Going Home':
The First West Indies Tour
of England, 1900 — An Intellectual History

It would be graceless not to acknowledge the contribution of a few white allies, who made a timely intervention or rendered a crucial favour to a few black or coloured cricketers, thus hastening their contribution to the building of the West Indies cricket team. However, these white allies could not influence how black West Indians, whether they played cricket or not, used the game to advance their political culture. All West Indians — black, white, coloured, Madeiran Portuguese or Indian — were necessarily political animals, whatever the tenor of their agenda: radical or conservative. Cricket, then, was inescapably a political instrument by the 1890s; and the first West Indies tour of England, in 1900, as the Boer War raged in South Africa, encapsulated many fascinating strands of these diverse, complex societies, as they sought to craft their conceptions of freedom in the context of Empire.

Indeed, it is arguable that the first tour to England of the West Indies cricket team, between June and September 1900, provides a window to the region at the end of the nineteenth century. It provides insights into race, colour and class; insularity — that bedevilling reality of West Indian life (see chapter seven); differential conceptions of cricket and varying interpretations of the tour in particular, by colonial officials, the local white elite, the black members of the team and the black population of the islands.

The five black (or coloured/mixed race) cricketers were: Lebrun Constantine and 'Float' Woods (Trinidad); C.A. Ollivierre (St. Vincent); W.J. (Tom) Burton (Demerara [British Guiana]); and Fitz Hinds (Barbados). As seen earlier earlier, Constantine, a batsman and wicket-keeper, and Woods, a fast bowler, had represented Trinidad against Lucas's team in 1895 and Lord Hawke's in 1897, as well as Trinidad and the first West Indies team against Priestley's team the same year.

The first West Indies team in England, 1900. The team had five black players: from left to right (standing): W.J. (Tom) Burton (black), C.A. Ollivierre (black), Hon Aucher Warner, W.H. Mignon, G.C. Learmond, P.I. Cox, M.W. Kerr, P.A. Goodman; (sitting): 'Float' Woods (black), Fitz Hinds (black) [dubiously identified?]; S.W. Sproston, G.L. Livingston, Lebrun Constantine (black)

Trinidad, a diverse society, with a countervailing French Creole presence that had helped to temper the superiority complex of the British, was probably the most liberal island, in spite of its sensitivity to colour. Black and coloured men were already playing for Trinidad; this was not the case in Barbados and British Guiana. So-called professionals, too, fast bowlers like Woods (and Cumberbatch, his fellow exile from Barbados), who bowled to white batsmen of the elite Queen's Park Club, at practice sessions, were selected for the island team. Fitz Hinds's selection, however, was a most controversial one in Barbados: the team to tour England in 1900 was dogged by the 'Fitz Lily' Affair.[1]

Hinds, a black man, had joined the Spartan Cricket Club, founded in 1893 by 'wealthy and influential coloured men', the only club in Barbados 'intended to serve the upper middle class black and mulatto families'. Sir Conrad Reeves, the famous coloured jurist, was its principal architect; but this club, as Sandiford observes, 'displayed all of the racism and snobbery of the older (white) clubs [Wanderers and Pickwick]'. It discriminated against Fitz Hinds, an artisan, both on grounds of colour and class. He was an apprenticed painter (of houses), so that although he gained admission to Spartan, a furore emerged in 1899, because some of the Spartan members deemed him an 'undesirable member' because of his low social status. Moreover, the white clubs, Windward and Pickwick, refused to play their front-line cricketers against a Spartan team with the lowly Hinds as one of their numbers, in the domestic season of 1899–1900, on the eve of the selection of the West Indies team for England. Sandiford remarks that the so-called Fitz Lily Affair encapsulated the race, class and colour prejudice against black cricketers (blacks generally), still prevalent in Barbadian society at the end of the nineteenth century:

> The early history of Spartan is dogged by the notorious 'Fitz Lily affair'.... Delmont Cameron St. Clair Hinds, then generally known as Fitz Lily, had worked as a Pickwick groundsman while serving his apprenticeship as a painter in his youth. He was still only 19 years old in 1899. By the regulations then in vogue he was ineligible to participate in the Cricket Cup competition as the committee considered him a 'professional'. The Challenge Cup Committee [founded in the 1892–93 season], in fact, branded as 'professionals' all groundsmen, as well as other black manual labourers, in a deliberate attempt to restrict the sport mainly to

white 'gentlemen'. Hinds was clearly one of the best cricketers in the Caribbean at that time and naturally he wanted to further his cricket career. He therefore left his job at Kensington [Pickwick] and applied for admission to Spartan. The Spartan membership was much divided over the issue but some remarkable lobbying brought the great Fitz Lily into the fold.[2]

Sandiford explains the turbulent repercussions that this seemingly trivial development had for domestic first division cricket in Barbados, in the eight season of the Challenge Cup, in 1899–1900:

Hinds's election to Spartan provoked an incredible uproar. The majority of the Pickwick and Windward cricketers refused outright to play against him and even some of the Spartan members refused to play *with* him [because of class and colour]. This kind of racism and snobbery destroyed the whole of the 1899–1900 season. The net result was that Spartan actually won the first division title for the first time that year because its major opponents often took the field without their key players. The Cup committee thereupon strengthened its rules to prevent any repetition of what many considered to have been chicanery on the part of the Spartan club. The new regulations made it impossible after 1900 for former groundsmen or 'professionals' to take part in the Challenge Cup competition. It did not matter, of course, that there was not a single professional cricketer (as the term was then used in England) in Barbados at that time.[3]

Sandiford concludes: 'Even though he was one of the best cricketers in the Caribbean his presence caused such a rift in the Spartan ranks that he actually decided to leave Barbados [in 1905].'

The furore had spilled over into 1900 and resulted in an accomplished white Barbadian batsman, H.A. Cole (1874–1932), a Pickwick player, who had been selected to tour England with the West Indies team, withdrawing on the spurious ground that Hinds was a 'professional' and not an amateur. On the eve of their departure for England in April 1900, Cole had written to the cricket committee on the matter, stating that he could not tour if Hinds were included as an amateur.[4] Burton and Woods, the two black fast bowlers selected, were also so-called professionals (ground bowlers to white men), but he seemed not to have objected to their selection as they were designated as such. They obviously knew their place; they were not aspiring above their station. White Barbadians played against the black Trinidadian, Lebrun Constantine, in their inter-colonial game in January 1900, played against black and coloured middle class Barbadians in their domestic cricket competition, and played with black men in composite West Indies teams in 1895 and 1897, but, unlike Trinidad, they had never selected a black or coloured Barbadian to represent Barbados. Cole had refused to play against Hinds in the Challenge Cup of 1899–1900 (Pickwick v. Spartan), which Spartan won for the first time. To play in the same team with a black Barbadian — amateur or professional — must have been unthinkable for Cole. In fact, the *Barbados Bulletin* of December 22, 1899 had bemoaned the lack of courage on the part of Barbadian selectors in failing to select Fitz Hinds for the inter-colonial tournament in Trinidad, although it was virtually certain that he would tour England with the West Indies in 1900:

> It is ... to be regretted that F. Hinds has not been selected. He is our best all-round cricketer. It is likely that he will be a member of the West Indies team to visit the Mother Country next year; indeed, our cricket committee here asked him whether he is willing to go if selected, and he has answered in the affirmative. *He is therefore considered eligible to appear at Lord's and the Oval in company with the nobility of England, and yet not good enough to go to Port of Spain.*[5] (emphasis added)

At the start of the final of the inter-colonial championship in 1900, between Barbados and Demerara (which the former won by seven wickets), a Trinidadian correspondent remarked: 'Who are to be the representatives of Trinidad in the West Indies team? I have seen a good bit of local cricket, and I am one of those who think the best should be selected, irrespective of social status or colour.'[6] This would have been unpalatable to Hallam Cole, who probably considered it even more repugnant to tour England with a team that included five black men. The basis of the objection, ostensibly, was that Hinds was being deemed an amateur, while he was, in fact, a 'professional'. It is noteworthy that the other white Barbadians selected, Cole's teammate, Percy Goodman (Pickwick) and William Bowring (Wanderers), raised no objection to the status of Hinds, and did go on the tour.[7] Cole withdrew. His prejudices would have been fortified by the colour and class bigotry that had been so evident in Hinds's own club, Spartan, as well as by the racist selection policy of Barbados in the 1890s. Hinds did make the tour, but the furore had undermined his confidence and it did affect the quality of his play in England. Percy Cox, a white Barbadian from the Wanderers Club, took Cole's place. The *Barbados Globe* was unequivocal in their denunciation of the latter's obscurantism:

> Cricket finds no charm for narrow-minded mortals, and if, for such a stupid reason, some withdraw, it will perhaps be better for the success of the tour; as such an individual must fail to find a sympathiser in broad-minded England.... [N]either Mr. H.A. Cole nor Mr. G.B.Y. Cox will be able to go with the team. This we expected, and *we confidently assert that the objection set out as the reason why one of these gentlemen* [Cole] *is not accompanying the team is only a popular ruse beclouding some other permanent deterrent.*[8] (emphasis added)

Observers in England were aware of the resilience of the race factor in West Indies cricket. On February 7, 1900 the *Times* unmasked the so-called amateurism in Barbadian cricket, the source of the 'popular ruse', tracing it to its racial antecedents in slave society. In a leader, they spoke of 'a feud between the black and the white resting on the traditional hatred of the past of the slave for his owner, and of the social hatred of the poor for the rich'. Now, however, the *Barbados Globe* was deeply offended, although they themselves had unmasked Cole's 'ruse'. The anger showed: they deemed the comment of the *Times* 'a stab in the dark'. But they did not offer an explanation of why black men of proven talent were still being excluded from the Barbados cricket team. In fact, in 1897, Trinidad was forced to exclude their two first-rate black fast bowlers when they toured Barbados — Woods and Cumberbatch (both Barbadian exiles), who had been superb against Lord Hawke's and Priestley's teams — because of the racism of Barbados's cricket administrators. The *Globe's* rebuttal of the *Times* was therefore hollow:

> [S]o far as Barbados is concerned the memories of slavery are lost in oblivion. The few who may have memories of that disgraceful period in English history are too ignorant to cope with the advance that the spread of education and enlightenment have scattered among us. Slavery is a word forgotten in British communities, for every

inhabitant, according to the laws of Great Britain, has an equal right to acquire the dignity of a landholder, and many a descendant of the despised slave ... has long ere thus been possessed of his own freehold which he has worked independent[ly] of his fairer brother proprietor.... They are a law-abiding, good and contented people, ever ready to arm themselves to the teeth to fight for their rights.[9]

To appreciate the depth of the prejudice of white Barbadians at the end of the nineteenth century, one has to explore the internal dynamics of the white community: the differential projection of power and the established hierarchy. The plantocracy, with claims to longevity in the colony's premier activity, the sugar plantation culture, constructed their identity in terms of a veritable Barbadian aristocracy: an extension of 'home'. They had tended to distance themselves socially from the later arrivals: the mercantile element, based in Bridgetown and engaged in the import–export trade (the bourgeoisie, so to speak). This distinction had found expression in the elite schools: Lodge was associated with the children of the plantocracy; Harrison College with the children of the commercial elite (and a sprinkling of those of coloured and black upper middle-class professionals). At the level of first-division domestic cricket, the sugar planters had founded Wanderers in 1877, while the white commercial element had their own club Pickwick (at Kensington), founded in 1882. Although the latter were no less accomplished cricketers, they still harboured an inferiority complex rooted in the old hierarchy. It is significant that the socially preponderant, and therefore more confident, Wanderers seemed to have evinced no opposition to the selection of a so-called professional (Hinds) by Spartan, the club of the coloured and black upper middle class, founded in 1893.

By the depression of the 1890s, however, the commercial elite had acquired substantial ownership of failing plantations and an impressive financial base, to make them credible competitors with the old planting families. Indeed, there was already considerable intermarriage to warrant a blurring of the social divide. But the differential social distinction lingered, in this parochial little world, fostering a resilient taint on the new money of the commercial elite. H.A. Cole belonged to the latter group: he attended Harrison College and played for Pickwick. Therefore, the inflexibility of his response to the selection of Fitz Hinds bore evidence of all the social insecurities of the rising bourgeoisie: wealthy, but still dogged by their lower status in the white hierarchy with its assumption of superiority of the old planting families. Beckles explains the escalating fortunes of this group, in the 1880s and 90s, but it is easy to imagine their gnawing insecurity:

> The economic depression of the 1880s and 1890s ... produced significant changes in the ownership of arable land and hence the social composition of the elite. The most important development of this period was the rise of the local merchant class as a new force within the social elite — merging with, and to a large extent, pushing aside, sections of the traditional plantocracy. The ascendancy of the local merchant capitalists was characterised by their forceful entry into the plantocracy by means of financial arrangements and marital links. This development had to do with two important features of the post-slavery order, the first of which was the ability of planters to retain the old representative system, and hence their control over the legislature. This meant that planters were able, by means of manipulating the organs of government, to ensure that estate ownership, even in the most difficult of times, stayed in local hands and was not transferred to foreign merchant houses to which they were indebted. Second was the development of local financial institutions and merchant companies that were able to rescue, and purchase, many estates before absentee interests were able to do so.... Many of the estates fell into the hands of the local urban merchant class, who hitherto had been slighted by the planter elite as an under-group, in spite of their obvious substantial financial worth and capacity. Bridgetown merchants had long been consolidating their economic base with an eye to buying into the plantocracy which was still considered, in spite of its economic decay, as the social elite. This of course had to do with planters' firm grip over the political machinery.[10]

As noted above, Percy Goodman, one of the three Barbadians selected to tour England in 1900, raised no objections to 'professionals' in the team. The pedigree of his family was impeccable: four of them had attended Lodge School, the school of the plantocracy; his elder brother, Aubrey Goodman, was one of the founders of Pickwick and Solicitor-General of Barbados. The other 'Barbadian' selected, William Bowring, was an Englishman who had recently settled in Barbados, so he could more easily elude the social and racial pretensions that constrained the responses of local whites. The young man who replaced Cole, Percy Cox, was also, like the Goodmans, from a family that was associated with Lodge School, with outstanding cricketing credentials. So that while Hallam Cole represented the more reactionary strand in white Barbadian racial attitudes, there were more secure whites who were prepared to go against the grain, to open spaces for blacks and coloureds to begin to participate in the game. And the victory of Spartan in the Challenge Cup Championship in 1899–1900, however diminished by the refusal of some of the best white cricketers to play against them, was a major psychological step, enhancing black people's conceptions of greater possibilities. In Bruce Hamilton's laconic remark, the Spartan victory was a 'happening full of portent for the future'.[11]

Keith Sandiford has observed that the seminal role of several liberal white families in the gradual erosion of prejudice against black working class cricketers was not insubstantial. Indeed, the Goodmans's response to the 'Fitz Lily affair' was exemplary; it helps us to comprehend the instinct for moderation of black Barbadians:

[I]t has to be said that some white liberals, such as the Goodmans, Hoads, A.B. St. Hill and George Walton, objected to the policy of segregation and tried their best to remove the barriers between Pickwick and the groundsmen [black 'professionals']. Attempting to undo some of the mischief caused by the 'Fitz Lily affair', Clifford Goodman [the Pickwick and Barbados fast bowler] arranged a friendly match between Pickwick and Fenwick (the most famous working class cricket club of the era) in November 1899. In his own team he also included two blacks, Stephen Rudder [who had played in Trinidad] and G.T. Cumberbatch, from Spartan. For this he received fulsome praise from another white liberal, the editor of the *Barbados Globe*, who remarked that the 'stubborn refusal of certain members of the Pickwick to take part in any game in which poor coloured [black] men are engaged is a persistent exhibition of artificial greatness that finds no place where intelligence encamps'. He consequently found [Clifford] Goodman's determination to change this attitude most praiseworthy. Clifford's elder brother, Aubrey, then President of the Pickwick Cricket Club, also made an impassioned plea to his colleagues in 1900 for sportsmanship and fair play, insisting that 'cricket should be played without regard to class, colour or creed'. His plea apparently fell on deaf ears since Clifford, who had led the club with great success for six years, was promptly replaced by the more conservative Clement Browne.[12]

Bruce Hamilton, too, remarks on the magnanimity of the Goodmans towards their social inferiors. Some years after the 'Fitz Lily affair', Percy Goodman was generous in his recollection of Fitz Hinds, who had encountered persistent humiliation from many white cricketers in Barbados: 'by his good behaviour, pluck and hard work in every department of the game, [Hinds] won golden opinions from even the bitterest of his opponents.' For black Barbadians, this was another milestone in their long apprenticeship within and beyond the boundary: Hinds remained gracious amidst the barbarism of his superiors. They would have been buoyed by his selection to represent the West Indies in England in 1900; so, too, by the fact that later that year Fenwick, a team of lower class black cricketers — deemed euphemistically 'professionals' — defeated all the first division white teams, Wanderers and Pickwick included, in non-representative matches. But these dark plebeians were ineligible to play those same teams in the local Challenge Cup or to represent Barbados in the inter-colonial championship against Demerara and Trinidad. Hamilton assesses the state of non-white Barbadian cricket at the end of the nineteenth century:

> With the Spartan victory of 1899 [–1900], may be taken a landmark in the history of a humbler class of cricket: both events foreshadowing a new development of the game in a new century. In this year several matches against the regular clubs were played, not of course in the Cup competition, by Fenwick, a team of [black] professionals. Their best player, Shepherd ... was actually at the head of the Island bowling averages for the year. Within a very short time, the team was to become extremely powerful, and its good example encouraged the formation of similar clubs.... [I]t should never be forgotten that under the most difficult conditions, with the scantiest resources, and sheer keenness to play as the main inducement, poor Negroes have for years been doing their share to create a background for the remarkable cricketing success of this little island.[13]

Hamilton noted that the following year, 1900–1901, Fenwick, though still excluded from the Challenge Cup, were just as driven by the will to win, in their encounters with the white teams (and a non-white one, Spartan), vying for first-division supremacy. Against the backdrop of continuing, if somewhat lessened, bigotry, the black working class players unobtrusively enhanced the argument for merit over race:

Wanderers won the Cup ... Spartan dropped back to fifth.... Echoes of the controversy over the alleged professionals [the 'Fitz Lily affair'] were still to be heard, and continued to mutter and rumble for the next few years. Pickwick and Windward were the clubs chiefly affected, and though they took second and third positions respectively, the refusal of some of their men to play regularly prevented them from offering a strong challenge to Wanderers.... So much for the amateur majority, but the real honours of the year were carried off by the professionals. Fenwick had a wonderful season. Not all their matches are on record, but of those which are mentioned they won every one, against Lodge, Pickwick, Wanderers, Spartan, and Windward, only Spartan giving them any difficulty. A strong Wanderers team was put out for 42 and 58 on a good wicket! It was brilliant bowling that brought Fenwick their successes. Both Shepherd and Layne had [bowling] averages of a little over 5; among the former's performances were 8 for 24 v. Wanderers, 8 for 26 v. Lodge, and 7 for 4 v. Windward; while Layne had 6 for 8 v. Spartan. The batting was weaker, Shepherd who did best, having an average under 25.[14]

The magnanimous spirit of the Goodmans was winning: though discriminated against, even poor, black players now had spaces within Barbadian cricket to demonstrate their mastery of the game. The fact that they could do so against white players, nourished their skills and fortified their resolve to win: the lowly Fenwick men knew that they spoke for all black Barbadians. This was probably all water on duck's back to Hallam Cole and his ilk, but it was symbolic shifts in attitudes encapsulated in seemingly minor innovations, that were the precursors to big changes in West Indies cricket, in the wider society as well. And there were others, like the white Guyanese, G.C. Learmond (Learie), the maternal grandfather of the West Indies batsman of the late 1960s and early 1970s, Stephen Camacho, who made a conscious effort to fight prejudice in cricket, and thus open the way for the lessening of bigotry beyond the boundary. Learmond's example is worthy of further attention.

George Learmond (1875–1918) was born in British Guiana to Scottish parents, but he was sent to Combermere School in Barbados, generally associated with a more practical or vocational curriculum, compared with the substantially classical orientation of the Lodge School and Harrison College. So that Learmond attended an institution which, by the 1880 and 90s, had become the key institution for the education of the coloured and black middle class in Barbados. This soon enabled him, more than most white men in the West Indies, to win the confidence of the coloured and black middle class on the island. When, in 1893, they founded the Spartan Cricket Club to compete in the Challenge Cup in Barbados, they chose 18-year-old Learmond as their captain. Sandiford reflects on this unusual appointment:

> Spartan was founded ... essentially for non-white players who had been excluded from Pickwick and Wanderers on purely racial grounds. Ironically, the club chose Learmond as its first captain despite the fact that he was white, foreign [from British Guiana] and inexperienced. This proved to be a singularly fortunate choice since all reports indicate that Learmond's leadership was a source of inspiration and had much to do with the club's early successes in the Challenge Cup competition. His value to the team was publicly recognised by Sir Conrad Reeves, President of Spartan, who presented him with a silver cup just before he returned to Demerara in 1896. Learmond went on to represent Barbados, British Guiana, Trinidad and the West Indies.[15]

It is clear that Learmond was a white man of broad sympathies, at ease with black people of a certain type. He made such a salutary impression on Lebrun Constantine, with whom he toured England in 1900, that when the latter's first child was born on September 21, 1901 he named him Learie, after George Learmond, whom he had befriended. He must have been perceived as impeccable on the race issue to win such respect from blacks and coloureds, though still a young man. Learmond was an extraordinary person because in the two places that shaped him — Barbados and Demerara — a black or coloured man could not represent these colonies against inter-colonial teams or even English touring teams, such as Lucas's, Hawke's or Priestley's.

For African and Indian West Indians any suggestion of discrimination spoke of the legacy of slavery and indentureship. But the fight for constitutional change, the repeal of draconian Crown land laws, strikes for better wages on the plantations, which often led to shootings by the colonial police, and the quest for redemption through a reaffirmation of their African and Indian heritage, were all aspects of the ongoing fight for the expansion of freedom. Slavery could not be forgotten and Indian indentureship was not terminated until April 1920; but the 'spread of education and enlightenment' was real, and black, coloured and Indian middle-class people were already engaged in the struggle for civil rights in the 1890s. The great depression of that decade gave urgency to these issues and created spaces for the articulation of the democratic impulse shaped by the culture of resistance. The fact that the *Barbados Globe*, generally progressive on questions of race, could so sanctimoniously deny the persistence of deep-seated bigotry was in itself a manifestation of the pernicious legacy of slavery, and the necessity to ameliorate, if not extirpate, it. The 1900 West Indies tour of England was necessarily an aspect of that broader goal: it reflected the struggles beyond the boundary and it quickened the impulse for reform; it would throw up its own popular heroes.

Black people were already deeply conscious of their place in the history of the region and were beginning to celebrate their own achievement, challenging the received wisdom of colonial authorities. In July 1900, for instance, a white planter in British Guiana, E.C. Luard, had published a series of articles on the Morant Bay Rebellion in Jamaica in 1865. He repeated the conventional version about the coloured agitator, George William Gordon's responsibility for the subversion of the peace of the island, while Governor Eyre was considered a hero for his necessary use of force to suppress the misguided black participants in the revolt. Hon A.B. Brown, a lawyer, the first black man to be elected to the legislature of British Guiana, in 1897, was moved to rebut what he considered Luard's 'limited', prejudiced chronicle of Morant Bay. He was responding emphatically from an anti-colonial perspective, attributing its origin primarily to popular outrage at perceived chronic injustice. This epitomized the new spirit of self-assertion and growing confidence of the 1890s, and represented a version of history that consciously attributed agency to African people:

> [Gordon] was a fearless speaker; he saw that his country was oppressed, the labourers were starving, the administration of justice corrupt; and he thought he should like to remedy these things.... Had Gordon not been born, there should still have been a rebellion ... in Jamaica in 1865. There was a variety of causes that led to the rebellion. But when it is stated that Gordon was the immediate cause, there is nothing more unfounded.[16]

Brown then assessed Governor Eyre's role in the suppression of the rebellion: he 'arrested [Gordon] most illegally and unjustifiably, and with a "comedy" of a trial caused him to be executed' — no hero of the black people, this champion of imperial rule. Brown concludes:

> We believe the Governor to have been a man of ability, of ability to commit the most shocking atrocities in the name of law and order and expediency. The [black] rebels are said to have killed 22 persons of all colour. 'On the other hand [he quotes from W.P. Livingstone's *Black Jamaica*] ... the superior whites who ought to have exercised the prerogative of self-restraint, killed first in rage, and then in cool deliberation, 439 negroes, scourged with great barbarity 600, including women, "punished" with more or less severity a large number of others, and destroyed in wantonness a thousand homes.' *All this is the act — the rash and unjustifiable act of a tyrant and oppressor who some are inclined to worship as a hero and a martyr....* But from all we could gather of his character we think he was a man of an irritable temper, destitute of tact and foresight.[17] (emphasis added)

Brown was challenging European monopoly of the right to define. So, too, were the five black players in the West Indies team to England in 1900. I have dealt at length with Plum Warner's defence of the right of black cricketers to represent the West Indies in England, and have argued that without his commanding stature the white authorities in West Indies cricket would have used the ruse of 'professionals' to exclude black men indefinitely. Warner had made the case for Woods and Archie Cumberbatch as the two best fast bowlers in the region, but the latter was still omitted; no reason was given. Both were so-called professionals; the selectors had already chosen two such: Woods and W.J. Burton, the fast bowler from British Guiana, like Cumberbatch, exiles from the racism of Barbados cricket. Warner considered Cumberbatch better than Woods, so did the *Barbados Cricketers' Annual* of 1899–1900.

At the end of the tour, Plum remarked that the absence of H.B.G. Austin (on duty in the Boer War), Cole and Cumberbatch 'prevented the side from being fully representative'.[18] Three black 'professionals' were probably too many; but three black Barbadian exiles would have been an intolerably robust riposte to the czars of Barbadian cricket orthodoxy. No whites were ever deemed professionals in the West Indies; blacks were categorized thus in order to keep them out. It was the badge of subordination, however impressive one's gifts. Therefore, black cricketers sought, wherever possible, to elude this construction. And in 1900 three of the five selected to go to England were able to do so: Lebrun Constantine, a batsman from Trinidad (the father of the great all-rounder of the 1920s and 30s, Learie); Fitz Hinds, the batsman from Barbados, of the infamous 'Fitz Lily Affair'; and C.A. Ollivierre, a batsman from St. Vincent, who had also played in Trinidad. These players had subverted the scheme designed to cripple their ambition. The names of these three, like all their white West Indian teammates, were prefixed by 'Mr'. That was not a small achievement, at the end of the nineteenth century. Moreover, by establishing themselves as batsmen, they were also subverting the old definition, going back to slavery, that had sought to limit them to fast bowling — a task not readily associated with gentlemen.

By stamping their credentials as batsmen, they were also making a broader statement that black people would not all succumb to limited and limiting procrustean, Eurocentric definitions. Indeed, 'Mr. C.A. Ollivierre' topped the batting averages on the 1900 tour: he made 883 runs, with a highest score of 159 and an average of 32.70; while 'Mr. L[ebrun] Constantine' came second: 660 runs, with a highest score of 113, at an average of 30.50. Constantine's century was the first by a West Indies player in England.[19] It is also memorable because it was achieved under very difficult circumstances, at Lord's, against 'Gentlemen of the MCC', which included 'Mr. W.G. Grace' and Lord Harris. MCC won by 5 wickets, but Lebrun Constantine's innings on June 23, 1900 was played with the flair and panache that belong to black West Indian style:

> For the first time during the tour one of the visitors made a hundred. This was Mr. Constantine, who, going in when the match seemed over in the second innings [at number nine], speedily took the measure of ... the bowling ... and in the brief space of an hour and a half scored 113 runs ... including a 5 and 17 fours. His hitting was hard and his timing good. He received the most valuable assistance from Burton [the black fast bowler, a 'professional': no 'Mr' here], who eventually carried his bat [for 64], after showing some very determined play.[20]

A member of the West Indies team recorded his impressions of aspects of their play in that historic match at Lord's. He wrote:

> Constantine and Burton played two magnificent innings at Lord's ... 162 in 65 minutes for the 8th wicket [9th]. Most of us had changed, as we were certain we would be licked by an innings; but in the end the MCC had 107 to get on a goodish wicket, and were in trouble in getting them [W.G. was bowled by Burton for 3]. Burton and Woods [the two black fast bowlers] bowled like demons, and I must say I have not yet seen better fielding anywhere than ours for those few hours. If we had caught Mordaunt (51) behind the wicket, I believe we would have pulled the match out of the fire. The bowling of the same pair at Northampton was something to be seen. In the first hour in their second innings, they only got 8 runs and we got 4 wickets.[21]

Northampton won by 61 runs, but the bowling of the two black 'professional' fast bowlers was exemplary: Woods 6 for 88; Burton 9 for 66. This was totally in character, as Woods got 72 wickets on the tour at 21.54 each, while Burton got 78 at 21.55. They bowled 1208.3 overs between them; 316 were maidens; and they took 150 wickets; only 80 wickets went to the rest of the bowlers, with the white Grenadian medium pacer, Mignon, getting 30 at 29.43. It is clear that the two black fast bowlers carried the bowling on their shoulders, while two black batsmen, Ollivierre and Constantine, came first and second in the batting respectively. 'Mr. Fitz Hinds', the controversial black Barbadian batsman, got a batting average of only 20.13, with a highest score of 79.[22]

In 1900 *Cricket* noted that the bowling was 'too little varied'. It is incredible, but true, that this team lacked a spinner and a specialist wicket-keeper. But 'Float' Woods seemed to have made a good impression from the first match at Crystal Palace: 'Woods is the fastest bowler. He takes merely a few steps as a run — a batsman has to be rather quick to be always ready for the ball — and with a slinging action not much above the level of the shoulder gets up a great amount of pace.' They were rather charitable to the novices, in keeping with Plum Warner's assessment in his book *Cricket in Many Climes*, published on the eve on the tour: '[T]he visit is made for educational purposes, and not at all with the idea of setting the Thames on fire.'[23]

Cricket carried its reports on the tour to the end, although many English papers, following the ignominious defeat of the West Indies in their early games, decided that they did not merit further attention. However, at the end of the tour, the paper observed that the tourists had learnt much: '[The] team in its last match was very much more formidable than in its first, for it is hardly too much to say that every one of its members was a far better player than he was when he reached England.'[24] The West Indies played 17 games, won five, lost eight and drew four.

Of Woods *Cricket* noted: 'On a queer wicket, Woods, the fast bowler of the team, was a player who was likely enough to dispose of any man, or a whole team if he met with a little encouragement, for although his run is very short, he gets a great amount of pace on the ball and, at times, gets up in a very awkward manner.'[25] It is inexplicable that so little was said of Burton of British Guiana, the other black fast bowler: he took 78 wickets to Woods's 72. I saw a sketch of him in the *Argosy*, one of the two main papers in his adopted homeland; he looks coloured (mixed race) and, by all accounts, was substantially less of an extrovert than Woods. However, that paper had no doubts that Burton was the star of the tour, way ahead of the popular Woods; they even stretched the facts a bit in their celebration of their local hero: 'To him fell an extremely heavy proportion of the bowling. He bowled a great many more overs than the Trinidad pro, Woods [true: 660.5 overs to Woods's 547.4, 113.1 overs more], whose average he overlaps by a long way indeed [not true: 78 wickets at 21.55 to Woods's 72 at 21.54]. Burton has done capital work, his performance is highly creditable from many points of view.... Woods was merely fast, straight and low — not good enough by any means for batsmen on the other side of the Atlantic.'[26] This was hardly an accurate verdict on Woods in this ungenerous assessment, but the Guyanese had satisfied themselves of the superiority of their adopted son. There would always be room in West Indies cricket for a recrudescent insularity.

Indeed, Woods's pace, resolve and obvious panache, key constituents of the great tradition of West Indian fast bowling, had stamped something of the black West Indian persona on the tour. As W.C. Nock, the white Trinidadian manager of the team, observed, the black players, in their exuberance, could sometimes exceed the requisite circumspection. He recalled an incident in which Woods was bowling

and the whole team appealed for a catch behind the wicket. The appeal
was disallowed and he reproached the umpire 'with much scorn': 'You
call yo'self a umpire!' Fortunately, the latter was apparently amused,
and Woods, though serious at the time, was soon mollified. Stanley
Sproston, a white Guyanese, acted as captain on many occasions in
1900; he related a similar tale, in the match against Surrey, which
West Indies won by an innings and 34 runs. Woods, 'bowling very fast',
earned very impressive match figures: 48 overs, 8 maidens, 116 runs,
12 wickets. Sproston recalled, though, that the bowler was not
impressed with at least one umpiring decision: 'Occasionally the
coloured members of the team were a little amazed at decisions which
seemed to them very bad, and when Shuter, in the Surrey match, was
given not out, Woods, who was bowling, was considerably excited at
what he thought was a fearful mistake on the part of the umpire, and
coming up to me, he said, "Mr. Sproston, if it had been in Trinidad, I
should have lick he down", at the same time pointing to the umpire.
But his anger was over in a moment.'27

But Nock recalled a funnier side to the fast bowler. In their first
match at Crystal Palace, Woods, with whom he was walking around the
ground, remarked: 'Mr. Nock, they *have* got a lot of white people in this
country!'28 C.L.R. James, too, relates a supposed hilarious tale from the
encounter between Woods and the great Gloucestershire and England
batsman, Gilbert Jessop, a prolific hitter. In a score of 619, Jessop made
157 in an hour — with 29 fours: 50 in 20 minutes, his century in 43
minutes. In 33 overs Woods conceded 141 runs. He was wicketless.
Hinds's 8 overs cost 72 runs (not 3 overs, as James cites from *Wisden*;
while Burton's 5 wickets cost 168, not 68 as James states.)29 Jessop's
torrential hitting allegedly prompted a desperate measure from Woods.
James tells a story of 'emotion prompting a return to nature':

On June 28th 1900 ... on the Bristol cricket ground, a West Indian
bowler went to his captain and asked permission to take off his boots.
West Indies captain Aucher Warner, a brother of Sir Pelham, asked
him why; he replied he could bowl properly only when barefooted.
Woods was making the best response he knew to a truly desperate
situation.... Aucher Warner promptly refused his request. Woods
returned to the bowling crease. Jessop despatched his fast balls over
the boundary, out of the ground, on to roof-tops. Woods made a last
attempt. 'Mr Warner', he pleaded, 'let me take off one — just one and

I could get him — just one, sir'. 'Out of the question. You can't do that here, Woods'. Dragging his feet, Woods had to endure this martyrdom, to the end encumbered by full armour.[30]

James remarks that the story is true, but it was 'perhaps of that higher order of truth which good fiction is'. He observes that Plum Warner was impressed with the skills of many of the black bowlers they encountered, at nets, on Lord Hawke's tour of 1897 (the so-called professionals), some of whom were 'definitely difficult'. He sketched the part played by several of the white creole families in giving these black 'boys' a start: 'The Warners [Trinidad], the Austins, the Goodmans [Barbados] and the Sprostons [Demerara or British Guiana] took over the best of them, shod them and clothed them, and brought them to England. Woods was one of these. His nickname was Float, after a local delicacy, as an Englishman might be called Chips from fish-and-chips.'[31]

It is interesting that the black cricketers were not detracted by the curiosity they attracted in England because of their race. During their first match, at Crystal Palace, against the London County Cricket Club captained by W.G. Grace, it was anticipated that Woods would bowl bare-footed. They were disappointed, for he bowled in the 'orthodox style'. The reporter elaborated: 'that is to say, with his boots on — a practice which his four coloured colleagues faithfully imitated'. He noted that Woods's pace was not affected by 'the disadvantages of the civilised buckskin. He only takes a four-step run to the crease, but this does not apparently affect his pace, which frequently deceived the champion himself [W.G.]'.[32] Another correspondent noted that although W.G.'s team made 432 for 8 on the first day, the effort of the West Indies bowlers never flagged, despite their inauspicious initiation (Woods and Burton bowled 61 overs between them and only got 2 for 227): '[T]he bowlers never lost heart, and to the last ball of the day they varied their pace with as much study as at the beginning of the match. Indeed, one could not help noting that only the really first class cricketers were quite comfortable with them.'[33] The talent was acknowledged, as the curiosity over the exotic was quickly spent.

It was Plum Warner who had kindled the curiosity around 'Float' Woods. The tale about his tendency to part with his boots when he bowled became so etched even in West Indian folklore, that C.L.R. James located it in the 1900 tour, when Woods supposedly beseeched

Aucher Warner, during the Jessop onslaught in their match against Gloucestershire — on June 28: 201 runs were scored in an hour while he was at the wicket. There is no record of Woods shedding his boots on that occasion or any other, but he did concede that he had no means of containing 'Mr. Jessop'. What is on record, in several newspapers, is the fact that the Jessop onslaught evoked a unique response from one of the black cricketers: 'The coloured members of the West Indies team have curious ways of expressing their admiration for the rigours of English batting.... One of them, who was fielding in the match against Gloucestershire, was almost convulsed with laughter when Jessop hit five 4's in one over, and when the fifth ball was struck hard over his head he threw himself on the ground and rolled about in the frenzy of merriment.'[34] All five 'coloured' members of the team played in the game in question, so it is not possible to ascertain the perpetrator of this bizarre piece of theatre. However, it is appropriate that the known source of the tale of Woods's boots be recorded — Plum Warner, in a piece for the *St. James's Budget* of June 8, 1900:

> The story goes that just before Lord Hawke's team arrived in Trinidad [in 1897] my brother [Aucher Warner], who was the captain of the island team, said to Woods: 'Now, remember you must wear boots when you play against the English cricketers'. To this he replied: 'Me, sah; but how am I to get a grip with my toes?' My brother, however, insisted, but when the match came off Woods appeared in a pair of tennis shoes, the soles of which were cut clean out! That, at any rate, is the story, so when Woods plays at Lord's the spectators ... must not be surprised if he takes off his boots and hands them to the umpire!

This was reproduced in the *Port of Spain Gazette* (Trinidad) of June 29, 1900, the day after Jessop's onslaught and the 'coloured' player's theatrics at Bristol, so it is comprehensible why the story entered Trinidadian lore: their 'Float' and his memorable encounter with Jessop. James was born in 1901, but it was one of the great cricket tales that lodged in his magnificent imagination. It spoke to the source of the West Indian cricket tradition: the poor black fast bowler, often, literally, 'a barefoot man', pitted against the white batsman. It encapsulated the spirit of the black West Indian endeavour — as usual, with a touch of self-deprecation and creative imagination.

Shortly before the West Indies cricketers left England, W.A. Bettesworth of *Cricket* interviewed 'Float' Woods (J. Woods) for his weekly column, 'Chats on the Cricket Field'. It is the only interview I have seen with him; and it reveals something of the strength of character and self-belief that possessed many of the educated black elite and cricketers at the end of the nineteenth century. Bettesworth's assessment of Woods corroborates this. He said that he was unable to include a picture of Woods in the article, as was the custom, because he was photographed once only by a professional photographer, and that picture could not be found. Instead, they placed a picture of the Hastings Cricket Ground in the interview: its relevance is not reachable. (A poor reproduction of a group picture with some members of the 1900 team appears in *The Cricketer* [May 1988]: Woods is sitting in the front row; the black face is evident, but it is hard to give it shape or to read anything into it.) However, if Bettesworth had looked at Plum Warner's recently published *Cricket in Many Climes*, he would have seen a very good picture of Woods with fast bowler, Archie Cumberbatch, his fellow black Barbadian who had settled in Trinidad.

Bettesworth compensated for the absence of a picture by an attempt to convey his physical attributes; he captured his intelligence too: 'Woods is a fine specimen of the darkest of the coloured natives of the West Indies, that is to say, he is very dark indeed. He has a good figure, which denotes strength in every movement. He is very solidly built, and is of medium height. When his face is in repose one can plainly see that his disposition is phlegmatic, but when it lights up it is full of intelligence. He speaks English accurately but slowly ... he does not make long speeches.' The columnist notes that his fast deliveries tend to move across from the leg, out-swingers; his slower deliveries tend to come in from the off, his in-swingers. He then added a curious fact: 'Although or perhaps because — he takes a very short run, he makes a pretty big hole in the ground.'

Woods evokes the spirit that is at the source of the great tradition of West Indies fast bowling. I have encountered nothing of note on him in the region's newspapers. This interview merits reproduction. Bettesworth first asked him how he learnt to bowl:

WOODS: Learn to bowl? I didn't learn. I taught myself. There was no one to give lessons. I saw my friends bowling and I thought I would like to bowl too. So one evening, when I was about fifteen, I went up to the cricket ground, with other boys, and took up a ball and began to bowl. That's how it was.

BETTESWORTH: How did you get on?

WOODS: Well, Mr. [Aucher] Warner [captain of the Queen's Park team, Trinidad] told me I'd come on as a good bowler, so I used to go every evening to the ground to practise. I was much faster then. But I was ill one time and caught a cold in my head, which was bad for me; so I couldn't bowl so fast afterwards. I learned how to make the ball break from my own idea. There was nobody to show me.

BETTESWORTH: Do you think you are as fast now as most of the English fast bowlers?

WOODS: I think I am faster than those I have seen. Richardson was, perhaps, the fastest, but he is not as fast as I am now. They tell me he used to be much faster. But I don't think he could ever have bowled as fast as I do if he had taken as short a run. I have tried to see what I could do with a longer run, but I don't like it. I like bowling on a fiery wicket best. We had one or two in England, and I did well on them. We had one at Stoke [against Staffordshire] but Hollowood played one of the pluckiest innings I ever saw, and made a hundred against us [103]. I hit him all about the ribs and legs, but he kept in all the same. Of course, I didn't try to do this, but you can't help it if you are a fast bowler when you get a fiery wicket.

BETTESWORTH: What have you learned in the way of bowling since you arrived in England?

WOODS: I think the two best things were to try to keep a good length and not to mind being hit. But this is not very easy. Mr. Stoddart hits very hard; but he did not hit as hard as Mr. Jessop [of Gloucestershire]. I did not know how to bowl to Mr. Jessop, for it did not seem to matter whether the ball was straight or not. He hit it somewhere or other, but you never knew where it was going to go. I tried to stop him all I knew, but nothing can be done when he gets going.

BETTESWORTH: Did you ever try to bat well?

WOODS: I can't bat well. But I sometimes make a few runs. My best innings this tour was 36 [going in last] at the Crystal Palace. Mr. Grace's bowling fooled us [he got 5 for 52 in the second innings].

BETTESWORTH: Were you much discouraged when London County

made so many runs against you at the Crystal Palace in your first match [432 for 8]?

WOODS: No. I thought that we should make as many runs as they did. But we had had very little practice and we got out. But it gave me pleasure to bowl in the match, and I knew I would do better when I had been able to practise more.

BETTESWORTH: Were any particularly good catches made off you during the tour?

WOODS: Burton took a nice catch off me at Southampton. It was at slip, very fast, and low down sideways. Hinds also took a pretty one at slip. That was low down, too, with the left hand. Another fine one was by Constantine at square leg, just in front of the umpire. This was very low and hard. And Mr. Goodman made a pretty one at point. There were several others, but I don't remember them now.

BETTESWORTH: Where do you like fielding yourself?

WOODS: Anywhere they put me. I like fielding very much. Once I got my feet wrenched in trying to turn quickly, but that was the only time I was hurt. We were all very lucky in not being hurt, but Constantine got a few blows when wicket-keeping. The only thing most of us ever suffered from was cold, though one or two had attacks of fever. But the climate did not upset us nearly as much as we expected.

BETTESWORTH: Did you enjoy the tour?

WOODS: I enjoyed it very much. There was the cricket and going about in trains; I liked the views on the way. The travelling didn't tire me much and I never had to be left out of the team [He played in all 17 matches]. I think I should like to live in England, though I don't know whether I could stand the cold in the winter. We did not like the cold weather when we first came over, but after a few weeks it was all right. Your sun seems to give a different kind of heat from ours, and makes you more tired after a day's fielding.

BETTESWORTH: What are your duties when you are at home? Are they like those of a professional in England?

WOODS: I have nothing to do with the ground, but I bowl at the nets. Sometimes I umpire and I like this very well. I think that the umpiring in England was very good, but the umpires sometimes made mistakes which worried me at first. But I knew they were doing their best.

BETTESWORTH: What did you think of the voyage to England?

WOODS: I liked it because I was not at all ill. Some of the team
played cricket on board, but I did not. I don't call that sort of
game cricket at all.[35]

In August 1900 the London *Dispatch* carried a cartoon captioned:
'The Surrey Captain Shaken'. It showed a massive Woods lifting Jephson
off the ground by his collar. He, in the eyes of the cartoonist, had
insulted the very competitive Woods by fielding a rather weak team
against the West Indies. Woods's pride, though, must have been
partially restored by the margin (an innings and 34 runs) and the
manner of their victory — the emphatic penetration of his own
bowling: he got 'twelve of Surrey's wickets, nine of them being clean
bowled, the stump on each of the nine occasions being knocked out of
the ground'. The cartoon was accompanied by the following perceptive
admonition attributed to Woods: 'P'raps, Massa Jephson, you put a
better team on the field next time I play you, Sah.'[36] The *Sporting
Chronicle*, too, emphasized that the demise of Surrey was attributable
largely to the fast bowling of Woods — 'unplayable':

Woods … is now justifying all Mr. Pelham Warner's predictions
and he with the tactful Burton at the other end make a capital
combination.… Apart from the batting of Ollivierre ['that
accomplished cricketer'] and Cox which was delightful, the result
was due almost entirely to Woods, whose bowling his opponents
simply found unplayable.… [I]n the two innings he took 12 wickets
for 112 runs. Now that he has accustomed himself to English
conditions, Woods is likely to justify all the good things said about
him by those who knew of his abilities at home, and he is a bowler
that every team in the country will have to seriously reckon with.[37]

This underlines the single-mindedness, utter commitment and
pride Plum Warner had observed in many black cricketers in 1897,
and others had recognized in those on the 1900 tour, even when an
ignominious defeat was irreversible. They knew that they were not
simply playing a game, however noble the motives. They all knew that
their cricket was necessarily at the core of black West Indian life,
integral to the educational and political struggles that they were waging
to advance their civil rights, only 62 years since they were freed. 'Float'
Woods knew that his cricket spoke for his people, whether he wished

for this or not. The intensity showed, but there was also a sincerity of purpose and a resolve to use the limited means to get as far as possible. He was not ashamed to admit his limitations: 'We come to larn, sir', as one cartoonist summarized the tour. Woods was a pioneer: on his and Burton's achievements of 1900 was built the great tradition of West Indies fast bowling. C.L.R. James locates him in this tradition:

> Woods was a very fine fast bowler.... The next generation of black men bowling fast was more sure of itself. In actual fact it produced the greatest of them all, George John. World War I interrupted his international career as it interrupted George Challenor's [a white Barbadian and graduate of Harrison College]. These two, the gentleman and the player, the white batsman and the black bowler, were the two finest cricketers the West Indies had produced up to this time, and the most characteristic. John was a man of the people, and an emigrant from one of the most backward of the smaller islands. It is only recent political events in the West Indies which taught me that John incarnated the plebs of his time.... [When John toured England in 1923, he was over 40, way past his peak.][38]

Woods was the father of West Indies fast bowling, as George Challenor was of West Indies batting. But no assessment of West Indies batting could ignore the contribution of Woods's black colleague on the 1900 tour, C.A. Ollivierre, the opening batsman from St. Vincent, who topped the batting averages in 1900 and stayed on to play county cricket for Derbyshire. In July 1900 Charles Ollivierre had made a major contribution to West Indies impressive victory over Leicestershire, by an innings and 87 runs. He scored 159 in an opening partnership of 238 in 2 hours and 15 minutes with Plum Warner (113), who played that one game for the West Indies in the summer of 1900. Plum acknowledged Ollivierre as 'a brilliant player, who ran between wickets like a deer'.[39] He also made 94 in an opening partnership of 208 with Percy Cox (142), against Surrey, in West Indies victory by an innings. Vincentians were very proud of the achievements of Ollivierre. They sent a congratulatory telegram to him after he had made his century against Leicestershire, as well as a cheque of £5 5s. 'as a mark of his countrymen's appreciation of his fine batting'.[40] It was clear that his batting reflected the black West Indian spirit, the flair and the

aggression to which I referred earlier. This was evident in a
correspondent's account of an innings of under 50 'the dusky player'
made against Warwickshire in June 1900:

> Sproston and Ollivierre were the first pair to bat, and the splendid
> crowd showed much interest in their debut. The dusky player
> aroused enthusiasm by having a 'go' at Ward's first over. He hit
> two fours and altogether made eleven off the over. The pair made
> 29 runs in 15 minutes when Sproston had the bad luck to pull one
> into his wicket. Cox also made runs and 50 went up in less than 45
> minutes, but at 60 Ollivierre's daring innings came to a close. He
> jumped out to drive Ward, only half got the ball, and was caught
> at cover slip [gully?] for 41 — *an innings of the kind crowds like.* He
> made his runs in 37 minutes and hit eight fours.[41] (emphasis added)

On August 23, 1900 *Cricket* reported that Ollivierre would remain
in England; he had got a post in the office of a Mr S.H. Wood in Glossop,
'with a view to qualify for Derbyshire'. Apparently, his devoted
countrymen had not heard of this; they were immersed in 'elaborate
arrangements' to welcome their hero back to St. Vincent. The *Port of
Spain Gazette* explained: 'Mr. Ollivierre ... will be received on board
the steamer by a reception committee, and then on his landing, he will
be entertained at breakfast, at which the Trinidad and Grenada
representatives will be invited to take part.'[42]

Such was the pride that West Indian cricketers already sparked in
their grassroots fans. So they must have been lifted by Plum Warner's
verdict on Ollivierre in 1900, attributing to him some of Ranji's qualities
as a batsman: 'Ollivierre was the best batsman in the eleven. He has
strokes all round the wicket, and in some ways remind one of Ranji.
His 159 against Leicestershire was as good an innings as was played
last summer. He was particularly strong in cutting and playing to leg,
and I shall be much surprised if he does not develop into one of the
best batsmen in Derbyshire, for which county he is qualifying.
Considering that his opportunities of playing cricket in St. Vincent
must have been very limited, his performance was remarkable.'[43] It is
interesting to note that Ollivierre had, in fact, worked for some time in
Trinidad, so it is arguable that the standard of cricket and access to
facilities, including the black and coloured clubs in that comparatively
tolerant island, must have enhanced the quality of his game. It is

C.A. Ollivierre (1876–1949): the first black West Indian to play county cricket (Derbyshire, 1901–07); toured England in 1900

noteworthy that Plum had witnessed every stroke played by Ollivierre in his innings against Leicestershire; they had opened the innings for the West Indies and posted a partnership of 238: Warner made 113; Ollivierre's 159 was, as *Wisden* records, scored 'in three hours and ten minutes without giving a chance'.

It is not possible, however, to ascertain black West Indian reaction to the success of Ollivierre during his years with Derbyshire, but, as in 1900, his achievement in county cricket must have given then abundant pride. He never represented West Indies again but, as the first West Indian in county cricket, he established a tradition of West Indian excellence in the English leagues and the county game, which has been enthralling ever since. The benefit was reciprocal: many West Indian cricketers made a living playing in the Lancashire League, from the 1920s, thus helping them too to develop their technical skills in varying conditions. Ollivierre played 110 matches for Derbyshire between 1901 and 1907, before eye problems forced a premature end to a distinguished county career. He played for some years as a club player in Yorkshire, and for 16 years, until the Second World War, he coached schoolboys in Holland. As Clayton Goodwin observes: 'Ollivierre's expert batting and together with that of S.G. [Sydney] Smith, the talented [white] Trinidadian all-rounder who joined Northamptonshire shortly afterwards [1907; he toured England with the West Indies team in 1906], put West Indian cricket on the international map at a time when Test matches were limited to Australia, England and South Africa.'[44]

H.S. Altham remarked in 1926 that from 1902, for three years, C.A. Ollivierre played 'some truly brilliant, if inconsistent, cricket', intimating that he had, indeed, captured the imagination of many by the character of his play: he 'recurs to memory'. Possibly, the inconsistency was the corollary of his spasmodic magnificence: the potential flaw was contained in his brilliance. Altham has left us a masterly depiction of this brilliance, from the 1904 season:

Derbyshire have never enjoyed any great measure of popular support, but if there is nothing very exhilarating in their cricket history, we can at least end it with a brief reference to one of the most amazing matches ever played, in which the county appears in an altogether triumphant light. It was at Chesterfield in 1904. Essex won the toss, and on a wicket that from the very first was distinctly lively put together the mammoth total of 597, of which Percy Perrin was responsible for 343 not out. Nothing daunted, Derby replied with 548, thanks chiefly to Ollivierre, who hit most brilliantly for 229. Then Warren and Bestwick proceeded to rattle Essex out for 97, and after Wright had been dismissed for a single, Ollivierre (92) and [Bill] Storer (48) knocked of the runs, and the side that had gone in against a total of virtually 600 triumphed by 9 wickets![45]

Only one white professional seemed to have vented any opposition to Ollivierre's playing for Derbyshire: the same Bill Storer, with whom he had won that memorable match in 1904. In 1931, the cricket writer, E.H.D. Sewell, observed of 'this coal-black batsman' that Storer, the Derbyshire and England professional, had objected to his presence in county cricket. He 'believed in England for the English and was not enamoured of importations, especially of the ebony hue'. Jack Williams concludes, however, that while there was evidence of racism, as reflected in this case, Ollivierre's achievement 'may well have created goodwill towards non-whites' among the white supporters of Derbyshire. I have no evidence of the number of black people in England in the early 1900s, but it must have lifted them to read of the achievements of this aggressive black opening batsman from remote, obscure little St. Vincent.[46]

In mid-August 1900, at the conclusion of the West Indies tour, a dinner in their honour was held at the Grand Hotel in London. There is no record of any of these cricketers speaking at the banquet, neither do we know how they reacted to the toasts proposed in their honour. What is clear, though, is what the ruling elite felt about cricket in the Empire and by implication the purpose of tours such as the current one. Lord Harris, former cricketer, colonial administrator and promoter of cricket in India, who was born in Trinidad, said that he wished the West Indians had not only learnt something about the game, but that they had learnt something, too, of 'the advantage of Empire'. He felt that cricket had a potentially great educative influence, as the people of England became aware of Australia largely through cricket tours; these had done 'more to draw Australia to England than all the treaties and the acts of Parliament of the past'. Harris even suggested that Australia's contribution to the Boer War was influenced by the goodwill that cricket was fostering between the two countries. He hoped that the current tour would have the same consequences for the West Indies.[47]

Lord Selbourne of the Colonial Office echoed those sentiments and underlined the place of sport in the imperial mission — in consolidating the Empire. He reportedly said:

[I]t would be possible to exaggerate the importance in our Imperial unity which our imperial sports might play; but he was sure that he would be a foolish man who denied that cricket, and our taste, as a race, for sport, had had a real influence in harmonising and in consolidating the different parts of the Empire. The West Indies might take an example from Australia.... They had now united into a great Commonwealth; and who could say a really important factor in that consolidation was the difficulty there once was in selecting a united Australian cricket team?[48]

This perception of the Empire was congruent with white West Indians' conception of it and their relationship to the mother country. It is impossible to ascertain how the black cricketers responded to this imperial definition. But, as I have argued, black intellectuals in the British West Indies, even in the 1890s, were already challenging the assumption that the Empire was sacrosanct. They were well aware of the unrepresentative character of colonial administration, of discrimination on the basis of race and colour within the colonial service, of the difficulties of land acquisition and a range of civil disabilities. But the battle was joined: education and cricket were at the core of the agenda for civil and political rights, instruments of mobility.

In October 1900, a benefit match for the successful black fast bowler on the English tour, W.J. (Tom) Burton, was played at the Georgetown Cricket Club (GCC), in British Guiana. He was a 'professional' with that club, so he did not have the status of its predominantly white or near white members. As noted above, he got the highest amount of wickets in England in 1900: 78 at 21.55, including W.G. Grace's, whom he bowled twice.[49] Plum Warner lauded the bowling of Woods and Burton, but he was especially impressed with the latter's consistency of focus, his thoroughly professional approach:

The bowling practically depended on Woods and Burton, both of whom did well. Woods on occasion was up to his best West Indian form, but at other times he seemed to lose heart very easily, though it must be confessed he was unlucky in the matter of missed catches. Burton was generally thought in England to be the better bowler of the two. His length was always excellent, and he possessed more finesse and headwork than ... [Woods]. He sent down a very good yorker, and it was with this ball that he twice had the honour of bowling W.G. Though Woods headed him by the merest fraction in the bowling analysis, it was pretty generally admitted that Burton on the whole accomplished the best work.[50]

On Burton's return to British Guiana, apparently many of his black admirers soon expressed, in letters to the press, what they saw as the failure of the Georgetown Cricket Club to honour their hero's magnificent achievement in England. They intimated that this absence of generosity was rooted in racial bigotry on the part of the white ruling elite. Burton's benefit match, unfortunately, was enmeshed in matters beyond the boundary, as cricket necessarily was in the West Indies. He was the recipient of $100, which was 'placed to his credit in the Savings' Bank'. The response of the acting Governor, Sir Cavendish Boyle, was instructive, as it demonstrated how far cricket was inescapably an aspect of politics in the British West Indies. He reportedly said:

> They had heard a good deal of talk about what the Club was doing and why it had not given Burton something. *Bis dat qui cito dat* was a good motto for most things, but in this case they had to wait. They had heard a good deal about the differences of class [race] lately in anonymous writings. But in the most conservative and at the same time liberal pastime, cricket, there was no such thing as class. If a man showed himself to be good he was welcomed, whatever he was and whatever his parentage might be. He thought ... the man who wielded the willow and trundled the ball was a better man than those who wielded pens and slung a lot of ink about class — all of which was nonsense and most of which was mud.[51]

Burton still could not represent the Georgetown Cricket Club or British Guiana because he was black, so it is inconceivable that his supporters could have accepted this belated assertion of equality; it would, however, have strengthened their commitment to the game and the fight for a freer society. The ruse of professionalism to exclude blacks was wearing thin; it had already been conquered in Trinidad. This was obvious in the contrasting warmth of the reception given the returning Trinidadian players, irrespective of race: Nock (the manager), Constantine, Woods and D'Ade. Aucher Warner, the captain, was recovering in England. In fact, in recognition of the greater need of the two black players, Woods and Constantine, testimonials to them were arranged before their arrival. The *Port of Spain Gazette* covered their arrival, dubbing the reception 'a right royal welcome'. It reported: 'The Gulf mail steamer, "Paria", was kindly placed at the disposal of the Queen's Park Committee to go alongside the inter-colonial boat so as to take "our boys" ashore…. The police band … also went off in the "Paria" and played many lively selections on reaching the "Esk" and on the way ashore…. A very large and enthusiastic crowd who had gathered to welcome home "our boys" cheered and shouted, and it was with great difficulty that one could pass.' Later that day a reception was held at the Queen's Park pavilion for the presentation of the testimonials to Constantine and 'Float' Woods. It was presided by the acting Governor, Sir C.C. Knollys, who complimented the West Indies team for playing as a unit in spite of their disparate composition; they deserved every credit; and of the irrepressible 'Float' Woods, he joked: 'It was always expected that "Float" would float'. Lady Knollys presented Constantine and Woods with a purse containing £13 10s. each. 'Float' then addressed the Lady in his inimitable fashion: 'I congratulated you for receiving this purse. I only hope the next time I will get more (cheers and laughter).'[52]

If we are to go by the depth of the black players' commitment to cricket, on the 1900 tour of England and beyond, it is incontrovertible that they saw their growing ascendancy in the sport as instrumental to their advance in the British West Indies. In July 1900, for instance, evidence of this black West Indian resolve was embodied in a catch Charles Ollivierre took in the match against Lancashire at Manchester, to dismiss Hallows off Mignon's bowling. The *Manchester Sporting Chronicle* observed that, with a bit more experience, he could soon be in the 'first rank', and celebrated his catch at long-on thus: '[He] was running backwards as the catch was made, with one hand, and the ball was going away from him all the time. The effort will rank as one of the best catches ever seen on the Lancashire ground, and thoroughly merited the applause so heartily bestowed on it. Such incidents as these show to what extent these West Indians have mastered the game of cricket.'[53] *Wisden* noted that Ollivierre 'was seen at quite his best'.[54]

Stanley Sproston, who captained the West Indies in several of their matches in 1900, including the five that they won, spoke 'enthusiastically of the keenness of the coloured members of the team'. He underlined their commitment, citing an incident from their match against Gloucestershire. It is worthy of note that it took place amidst the Jessop onslaught in which the bowler in question delivered 9 overs for 72 runs. Sproston recalled: 'Hinds [the black Barbadian] went on to bowl and would not have a man out in the country. Townsend [who made 140] hit a ball which went past him towards the boundary, and two or three of the team were proceeding to go after it. But Hinds waved them back, calling out, "Leff all to me, I'm going for it", and he went after it at a tremendous pace, leaving everybody else far behind.'[55] At the conclusion of the 1900 tour, W.C. Nock, the white Trinidadian manager of the team, was asked by W.A. Bettesworth of *Cricket*, 'Did the coloured members of the team quickly fall into English ways?' He responded:

> Very soon. They are thorough sportsmen, and have given no trouble whatever during the tour. Truth to tell, I was a little afraid that they would be spoiled by the hospitality which has been so freely offered, but it has not had this effect at all, for they knew when to pull back. They are very keen cricketers.... In one of the towns where we were playing I went to the coloured members of the team and said, 'I have got tickets for us all tonight at one of the theatres, and [we] will have an enjoyable evening'. To my surprise they one and all said that they thought they would rather not go, as they were very anxious to win the match.[56]

Writing many years later on the lessons learnt from the 1900 tour, Sir Pelham Warner identified five players, four of whom were black, whose performance, he thought, had laid the foundation for the advancement of West Indies cricket: Lebrun Constantine; C.A. Ollivierre; P.I. Cox (1878–1918), a white Barbadian batsman; and 'a pair of capital bowlers', 'Float' Woods and W.J. Burton. Warner added that 'the lessons learned on the tour were absorbed', thus creating the basis for several outstanding batsmen and bowlers between the Wars: the white Barbadian batsman, George Challenor, a master of 'style, hitting-power and defence', as *Wisden* characterized his batting in 1923

Lebrun Constantine (1874–1942): father of the great Learie; first black first-class cricketer; toured England in 1900 and 1906

in England; the fast bowlers, George John (Trinidad), George Francis and Mannie Martindale (Barbados); and Learie Constantine, an all-rounder, whom he considered a 'glorious' fieldsman, the 'finest in the world' (Trinidad).[57] It would take decades before the West Indies team cohered into a united force, but the legacy of 1900 was taking shape.

Both Learie Constantine and C.L.R. James assessed this legacy and spoke authoritatively on the attitude of one of the 1900 (and 1906) tourists, Lebrun Constantine ('Old Cons' to most in the West Indies). Learie recalled that his father had created his own pitch so that they could play as intensively as possible. Lebrun was an overseer on a cocoa estate but he practised assiduously after work. He also coached Learie and his friends, but did not try to expunge the spontaneity and flair out of their respective play: the peculiar style was admired and encouraged; it was a matter primarily of tightening the defence and mastering the basic skills. He showed them how to break the ball, the importance of good line and length. In one area, though, fielding, Lebrun was a 'martinet':

> You were not allowed to miss anything. If one ball got away from you and then another, it was as well if you were far from him, for if you were near he would give you a rap on the head. 'Sheer carelessness', which to him was the unforgivable sin. Often he put us to stand a few feet behind his back and hit the catches over his shoulders while we caught them behind. With his strong wrists and forearms he could hit fairly hard in any direction. They were awkward to judge, but that was not accepted as an excuse for missing, my father's theory being simplicity itself: if you were paying attention you did not miss. 'Pay attention!' 'Pay attention!' and again 'Pay attention!' To this day I pay attention, and when I don't my side suffers.[58]

The competitive spirit was fostered relentlessly, passionately, even on Sundays — after church. The pursuit of excellence was a family affair: all were involved, as was the case in another household, earlier, in England: the Graces. Learie recalls:

> Sunday was a field day. Uncle Victor [Pascall, his mother's brother who toured England with Learie in 1923], now a full-fledged intercolonial and a great man (though not as great as my father),

would come over sometimes and we played after breakfast [lunch] ... till dark. Often my mother kept the wicket, and in those days my sister was as hard to get out as any of the younger group.... My father would give us a chance to get each other out, and then when the failing strength of the attack showed ... he would take the ball himself.... [He] bowled and bowled, and you gripped your bat and played him for your life, with the others in the slips and close in at cover and short leg waiting hungrily for your downfall. You might last three overs. 'Humph! This boy is getting on!' my father would say, but the pleasure of the compliment would be overshadowed by the knowledge that the words were but the preliminary to a more concentrated attack.[59]

Learie continues: 'Still you held on. The off-break, fast as it left the pitch, you could manage; the straight one that should have been an off-break, but was not, you dug out just in time and grinned in triumph at your brother in the slips who thought his innings had come at last; until a ball floating uncertainly over the blind spot warned, and the crash of the wickets behind confirmed, that the old man had got through at last.'[60]

Lebrun Constantine was the architect of Shannonism. James has observed that the main cricket clubs in Trinidad in the early twentieth century were, like those in Barbados, a reflection of the race, colour and class stratification of Trinidadian society. Queen's Park represented the white elite or the very light; Maple was the club of the coloured middle class but it admitted a few dark people on the basis of class; Shannon (formerly Victoria) was the club of lower middle-class blacks, like the Constantines and the St. Hills, who played Test cricket for the West Indies in the 1920s and 30s; Stingo represented the very dark, the black plebs: they had great talent but no status; their key players included George John, the demon fast bowler, and Joe Small, the West Indies Test player. James should have gone logically to Constantine's club, Shannon. He did not. He went lighter, to Maple. He was counselled that they were the people of the future: if you had ambition that's where you went. He regretted it later, for Shannon, of darker hue, carried with it the hopes of most black Trinidadians, the dream that they could lift themselves to a position that would give them security and dignity. It evoked the same aspirations they cultivated of liberation through education.

Shannonism, as James argues, was at the core of the black endeavour; by merit alone they could lift themselves, underlining for their detractors — white and brown — what Learie once said to James: 'They are no better than we.' James assesses the meaning of Shannonism, the unconquerable resolve embodied in Lebrun and Learie, within and beyond the boundary:

Shannon opened their bowling with [Learie] Constantine and Edwin St. Hill, both Test players.... First change was Victor Pascall [Learie's uncle], for long years the best slow left-hander in the West Indies, who had visited England in 1923. Then might follow Cyl St. Hill, well over six feet, fast left hand, his arm as straight as a post. When he dropped the ball on the off-stump it might straighten, to take the outside edge of the bat, or continue to the inside of your ribs. Cyril Fraser, genuine leg-spinner, sound bat and brilliant field anywhere, would be welcome in most English counties.... At their best ... the Shannon bowling and fielding would have made a shambles of most English counties then or now.

It was not mere skill. They played as if they knew that their club represented the great mass of black people in the island. The crowd did not look at Stingo in the same way. Stingo did not have status enough. Stingo did not have that pride and impersonal ambition that distinguished Shannon. As clearly as if it was written across the sky, their play said: Here, on the cricket field if nowhere else, all men in the island are equal, and we are the best in the island.... They missed few catches, and looked upon one of their number who did as a potential fifth columnist. Wilton St. Hill chased a ball from slip to third man as if he were saving the match and not a possible single.... The crowd expected it from them, and if they lapsed let them know.... Queen's Park were the big shots.... They would bowl them out, and show them some batting too. As for Maple [James's club], with our insolent rejection of black men, they would show us. They usually did.[61] (emphasis added)

It was a measure of the avidity of purpose — the resolve of Shannonism — of Lebrun Constantine that he persevered as a cricketer although the demands of a growing family made it increasingly painful for him to do so. In this regard, however, it is necessary to correct a key factual error about his tour of England in 1900, which has persisted

because of a version that appears in *Beyond a Boundary*. It relates to
the means by which he was able to make that tour. James's version is
fundamentally different from Learie Constantine's, but it is the latter
that must be accepted. James narrates:

> The boat with the team to England in 1900 had left [Trinidad] and
> 'Cons' [Lebrun] ... though chosen, had remained behind.... He was
> not a rich man who could pay his own way.... He had not gone
> because he couldn't afford it. People who thought he had gone saw
> him standing in the street. A public subscription was organised on
> the spot, a fast launch was chartered and caught the boat before it
> reached the open sea. Constantine Snr. scrambled on board to hit
> the first West Indies century made in England (st. Reynolds b.
> Grace, 113) at Lord's of all places.[62]

The last point is correct (Lebrun made the first century by a West
Indian in England, in 1900), as is the fact that a launch was chartered
to get him on to the boat for England. However, Learie's version, which
is no less enthralling, is certainly nearer the truth. He recalls his father's
epic tale of resilience, but the year is 1906, Lebrun's second tour of
England, when his highest score was 92 — not 1900:

> He visited England in 1900 with the West Indies side and was again
> invited to go in 1906, but he could not see his way to make the trip.
> Whereas in 1900 he had one child, in 1906 there were four.... On
> the morning the boat was sailing, he left Maraval and went to Port
> of Spain. He would have liked to join the boys but he could not afford
> it. So ostensibly he went into town to have a few drinks with them
> and finally to see them off.... He arrived in town too early for the
> players who were sailing that day. He felt lonely and isolated. At
> the bottom of Frederick Street a Mr. Michael Philip Maillard, [a
> white] merchant, a great supporter of cricket and an admirer of the
> Constantine family, stood in front of his business premises. He saw
> my father and called him in to say goodbye to him. But my father
> informed him that he was not going. 'Not going. Impossible!' said
> Mr. Maillard. My father explained the position and Mr. Maillard
> told him that he had got to go. There was no question. My father
> protested that he had made no provisions, no preparations at all,
> and the answer came: 'Never mind that, you have got to go'.

Learie concludes the remarkable tale of generosity to a great hero:

> Mr. Maillard sent for his carriage and one of his fastest horses, and
> into the carriage jumped my father, and off to Maraval they raced.
> Meanwhile, Mr. Maillard did a bit of shopping, and by the time my
> father returned a trunk was packed, a sum of money collected to
> cover the family's and my father's needs, and so my father was
> ready to sail. Off to the jetty they went, but the boat which carried
> passengers to the sailing ship two or three miles off-shore had gone,
> and the ship had sailed. Chartering a fast launch they set out in
> chase, and before the steamer had got out of the Bocas into the open
> sea they caught up with it, a rope ladder was lowered, and my
> father joined the others on board.[63]

James's version, suggestive of the masses spontaneously pooling
their pennies for their hero, who repays by scoring a hundred as soon
as he gets off the boat — at Lord's, is a finer rendition, though
embroidered. But the inspiration for Lebrun Constantine's iron will to
succeed definitely has its promptings in black people's perception of
him as a pioneer within and beyond the boundary. He was the first
black cricketer to represent Trinidad, in 1895, one of the first to play
for the West Indies, in 1897, and the first to play in an inter-colonial
match, in 1900, on the eve of the English tour. His place in black West
Indian society was necessarily, therefore, one that transcended bat
and ball. Learie's career would follow a similar pattern.

I will cite one other Trinidadian example of Shannonism — in
education — the case of Eric Eustace Williams (1911–81). His father,
like Lebrun Constantine, carried in him the fears and hopes that his
son would achieve excellence in an area deemed central to colonial
society. In these boys were invested the hopes and aspirations of
several generations of black parents, but they were claimed by all
black people, exemplars of their own arrival. Failure could not be
countenanced; it was too evocative of the stain of the universe of the
slave plantation. These gifted boys — scholars or cricketers — were
expected to atone for what George Lamming sees as the 'psychic shame
which burns the hearts of men whose lives have been a history of
genuflection and an apparent subservience of spirit'. Eric Williams
tells the story of the strain engendered by his educational endeavour
— a collective project — and the pain it inflicted on his father, from

the cradle until the day he became the Island Scholar in 1931:

> My father knew that what he had never been given an opportunity
> to achieve with his brains, he might with his loins. The island
> scholarship for his son [to study at university in England] became
> the dream of his life. The first hurdle to overcome was the
> government exhibition from the primary to the secondary school....
> I was never allowed to forget that I was the rising hope of my stern,
> unbending relatives.... In my final try at the crucial scholarship ...
> [my father's] concern over my performance in each paper, the
> rest of the family listening the while, was such an intolerable strain
> that I refused point blank to answer any question and remained
> silent; at the end of the examination he asked me, not unkindly,
> whether I wished to discuss the prospects, and I told him that I did
> not.... I had a distinguished record at Queen's Royal College, both in
> the classroom and on the playing field.... [So] it was a day of jubilation
> ... October 19, 1931, when the news of my scholarship victory was
> brought to me. Jubilation, particularly for my father, who arrived
> home for lunch bewildered by the congratulations from people on
> the way. His twenty year old dream had come through.

Williams drew the lesson for his father of the pain and privation
that the whole family had endured for two decades, in the campaign to
take him to the summit of educational attainment in colonial Trinidad.
He was speaking for most black people in the British West Indies:

> Underpaid, tired, demoralised by the sight of younger people
> promoted out of turn over his head, because he lacked the necessary
> pliancy to ingratiate himself with the powers that controlled his
> destiny, he looked upon my victory as a decisive proof of his
> manhood. His bearing was more erect thereafter, his confidence in
> himself restored, and he often told me that, whatever his rivals
> had, they had not an Island scholar as their son.[64]

Eric Williams went on to Oxford in 1932, earned his doctorate in
1938 and became an outstanding scholar of West Indian history, the
author of *Capitalism and Slavery*, and the first Prime Minister of Trinidad
and Tobago. After his cricketing conquests, Learie Constantine became
a lawyer in 1954, a minister in Williams's government in 1956, then his
country's first High Commissioner to London in 1962; he was knighted

the same year and was elevated to the House of Lords in 1969.

On August 24, 1900 the *Port of Spain Gazette* in Trinidad carried an article from the Barbados *Bulletin* on the lessons to be learnt from the 1900 West Indies tour of England, and the possible legacy of this seminal event. Paradoxically, for a piece originating in Barbados, it was a very perceptive and imaginative assessment, with revolutionary projections toward a more democratic culture in the region. I have not been able to ascertain the pedigree of the *Bulletin*, but this piece would have struck a chord with the fathers of Learie Constantine, C.L.R. James and Eric Williams, and many other black, coloured, Indian, Portuguese and progressives whites, a few of whom were present in most islands. It was a vindication of the struggle of submerged groups to achieve, within and beyond the boundary. They remarked that Lord Harris's characterization of the tour as 'successful' accorded with the facts; but it was also the fact that 'the sportsmanlike conduct and sturdy play of our men have conquered the prejudices and won the approval of the public at home [England]'. Moreover, they envisaged that the 1900 tour would have profound ramifications for all West Indians:

> What will be the effects on West Indian cricket of the tour? Well, the superstition that the West Indian cricketer is inherently inferior to the English cricketer will vanish forever from the minds of West Indians. Everyone will grasp the fact that with equal advantages of training and practice, the West Indian can play the cracks of Australia and England on equal terms.... *This firm conviction of capacity for the accomplishment of what other people in the Empire have succeeded in doing will, in the future, be a source of great strength to West Indians. It will be an attitude of mind rendering them self-respecting and ambitious in other domains of thought and action than cricket merely. We have so long been told by supercilious Europeans that we are an inferior people, unable to wing our way in regions where superior races soar easily, that we have perhaps underrated our powers.*[65] (emphasis added)

The paper was anticipating a democratizing of the game in keeping with a broader conception of civil rights: 'cricket would take on many changes here with the progress of the age, which would be resented by sticklers for local conservatism'. And they advocated an end to the spurious notion of the professional, which kept many gifted cricketers out of the game because of their race. This was a radical proposal; they were following where Trinidad was leading, but the fact that the advocacy of reform was coming now from conservative Barbados was, in itself, reflective of the impetus for change in the British West Indies, at the end of the nineteenth century:

> The tour will bring forcibly before the minds of the cricket authorities of the leading colonies the status and rights of West Indian professionals. This question demands settlement, and until it is settled we cannot expect to see much progress made in West Indies cricket. We have no doubt that the authorities in Demerara and Trinidad have had their attention directed to it, and that the near future will see a most important reform passed, which will strengthen the cricket in these islands. It is needless to add that Barbadian cricket will be influenced for good by this tour.[66]

In fact, Trinidad, always the pioneer in undermining 'the Chinese wall of exclusiveness', having pioneered the selection of black players against English touring teams since 1895, had picked Lebrun Constantine to represent them against British Guiana (Demerara) in the inter-colonial championship of 1900, on the eve of the tour of England. It is true that he was not deemed a professional, but the fact that British Guiana, like Barbados, traditionally all-white by choice, played against a Trinidadian team which included a black man, had already given ground for the assumption of the *Bulletin* that racism in West Indies cricket would be challenged in the aftermath of the 1900 tour. It is noteworthy that on the return of the team in early September 1900, the Manager, W.C. Nock, a white Trinidadian, remarked that the English people 'were most hospitable to the team ... without any [racial] distinction whatever'. And at a banquet given in their honour by the Surrey Club, Lord Alverstone propounded the idea of an inclusive Empire, that 'West Indians and all other colonists, irrespective of colour or other differences, should think of England as their home. It was the head of the Empire and therefore the home of every British subject'.[67]

It was impossible to treat black cricketers as equals in England and expect them to remain second-class subjects in the West Indies. Such carrots of inclusiveness had immediate repercussions in the British West Indies. Within the boundary, too, the 1900 tour had a profound impact: although the spurious distinction between amateurs and professionals would remain for some time, as early as September 1901, two black cricketers represented Barbados in the inter-colonial final against Trinidad in Georgetown, British Guiana. These were S.A. Rudder, a fast bowler, and Fitz Hinds, who had toured England in 1900. Nothing encapsulated the aptitude of the British West Indies for compromise than the fact that the same Hallam Cole who had refused to go to England in 1900 because he had rejected Hinds's claim to be an amateur, now played in the same team with him, as he would in 1904. It is also noteworthy that Trinidad's victory by 172 runs in the final of 1901 owed much to an innings of 71 by Lebrun Constantine. The discipline in his play earned recognition from the Barbados *Globe*. It was an innings that vindicated his character — vintage Shannonism: 'He was batting for one hour and fifty minutes, and during that period displayed the form which has made him justly famous in the West Indies as a batsman of exceptionally sound defence and good judgement. His score of 71 was not obtained by brilliant cricket; it was rather a steady, sound display of all-round batting. He mastered the Barbados bowling completely, and although he gave a chance at 36, yet his innings was remarkable for the splendid defence he maintained, and the manner in which he played every bowler the Bims could put on all round the wicket.' This was no mercurial adventure by a volatile Negro: it bore the imprint of a people increasingly confident of their capacity for a measure of self-government.[68]

On the issue of race in politics and education, progressive promptings were already being disseminated by September 1900. On the day the Trinidad members of the team landed in Port of Spain (Nock, Constantine, D'Ade and Woods), the *Port of Spain Gazette* carried a leader rejecting the Crown Colony system of government on the island:

> [T]he surest way, indeed the only way, to eventually arrive at true representative government is to sweep away the mockery of it with which the people of Trinidad have been befooled for the last seventy years. It is no reproach to the individuals to say that the Unofficial members since they first took their seat ... in December 1834, have never, in the true sense of the word, been representative of the popular voice. Nominated by the Crown, they had no mandate from the people, and any good the long succession of Unofficials may have done since that date, has been due to their individual honesty and fitness for the position awarded them.[69]

Later that month, J. Wood Davis, a progressive white creole senior civil servant, admonished the conservative, pro-planter *Argosy* in British Guiana, for their support of the government's reduction of the education budget, and their vilification of Rev H.J. Shirley, a radical Congregational minister, an Englishman, an open ally of the black working class in British Guiana. Davis's contention was that discrimination was still being perpetrated against blacks, but an increasingly educated black populace was already conscious of their rights of citizenship; therefore, a perceived abridgement of their educational opportunities would aggravate their aggrieved sensibility within the British Empire:

> [T]he British flag floats over our colony, and this is a guarantee of liberty and equal rights. Can it in candour be asserted, however, that the black man has the same privileges and opportunities that belong to his 'pale-faced brother'.... [S]eeing that there is nothing in the constitution and laws ... to justify the position of inferiority created for black colonists, they suffer a grievance which ought to be exposed and removed. There may have been a time when their wants of education and unappreciation of the duties of responsible citizens were natural reasons for keeping them in the background. That time, however, belongs to past history and if not given fair play by reasonable appeals to the local Government, recourse must be had by them to the liberty-loving British nation. Mr. Shirley contends that hardships will never be remedied by petitions through the regular channel. If the Secretary of State [Joseph Chamberlain] had not proved his determination to uphold the actions of colonial Governors no matter how arrogant or ignorant they may be, such an assertion would have been uncalled for.[70]

Davis was arguing that black people had justifiable grounds for harbouring grievances, and that they were now capable of representing themselves. The culture was changing; it was unacceptable to attribute their political awareness to the machinations of agitators:

> The fervour with which you denounce Mr. Shirley as fomenting mischief among the people, carries with it the idea that that they are easily moved by an outburst of passion. Such a notion cannot but be resented as unjust and almost malignant. It would take much more than the declamations of an orator ... 'to rouse the

people to any action resulting in considerable trouble and mischief'.... Judging from remarks which frequently appear in the press that the children of the poor (which mean the offspring of the black race) are being too highly educated for the field [menial labour], which by some peculiar law of nature, is their special heritage, it is not to be wondered at that ulterior motives are imputed to the government regarding the reduction of the education grant. Mr. Shirley moves among the class of people whose feelings would be bitter on the question as affecting the most.... You cannot believe that the people are content that educational facilities granted to their children should be curtailed, when the bill paid for the upkeep of Queen's College, the school provided for the sons of the well-to-do, remains intact.[71]

It was not fortuitous that as the black cricketers were opening new space for their people by their courageous play in the 'mother country', thus establishing their credentials to civilization — mastery of a difficult craft and the right to greater respect — the first Pan-African Conference was taking place in London, from July 23 to 25, 1900. A Trinidadian lawyer in England, Henry Sylvester Williams, was the prime mover behind this meeting of Africans in the diaspora primarily. For them, with a growing degree of self-confidence, it was important to gain the attention of Englishmen at the heart of Empire on the problems of blacks universally. As C.E. Quinlan of Saint Lucia remarked on the eve of the Conference: 'It was the desire of the black people to explain to the English public the grievances of the coloured races in different parts of Her Majesty's Empire, and they sought to assist the work of the Anti-Slavery Society, the Aborigines Protection Society and other organisations which were working to redress the grievances under which black men had for so many years laboured.'[72] Sylvester Williams added that the Conference was 'the first occasion upon which black men would assemble in England to speak for themselves and endeavour to influence public opinion in their favour'. He also noted that they would definitely address the question of the position of blacks in South Africa. This underlined the centrality of the question in the context of the Boer War and the difficulties engendered by it for black South Africans. Moreover, it reflected the importance for educated Africans in the diaspora of crucial issues in the ancestral homeland. This concern would, of course, be manifested much more intensively with regard to

South Africa in the latter half of the century; but the return-to-Africa strand in Garveyism in the 1920s, the Abyssinian (Ethiopian) issue in the 1930s and the emergence of Nkrumah's Ghana in the late 1950s, would also command their attention.

Thirty delegates, including a few women, representing Abyssinia, Liberia, West Indies and the United States, attended the Pan-African Conference held in Westminster Town Hall. It was convened 'to consider the present social, political and financial condition of the coloured people all the world over, and to discuss a process of amelioration'. It is noteworthy, however, that among the papers discussed was one, 'Our Women', and that Mrs Anna J. Cooper, 'a coloured principal of a college in Washington, D.C.', read one entitled, 'The Negro Problem in America'. Miss Ann Jones, BA, another black woman who taught rhetoric at a high school in Kansas City, reportedly delivered a 'bright speech'. Another woman contributor was Mrs Coleridge Taylor, wife of the black British composer of 'Hiawatha', who sang a song 'to the delight of an audience largely composed of white ladies and coloured gentlemen'.[73]

R.E. Phipps, another Trinidadian barrister, told the conference that in the Empire, 'the worst positions in the Civil service were set aside for the coloured [black] people, and then they were appointed on the understanding that their action should be controlled'.[74] Sylvester Williams, who had spent some time in South Africa, addressed the Conference on the condition of blacks there, noting that 'they were not allowed to go on the side walks, and [that] in Natal there was a post office with one door for the natives and one for the whites'.[75] It was a measure of their growing stature that the Conference, 'comprising men and women of African blood and descent', sent a petition to Queen Victoria, to 'respectfully invite your august and energetic attention to the fact that the situation of the native races in South Africa is causing us and our friends alarm ... [and] Your Majesty's humble Memorialists pray your influence be used in order that these evils, to which we have respectfully called your attention, be remedied, and thus foster the purpose of a true civilisation amongst Your Majesty's native subjects'. The Queen did not reply, but she did when Sylvester Williams wrote to her again, in January 1901. He received her reply the day before she died.

Two other papers discussed at the Conference were indicative of the sense of possibilities that permeated the vision of these ascendant men and women: 'The Progress of Our People in the Light of Current History' and 'The Condition Favouring a High Standard of African Humanity'. But it was the following assessment that really conveyed the momentous nature of this Conference for black people: 'The coloured gentleman has at last determined to shift the burden of his race from the shoulders of the white man on to his own.'[76] And in a spirit totally congruent with this bold assertion of their right to repossess their past and control their future, a delegate, Hon H.F. Dowding, said that 'the black race had no intention to comply with the wish of those who desired that they should remain slaves in perpetuity.... They did not seek freedom by force of arms; they would win it by deserving it [on merit]. In their humility and long-suffering, they had risen from the lowest depths. The time would come when the world would see their worth'.[77]

James R. Hooker, a biographer of Henry Sylvester Williams, has reflected on the summer of 1900 and deemed it 'a good one'; 'there was reason for growing self-confidence ... and the Conference showed it': the Boer War was moving towards a conclusion, in Britain's favour; and, he adds, the 'first-ever West Indian cricket team had come to England and despite severe self-doubt, had done well (8 lost, 5 won, 3 drawn, 1 abandoned)'. He adds that although the 'connection between war, cricket, Empire and black advancement may not be apparent to [those] unfamiliar with the social significance of the game in the Islands ... [t]his quintessentially English sport stood for all that black Englishmen ... admired in British life'. Cricket stood for more, as I have argued, for Hooker missed the subversive element that permeated the West Indian game, as he failed to recognize the deeper promptings of middle-class West Indians' Pan-African cravings: the quest to infuse their achievements within the context of Empire with intimations of ancestral greatness, the importance of an imaginary homeland. This was not meant for the African in the ancestral land; it was exclusively a diasporic endeavour, and it was combined, often in a personal, idiosyncratic manner, with their mastery of diverse facets of the English tradition: in sport and in education.[78]

It was probably fortuitous that the issue of the *Port of Spain Gazette* (August 24, 1900) that had carried the perceptive retrospective from the *Barbados Bulletin* on the 1900 tour, also had a piece on the outcome of the Pan-African Conference in London. But it is difficult not to see in them a glimpse of the 'growing self-confidence' when viewed in conjunction with another piece on the 1900 tour, from the London *Standard*, that appeared in the same issue:

> The West Indians have done well. We consider them courageous to have tried conclusions with some of the leading teams. Though they were often outplayed they showed promising form, fully justifying their estimate of themselves in arranging the tour. Ollivierre is considered to be the prettiest bat, while Burton is defined as the best bowler for pure headwork.... The West Indians are sure to visit us again, and in course of time will be worthy opponents of our best teams.

When W.C. Nock and Lebrun Constantine returned to Trinidad they were interviewed for the *Port of Spain Gazette*. Their reflections on the knowledge they had acquired on the varying conditions of play, the mercurial pitches and the discipline and stamina bred by a constantly competitive game over several days, were crucial to the advancement of West Indies cricket. Nock had remarked that the tour 'would effect more good than 50,000 books written'; and he expressed pride in Charles Ollivierre's engagement to play for Derbyshire through the instrumentality of 'Mr. Wood, a well known and thoroughly good cricketer'. He was qualifying as an amateur, and had secured the position of a clerk in a counting house, at £150 per year, to enable him to do so. Nock concluded: 'Does this alone not prove that the West Indies cricket tour to England commenced to bear fruit before their departure for their homes? The tour, if nothing else, has proved to the never travelled Englishman that the West Indians are not a despicable lot. I am certain that what our men have learnt in England will tend to greatly improve cricket as played in the West Indies.' An English paper had also commented on Ollivierre's impending advent to county cricket '[He is] ... the best bat in the West Indies team.... [W]hatever one may think of the policy of robbing the colonies of the best players in order to enrich the county teams, there can be no doubt that Derbyshire have obtained the services of a most valuable man.'[79] Lebrun Constantine said that he was 'pleased beyond measure with the tour', and that he had 'learnt a lot about cricket'. In Lord Hawke, who 'took much interest in the tour personally', they had a 'friend in the true sense of the word'. He explored the experience of playing in a vastly different environment:

> [T]he climate and especially the light had a somewhat great effect on me and it took some time for me to become accustomed to it.... [W]ith these totally new conditions and for the first time having to play such long matches, a fellow must feel shaky at the beginning; but I believe I picked up well afterwards and if I had not been ill for six days, thus preventing me from playing in all the matches, as Ollivierre had the good fortune to do, I could have topped the batting average. [They were the top two: Ollivierre played 16 matches, and made 883 runs with an average of 32.70; Constantine played 13, and made 610 runs at 30.50.] Cricket in England is vastly different to that in Trinidad and one has to learn the pitch to be able to bat and bowl effectively. [N]ot only have I enjoyed the tour but I have benefited from it.[80]

Tom Burton, most self-effacing although he had taken the most wickets on the tour, told the *Daily Chronicle* in Georgetown that playing in England really was an education:

> The tour has taught us one important lesson. We have learnt to be more patient. Our great mistake is we are in a hurry to make runs. That comes about by our being accustomed to half-day matches, playing on a Saturday afternoon. In England we had three-day matches and it does not generally matter how long a man takes to knock up fifty. He plays to get runs and he does not risk getting out if he can avoid it.... With another fortnight in England I think we would have shown vastly improved form. We gained experience as we went on, and a lot of it too.

His own outstanding bowling was, he said, a consequence of his patience against the best batsmen: it bears repeating, he yorked Dr W.G. Grace twice on the tour.[81]

Lebrun Constantine had noted that among the places they visited in England in 1900 was the House of Lords. He could not have known that his eldest son, Learie, born in 1901, would be elevated to that institution nearly seven decades later, in 1969. It is to that son, Lord Constantine of Maraval and Nelson, to whom I give the final word on the legacy of 1900. The year was 1958; Learie was the Minister of

Works and Transport in Dr Eric Williams's cabinet; and the Leader of the Opposition in Trinidad, Bhadase Maraj, an Indo-Trinidadian, had made a disparaging intervention in the House, asserting that although Learie had a great reputation as a cricketer, he was a novice in political affairs. Constantine responded sharply, emphasizing what most West Indians had long known: cricket was a very political matter; the great West Indian cricketer was necessarily a political person; he carried with him, at home and abroad, the hopes and aspirations of West Indian peoples long after he had laid down bat and ball:

> [T]he Leader of the Opposition said that I took this game of politics for bat and ball. I want to say that whatever reputation I have made, I have made it because of bat and ball. I have been to India, I have been to Ceylon, and I want to issue a challenge to the Leader of the Opposition. Let him land in India, his Mother Country, at any time; and let me land in India at any time, and compare the welcome that would be given to him in his Mother Country with the welcome that would be given to me. If he gets a better welcome than I, I shall pay some money into any charity he names. I have mixed with Dukes, with Princes, with Kings and Queens because of my cricket; and I want to say that it is an indication of the mentality of the Opposition when they try to reduce one of England's greatest cultural games to a mere game of bat and ball.[82]

Later, when another legislator cast doubt on his integrity, he countered with what he saw as unimpeachable qualities engendered by his life as a cricketer of international repute. Learie said: 'I am not going to say much except to remind him that at one period I was a sportsman, that I moved around the five continents as a sportsman, and that I became respected by people in those five continents as a sportsman. I am accepted today in all five continents as a sportsman, as a man of integrity, and as a man of probity.'[83] In 1930–1931 Learie played four tests for West Indies on their first tour of Australia, a series that the latter won 4-1, three of them by an innings. Learie's performances with bat and ball were not memorable, yet Australians were still entranced by the style of the man's cricket. Johnnie Moyes who saw him then recalls:

INHERITORS OF THE LEGACY OF MUSCULAR LEARNING

Left: Sir Frank Worrell (1924–67), first black captain of the West Indies team, and Lord Constantine (Learie) (1901–71) in London, 1963

C.L.R. James (1901–89), the author of Beyond a Boundary *(1963): the bible of muscular learning*

Constantine gave you pleasure because his own joy was so evident, because he sought the unattainable and was full of adventure. If he failed he failed gloriously.... [B]y and large he was the showman exploiting his manifold talents, breaking away continually from the normal to attempt the impossible.... In Australia, under the hot sun, he was indefatigable as in England, though the wickets were not as fast as he had hoped. Now and again he looked hostile. His fielding was always a sight for the gods. Sometimes he hit well, but our recollection of him is not one of achievement so much as genius badly directed. Nevertheless we can be glad of the genius. We can recall some of the many grand things he did — not runs scored or wickets taken, but his manner of playing cricket. He played in Australia in 1930–1, and eighteen years later he was still remembered because of the joy he gave.[84]

This would have made Lebrun Constantine just as proud as Eric Williams's father was, that day in 1931, when Eric won the Island scholarship that sent him to Oxford. For in Trinidad, as Ivar Oxaal argues, cricket and education were at the core of the shaping of the 'island civilisation':

Someday, perhaps, a Trinidadian writer will attempt a full-scale social history of the complex little island civilisation that was Trinidad in the early years of the [twentieth] century. In his cricket memoirs, *Beyond a Boundary*, James provides glimpses into such facets of the period as the puritanical code impressed on the Q[ueen's] R[oyal] C[ollege] schoolboy, the metropolitan sophistication of a group of local intellectuals [the Beacon Group], and the manner in which membership in the various local cricket clubs was determined by very fine class and colour distinctions. The excellence of the cricket played was a product of the sublimated class conflict which found an outlet in the keen rivalries between the clubs; also of importance was the ready, informal, availability of top players for matches at every level. Under the veneer of class and caste there had taken shape a self-confident, robust, uninhibited national character for which cricket ... provided a disciplined, formalised, means of expression.[85]

I have sketched the rudiments of what education and the great imperial game meant to West Indian peoples at the end of the nineteenth century, and by so doing have taken a small step towards the comprehension of the shaping of these extraordinary island civilizations in the British Empire, only half a century or so after their liberation from slavery. This was not a small achievement in these little islands, the meeting place of African, Amerindian, Asian and European civilizations: out of racial obscurantism and savagery, hybridity and enlightenment were in the making.

Chapter Seven

The Shaping of West Indies Cricket:
The Pitfalls and Challenge of Insularity, the Jamaican Case, 1900

These disparate islands under British control had very few opportunities to work together. Jamaica, for instance, was a thousand miles from the eastern Caribbean, and 1,400 miles from British Guiana, the colony of my birth. Before I went to university in Canada in 1970 I had never met a Jamaican. Although I knew Trinidad to be an island with as many Indians as Guyana, I can recall meeting no more than five or six of them before the deluge in Canada, when for the first time I discovered several thousands 'West Indians', at university and in the streets of Toronto. Yet I felt strangely drawn to these people, whatever their racial background. There was something in the history — a common thread — that drew us: slavery, indentureship, the colonial curriculum, the anti-colonial movement, the aborted effort at a West Indies Federation in the late 1950s, the University of the West Indies and recent grandiloquent expressions, apparently another initiative in regional cooperation, such as 'Caribbean economic integration' and 'the harmonization of fiscal incentives', our familiarity with the current black power iconography spiced with idioms from the received 'Afro-American' lexicon of rage. But most powerful of all the commonalities was the currency of West Indies cricket: here we really had a common language, enough heroes to accommodate all the bigger territories, all the races, too: Learie Constantine, George Headley, the three Ws, Ramadhin and Valentine, Hall and Griffith, Kanhai and Sobers. On this score we were definitely West Indians; we did not need a state. For many of us at university in Canada, an axis of pride in West Indies cricket was a vital component in our constructions of identity: our conquests of the 1960s, under Frank Worrell and Garry Sobers, were fresh and inviolable.

What we did not examine, however, was why this institution, the West Indies cricket team, had become the single most important instrument in the making of the British West Indies; how, indeed, it had encountered all the debilitating indices of insularity — island chauvinism on virtually every issue, race and colour prejudice, aggravated fissiparous tendencies at times of stress — yet it had survived. It was years before I tried to explore this phenomenon. I settled on the idea that the inter-colonial cricket championship, between the larger islands initially, was crucial in fostering contact between peoples who, in its absence, would have had virtually none: all strings radiated from individual colonies to the metropolis, mediated by the Colonial Office in London. The inter-colonial championship was unique in fostering intra-territorial links between Barbados, Trinidad and British Guiana (Demerara). However, geographical distance and the decline of Jamaica as a sugar-producing island by the last quarter of the nineteenth century, meant that while inter-territorial cricket advanced among these three territories in the 1890s — the foundation of West Indies cricket — Jamaica played virtually no part in this process. This erected a wall in the minds of the cricketing elite of the West Indies with regard to the state of cricket there, leading to the marginalization of Jamaicans in the emergence of the West Indian game in the late 1890s and beyond. The upshot was that cricket in that island stagnated. They lost all but one of their games against Lucas's English touring team in 1895; they lost all their games against Priestley's team in 1897, by massive margins; Lord Hawke's team of the same year did not even bother to visit them; and when the first West Indies team went to England in 1900, the two Jamaicans selected were virtually ignored for most of the tour.

I start from this humiliation of Jamaica on the 1900 tour of England then work back to the state of their domestic game in the 1890s, in order to demonstrate the dominance of Barbados, Demerara and Trinidad in the making of regional cricket. Special emphasis will be placed on the nexus between success at the regional level and the organization of their respective domestic game. I will conclude with an ascendant facet of Jamaican cricket, primarily the rise of the black artisan team, Lucas (similar to Fenwick in Barbados and Stingo in Trinidad), in order to adumbrate the contours of the future of West Indies cricket. The race issue necessarily will be explored to show, too, why this elevation would be retarded for some time, as merit was subordinated to white supremacist assumptions. The democratizing of West Indies cricket was attenuated because the democratizing of British West Indian societies was measured. But the fact that blacks and coloured cricketers could participate in some spheres of domestic cricket, however limited, made them work harder to lift the quality of their play. As this improved, popular response intensified: black cricketers were conspicuous heroes to their disenfranchised fans. This made the game fundamentally political: it could not be separated from the reforming impulse emerging among the submerged groups in the region, by the 1890s. In turn, it accelerated that impulse for change.

In 1900 two white Jamaicans were selected to go to England: M.M. Kerr, a batsman primarily, who had a batting average of 33.96 from 35 innings in domestic cricket in Jamaica, in 1899. He had also taken 54 wickets at 9.57. The other was G.V. Livingston, a fast medium bowler, who had taken 105 wickets at 6.86, and had a batting average of 11.2 from 26 innings.[1] These were impressive figures, but had obviously made little impression on the West Indies captain and the manager during the tour of England. M.M. Kerr played in only four of the 17 matches. He was not ill. He made a paltry total of 29 runs on the tour, with a highest score of 20 and an abysmal average of 4.83. The only other player who fared worse was his countryman, G.V. Livingston, who played in two matches and bowled a mere 18 overs, took no wicket for 65 runs and had a batting average of 3.33.[2] Not only were the Jamaicans ignored; they were made to feel that they lacked the credentials to be there. At the conclusion of the tour, Lebrun Constantine was forthright in asserting their lack of merit: 'The Jamaicans are good fellas — rather quiet; but they seem to know very little of cricket. If they are really representatives in the strict sense, of Jamaica, I say Jamaica possesses no cricketers. Our skipper [Aucher Warner], to uphold the honour of the West Indies — too late I think — wisely decided to keep them out a bit, but Livingston got somewhat angry about this and went about his own business.'[3]

In Livingston's first match, against Warwickshire, on June 18–20, 1900, he bowled 14 overs for 46 runs without taking a wicket; in his second — and final match — against Wiltshire, on July 12–14, he only bowled 4 overs for 19 runs; again, he was wicketless. He never played another game. In Kerr's four matches his scores were 3, 2, 0, 1, 20 and 3. It was clear that he, too, had not endeared himself to Aucher Warner, and this had fed allegations that both Jamaicans were 'being treated shabbily by the skipper'. The following excerpts from two letters sent to Jamaica from England, reflecting the feelings of Livingston, suggest an irreconcilable state of affairs. One was probably written by Dr Gibb, captain of the Kensington Cricket Club (Livingston's club), who was visiting England and went to several of the games:

> I went to see the West Indies on Thursday. But it rained all day, and so we saw no cricket; but we saw Livingston and Kerr. I guess they are both sick of it. I believe the captain [Aucher Warner] has a grudge against them. There is sure to be a row about it. Kerr was batting last match for 45 minutes for 3 runs. It rained all the time; so he had to be very careful. He has not been played again. I think it a shame. If a man can stay in so long he must be very good....
>
> Our Jamaican contingent have not been treated well. They have only played in one match. Kerr was sent in, when they requested him to play for a draw, and he was at the wicket three-quarters of an hour, and scored 3 [v. Worcestershire]. But, as you know, this is not his game. Livingston was put on to bowl [v. Warwickshire], and after 3 overs was taken off. After a while he was put back again. This occurred three or four times during the innings. When he was bowling, three chances were missed which would have been his wickets.[4]

Indeed, Livingston left England before the rest of the West Indies team, having virtually withdrawn from the tour. He had written to his father in Jamaica, as well as the Kensington Cricket Club, concerning what he deemed the disgusting treatment he received from Aucher Warner which forced him to abandon the tour. The *Jamaica Daily Telegraph* of July 11, reported thus:

> In both letters Mr. Livingston complained of the treatment he was then receiving from the captain of the team. Up to the time of writing ... he has only been selected to bowl in two matches [that remained unchanged]. On the last occasion he bowled for six overs, and although he was not disappointed at the result ... he was removed. In the six overs only nineteen runs were made from his bowling. Mr. Livingston, it appears, was so disgusted with the treatment that he practically dissociated himself from the team and started to visit other places in England with Dr. Gibb, the captain of the Kensington Club, who was present at several of the earlier matches. Dr. Gibb sailed from England on Wednesday, and it is presumed that Mr. Livingston sailed with him.[5]

The omen was never very auspicious for Jamaica. As early as July 1899, Trinidad's Aucher Warner, who captained the West Indies team to England in 1900, had established the basis for selection as the inter-colonial triangular tournament in Trinidad in January 1900. While he was prepared to make an exception of Mignon from Grenada and one of the Ollivierre brothers from St. Vincent, as well as so-called black professionals, such as the fast bowlers from Trinidad, Woods and Cumberbatch ('professionals' could not play in these matches), he was not very optimistic about the chances of Jamaican players, as they had never participated in the inter-colonial tournament initiated in 1893. Warner explained:

> The inter-colonial matches will be played here [Trinidad] in January [1900], when the three colonies of Trinidad, Demerara and Barbados will be represented. There will be then every opportunity of observing the play of the men taking part, and full opportunities for meeting and discussing and selecting the very best team that can be got. Of course, the representatives going over next year will make these inter-colonial matches unusually interesting, as with the exception of Mignon and Ollivierre and possibly one or two others from the other islands, all the men likely to go to England will be taking part in the matches in Trinidad.

> *Jamaica will be a somewhat negligible quantity, and practically will be out of it, as they have had no organisation such as the inter-colonial matches afford....* As for the composition of the team, speaking entirely for myself, and expressing opinions liable to be changed by future form, it seems to me Mignon of Grenada [a white medium pacer] will undoubtedly be chosen. Mignon is just about up to the first class form of amateur bowlers in England; he can bowl all day and uses his head. There can be no doubt of his selection, nor of Woods (Float) and probably of Cumberbatch and D'Ade and there are other Trinidadians whose claims must be considered. One of the Ollivierres from St. Vincent [Charles, the batsman or Richard, the pace bowler] at least will have to go, and for batting we have not got to go very far from Barbados where ... they can supply any number of good bats.... I have seen very little of Demerara cricket lately.... No doubt, however, they have five or six men fully competent to form part of the team.[6] (emphasis added)

Hon Aucher Warner, the brother of Plum and captain and Vice-President of the prestigious Queen's Park Cricket Club (QPCC) in Port of Spain, Trinidad, was probably the most authoritative person in West Indies cricket. He was also a nominated member of the Legislative Council. Six months before the inter-colonial tournament, he felt that several players from the Windward Islands could be selected for England, but he was categorical that 'Jamaica ... practically will be out of it'. It is clear that Jamaica was not prepared to participate in the crucial tournament and that fact had clouded the minds of key people like Warner and others in the QPCC against their inclusion. The Club had, in fact, written to the cricket authorities in Jamaica, Saint Lucia, St. Vincent and Grenada, to form a 'combined' team in order to participate in the inter-colonial tournament. Jamaica indicated that they would be unable to do so. This certainly had prejudiced the perception of the Trinidadians, and possibly the Barbadians and Demerarians, against the inclusion of Jamaicans in the team. For these three territories, by the end of the 1890s, this triangular tournament was sacrosanct. In fact, Barbados and Demerara (British Guiana) had first competed in a match, at the Garrison Savannah, Barbados, as early as February 15–16, 1865. Barbados won by 138 runs. In a return match, in Demerara in September 1865, Barbados lost by 2 wickets. The third match between the two colonies was played in 1871; Barbados won by 8 wickets. The contest was not renewed until 1883, and by the early 1890s Trinidad had also entered the inter-colonial tournament. A pillar of West Indies cricket was in the making and those outside of it were gravely handicapped. The standard of Jamaican cricket could not therefore be properly assessed.[7]

Jamaica's case was not enhanced by their Governor's constant meddling in their cricket, a pattern set when he was Governor of British Guiana in the late 1890s. In response to the invitation from Queen's Park Club, he had virtually subverted the popular idea that the inter-colonial matches in January 1900 be the basis for selection. His proposal was absurd and reflected the narrowness of Governor Hemming's vision, especially reprehensible in the context of an environment of change in the British West Indies. He suggested that 'each colony should select four or five of their best men, and write down a full description of each man's capabilities, and send them to a Committee at home [England], composed of Lord Hawke and others, to select the team out of these names submitted'. This was a backward step when the basis for a more rational and fairer selection process was already available through the biennial triangular tournament. Trinidad rejected it categorically: 'The form of many men prominent when Lord Hawke was here [in 1897] has changed and new stars have arisen in the cricket firmament, so that it is imperative the West Indian team shall be selected by West Indians who know the form of the men up to the time of selection.'[8]

Of course, Trinidad had the moral authority to demand local autonomy in the selection process, for they had demonstrated courage in selecting black men, including so-called professionals, to play against visiting English teams: Lucas's (1895); Lord Hawke's and Priestley's (1897). And, as seen above, Aucher Warner was anticipating an escalation of the process of reform through the selection of black men, amateurs and so-called professionals, on merit, for the 1900 tour of England. Distance alienated Jamaica from the rest; the feeling was mutual at the end of the 1890s; but the members of the established three did not make it easy for Jamaica, always sensitive to slights from smaller islands, to enter the tournament: they had advised Jamaica that she should combine with several of the small Windward Islands in order to participate in the regional tournament. It is noteworthy, too, that the 'West Indian Challenge Cup', the symbol of cricket supremacy in the region, was adorned on one side with the coat of arms of the three pioneers only: Barbados, British Guiana (Demerara) and Trinidad. This must have exacerbated Jamaica's sense of isolation.[9]

However, there was no doubt that most of the islands were desirous of participating in the West Indies tour of England, for by August 1899 Barbados, British Guiana, Jamaica, Trinidad, Saint Lucia and St. Vincent had responded positively to Lord Hawke's invitation for a 'representative' West Indies team to tour England the following year. The Lord had written in his capacity as Chairman of the Sports Committee of the West Indian Club (affiliated to the prestigious West India Committee in London), to the leading West Indian cricket clubs.[10] In fact, by September 1899 members of the West Indian Club, Lord Hawke and others, had already contributed some funds towards the tour.[11] The Lord, as seen earlier, had played against a Trinidad team that included black men, amateurs and 'professionals', in 1897. On the eve of the first West Indies tour of England he was emphatic that the West Indies team must include 'amateurs and professionals', and that 'great interest would be centred on the work of the coloured [black] players'. Lord Hawke was pleased that black players had played in some of the teams he encountered in 1897, for as he remarked to *Titbits* in August 1899, he had no time for the 'colour line'; he wished 'to play against the best teams that can be got together, whatever may be the colour of their skins'.[12]

Trinidad as a whole had made a great impression on the Lord; Plum Warner's influence would have heightened that impact; but it is arguable that the comparative inclusiveness of their cricket had elevated them in Hawke's eyes. This positive perception of Trinidadian cricket, stimulated by their selection of black players, was decisive in his resolve to get a West Indies team to tour England. It will be recalled that his team was defeated twice by All-Trinidad in 1897. It is hardly surprising, therefore, that Algernon Aspinall, Honorary Secretary of the West Indian Club, would write to W.C. Nock, Secretary of Queen's Park, in September 1899, to endorse their position with regard to the basis for selection of the team: 'That the team be chosen in Trinidad when the cup matches [Inter-colonial Tournament] are played there in January next'. This is the backdrop, then, to the following report carried by the *Port of Spain Gazette*, possibly emanating from the West Indian Club: 'We learn it is thought in England that Mr. Aucher Warner should captain the team and Mr. Nock manage it as suggested in *Cricket*.'[13]

As noted earlier, Lord Hawke (and Plum Warner) had not visited Jamaica in 1897; his rival Priestley did. So Jamaica remained not only a backwater in the eyes of West Indian cricketers, but also those who mattered in England: Lord Hawke, Plum Warner, H.N. Lubbock and Algernon Aspinall (the latter two of the West Indian Club and the West India Committee). Jamaica did not enhance their case for recognition when the Kingston Club in Jamaica, their key club representative of the upper-class white, urban mercantile community, sent a telegram to the highly respected W.C. Nock of Queen's Park, in October 1899, that they would participate in the selection of the team but would not contest the tournament in January 1900: 'Jamaicans visit to Trinidad impossible, but will send reps to select team in January.'

Meanwhile the Trinidadians continued to enhance their stature as promoters of a more inclusive, racially tolerant approach to cricket. In November and December 1899, for instance, although Queen's Park Cricket Club still engaged Woods and Cumberbatch as 'ground bowlers', so-called professionals, and did not include black players in their team, they reportedly competed against a number of black teams: Stingo, representing working class backs; a 'Float' Woods XI; and a H. Attale XI. In December the Trinidadians, on the eve of the inter-colonial games, had indicated their opposition to the continued exclusion of 'professionals', black fast bowlers like Woods and Cumberbatch, from the tournament. Trinidad had defeated all the English touring teams in the late 1890s, because of the supremacy of their black fast bowlers, but had failed to reproduce their excellence in inter-colonial matches because of the exclusion of these black players. Consequently, they were predisposed to reform more than others in the West Indies, especially all-white Barbados, which had benefited from the continued exclusion of gifted black cricketers. This, indeed, was what had captured the imagination of Lord Hawke and Plum Warner: it was precisely Trinidad's demonstrated, enlightened attitude to race that their English guests wished the composite team to reflect. The *Port of Spain Gazette* had observed: 'unless the rule excluding professionals be rescinded, there is little prospect of Trinidad obtaining premier position in future. We shall not be surprised, therefore, to learn that the Trinidad cricket authorities desire a change in their own interests and in that of the game in the West Indies'. However, the black 'amateur', Lebrun Constantine — the first black cricketer to play inter-colonial cricket — represented Trinidad, and the fact that Barbados and British Guiana (Demerara) raised no objections to his playing in January 1900, epitomized the gradualist temper in favour of reform being shaped in these British West Indian societies.[14]

As expected, Trinidad, without Woods and Cumberbatch, lost to Demerara; Barbados won the Inter-colonial Challenge Cup for the fourth time by defeating Demerara. Jamaica, as they had warned, did not participate, but in December 1899, before the start of the tournament, they announced their players in order of preference, for consideration by the selection committee scheduled to convene in Trinidad after the tournament. The joint committee of the first-division clubs, Kingston, Garrison (British soldiers stationed in the island), Kensington, Melbourne, including the irrepressible Governor Hemming, recommended six players and they 'held strongly to the view that Jamaica should have at least three representatives in the team to England'. The six nominated in order of preference were: M.M. Kerr, G.V. Livingston, F.L. Pearce, J.J. Cameron, S.C. McCutchin and C.E. Marshall. All were white 'amateurs', including Kerr of Melbourne, like Spartan in Barbados, a club of the coloured professionals primarily.

They argued thus for the first three players: 'Mr. Kerr ... [is] decidedly the finest all-round bat in the island, Mr. Livingston [of Kensington] the best bowler, and Mr. Pearce's [of Kingston] experience, steadiness and fielding entitled him ... to third place.'[15]

The day before the team for England was selected, a knowledgeable correspondent to the *Port of Spain Gazette* attributed the defeat of Trinidad by Demerara in the inter-colonial match to 'the want of judgement of the captain', Hon Aucher Warner. Moreover, he expressed reservations not only of his skills as captain, but even his merits as a player for Trinidad. While endorsing his fellow Trinidadian, W.C. Nock, as manager of the West Indies team, he was sanguine that Aucher Warner did not deserve selection in any capacity. His stance seemed not to have been actuated by any prejudice against Warner, but sprang from the generally progressive temper of Trinidadian public discourse at the end of the nineteenth century:

> I have seen a good bit of local cricket, and I am one of those who think the best should be selected, irrespective of social status or colour. The West Indies team are on a cricketing, and not a social tour: it behoves the selection committee of the Queen's Park Cricket Club to sink social prejudices, and for some of them who may be playing members to forget themselves if it be for the benefit of the island and West Indies cricket [an allusion to Aucher Warner].... Mr. Warner is admittedly a jolly good fellow, but is he good enough for the team? Can he as captain be compared with S.W. Sproston [British Guiana], Learmond [British Guiana] or G.B.Y. Cox [Harrison College and Barbados]? As a batsman is he good enough to represent Trinidad in particular and the West Indies generally?[16]

At the completion of the triangular tournament the following 15 players were selected to tour England that summer: G.B.Y. Cox, P.A. Goodman, H.A. Cole, F. Hinds, W. Bowring, captain (Barbados); S.W. Sproston, G.C. Learmond, W.J. Burton (British Guiana), W.H. Mignon (Grenada), M.M. Kerr (Jamaica), C.A. Ollivierre (St. Vincent), L.S. Constantine, L.S.A. D'Ade, 'Float' Woods (Trinidad), and the Barbadian batsman, H.B.G. Austin, who was already in England.

The reserves were: W.E. Goodman (British Guiana), brother of Percy and Clifford of the Barbadian cricket dynasty, G.V. Livingston and F.L. Pearce (Jamaica), and P.I. Cox (Barbados). There were two notable omissions: Hon Aucher Warner and Clifford Goodman (1869–1911), the Pickwick and Barbados fast bowler, the best bowler in the region until the mid-1890s, who many felt had passed his best. Apart from the Jamaicans, who had secured only one place, M.M. Kerr, most West Indians seemed to have concurred with the selection, apart from overwhelming opposition to Bowring, an Englishman recently resident in Barbados, as captain. Even in Barbados, where he played for Wanderers, they felt that his record did not merit selection even as a batsman. There was no discernible public opposition to the inclusion of five black players: Lebrun Constantine, Woods, Burton, Charles Ollivierre, and Fitz Hinds. The fast bowlers, Woods and Burton, 'ground bowlers' with QPCC and Georgetown Cricket Club (Demerara) respectively, were deemed 'professionals'. As seen in Chapter Six, Hallam Cole, a talented white Barbadian batsman from the Pickwick Club, withdrew from the tour on the pretext that he objected to the Barbadian batsman, Fitz Hinds, being deemed 'amateur'. G.B.Y. Cox withdrew for personal reasons. Cole was replaced by the 21-year-old white Barbadian batsman, P.I. Cox, while, strangely, G.B.Y. Cox, also a batsman, was replaced by the Jamaican fast bowler, G.V. Livingston. Bowring remained in the team, but Aucher Warner replaced him as captain, having been included when H.B.G. Austin left for the Boer War. However, the resolution of these problems occasioned considerable acrimony, especially the selection of the two Jamaicans, Kerr and Livingston, which underlined the fragility of early West Indies cricket.

As noted earlier, on August 17, 1899 Queen's Park Cricket Club of Trinidad wrote to the Kingston Cricket Club, suggesting that Jamaica, Saint Lucia, St. Vincent and Grenada form a combined team to play against the three regular participants, Barbados, Demerara (British Guiana) and Trinidad. QPCC were unequivocal that this tournament offered the best means of selecting the composite West Indies team to England: 'We think such a visit [to Trinidad] will afford an excellent opportunity of arriving at the merits of each island, and would materially assist the choosing of the team to send to England. Should such a visit take place the whole cost would have to be borne by the colonies participating.' The Jamaicans were also in receipt of a letter from the West Indian Club in London, dated September 5, 1899, proposing the same mechanism for selecting the team: 'That the team be chosen in Trinidad when the cup matches are played there in

January next [1900]'.[17] The Trinidadians, in a letter of September 28 to the Jamaicans, endorsed the argument of their English patrons that 'the results in January [1900] will be a good basis for the choosing of the bulk of the team'. The Barbados Cricket Committee, too, sanctioned this suggestion and on October 2, informed F.L. Pearce, captain of the Kingston Cricket Club, of their concurrence '[that] each colony be represented at Trinidad in January next to select the team.' The Georgetown Cricket Club of Demerara also made the same suggestion.[18] It was clear that the three teams in inter-colonial cricket, in conjunction with the West Indian Club (Lord Hawke and Plum Warner included), were firmly of the opinion that Jamaica should participate in the tournament. The Kingston Club convened a meeting on October 6, 1899 that included the captains of the other first division teams in Jamaica, Garrison, Kensington and Melbourne, to discuss the question. F.L. Pearce presided, but Jamaica's insularity prevailed: they feigned acceptance of the proposal while refusing to send a team.

They approved of the 'suggestion that the team should be chosen in Trinidad *during* the Inter-colonial Cup Competition in January [1900]' (emphasis added). However, they could not send a team to participate in the games: '[I]t was decided that it will not be possible to accept this invitation; but it was agreed that a representative should be sent by Jamaica to join the other colonies in the selection of the team to go to England.' That representative would be F.G.M. Lynch, who along with Governor Hemming and Lieut W.K. Tarver were delegated to select the best candidates from Jamaica purely on the basis of their performance in domestic first-division cricket.[19] Jamaica had, in fact, deftly exploited the West Indian Club's loosely phrased proposal that the team be chosen 'in Trinidad *when* the cup matches are played there in January next' (emphasis added); but they studiously ignored the circulars from Trinidad and Barbados that Jamaica's participation in the competition be the basis of selection. By not sending a team to Trinidad they were, in effect, rejecting the proposal.

It is necessary to recall that Governor Hemming was the source of the absurd proposal that a West Indies team be selected by Lord Hawke, on the basis of recommendations by the respective island Boards with regard to the merits of their best players. That the established inter-colonial competition offered the best mechanism for fair selection was not seriously contemplated in Jamaica. They would later claim that distance precluded their participation, but were passionate in advancing the case of their best players and would lobby with persistent vigour in this regard. Interestingly enough, one such indomitable advocate was himself a candidate for selection, F.L. Pearce, captain of the elite Kingston Cricket Club, and a senior civil servant in the Colonial Secretary's Office in Jamaica. It would have been impossible for him to escape Governor Hemming's ubiquitous shadow. On August 29, 1899, in a letter to Herbert Emtage, Secretary of the Barbados Cricket Committee, Pearce noted that the Governor was in favour of Plum Warner as captain of the West Indies team in England, a suggestion with which he concurred. The fact that Plum was already a key player for Middlesex, with excessive demand on his time, and already an English Test player, apparently did not cross Hemming's mind, nor Pearce's for that matter: 'I think he is undoubtedly *the* man for the post.'[20]

Pearce had also sought to introduce one of his friends and potential lobbyist for Jamaica to Emtage. He was Lieut Evan Gibbs, an Englishman who had captained Garrison to the top of the Jamaica Challenge Cup in 1899. All his teammates would have been English military personnel stationed temporarily in Jamaica, but he had played against Kingston, Kensington and Melbourne, the first-division teams. As Pearce pointed out to Emtage: 'He will be able to give you an idea of our cricket here and of the form of the men likely to be chosen here for the West Indies team.' Pearce was one of those 'likely to be chosen'. Lieut Gibbs did not get to land in Barbados but he sent a letter dated September 2, 1899 to Herbert Emtage; as expected, he made as strong a case as he could for Jamaica. He remarked that he had been informed that Jamaica may not get any representation on the West Indies team to England; moreover, that they would have no input into the selection. He considered that 'absurd'. To him, 'an outsider', it appeared 'radically unfair'. Gibbs rejected any assumption of inferiority with regard to the best Jamaican cricketers:

> I was in Jamaica for a year during which time I played a great deal of cricket and had ample opportunity to compare the best Jamaican men with English cricketers who had played in good class cricket at home ... and must say I was very favourably impressed with the Jamaicans' cricket. I understand, though, on what authority I cannot say, that Jamaican cricket is not up to the standard of the other islands, of which I had no opportunity to judge. Whether this

is the case or not, I am quite certain that Jamaica can boast of four or five individual cricketers who can compare and compare favourably with any four or five any island can produce. In fact, M. Kerr of the Melbourne Club is very nearly a first class bat; with a little coaching he certainly would be, and is quite worth his place in several good teams at home. If the West Indies can produce eleven better men than he, they must have a precious hot team and the sooner they get to work and show the people at home what they can do the better.... I can only hope that Jamaica will be treated fairly when it comes to the final selection.[21]

Apart from Kerr, Gibbs also recommended the bowler, G.V. Livingston, whom he considered 'excellent': 'very steady, always keeping a good length, and bowls with his head ... a fair bat and a good field'. He also advanced the claim of F.L. Pearce, the captain of Kingston Cricket Club, as 'a very good steady all-round man ... always a difficult ... [wicket] to get ... excellent field and useful change bowler'. In fact, Livingston was considered the best bowler in Jamaica in 1899, having secured 105 wickets at an astounding average of 6.85 runs per wicket.[22] This, however, seemed to have made little impression in Barbados, Demerara or Trinidad; it was probably seen as a reflection of the poverty of batsmanship in Jamaica, rather than a reflection of the intrinsic merit of Livingston's bowling. Yet the Jamaicans had no doubts of their merit and right to representation in a composite West Indies team, their non-participation in inter-colonial cricket notwithstanding. They anticipated that they would have at least two representatives. Pearce recognized the potential benefits of the experience: '[T]he interchange of visits with the mother-country will not only result in the improvement of the game played in the colonies, but must also prove beneficial to the interests of the islands generally in making them more widely known to the English people.'[23]

The imponderables immanent in the selection of a team representing so many geographically dispersed colonies, several of whose players were unknown to those in other territories, militated against a rigorous exploration of individual merit. Jamaica particularly had no means of establishing their claims: being a non-contestant in the regional inter-colonial cup, their competence was indeterminable. The impasse was compounded by inconsistencies in establishing the criteria for selection. Soon after participation in the tournament of

January 1900 had been advanced as the basis for selection, Jamaica's intransigence forced a retraction from Demerara and Barbados, which seemed to have rendered the tournament a white elephant, although Trinidad did not waver. This was exacerbated by the fact that so-called professionals (black players), whose inclusion the West Indian Club in London had identified as a defining feature of the tour, were still excluded from selection by these two participants in the tournament: Barbados and British Guiana (Demerara). Race still dominated West Indies cricket in 1900, as it did the politics of the region. Rather than select black men to play in the tournament, these two all-white teams preferred that the agreed mechanism for selection be rendered toothless.

On October 9, 1899 Walter M. Steele, Honorary Secretary of the Georgetown Cricket Club (GCC), in British Guiana, informed the Kingston Cricket Club in Jamaica that the inter-colonial matches in Trinidad were not going to be an adequate instrument for selecting the West Indies team. British Guiana was conceding that the inherently flawed proposition of nominating potential representatives, by respective territorial selection committees, based exclusively on domestic, rather than regional, performance, was admissible for non-participants such as Jamaica. Steele was expressing the position of the GCC:

> [O]nly Barbados, Trinidad and Demerara will be playing, while Jamaica and the Windward Islands will be absent altogether, and it is more than probable that they will have some men amongst them good enough for places in the team. Again, of the three colonies playing in January, it may happen that that some of their best men may not be able to take part for various reasons ... to say nothing of the fact that *no professionals will be playing in the cup matches, whereas a certain number will certainly be included in the team for England.* It is quite evident that all the best cricketers in the West Indies cannot be brought together in one place and on one particular occasion, for a selection to be made from them, and a good deal must therefore be left to each place, in the way of putting forward only the names of those whom they honestly consider to be up to the highest standard of West Indies cricket.[24] (emphasis added)

The committee of the Georgetown Cricket Club, apparently acting alone — the West Indies Cricket Board was not founded until 1927 —

was inadvertently undermining the regional cricket tournament as the most equitable mechanism for selecting a composite team. They were, moreover, with the support of the Barbados Cricket Committee (Trinidad, as noted above, was consistent), creating the basis for a contentious nomination procedure, at variance with the principle of selection on merit. The GCC had prepared a questionnaire to aid the nomination process, thus playing into the hands of the Jamaicans who assumed that all constituent parts of the British West Indies had a natural right to representation. The Demerarians explained: '[I]t will at least enable us to know before the meeting in January who the best men are in each place ... and will furnish some data to work upon. With this information before us, we consider that, say, nine men of the team might be chosen finally in January, the remaining five places being left over to be filled as near to the last moment as possible.' The key questions posed by the GCC were: 'the names of the four best cricketers in your island or colony and their ages'; whether they were amateur or professional; those who were 'worth their place in the team'; and the basis of their qualification.[25]

This was ridiculous, as the selection by instalment would have had no reference to the matches to be played in Trinidad; and no other matches that could have enhanced the selection process were scheduled before the departure of the West Indies team for England. Had the GCC's proposal been accepted, it would only have inflamed the feelings of Trinidadians who were deeply convinced of the superiority of the regional system. Moreover, Trinidad was showing imagination, in keeping with the vision of Lord Hawke and Plum Warner, by democratizing its cricket away from the old racial assumptions: as in politics, the principle of nomination was a vitiation of that spirit. The problem here was not merely West Indian insularity, but also the issue of the non-acceptance of 'professionals' in inter-colonial games. The latter, of course, had its origins in the old class prejudices of the higher orders of English society. But in the West Indies the concept of the professional cricketer had a hollow ring — black bowlers employed to bowl to white men at practice sessions in elite clubs, such as Wanderers, Pickwick, GCC and QPCC — and it appeared to blacks as a ruse to exclude them from the highest levels of the game. Pressured now by Lord Hawke and Plum Warner, the white West Indian 'aristocracy' had to select these humble dark folks, who had demonstrated their skills against some of the best in English cricket but were still not eligible for selection in the regional tournament. Trinidad — with Aucher Warner at the helm — had taken the initiative to erase racism in cricket; they did not have patience with the lingering obscurantism: they were not inclined to accommodate Jamaica.

Meanwhile, the Barbados Cricket Committee (BCC) had informed the Kingston Cricket Club that they concurred with Demerara. They observed: '[T]he form of the men at Trinidad should not be the criterion on which the selection should be made, but only as an opportune time for bringing our representatives together; but as far as we are concerned we shall know by then our likely men, as our [domestic] season will be practically at an end.'[26] Barbados, too, were reducing the matches in Trinidad to a charade, a sort of rendezvous, a pleasant social encounter among white players (Lebrun Constantine notwithstanding), rather than the site for a rigorous display of skill and resilience, essential for a demanding tour of England. As in Jamaica, the domestic competition, not the more demanding regional one, was now deemed paramount. West Indians had no previous encounter with the vagaries of the vastly more rigorous English game, yet the selection process was being tinkered with in a manner potentially detrimental to the team.

On October 16, 1899 Emtage of the BCC had expressed regret that Jamaica would not participate in the inter-colonial games in Trinidad, but added that he recognized 'the difficulty of working the matches in'. Jamaica had tabled their tired claim in seeking exemption — that the time required for them to travel and take part in the competition was three weeks; that was not feasible for amateurs. Apparently, unilaterally, the Barbados Cricket Committee, in a cable on October 23, had attempted to persuade Jamaica to play in Barbados, on the assumption that the tournament could be moved from Trindad. Jamaica was immovable: '[T]he same obstacles that exist in the case of the proposed visit to Trinidad are also present — i.e. that of three weeks being required for the visit.' Demerara and Barbados had already conceded Jamaica an impregnable defence, reinforcing their standard submission against participation in inter-colonial cricket, and they exploited it adroitly:

> It was thought that in view of the possibility of the best team in the island being unable to go to Barbados and also that as the form of those men who did go, as exhibited during the proposed games there, could not be taken as a criterion on which the selection

should be made, it did not appear that the object of assisting the final selection of their contingent would be secured.[27]

Whatever the persistent logistical obstacles to Jamaica's participation in regional cricket, it seemed that their case for representation in the West Indies team was enhanced by a process of nomination, rather than by one based on merit determined by the regional competition. It is also arguable that similar pressure for black and coloured participation in local, regional and West Indies cricket, so evident already in Barbados and Trinidad, did not obtain in Jamaica at the end of the nineteenth century. The admirable strides in education and politics made by black and coloured Jamaicans were not reproduced in cricket, certainly not as markedly as elsewhere. In 1898–99, for instance, in the Jamaica Challenge Cup Competition, the symbol of cricket supremacy on the island, the batting seemed palpably mediocre. C.E. Marshall, who had the best batting average, secured a rather unimpressive 29.5. The two batsmen nominated by Jamaica as candidates for the 1900 tour of England, would not have been seen, in the precocious cricket world of the eastern and southern parts of the region, as manifestations of excellence:[28]

	Matches	Innings	Total	Highest Score	Average
M.M. Kerr	6	6	177	97	29.5
F.L. Pearce	6	6	84	29 not out	16.8

It is noteworthy, too, that the Jamaica Challenge Cup Competition for 1899 was won by Garrison, a team comprising British military personnel temporarily resident in the island. It suffered from yearly 'migrations'; but the team that came second, Kingston Cricket Club, of which F.L. Pearce was captain, had obviously not mastered two of the basic skills of the game: bowling and fielding. The Club's Report for 1899 noted: 'The club is ... sadly in need of a good first class bowler.... [And its] performances in the department of fielding have been more than deplorable ... the committee would earnestly impress upon members the absolute necessity for obtaining proficiency in this important branch of the game by constant practice.'[29]

It is necessary to underline that Trinidad which had boldly pioneered the selection of black players against English touring teams since 1895, and were now hosting the 1900 tournament, continued to show no sympathy for Jamaica's case for non-participation, and probably interpreted their intransigence as a reflection of their limitations. But Trinidad were encountering some difficulty themselves in securing the approval of their candidate for manager of the team to England, W.C. Nock, secretary of the Queen's Park Cricket Club, of which Aucher Warner was captain. They were anxious to resolve the matter, and had written to the Barbadians to establish the managerial credentials of Nock:

> [We] are of [the] opinion that no better selection could be made than that of Mr. Nock. The idea of a West Indies team visiting England was proposed by him to Lord Hawke on the occasion of the former's visit to Trinidad [1897]. Lord Hawke fell in with the idea, and the project has ever since been the subject of frequent correspondence between him and Mr. Nock, and of consideration between them on the occasion of Mr. Nock's visit to England last year [1898]. When in England Mr. Nock acquired information on cricketing affairs as managed there, which will be most useful to the team.[30]

The Barbadians essentially rejected their submission while, strangely, claiming that they had 'no objection to Mr. Nock as manager'. Nock was not a player but apparently a first-rate administrator, in cricket and in the colonial civil service. But the Barbadians suggested that if a manager were to be appointed in the West Indies that person should be a player/manager. Indeed, they were disinclined to support the case for Nock: '[T]hey did not at all think it necessary to carry such an official with the team, but it should be left with the West Indian Club to appoint someone on their side [in England], as such a one would have more knowledge of what was required, and they would be the ones responsible for the financial success of the tour.' The Barbadians had a substantially narrower conception of what the Trinidadians defined as a 'very responsible and arduous post' for which they felt their man was eminently qualified.[31]

On November 4, 1899 Algernon Aspinall of the West Indian Club noted that P.F. Warner (Plum) could take 'no active part' in the matches, as he had been appointed captain of Middlesex. The Club virtually endorsed the case of the Trinidadians, for they observed that the appointment of a manager in the West Indies was 'absolutely essential to the success of the tour'.[32] The Jamaicans responded in their customary convoluted manner: 'as the West Indian Club thought it essential that a manager should accompany the team, they had no objection to the proposal'. Yet, in a bizarre note, they *'strongly urged that a gentleman fully qualified for the position should be selected in England by the West Indian Club.'*[33] (emphasis added) Mr W.C. Nock got the job only because the West Indian Club supported him. This issue and the manner of its unfolding demonstrate how bedevilling virtually every action could become as the process of selecting the first West Indies team to England meandered towards a conclusion. Insular perceptions, consciously or unconsciously, would seep into seemingly clear-cut issues, throwing up irreconcilable stances.

R.W. Bradley had replaced Lynch as Jamaica's selector in Trinidad in January 1900, to choose the team for England. As noted earlier, only one Jamaican was selected initially: M.M. Kerr, the batsman from the Melbourne Club. This was precipitately interpreted as a deliberate slight to the island. As the *Gleaner* remarked, such prejudicial treatment had eroded Jamaican interest in the tour:

> We have always felt rather dubious as to Jamaica's chance of proper representation in the West Indies cricket eleven ... and therefore we are hardly surprised at the news that only Kerr has been chosen. Mr. Bradley says that only cricketing merit was considered by the selection committee. That is very right and proper, but on cricketing merit both Livingston and Pearce deserved places in the team. Jamaican cricketers feel they have been badly treated, and we do not wonder.... We await the action of the Kingston Club. At all events, Jamaica's interest in the tour is effectively killed by such shabby treatment.[34]

The paper had nothing to say about the omission of one of the best fast bowlers in the region, the Barbados-born Trinidadian, Cumberbatch, whose performance against all the English teams that toured the West Indies in the latter half of the 1890s was acknowledged as formidable. They obviously considered Livingston better than him, although Lord Hawke and Plum Warner had offered a high assessment of Cumberbatch's demonstration of the art of fast bowling. There were already five black men in the team — that was probably sufficiently irksome for them. But on merit alone, this black bowler deserved his place before Livingston of Jamaica or Mignon of Grenada, both of whom were white. The Jamaican selector, R.W. Bradley, presented a confidential report on the selection process to the committee representing the local clubs, which deemed the inclusion of only one local cricketer a 'slight ... cast on Jamaica'. In keeping with their modus operandi of continually looking for solutions in England (Governor Hemming was again instrumental), the Jamaicans cabled Lord Hawke in London, on January 25, 1900, to protest against the exclusion of Livingston and Pearce, and threatened to withdraw from the tour:

> Jamaica strongly protests against selection of West Indian cricket team; only one selected from Jamaica, while five are chosen from Barbados [six], three from Trinidad, three from Demerara. Sir Augustus Hemming [the Governor] considers Jamaica can send three cricketers fully qualified to represent West Indies with credit and success. *Under the circumstances Jamaica will withdraw, unless more fully represented.*[35] (emphasis added)

The Barbados Cricket Committee regretted Jamaica's action, but seemed to have poured salt in their wounds by pointing out an error in their arithmetic: the Barbadians selected were 'in reality six and not five', because H.B.G. Austin, who was already in England, had to be added to the list. The *Gleaner* claimed that the Jamaican selector 'knew nothing of Mr. Austin in the team'. The *Barbados Bulletin* predicted that the Jamaican protest would prove abortive. They were neither impressed with nor even mildly sympathetic to their action:

> The despairing appeal to Lord Hawke is useless, as he cannot help the distressed Jamaicans. Their withdrawal from the tour would be a peevish display on the part of our unhappy neighbours. Sir Augustus Hemming's indignation is quite wasted on colonists in these parts who do not care a rap for his thunders, whether real or simulated for the occasion.[36]

The *Argosy* of British Guiana was even more unequivocal in its dismissal of the Jamaicans' threat. They did not deserve selection on merit; therefore, the paper welcomed their withdrawal:

It would be a good thing for the team if Jamaica did withdraw; thereby the team will be strengthened. It was of course anticipated that the Selection Committee would have an almost impossible task to perform. The intention was never that every island should be represented, but the best cricketing talent.[37]

Himself a candidate, Pearce responded publicly to the imbroglio in an article in the *Gleaner*. His contention was that the whole issue rested on whether the selection had been made on the basis of 'true cricket merit', and whether by 'a disinterested body of gentlemen'. He quickly took exception to the composition of the selection committee:

Trinidad   —   *Aucher Warner (chairman)
Demerara   —   *S.W. Sproston
Barbados   —   *W. Bowring
Grenada   —   G. de Freitas
St. Vincent —   H. Hazell
Jamaica   —   R.W. Bradley
(The Leeward Islands were not represented, neither were Dominica and Saint Lucia.)
* denotes cricketers who were candidates for selection

Sproston and Bowring were selected or helped to select themselves; the latter, inexplicably and most controversially, was appointed captain. But, as noted earlier, under mounting public pressure even in Barbados, his recently adopted home, Bowring, an Englishman, was forced to withdraw as captain although he retained his position as a player (batsman). When H.B.G Austin withdrew because he had to go to the Boer War, Hon Aucher Warner joined the side as captain. All three of the candidates for selection who were members of the committee were therefore now selected for the tour. Pearce's indignation at the composition of the team is comprehensible:

[T]he first three named gentlemen were candidates for places on the team, and however fully qualified they may have been to take their places on that team it was manifestly not according to the fitness of things that they should form part of a committee to select themselves to the exclusion of other candidates. This was the view we in Jamaica took to the matter from the beginning, and more than one gentleman fully qualified to represent Jamaica at the

conference in Trinidad [himself included], declined the invitation
to do so on the ground that he was one of the six selected as Jamaica's
best cricketers and as such was a possible candidate for a place in
the team.... As for the care bestowed on the selection we learn from
Mr. Bradley that the meeting was 'indolently' put off until the last
evening ... when it was manifestly impossible for him to have
consulted his committee by cable if he had wished to do so, and
furthermore the meeting lasted only 45 minutes, an abysmally
inadequate period for the proper consideration of the matter. *It is
evident that the so-called conference was a mere form so far as we
are concerned, and that no pains were taken to duly weigh the claims
of the cricketers nominated by Jamaica.*[38] (emphasis added)

The West Indian Club, of which Lord Hawke was a key member,
were not sympathetic to the grievance of the Jamaicans, neither did
they consider it appropriate for them to overrule the decisions of the
selection committee in the West Indies. They hoped that Jamaica would
abide by their ruling. Consequently, the joint committee of the Jamaican
cricket clubs passed a resolution accepting their one place on the team
(Kerr), but to continue to 'vigorously urge our claims to further places'.[39]

Yet the controversy persisted. R.L. Greaves, a prominent Jamaican
who had been in Barbados for two months in early 1900, claimed that
he was reliably informed there that Jamaican pace bowler, Livingston,
too, would have been selected had Bradley not insisted that Pearce be
given a place. He contended that the selectors were prepared to select
Livingston 'on the strength of his reputation', although they had never
seen him play. Greaves asserted: '[Bradley] said Mr. Pearce must come
first, and he declined to consent to Mr. Livingston being in the team if
Mr. Pearce was not.... The Committee said they would not have Mr.
Pearce, and so both were excluded.' The *Gleaner* challenged Bradley
to respond to Greaves's charges, for if the latter were accurate, he
'must share the odium for Jamaica's unfair representation'.[40] Passions
had become inflamed.

Walter Bradley rejected the charges and tried to explain the
circumstances in which he was forced to give priority to Pearce's case
above that of Livingston. He referred to his brief from the joint
committee of the Jamaican clubs in order to establish that his action
in Trinidad was totally compatible with his mandate: 'The committee
support the recommendation of the selection committee [chaired by

Governor Hemming] that the three gentlemen first named by the latter, Messrs Kerr, Livingston and Pearce should be the first chosen to represent Jamaica. If, however, you find that a sufficient number of bowlers apparently superior to Mr Livingston are selected by the Conference [in Trinidad] from other colonies, you will be at liberty ... to omit his name.'[41]

Bradley submitted that he had 'difficulty even in getting Mr. Kerr elected', and that there was no way Jamaica could procure more that one place. All the bowling places were filled; Livingston had no chance whatsoever. The last place to be filled was that of a batsman, and that was the context in which he 'strongly pressed' Pearce's case against that of the Barbadian, H.A. Coles [sic] [Hallam Cole]. The merits of the latter had already been established in the inter-colonial tournament: he got the place.[42] As was seen earlier, the racial prejudice of Cole led to his withdrawal from the team and his replacement, ironically, by G.V. Livingston, not a batsman as was the logical step.[43] The case for the selection of Archie Cumberbatch, the Barbados-born black Trinidadian fast bowler, was infinitely stronger than Livingston's, but it is highly likely that in order to win Jamaican support for Aucher Warner to succeed Bowring as captain, Trinidad acceded to Jamaica's demand for the inclusion of another of their player: Livingston was next on their list, hence the unusual replacement of Cole by Livingston.

Aucher Warner informed Bradley, the Jamaican selector, that in view of Cole's withdrawal he was recommending Livingston for the place and wished to know his view on a replacement. But he also indicated, astutely, that he was willing to defer to the wishes of the West Indian Club and make himself available for the captaincy. Warner explained why he was supporting the Jamaican bowler: '(i) He was very nearly included in the team at the original meeting [Bradley had denied this]; (ii) Jamaica has at present only one representative in the team [the Trinidadians did not think they merited more]; (iii) the selection would meet the view of the sports committee of the West Indian Club [this is doubtful]'. This version by Warner was not compatible with Bradley's account of the proceedings of the selection committee in Trinidad in January 1900. Therefore, Warner's belated conciliatory gesture towards Jamaica could only be read as a quid pro quo necessitated by his need for Jamaican support for his belated inclusion and simultaneous elevation to captaincy. He had reportedly written to Bradley: 'Mr. Bowring, in deference to the views of the sports committee of the West Indian Club, had resigned the captaincy of the team. Mr. Warner added that in compliance with the wishes of the West Indian Club, he was willing to place himself at the service of the Selection Committee. A reply by cable was asked for.' He had skilfully and expediently tied the selection of Livingston to his own case. It is hardly surprising that the response was totally in his favour: 'Jamaica approves of Warner replacing Bowring in team and as captain also and of Livingston to fill remaining vacancy.'[44]

Indeed, even the *Barbados Advocate* [February 3, 1900] was appalled both at William Bowring's (1874–1945) selection and his elevation to captaincy of the West Indies team. They alleged that he had exploited the authority given him, ignored his brief and conducted himself dishonourably by seeking to represent the West Indies:

> Mr. Bowring had at the last moment been asked to act as our delegate [in Trinidad].... It is said that Mr. Bowring received certain definite instruments from our Cricket Committee as to the men who should represent Barbados; and, needless to add, he was not one of them. There is therefore an element of grim humour in the situation, when, as a result of his mission, Mr. Bowring succeeded not only in including himself in the team, but also in obtaining the position of captain.... Bitter criticism of his action has followed, and loud demands are being made for the recision of his nomination. For ourselves, we put aside as altogether irrelevant, the question of Mr. Bowring's capacity as a cricketer. The avowed object of the tour is to demonstrate to the English public the standard of West Indian cricket, that is *native* talent. Now, Mr. Bowring is an Englishman whose connection with West Indian cricket hardly exceeds one short year. [He was born in St. John's, Newfoundland and educated in England.] He learnt his cricket in England, and played there all his life until 1898. He no more really represents West Indian cricket than do Messrs A.E. Stoddart, Sammy Woods, Leveson-Gower or any other member of the three English teams that have toured in these islands. To include him in a West Indies team got together for the above object is clearly therefore to violate first principles. To make him the captain of such a team is burlesque.[45]

The Bowring issue was resolved with the appointment of Aucher Warner as captain, although he did go to England as a member of the team. Livingston got his place, and the *Gleaner* remarked that this would strengthen the West Indies team.[46] A correspondent to the *Argosy* in British Guiana saw it differently: Livingston's belated selection was made 'not without much grumbling and dissatisfaction'. He was not impressed with the belated placating of Jamaica: 'At present the standard of the game in that island is poor but no doubt the present Governor [Hemming] who is an ardent cricketer, will endeavour to make things "look up".'[47] But the Jamaican imbroglio was not amenable to speedy resolution. It soon assumed an internecine character as M.M. Kerr, the Jamaican batsman selected, seemed to be encountering continued opposition from some elements in the Kingston Cricket Club, of which his rival for a place to England, F.L. Pearce, was captain. It is important to recall that Pearce had strong connections in government, including Governor Hemming. His club was the home of the elite of the island: they would have looked down on Melbourne and Kensington, the clubs of Kerr and Livingston respectively. The latter two were white or near-white clubs, but they did not have the status; they were not upper crust and would have admitted a few light coloureds. The failure of Kingston Cricket Club to get Frank Pearce on the team to England in 1900 would have been interpreted by the elite as a 'slight' to their status at the pinnacle of Jamaican society. Beckles has delineated the race, colour and class criteria that shaped the composition of the first division cricket clubs in Jamaica in the 1890s:

> The establishment of a network of cricket clubs had a great deal to do with the transformations taking place in West Indian social life at the end of the century. The convergence of an urban professional middle class of whites, coloureds and blacks challenged the dominance of the planter–merchant elite within the cricket culture. In Jamaica ... St. Jago, and Vere and Clarendon Clubs [both established in 1857] were represented exclusively by the planter elite, while the Kingston Club [1863] catered for their wealthy urban mercantile allies. While the Kensington Club [1878] maintained a largely upper middle class white membership, the Melbourne Club [Kerr's, founded in 1892] was the facility of the coloured professional classes who, from the slavery period, considered attractive the skin-lightening miscegenation approach to social mobility into elite white society. Not surprisingly, the Melbourne Club harboured as many anti-black attitudes as the

whites-only clubs — the colourism that separated the different shades of non-white society being as potent ideologically as the racism that divided blacks and whites. Not one black person ... could be found among the 58 members of the club in 1894. Whereas in Jamaica Melbourne used the technicality of a complex fee structure to rationalise the absence of blacks from the club, in Barbados white officials categorised blacks as professionals not suited to participate in amateur competitions.[48]

In turn, Kingston would have looked down on Melbourne because of their predominantly coloured pedigree and recent vintage — a taint that had its roots in the West Indian scheme of colour/class hierarchy — Kerr's whiteness notwithstanding. This was the context, then, in which 'Umpire', a well-known cricket correspondent to the press in Jamaica, wrote to the *Jamaica Daily Telegraph*, in May 1900, to debunk the allegation perpetrated by the local selection committee that M.M. Kerr was unwell, and therefore had to prove his fitness before embarking on the tour of England. He obviously had the benefit of confidential information provided by Kerr. The selection committee of which Governor Hemming was chairman had passed the following condescending resolution: 'That this Committee, while regretting to learn of the recent illness of Mr. M.M. Kerr, request that he will be good enough to furnish to this Committee a satisfactory medical certificate to the effect that he will be able to stand the strain of a three month's cricket tour to England, i.e, six days play and at least two nights' journey per week.'

On April 25, 1900 S.C. McCutchin, the Secretary of the Kingston Cricket Club, sent a copy of this resolution to Kerr, with 'a polite invitation "to comply with the request contained therein"'. On April 27, Kerr responded sarcastically but firmly:

> Whilst I have no personal objection to complying with the resolution of your Committee, conveyed to me in your letter of the 25th inst., before doing so I must ask that you will furnish me with the authority of your Committee to demand such a certificate as that required. I shall also be obliged, if not asking too much of you, if you would supply me with the names of the mover and seconder of the resolution, so that I might personally express to them my sincere thanks for their regret at my recent illness.[49]

'Umpire' observed that most of the members of the selection committee were members of Kingston Cricket Club who could not accept that Kerr was 'the best all-round cricketer' in Jamaica. Moreover, he argued, they were still not reconciled to the idea that their candidate, Pearce, was not in the West Indies team: '[T]he majority of the local Committee have resolved deliberately (ever since the date of Kerr's selection) to leave no stone unturned to get that young player out of the team, and to force the hands of the West India Committee in London to accept Mr. F.L. Pearce as one of Jamaica's representatives'.[50]

The correspondent contended that although Kerr had been unwell for some time, the nature of the illness, 'grippe' (influenza), which confined him to bed for a short time, should not have occasioned such 'a despicable subterfuge'. He deemed the resolution 'mean-spirited, contemptible, ungenerous and unsportsmanlike'. 'Umpire' saw this measure as a 'subterfuge' to discredit Kerr in order to enhance the chances of Pearce superseding him. He alleged also that a member of the committee had planted a paragraph in the *Gleaner* that Kerr was 'seriously ill with pneumonia', the underlying motive being the same. He then implicated Governor Hemming in the machination to supplant Kerr:

> I hear that a letter from His Excellency the Governor was read at ... [the committee meeting], suggesting that on account of the critical state of Kerr's health F.L. Pearce should be sent to represent Jamaica. *I can quite believe that Sir Augustus Hemming would be stupid enough to write such a letter.* His whole career in the West Indies has certainly not impressed me with the fact that he is a superlatively wise man.... I have no hesitation in saying that no committee of so-called gentlemen ever resorted to a meaner and more despicable subterfuge to get rid of one man for the purpose of advancing the interests of another.[51] (emphasis added)

On May 12, 1900 Kerr had silenced his critics by scoring 81 not out in a match between his club, Melbourne, and Lucas Cricket Club, a rising team of artisan blacks. The *Jamaica Daily Telegraph*, which had never given credence to rumours of the 'critical' state of his health, responded with biting sarcasm to his triumphal return to cricket: 'It is quite evident from this that his health is in a rather precarious condition, and that it is highly necessary that he should produce a medical certificate to allay the brotherly anxiety entertained regarding

him by some members of the Kingston Cricket Club.'⁵² The *Daily
Chronicle* of British Guiana suggested that the campaign to cast doubt
on the fitness of Kerr was fed by the selection committee of Jamaica of
which Governor Hemming was chairman; they had allegedly received
support from the *Gleaner*. The latter, after it was clear that Kerr would
make the tour, still sought to rationalize the original demand for a
medical certificate: 'The Selection Committee has been roundly abused
for asking Mr. Kerr for a medical certificate as to his fitness to stand
the ardours of the English cricket tour, for which he must leave Jamaica
on 22nd inst. [May]. In view of Mr. Kerr's indifferent health for some
time past and his recent attack of influenza there was some justification
for the request; because if Mr. Kerr were not likely to be strong enough
for the strain of the tour, steps would have to be taken early to appoint
his successor. As it turns out Mr. Kerr is almost certain to go.'⁵³

Kerr did go with Livingston to England, but the omen was not good;
it would not be an auspicious tour for the two Jamaicans. If anything,
the fissiparous tendencies permeating the selection of the first West
Indies team to England, in 1900, were exacerbated. As noted earlier,
Lebrun Constantine had seen no merits in the cricket of Kerr and
Livingston, and was categorical in saying so at the end of the tour. Tom
Burton, the Barbadian-born fast bowler from British Guiana, also shared
similar sentiments about the two Jamaican tourists, stating that they
were not treated unfairly. In an interview with the *Daily Chronicle* on
September 5, 1900 he, too, was unflattering in his impressions of the
Jamaicans. The *Daily Gleaner* reproduced Burton's and Constantine's
remarks in the same issue. Burton observed: 'The G.C.C. [Georgetown
Cricket Club] could turn out half-a-dozen better bowlers and batsmen
than either Livingston or Kerr, and so could Barbados or Trinidad, I feel
sure. If they had been played oftener they might have come off some
day, but there were better and surer men for the places.'⁵⁴

It was totally admirable of M.M. Kerr (a white man) that he made
no excuses for his failure in England, was most generous in assessing
the performance of his black team mates, while making a strong case
for Jamaica to participate in the inter-colonial tournament with their
best players, including blacks, if they were to reach the level attained
by the southern colonies: Barbados, Trinidad and Demerara (British
Guiana). Strangely, he was not quoted as saying anything about his
white compatriot, Livingston, who had abandoned the tour. It is

arguable that the treatment he had received from his elite enemies in Jamaica (including the Governor) shaped his magnanimity, but it is even more plausible that those attitudes were already lodged in him and, like his remarkable colleague on the tour, George Learmond, had influenced his decision to join a predominantly coloured club, rather than Kingston or Kensington. The following are excerpts from his long interview with the *Daily Gleaner* [DG]:

DG: What are your impressions of your fellow players, Mr. Kerr?

KERR: The best man of the team, I think, was undoubtedly [Charles] Ollivierre, the black man from St. Vincent. He is a unique bat. [Percy] Cox was very good, too, and so was Constantine, another black player from Trinidad. I need hardly say that the blacks were the favourite of the British public. I think most of them suspected us all to be black. The people we met had queer ideas about the West Indies and used to ask us some very quaint questions sometimes. But to return to the team. I think Burton was the best bowler we had. He played havoc with the Norfolk wickets when they were all bowled down for 33. Woods is a good medium-fast bowler, but rather erratic. Undoubtedly we were badly off for bowlers. Burton and Woods had to do practically the whole work throughout the tour. It would have been a good thing for us to have had a good slow bowler as well, so that we could have taken more advantage of the wet wickets....

DG: Some people here [Jamaica] think you were badly treated, Mr. Kerr.

KERR: Yes, I know that. I saw a letter in the *Gleaner* while I was in England, in which the writer recorded that Livingston and myself hadn't come off, and he hope we wouldn't make any excuses when we got home. Well, I've got no complaints or excuses to make. As I say, I had a good time and enjoyed myself. I was played in four matches, and it is quite true that I did not come off. They had a right to play other men whom they thought better. I have only this to say — that I never played on a decent wicket. Three of them were wet, and the fourth, at Stowe [against Wiltshire], was very bumpy. The English bowlers have a wonderful knack of taking advantage of a damp wicket. They were much better than we were in that respect.... [We were most hospitably treated everywhere we went, and I had a very good time, thoroughly enjoying the tour.]

DG: Which of the English players struck your attention most forcibly, Mr. Kerr?

KERR: Jessop [of Gloucestershire]. He is a wonderful hitter. He can always place the ball in the exact spot he wishes. His accuracy is marvellous, and so is the vigour he puts into his strokes.... Gunn [of Nottinghamshire] worked mischief among us with his [underhand] lobs. We didn't understand them at all. Naturally I was very much interested in meeting Dr. Grace. He is getting old for cricket [aged 52 in 1900] and I suppose he does not play up to his old form, but he is still a fine bat and his experience tells for a lot.

DG: What do the men from the other colonies think about Jamaican cricket?

KERR: They say we don't play cricket enough here; that we are not sufficiently keen on the game; and they want to know why we do not take part in the inter-colonial matches. I am very strongly of opinion that we ought to arrange to do so without delay, before Lord Hawke brings his team out [in 1902; it did not materialize]. Most of the other colonies seem to think they are better than Jamaica in cricket, but I should not like to say that. There were several men in the team who, in my judgment, were no better than many Jamaican players I know. *If we take part in the inter-colonial matches, I don't think we shall come out so badly, providing an eleven really represents the whole of Jamaica.* I quite agree with the *Gleaner* that the committee to arrange matters in connection with Lord Hawke's visit should represent not only all the Kingston clubs, but the leading country clubs as well.... There is another point I would like to make. *We ought to search for new talent in Jamaica as vigorously as they do in the other colonies, and we ought to encourage black players as they do. As you know, the men who came off best on the tour were black men. There are, I believe, plenty of black cricketers in Jamaica who would do credit to the island if they were only given a decent chance.*[55] (emphasis added)

There was obviously much to what Kerr was saying about the state of Jamaican cricket and its isolation from the West Indian mainstream. The day his interview appeared, a correspondent to the *Gleaner* expressed similar views on the matter: 'If it were possible I should like to see a combined team from the sister colonies visit us. We would be then in a position to judge our form with theirs. We, in Jamaica, do not receive the support from the public as the others do.'[56] It is very likely that the continued exclusion of black Jamaican cricketers at the club, national and international levels was at the heart of a discernible lack of patriotism in the island's cricket. However, as Brian Moore and Michele Johnson argue, in spite of the domination of Jamaican cricket by whites, coloureds and blacks were already playing the game, infusing it with their distinct cultural codes, however unpalatable to the ruling elites. By 1892 'well-to-do coloureds' had created the Melbourne Cricket Club but, like Spartan, the coloured club in Barbados (founded in 1893), they were no less punctilious in their resolve to exclude black men: 'those who were less well-off and of darker hue'. The prejudice of whites and coloureds was, in fact, instrumental in the rise of Lucas Cricket Club, a team of 'black artisans in Kingston', towards the end of the 1890s. It is noteworthy that the team was named after the captain of the first English team in the West Indies, in 1895,[57] a vindication of the impact of the early English touring teams with their broader attitudes towards non-white cricketers. Lucas Club went on to win the Senior Cup cricket in 1904, 1905, 1906, 1911, 1913, 1914 and 1915: seven times in 11 years (no games were played in 1907, the year of the earthquake).[58] Moore and Johnson are brilliant in their assessment of the impact, within and beyond the boundary, of the play of those of 'darker hue':

> Lucas's dominance in the first two decades of the [twentieth] century astounded the elites [white and coloured] and shattered the racial myth of black inferiority/white superiority upon which Jamaican society had been premised since the days of slavery. They proved that if literally given a level playing field, they could be better at the imperial game than those who had brought it, and they introduced a new aggressive attitude and determination to win that had been theretofore absent. There could be no pretence at forging camaraderie with the elites because the latter refused to socialise off the field with members of the Lucas team.... The 'gentleman's' world of cricket was being turned on its head. It was being proletarianised *and* further creolised and, not surprisingly, the officers of His Majesty's forces withdrew from Senior Cup Competition in 1909; while Melbourne, their duskier companions at arms [coloureds], ever so sensitive of their undesired social proximity to their [black] Lucas 'cousins', threatened to follow.[59]

They explore the political implications of Lucas's growing confidence:

> A deeper reason might have been that the representatives of colonial authority and elitism could not allow the 'benighted' people over whom they ruled to beat them at the quintessentially imperial sport.... The rise of Lucas was symbolic of a process of democratisation which constituted a challenge to the existing social order.... This challenge was just beginning in Jamaican cricket. Blacks no longer acquiesced in their relegation to the sidelines, or behind fences; they were at centre stage and their supporters made quite sure that everyone knew that. However, that they chose the imperial game *par excellence* to mount their challenge to the *status quo* was itself laden with inherent contradiction. For while *demanding* recognition and respectability within the colonial order, they were required to adopt some of its cultural forms, symbols and values.... But at the same time, they brought to it the values and behaviour of the streets and yards of the towns and rural villages ... which threatened to subvert the Victorian code of ethics in which cricket was enveloped.... [L]ike so many other aspects of life and culture in Jamaica, [cricket] reflected two different systems of ethics — one modelled on an imported Victorian culture, the other based on an indigenous Jamaican cultural fabric. But while providing a field of contestation between the two, cricket also facilitated their commingling which gradually obfuscated the boundaries that differentiated them.[60]

Jamaica would remain for a while yet at the periphery of West Indies cricket, although its influence as a pioneer in the educational and political development of black West Indians would remain strong. At the level of ideas about black identity, political evolution and approaches to colonial development, Jamaica would occupy a prominent place, and the daily newspapers in the British West Indies were punctilious in their coverage of inter-colonial discourses that helped to sustain intellectual curiosity among the rising non-white middle classes. Jamaica, though distant, would ever impinge on the consciousness of those British islands to the south. Intellectually and psychologically she helped to shape them.

This world created 'Float' Woods, the Constantines (Lebrun and Learie), George Headley, The Three W's, Garfield Sobers, the great fast bowlers — the whole tradition of West Indies cricket; but it also produced intellectual brilliance: Samuel Jackson Prescod, C.L.R. James, Dr Eric Williams, V.S. Naipaul (Nobel laureate in literature), Professor Arthur Lewis (Nobel laureate in economics), Derek Walcott (Nobel laureate in literature), Professor Elsa Goveia, Dr Walter Rodney and many more. The clash of insularities was often frustrating, but these British West Indian islands, though small and not gifted with natural resources, have shaped their own universe of achievement, creating a benchmark of excellence in cricket and education — a world in which, with the singular exception of Guyana, the politics of gradual reform and tolerance has taken root, establishing a reputation for democratic continuity in post-colonial governance. In this age of rampant nationalism, religious, tribal and racial bigotry, and recurring genocide, it is worthwhile to ponder the example of these little islands in the Caribbean Sea: the legacy of their muscular learning.

In March 1897, during Lord Hawke's tour of British Guiana, the *Daily Chronicle* reflected on the merits of this muscular learning, at a time when some were concerned that cricket had become such an obsession that intellectual attainments would be jeopardized. The paper sought to reassure them that athletic excellence is compatible with the highest manifestations of intellect; indeed, often, they are inseparable:

> To those who argue that indulgence in manly sport is incompatible with a high standard of intellectual superiority, it is only necessary to point out the example of the ancient Greeks. Unrivalled for their skill and prowess in feats of physical strength, they stood at the same time from an intellectual eminence which has not since been reached. The orator who one day might be heard holding a highly educated and cultivated audience enthralled beneath the spell of his eloquence in the Temple of Minerva might the next day be seen competing for the garland of the strong in the Grove of Olympia. Even that great philosopher himself [Plato] ... recognised how close is the connection between the physical and the mental parts of man's nature, and how very necessary it is that the body should not be neglected if a just equilibrium is to be maintained between both. For these reasons we think the tendency that our people show to engage in manly sport should not be discouraged. The qualities of generous emulation, energy, ambition, and the desire to excel, will prove useful in spheres other than the cricket field.[61]

Chapter Eight

A Temperament for Gradualism in the British West Indies:
The Intellectual and the Cricketer

I return to those immortal lines from James which I quoted at the beginning of Chapter Two: 'By standing on a chair a small boy of six could watch practice every afternoon and matches on Saturdays.... From the chair also he could mount on to the window-sill and so stretch a groping hand for the books on the top of the wardrobe.'[1] The chair, a seat of learning, so to speak, offering a 'window' unto cricket — and beyond the boundary — was planted in the British West Indies by the non-conformist missionaries and public school/Oxbridge headmasters, who worked assiduously to inculcate the public school code — muscular learning — into the minds of white West Indian boys, like Plum Warner; but, gradually, it percolated to a minority of coloured and black boys, too. It left its imprint here more than anywhere in the Empire.

By the late 1890s, aspects of the code would also reach a minority of girls. Yet this process could never be absorbed as seamlessly as James suggests. The mere fact of their being shaped by it, within the parameters of the creolization process, speaks to a necessary hybridity with possibilities for distortion of the received learning. This, however, was potentially enriching. The adapted code could be marshalled, as I have argued, to meet the vagaries of identity constructs of the diverse groups that shaped these British West Indian societies. The common denominator of education and cricket civilized all peoples in these British colonies that were made by slavery and indentureship. The latter were a salutary reminder not only to Africans but also some Europeans, Madeiran Portuguese, indentured Africans imported after slavery, Indians and Chinese that a history of bonded labour claim virtually all who would seek to extricate themselves from the ancestral taint of slavery. But so powerful a symbol of belonging is the latter, that it now seems necessary for all West Indian peoples to seek to establish a strand of 'suffering' as a criterion of belonging. 'All are involved; all are consumed', as Martin Carter poses the question of engagement. Cricket, however, would confer on those who could not locate themselves within the narratives of oppression, a surrogate text that validates the endeavour to belong.

Cricket goes to the roots that have shaped these former British islands. Black people have used the game to speak to their own identity, to advance their political and social agendas. But the game has carried those burdens only because, as C.L.R. James observes with his usual magnanimity, West Indies cricket is an edifice painstakingly built up by all its peoples and enhanced through its links with the English game. He explored the problem of the mastery of the greatest West Indian cricketer, the black Barbadian, Sir Garfield Sobers (born 1936), in order to comprehend the process. It is by no means the full story, but the rudiments and complexity of a comprehensive exploration are discernible.

James argues that one has to grasp the source of the original inspiration, the elite schools and their Oxbridge masters imbued with their Victorian code of muscular learning: the classics and cricket, as propagated by the indefatigable Horace Deighton and Somers-Cocks (Harrison College, Barbados), and William Burslem (at his own Queen's Royal College, Trinidad). The peripatetic Bajan artisan and schoolteacher must also be fitted into this complex tapestry, as well as the energizing English Leagues. James is saying that the great West Indies cricketer is at the heart of West Indian history, shaped by the vicissitudes of that process, inevitably a political person in the way the hero is made by the crowd to play representative roles that he may never fully comprehend. For the submerged peoples of the region, that role is constructed of elements chipped out of the long struggle for the recovery of West Indian humanity and individuality — in the context of slavery and its aftermath — and the later nationalist project: an alloy of sharp individuality tempered by the hopes and aspirations of West Indian peoples. The great cricketer was saddled with the burden of history. In 1967 Sobers captained a World XI at Lord's; James had no doubts of his 'competence or his moral right to the distinguished position'; but it stirred him to explore the source of the great man's gifts, its pedigree:

> I thought of cricket and the history of the West Indies. I cannot
> think seriously of Garfield Sobers without thinking of Clifford
> Goodman [1869-1911], Percy Goodman [1874–1935], H.B.G.

Austin [1877–1943] (always H.B.G. Austin), Bertie Harragin and others [all white West Indians].... They systematically built up the game, played inter-island matches, invited English teams to the West Indies year after year, went to England twice before World War I [1900 and 1906]. I remember too the populace of Trinidad and Tobago subscribing a fund on the spot so that 'Old Cons' [Lebrun Constantine] would not miss the trip to England [1906; not 1900 as James states]; and that prodigious [black] St. Vincent family of the Ollivierres [Charles toured England in 1900; Richard in 1906]. The mercantile planter class led this unmercantile social activity and very rapidly they themselves produced the originator of West Indian batting, George Challenor [1888–1947; a white Barbadian]. In 1906 he was a boy of eighteen and made the trip to England. He saw and played with the greatest cricketers England has ever known, the men of the Golden Age. Challenor returned to set a standard and pattern for West Indian batting from which at times it may have deviated, but which it has never lost.[2]

James then examines the rise of the black cricketer, although he does not go back to the source, the slave plantation, as I do in Chaper One:

The local masses of the population, Sobers's ancestors and mine, at first looked on; they knew nothing about the game. Then they began to bowl at the nets, producing at that stage fine fast bowlers. Here more than anywhere else all the different classes of the population learnt to have an interest in common. The result of that consummation is Garfield Sobers. There is embodied in him the whole history of the British West Indies... [But] Sobers, like the other great cricketers of the present-day West Indies, could develop his various gifts and bring them to maturity only because the leagues in England offered them the opportunity to master English conditions, the most varied and exacting in the world. Without that financial backing, and the opportunity systematically to consolidate potential, to iron out creases, to venture forth on the sea of experiment, there would be another fine West Indian cricketer but not Garfield the ubiquitous.... The roots and the ground he now covers ... go far down into our origins, the origins of all who share in the privileges and responsibilities of all who constitute the British version of Western civilisation.[3]

James had the privilege, day after day, to observe, scrutinize and write imaginatively about the mastery of many West Indian players;

to read and criticize many West Indian writers and scholars; indeed, to meet with and talk to them, about their work and the source of their creative energy. This was not the case with many of the humble admirers of West Indian cricketers, intellectuals and writers. In these poor societies, visual images, apart from pictures in newspapers, were sparse until recently; most people could not afford to travel to Georgetown or Kingston to see a Test match — the exploits of their heroes had to be imagined. James understood this too well and, as if to assuage the frustration of the image-bereft masses in the West Indies, he located an eloquent parallel — a resonant tale of hope embodied by the great Australian batsman, Sir Don Bradman, and one of his countrymen, Philip Lindsay (later a prolific novelist), a self-proclaimed disciple, languishing in poverty in London during the hard times of the 1930s, too poor to go to Lord's or the Oval. But he was sustained and pulled back from utter despair by the excellence of his hero, as he reduced English Test bowlers to mediocrity:

> Most of us need an ideal ... and to me Don Bradman became that symbol of achievement, of mastery over fate, all the more powerful because it was impossible for me, a cricketing rabbit, to compare myself with him.... That during those months of misery I did not lose faith in myself and abandon all hopes of success by writing I must thank Don Bradman. That I never made the final desperate choice between hunger and ambition and pawned my typewriter, as often the devil gnawing in my empty belly prompted me to pawn it, I must thank Don Bradman. Not entirely of course. A man's resolutions are made of many promptings and dreams of hopes, but Bradman helped to keep my faith alight, and this association of myself and him as nearly of an age and of the same country made me feel somehow that I must not let him down as he had not let me down. Yes, sport can do that to a young man, to one of those despised inactive watchers so often attacked as being bone-less sitters on their bottoms: it can stiffen the backbone and exalt the heart.[4]

James recognized a parallel in the way black Trinidadians were sustained by the elegance of Edwin St. Hill's batting in the late 1920s. Although a failure at Test level, he was mesmeric when he played for Shannon (formerly Victoria), the black lower-middle class club of the redoubtable Constantines. James, as usual, caught the larger picture beyond the boundary: 'I know that to tens of thousands of coloured [black] Trinidadians the unquestioned glory of St. Hill's batting conveyed the sensation that he was one of us, performing *in excelsis* in a sphere where competition was open. It was a demonstration that atoned for a pervading humiliation, and nourished pride and hope.'⁵ There is poignancy to this remark that would have resonated throughout the British West Indies, from the 'logies' of Indian workers in British Guiana absorbing tales of Prince Ranjitsinhji's conquests in England before the First World War to Jamaican immigrant workers in Panama and Costa Rica voraciously absorbing every trickle of news of George Headley's unfailing mastery in the 1930s, whoever the opponent, whatever the state of the pitch.

James was a courageous thinker. Even when one disagrees with him profoundly, immured as he could be by the dogma of the universality of the class struggle and, consequently, a tendency to misread the political instincts of British West Indians, one is impressed by his bold departures that stimulate broader, innovative ways of looking. It was as if his irrepressible intellectual vigour would eventually shoot through the overburden of moribund Marxist theology. This wider, human dimension was marked by a magnanimity and total freedom from the tired dogmas. It was reflected best and most consistently when he sought to relate to diverse strands in his education, especially what he owed to the Western intellectual tradition in all its magnificence and its capacity to reach the loftiest aspirations of the human imagination. Paradoxically, if there was one West Indian for whom the epithet 'Renaissance man' was unreservedly applicable, he was that man. At his best, he took a subtlety of perception, breadth of imagination and astoundingly wide learning — much of it unencumbered by the strictures of academia — both to his cricket and his eclectic intellectual endeavours. Therefore what he had to say of his great work that encompassed both of these elevating passions, *Beyond a Boundary*, must stand at the core of his interpretation of the best of the British West Indian tradition. In a letter in 1963 to his fellow Trinidadian writer and graduate from his alma mater, Queen's Royal College, Nobel laureate V.S. Naipaul (born 1932), he wrote:

> The book is West Indian through and through, particularly in the early chapters on my family, my education and the portraits of West Indian cricketers of the previous generation, some of them unknown. But the book is very British. Not only the language but on page after

page the (often unconscious) literary references, the turn of phrase, the mental and moral outlook. This is what we are. And we shall never know ourselves until we recognise that fully and freely and without strain.... I believe that, originating as we are within the British structure, but living under such different social conditions, we have a lot to say about the British civilisation itself which we see more sharply than they themselves. I believe I have made that clear in the treatment of W.G. Grace. [But James is categorical that] ... it is my West Indian origins that gave me the premises and impetus, though it "was in England and in English life and history that I was able to trace them down to test them" [Preface].[6]

Indeed, James had no doubt that West Indians were very well equipped for 'independent growth'. And in his Preface to *Beyond a Boundary* James observes: 'To establish his own identity, Caliban, after three centuries, must himself pioneer into regions Caesar never knew.' West Indians were not 'mimic men'; and in the great tradition of West Indies cricket and their solid grounding in the English intellectual tradition, he saw possibilities for the emergence of a genuine West Indian civilization. It is that amalgam of West Indian and English codes ('all the inhabitants of the British West Indian territories are expatriates', he says), inculcated by the elite schools, that gave these islands the intellectual security to adapt British institutions, which would give them continuity and security as independent states. British civilization was more than skin deep here. James was fond of celebrating this; even the Marxist meanderings could not divert him from the source of his truly magnificent intellect:

At these schools for many years there were some two hundred boys, children of Englishmen and local whites, many sons of brown-skinned middle class, Chinese, Indians, and black boys, often poor who had won some of the very few scholarships to these schools, and others, not too many, whose parents could afford it. These Oxford and Cambridge men taught us Latin and Greek, mathematics and English literature, but also taught, rather diffused, what I can only call the British public-school code. The success of the code inside the classrooms was uncertain. In the playing-fields, especially the cricket field, it triumphed. Very rapidly we learned to 'play with the team', which meant subordinating your personal inclinations and even interests to the good of the whole. We kept a 'stiff upper lip' in that we did not complain about ill fortune. We did not denounce failure but 'well tried' or 'hard luck' came easily to our lips. We were generous to opponents and congratulated them on victories, even when we knew they did not deserve them.[7]

James elaborates:

We absorbed the same discipline through innumerable boys' books: books by G.A. Henty, the 'Mike' stories by P.G. Wodehouse, school magazines like *The Captain*. Generation after generation of boys of the middle class went through this training and experience, and took it out into the West Indian world with them, the world of the games they continued to play and the world outside. The masses of the people paid little attention to this code but they knew it, and one condition of rising to a higher status in life was obedience or at least obeisance to it.... [C]ricket was a field where the social passions of the colonials, suppressed politically, found vigorous if diluted expression. On the cricket field all men, whatever their colour or status, were theoretically equal. Clubs of the lower middle class or black men [like the Constantines' Shannon], who achieved international status were passionately supported by the mass of the population, and in return this section seemed to play with an energy and fire which indicated that they were moved by the sense of being representative which circumstances had thrust upon them.... Individual players of the lower class, often black men became popular national heroes in whom the masses of the people took great pride. Yet it is doubtful if any player was more nationally admired and more of a popular idol than the late George Challenor, a white Barbadian and a member of the most exclusive of Barbadian clubs [Wanderers].[8]

James did not or could not acknowledge that what he admired so passionately in his colonial education was, indeed, the intellectual provenance of the British West Indian political temperament: the gradualist appeal of Olivier rather than the revolutionary fulminations of Lenin, as James would have preferred. This grounding in the British intellectual tradition, in the absence of any coherent parallel indigenous one, rendered these colonies unique. That was why Jamaicans would respond to the Fabian socialism of Norman Manley and not the Marxist disquisitions of Richard Hart or the Hill brothers;

why, too, Trinidadians would respond to the capitalist-oriented, liberal constitutional politics of Eric Williams and reject James's Workers' and Farmers' Party and his brand of Marxism: he lost his deposit in 1966, in the only elections he contested in Trinidad. British West Indian gradualism was born when the enslaved African first bowled to a white batsman, and it had political foundations as early as the 1850s, in the tradition of parliamentary government. Gordon K. Lewis remarks that the political legacy of the British in the West Indies was 'highly Roman', but he rejects the tendency to magnify this at the expense of the tradition of honouring civil liberties evolved under their rule:

> The Fabian Colonial Bureau helped to counterbalance ... [the ignorance of the Imperial administration on colonial issues], publishing, as it did, a multitude of critical books and pamphlets on the colonial problem, while books like those of Olivier [*Jamaica: The Blessed Island*], Macmillan [*Warning from the West Indies*] and Simey [*Welfare and Planning in the West Indies*] enabled many [British] West Indians to see their problems afresh.... On its positive side ... [the colonial administration] was incorruptible, highly motivated, passionately conscious of duty and conduct. It was determinedly constitutionalist, although the Crown Colony system placed severe strains upon constitutionalism. It cared for civil liberties.... It was not even afraid to declare its own faults and its West Indian critics have perhaps not sufficiently appreciated the fact that most of the ammunition they have used in their indictment of colonialism have come from the voluminous Blue Books or innumerable official reports.... It is the weakness of books like Dr. Williams's *History of the People of Trinidad and Tobago* [1962] that, conceived more in a spirit of hatred rather than of anger, they consistently underestimate the contribution, however minor, of the best of the British spirit to West Indian life.... The British, in all conscience, were colonialists. But it is at once historically inaccurate and psychologically unconvincing to write about them as if they were devils in human form.[9]

This is the foundation of today's political stability engendered by the general sanctity of the electoral process. It is necessary, therefore, to recall that whites were a minority in all of the British islands; and in a place like the Leeward Island of Montserrat (32 square miles), for example, they were very few, indeed. Yet it was a demonstration of an imaginativeness and flexibility unique to the British West Indies, paradoxically, that in January 1838, the year slavery was abolished, Edward Dacre Baynes, a white man, a stipendiary magistrate in Jamaica, founded a newspaper called *The West Indian*, for the following purpose: 'to spread useful knowledge, and to show that distinctions of race were not fundamental to human society; and also to help the Negroes to understand their duties and responsibilities.' Twenty years after the end of slavery, Baynes was the 'President' of Montserrat, and in an address to the Assembly on October 31, 1858 made the following extraordinary remarks:

> I see with much gratification, in the result of the late general election, an irrefragable proof of equality, not only by right, but of actual participation in power on the part of that class who for so many years were denied the possession of all political privileges. The present Assembly is composed of six white and the same number of coloured gentlemen, an unerring sign that the age of prejudice has passed away, and that the day is near at hand when all distinction of colour between members of the human family will cease to exist; black and white will be no more remarked in our political and social relations than in the accidental differences of complexion between Europeans at the present day — a day when it shall be fully recognised that Virtue, Talent and Education only should open the path of public honours and private respectability.[10]

Baynes was certainly too optimistic about the eradication of prejudice. But whatever the limitations of the constitutional role of those elected 'coloured gentlemen', it was a revolutionary step even if 'coloured' here meant mixed race. It was a profound signal that in these little islands non-white people could begin to educate and elevate themselves to positions of authority in colonial society. It was a big step in the dismantling of the ancient notion that Africans or people of African descent were naturally incapable of self-government. It would feed the idea that they were, indeed, capable of shaping their environment. This was a world to be remade and they had a part to play in it. Effort was worthwhile: 'virtue, talent and education' were worth striving for. Cricket and education were at the core of this enterprise. What do they know of cricket who only cricket know? James's dictum always to look beyond the boundary is inviolable in comprehending the history of the British West Indies.

As the West Indies team were preparing for the tour of England in early 1900, a near-white Jamaican writer, H.G. deLisser, published an important article captioned 'The White Man in the Tropics', in *New Century Review*. It was a timely piece as coloured and black middle-class leaders in the British West Indies pursued a greater measure of representative government. As noted earlier, the Pan-African Conference in London in the summer of 1900 encapsulated that growing African awareness of the necessity for assuming greater responsibility for their welfare. DeLisser's contention, largely an extension of Benjamin Kidd's and Joseph Chamberlain's theses, that the guiding hand of Europeans was indispensable for the moral, intellectual and political elevation of 'uncivilised races', was, in fact, being challenged before his very eyes as non-white West Indians gradually earned competence in a range of spheres: education, cricket, administration and politics. He argued thus:

> [A]lthough the white man cannot be acclimatised in the tropics, and cannot work there as a labourer, yet — provided he be kept closely in touch with the moral and ethical principles of the environment which has produced him, and providing there is a constant infusion of new blood from Europe, he may live successfully in the tropics for generations.... There are still almost unbounded fields for energy and enterprise in the tropics. And there is something infinitely more worthy to strive for than mere material gain. *That is the setting of a high example before uncivilised races, and the helping them towards the highest plane of civilisation of which they are capable.*[11] (emphasis added)

DeLisser had sought to demonstrate the rightness of his argument by citing the dichotomy between the degenerate white labourer in Barbados and the prosperous, energetic advancement of the planter-mercantile elite in that island. He observes that the latter 'have generally inter-married with English families, and so ... infused new blood into their own families. They have also kept up a close connection with the mother country. Their children have generally been educated in England, and so by these means they ... have always preserved themselves against degeneration'. The *Daily Chronicle* of British Guiana had endorsed these propositions, arguing that 'social relapse' was impossible for the higher class of whites in the region, and that this bode well for the future of 'the Negroes in these latitudes', for 'the vitalising influence' would not be eliminated.[12]

Implicit in this argument was the indispensability of imperial trusteeship embodied in Crown Colony Government: the subordination of the representative principle to the supposedly disinterested official and nominated element in colonial governance. This, of course, was subversive of the initiatives for the devolution of authority to local people so ardently canvassed in the 1890s. It is significant, therefore, that the *Jamaica Daily Telegraph* had challenged the assertions of DeLisser and Joseph Chamberlain with regard to the necessity for indefinite 'white superintendence' of tropical peoples. They were convinced that a democratic culture was already being forged in Jamaica and, therefore, were disinclined to acquiesce in the imperial definition that left the 'political destiny of a tropical population ... to be determined and directed by periodic relays of nomadic officials.' The paper was sanguine that with the emergence of an educated middle class drawn from all races, the democratic temper was irrepressible; moreover, that the new century would see the expansion of elected parliamentary government:

> Jamaica, up till 1866, possessed a purely representative form of government, and Jamaica has at this present [time], a mixed tropical population united in a sentiment of devoted loyalty and inspired with the love of free institutions as well as the memory of proud historic traditions. Young Jamaicans — no matter to what class and colour they may belong — meet on the same educational platform and hold their own — in open competition with young men and women from all parts of the Empire. It can be truly said of the tropical population of Jamaica that in feeling, disposition, predilection and prejudice, they are as thoroughly English as the inhabitants of Norfolk or Aberdeenshire [sic]. We have during the present session been having in our local Legislature a significant object lesson which cannot fail to have convinced the more intelligent of Mr. Chamberlain's 'white superintendents' that it is impossible for a small body of officials, however able and conscientious, to administer the Government of a country like Jamaica, without the aid of men thoroughly acquainted with the needs, wishes, requirements and aspirations of the colony.[13]

The intellectual uniqueness of the British West Indian colonies of which James spoke so often, was conceived within the interstices of an emerging liberalism, with its muscular educational ethos, and Olivier's Fabian socialism, which was a vital component from the late 1890s and beyond. As Paul Rich observes of the latter:

> [T]he West Indies ... acted as a forum of some significance in an increasingly sophisticated debate on the nature and functions of imperial government and its ultimate political objectives. In this debate, the model of colonial administration in Jamaica proved to be an important one by the early years of the twentieth century, especially under its Fabian [G]overnor from 1907–13, Sydney Olivier.... Olivier ... [was] an ardent exponent of the peasant model of economic development ... [as late as 1939, he advocated] in evidence to the Moyne Commission ... peasant settlement combined with a programme of 'liberal education' by which 'people can write and talk in a manner which appeals to the intelligence of educated men all over the world'. An increasingly bitter critic of the Colonial Office, which he felt had sold out to financial interests.... Olivier's voice remained one of radical protest until his death in 1943. In many respects he helped found a tradition of liberal debate and analysis in the British West Indies.... [He] should be considered a figure of considerable importance in both the Jamaican and West Indian intellectual and political tradition.[14]

This progressive strand in West Indian thought was also evident in the illumination the *Jamaica Daily Telegraph* reflected on the education of girls, the role of physical education and a widening curriculum. The following, in May 1900, speaks to a profound recasting of the imagination, a revolution in thinking at the end of the nineteenth century that created the foundation for submerged groups to build self-belief and to begin to aspire to self-government:

> The effect of such training is to give symmetry to the form, strength to the muscles, tone to the nervous system, and health to the entire bodily constitution.... Of late years the education of women has been arranged to cover a wider field and to include a larger curriculum of subjects. This, also, is as it should be. We do not see why in the olden time there should have been so great a difference made in the education of the two sexes. *A woman's intellectual*

capacity is as great as that of a man, and it is only right that every means should be taken to cultivate the mental powers of both men and women to the highest possible degree of perfection.[15] (emphasis added)

It is noteworthy, too, that Joseph Ruhomon, the young Indo-Guyanese intellectual, had, in his seminal lecture of October 1894, implored his Indian compatriots to change their attitude to women, to be bold to hasten their education:

[Parents] should see that their sons and their daughters — the future men and women of the Colony — get, not only that education which would enable them only just to eke out a common living in the future, but that sound, broad and liberal education, which would make them mighty pillars of the fabric of society.... You have the glorious gift of intellect — cultivate it by the numerous means which are at your disposal.... In association with our young women — and woman, you know, is one of the most important factors in society, and one of the most powerful of the forces at work in this nineteenth century, not only for the emancipation of her sex but in the common cause of humanity — in association with them ... you will obtain far better results in seeking to advance your own interests and the interests of our people than you can by working alone.[16]

This is why these islands in which virtually everyone belonged elsewhere, the victims of slavery and indentureship, would become authentic liberal democratic states. Everyone had to re-belong: compromise — negotiated incremental change — was necessarily indispensable to the process. Cricket and education, at the heart of the imperial mission and unmediated by resilient indigenous cultures, as in Africa and in India, would become the instruments for the construction of a rudimentary British West Indian identity.

In Frank Worrell (1924–67), a graduate of Combermere School in Barbados (founded in 1695) and Manchester University, and the first black captain of the West Indies cricket team, aspects of that fledgling identity cohered. In 1960–1961, although they lost the series 1-2 in Australia, he had captured the admiration and imagination of the Australian nation, as well as his rival, the Australian captain, Richie Benaud:

Had Frank failed on that tour it would have set back West Indies cricket, and especially the black cricketers, by twenty years.... Captaining Australia against his side that series, I saw for the first time that West Indies had been moulded into a team. Frank was a good tactician with a very calm exterior.... He had a calm influence on excitable individuals.... They did exactly what he asked of them.... It was because of Frank they never collapsed when the tension mounted, as had been their wont in the past. They did much for our cricket in Australia.[17]

Worrell's gifts, as James saw it, were, like Garfield Sobers's, a unique product of the African-European encounter — a lower middle-class Barbadian solidity shaped by British colonial culture, tutored in the ways of gradualism, fortified now by principles of moderation, the source of self-belief and quiet authority. Therefore, in his evocation of Worrell's leadership, in a foreign land, before white people, James was celebrating West Indian cultural, intellectual and political arrival, on the threshold of Independence in the early 1960s, the impending collapse of the short-lived Federation notwithstanding:

The West Indies team in Australia, on the field and off, was playing above what it knew of itself. If anything went wrong it knew that it would be instantly told, in unhesitating and precise language, how to repair it, and that the captain's certainty and confidence extended to his belief that what he wanted would be done. He did not instil into but drew out of his players. What they discovered in themselves must have been a revelation to few more than to the players themselves. When the time came to say goodbye some of the toughest players could only shake the captain's hand and look away, not trusting themselves to speak.

James, as usual, sees much more than meets the eye:

We have gone far beyond a game.... Frank Worrell, speaking last, was crowned with the olive. Beauty is indeed in the eye of the beholder. I saw all the West Indian ease, humour and easy adaptation to environment.... I could see his precise and uncompromising evaluations, those it seems are now second nature. But they were draped with that diplomatic graciousness which has so impressed the Australian Prime Minister [a passionate student of cricket, Sir Robert Menzies (1894–1978)]. If I say he won the prize it is because the crowd gave it to him. They laughed and cheered him continuously. He expanded my conception of West Indian personality. Nor was I alone. I caught a glimpse of what brought a quarter of a million inhabitants of Melbourne into the streets to tell the West Indian cricketers good-bye, a gesture spontaneous and in cricket without precedent, one people speaking to another. Clearing their way with bat and ball, West Indians at that moment had made a public entry into the comity of nations.[18]

It is of significance that some of James's people were of Barbadian artisan stock, including a versatile engine-driver on the Trinidad Government Railway, Josh Rudder, his maternal grandfather. It is not far-fetched, therefore, to suggest that he had a special empathy for the great Barbadians, Grantley Adams, Frank Worrell and Garfield Sobers, because he identified in them some of the attributes he saw in himself or aspired towards: the 'Englishness', too. It took an outsider, the Jamaican novelist, John Hearne, to seek to delineate what he considered 'characteristic Barbadian responses'. He is the equal of James in the manner of his intellectual exploration:

[I]n his obstinate 'Englishness', in his more civil and socially responsible behaviour — the Barbadian geography ... had played a significant role.... You have a small, flat island, every square foot of which is cultivable; your water is good; your climate one of the healthiest in the world. People bred easily and lived long in Barbados. The virtues of industry, thrift, honesty, care of inheritance, co-operation, strict regard for orderly debate, a compelling sense of your neighbour's rights and integrity *had* to be acquired by the Barbadian. These were not simply pious actions inspired by sermons. They were the only possible instincts for successful survival in a territory such as yours. People, in Barbados, could not *remove* themselves from one another as they could in, say, Jamaica until very recently, up into high, remote mountain valleys of virgin soil, and create lives that had small reference to the lives of their fellow citizens.[19]

It is entirely appropriate that James's book, *Beyond a Boundary*, a study of a life rooted in West Indian education, should have as its base cricket and the making of the West Indies. I do not go beyond the West Indies tour of England in 1900, the year before the birth of C.L.R.

James, but many of the forces that shaped the man himself are contained in the exposition here on cricket and education at the end of the nineteenth century. And I do explore that legacy. Alan Metcalfe's tribute to his great work of 1963, therefore, is indirectly a celebration of the muscular learning that made the British West Indies in all its intellectual richness and complexity:

> I am sure we can all identify writings that acted as catalysts to our thinking; books that say such things in ways that we dreamed of but have never been able to achieve. Such was the impact of C.L.R. James's *Beyond a Boundary* upon me. Here was a book ... that incorporated ideas I had been struggling with for years but have never been able to express in a clear, lucid fashion and, in all probability never will.... He provides in segments ... examples of history as I believe it should be written. Interestingly, the book is not in the final analysis history, but a view of life and the dominant forces within which a life is created and sustained told within an autobiographical framework.... *Beyond a Boundary* is the product of a true renaissance man. A man steeped in the literature of the ages but also experiencing the realities of life and combining them together with life. Sport, art, literature, politics, economics and life itself cannot be divorced from each other. It is in his denial of categorisation and specialisation and his emphasis upon the interrelationships between all aspects of life that C.L.R. James makes his most significant contributions.[20]

Beyond a Boundary is not a book that could have been written about anywhere else. And, as even V.S. Naipaul could recognize on its publication in London in 1963, it goes to the heart of the Anglo-West Indian encounter: '*Beyond a Boundary* is one of the finest and most finished books to come out of the West Indies, important to England, important to the West Indies. It has a further value: it gives a base and solidity to West Indian literary endeavour.'[21] The origins of this masterpiece could be located in the two cardinal strands in the making of the British West Indian: education and cricket in post-Emancipation society, especially the last quarter of the nineteenth century.

Elsa Goveia's powerful assessment of the place of the enslaved African in the West Indies got to the core of the inspiration of West Indian people to remake themselves, to reassert their humanity — to establish that their capacity for intellectual attainments was in no way inferior to their British rulers. She observes: 'In the West Indies, the slave was a 'thing' rather than a person, a 'property' rather than a subject.... The legal nullity of the slave's personality, except when he was to be controlled or punished, was the greatest obstacle to his adequate personal protection.'[22] Mastery of education and cricket, therefore, because these were central to 'the civilising mission' of the English, demonstrated that one had a mind, that one was not just a 'thing'. James was celebrating his intellectual pedigree in his great work. It was encapsulated in Shannonism, the parallel of which, in Jamaica, was epitomised by the hard play of Lucas Cricket Club and, in Barbados, by the consistency of focus of the black artisan 'professionals', Fenwick, from around 1900: studies in a resolve to win in their own way: with passion and style — the highest manifestations of which were the black players who toured England in 1900: Lebrun Constantine, C.A. Ollivierre, 'Float' Woods, Tom Burton and Fitz Hinds.

I have already explored the indefatigable play of Shannon and Lucas; a brief assessment of Fenwick will suffice as a reminder of the strength of character of many black players, in spite of the discrimination still prevalent. I have noted how resilient this was in Barbados, where the coloured team, Spartan, had won the Challenge Cup in 1899–1900 because many of the top white players from Pickwick, the foremost being Hallam Cole, refused to play against them on the spurious ground that Fitz Hinds was a professional. However, by selecting Hinds to tour England in 1900 white West Indian selectors were, indeed, establishing the right of merit to triumph over assumptions of white racial superiority. And it is to the credit of the Goodmans, the premier white Barbadian cricketing family from Pickwick (Clifford, Percy and Evan, who migrated to Demerara), that they rejected the obscurantists and continued to play against Spartan. Clifford Goodman 'fired a shot at the "deserters"' at the presentation of the Cup to Spartan in March 1900.[23] Moreover, Clifford and Percy Goodman played in the celebration match for the Rest of the Island v. Spartan, which the latter won by 89 runs: Stephen Rudder, 7 for 30; Hinds 3 for 26.[24]

But coloured Spartan themselves were not immune from this kind of prejudice. They excluded many cricketers of merit both on class as well as grounds of colour. However, as in Trinidad and Jamaica, black cricketers were beginning to demand a place centre stage. In June 1900, during the West Indies tour of England, it was announced that 'there is a movement on foot to admit a team of [black] professionals to the Cup Competition'. They would be captained by Willie Shepherd, a 'well-known Spartan groundsman'. A correspondent noted: 'Shepherd is, and always has been since I have had any knowledge of him ... a civil and well-behaved young man; apart from that he is a cricketer of no mean abilities.... The question of another professional does not crop up as, of course, they would play as professionals. These players would not be of any direct help to us in inter-colonial matches [against Trinidad and British Guiana] as the Rules preclude them *but against English teams they would, I suppose, be played as in Trinidad to the undoubted advantage of the Colony.*'25 (emphasis added)

Fenwick played in the Barbados Challenge Cup as an associate member in the 1900–1901 season, and defeated all three of the top teams: the all-white Wanderers and Pickwick, as well as Spartan. However, as they were not admitted as full competitors, the Cup could not be awarded to them. Even after their first game, a correspondent had remarked thus on the quality of the black novices' play:

> I expect to see the Fenwicks beat all the clubs except the Pickwicks.... They have ... the best bowling in the island, good batting and splendid fielding. Shurland, is to my mind, a better bat than [Fitz] Hinds and had he been put in a club where his cricket would have come out, I do not think Hinds would have gone to England. But there is another man who is also ... better than Hinds and he is the captain Shepherd. As a bowler he has also inspired me.26

When Fenwick played Pickwick, they defeated them, but the old issue of race and colour ensconced behind the ruse of professionalism cropped up again. Most of the top Pickwick players failed to turn up for the match against the black plebs: 'There was a lot of trouble experienced in raising a team and that which eventually walked out of the Pickwick pavilion was very different looking from a Pickwick eleven.'27 When the Barbadian players returned from England, Percy Goodman turned out for Pickwick and Fitz Hinds for Spartan, but in the match between these two teams 'the opposition', Cole's gang of bigots, still refused to play against Spartan.28 It was clear that because it was not all cricket within the boundary, the black masses beyond the boundary were beginning to vent their feelings in their peculiarly forthright manner. When Spartan played Pickwick, the people's hero, Fitz Hinds, was given out for 43. It was not taken well by Hinds's black admirers:

He was out lbw to Willie Hoad [a white man] and there was a deal
of dissatisfaction at the decision of Sam Moore [another white man],
who was umpiring; but he was clearly out and Hinds admits it.
But when a man is batting well and is a favourite with the crowd
you must not get him out lbw, or stump him or catch him at the
wicket or take a hard return low down on the ground. You must
either catch him in the country off a tremendous hit or clean bowl
him, neck and crop. If you don't all round the ground you will
hear: "He ent no ampire! Dey teef he out!"[29]

Hinds was out, but the incident was indicative of a new spirit: black
people were now sufficiently confident to challenge old assumptions
— attitudes mired in racial prejudice could no longer be tolerated.
And the quality of play of Fenwick was already strengthening their
resolve to fight elevated mediocrity with merit. They defeated the
team of the richest whites in Barbados, Wanderers, with their captain,
Shepherd, taking 8 for 24. They also beat Spartan, who continued to
discriminate against them on grounds of class and colour, Hinds's
controversial admission by them notwithstanding. In a close game,
Fenwick won by 2 runs. The skills and ferocity of their fast bowler,
Oliver Layne, on a difficult pitch, posed problems for all the Spartan
batsmen, even Fitz Hinds, who made 24:

The Spartans, no doubt, thought that they would win after they
had 54 up and only five wickets had fallen, but they reckoned
without Layne, who on a bad wicket is a beastly bowler to stand up
to. It takes a mighty lot of pluck and a mightier lot of skill to make
runs off him, and when he is not hitting your wickets, he is blasting
your person from head to heel. Such is the array of bowling that
Shepherd has at his command that teams need not consider
themselves the winners until the Fenwick score had been passed.[30]

Layne got 6 for 8. He, Shepherd and Thornhill were among the top
four bowlers in the Barbados Challenge Cup for 1900–1901. Layne
toured England in 1906 with the West Indies team, and was second in
the bowling averages after the black Vincentian, Richard Ollivierre,
brother of the 1900 tourist, C.A. Ollivierre. It was the iron will to
defeat their social superiors that drove men like Layne, but it was
clear that even in their first season Fenwick had also scored a major
psychological victory beyond the boundary through the resolve in

their play. They defeated Pickwick in their return match by 91 runs: only one player reached double figures. But the match was memorable for the fact that some of the 'deserters' who had objected to playing against so-called professionals, black men, played in that match. As a correspondent observed: 'The Pickwick and Fenwick match afford us another proof, if further proof were wanted, of the great strength of the Fenwick, who continued their victorious career by badly beating the Pickwicks.'[31] Merit was winning. In December 1900, for the first time in two years, a full strength Pickwick team, including the infamous Hallam Cole, participated in their return game against Spartan.[32] The black artisans were already establishing that ability and commitment were the only valid criteria in determining quality.

This — Shannonism — was what shaped C.L.R. James and gave him the will and moral courage to pursue intellectual excellence. And he was fortunate that he came under the wings of a number of distinguished, if largely unsung, black scholars in Trinidad, in the early years of the twentieth century, men made by the British intellectual tradition of the late nineteenth century. James celebrates the contribution of his early heroes, but also acknowledges his debt to the wider European scholarship:

> I want to make it clear that the origins of my work and my thoughts are to be found in Western European literature, Western European history and Western European thought.... It is in the history and philosophy and literature of Western Europe that I have gained my understanding not only of Western Europe's civilisation, but of the importance of underdeveloped countries.... I didn't learn literature from the mango-tree, or bathing on the shore and getting the sun of the colonial countries; I set out to master the literature, philosophy and ideas of Western civilisation.[33]

In paying his debt to the black teachers and scholars who set the example for him, one discerns the roots of James's apprehension of the West Indian achievement, an extraordinary journey from slavery to independence in less than a century:

> In a West Indian island in those days there would be certain small towns and villages where the schoolmaster was an important person. Next to him were the Anglican parson and the Catholic

parson, but the third stage was the teacher. If you wanted to know what was happening in the British Parliament, or if you wanted to know about the revolution in Turkey, or if you wanted to know what was happening in Barbados, or who had written this or that book ... whatever it was, you came to the local teacher to find out. And if he didn't know — well, nobody knew. That was the intellectual life of a rather narrow area. But the local teacher recognised his responsibility. There is a wonderful list of black teachers in Trinidad. My father was one. I knew them all. There was E.B. Grosvenor, there was Nelson Comma, there were the two Regises, there was Napoleon Raymond, there was old De Suse — a whole bunch of them, including my godfather, Mr. Poyer, and the man who married my aunt, Mr. Richard Austin.... They taught you everything you needed to know: reading, writing, arithmetic, proper behaviour, good manners, how you were to wear your clothes — everything. Those teachers educated the present generation of Caribbean people who are now between fifty and sixty years of age. Few today remember them. I knew all of them extremely well, and it is from their world that I and Grantley Adams and George Padmore have come, so that from early on we had a sense of intellectual and moral responsibility to the community — it was the atmosphere in which we grew up.[34]

This was the world of *Beyond a Boundary*. I am proud to be an inheritor of this rich legacy of muscular learning. *What do they know of cricket who only cricket know?*

Appendix

The West Indian Cricket Team.
Full Report of their First Tour in England,
June-August, 1900

THE WEST INDIAN CRICKET TEAM.

Burton, C. A. Ollivierre, Hon. R. S. Warner, (capt.), W. H. Mignon, G. C. Learmond, P. J. Cox, M. W. Kerr, P. A. Goodman,
Woods, F. Hinds, S. W. Sproston, G. L. Livingstone, L. Constantine.

W. Bowring and L. S. D'Ade Absent.

THE

WEST INDIAN CRICKET TEAM.

FULL REPORT

. . OF THEIR . .

FIRST TOUR IN ENGLAND,

June=August, 1900.

WITH INTRODUCTION

BY

PELHAM F. WARNER,

AUTHOR OF

"CRICKET IN MANY CLIMES."

"They have fully justified my high opinion of their ability to play a grand sports-manlike game."—Lord Hawke in a telegram to Lord Harris, G.C.S.I., G.C.I.E., August 13th 1900.

WEST INDIAN CLUB, HOWARD HOTEL,

NORFOLK STREET, LONDON.

PRICE ONE SHILLING.

THE WEST INDIAN CRICKET TEAM,

REVIEW OF THE TOUR

BY

PELHAM F. WARNER.

When the West Indian Club was formed in London in 1898, one of its objects was " to afford facilities for organising in connection with the West Indies and British Guiana, Annual Cricket Matches and other kindred amusements recognised by our English Universities and Public Schools," and the name of Lord Hawke figuring as Chairman of the Sports Committee was an assurance that this professed object would be faithfully carried out.

In the early part of 1895, previous to the formation of the Club Mr. R. S. Lucas' team had visited the West Indies. I had returned home enthusiastic about the good time they had, both from a cricket and social point of view. The results of the tour had shewn that there was plenty of good cricket scattered over the West Indies, which only needed encouragement and development to become first-class. But that a West Indian Eleven would come over to England and tackle our leading counties, was, it may safely be said, at the time unthought of. So enthusiastically had the praises of the West Indies been sung by Mr. R. S. Lucas' team, that in January 1897 we find both Lord Hawke and Mr. Priestley taking out elevens to the West Indies. That the dual visit was a mistake there can be little doubt, but at this distance of time it would serve no useful purpose whatever to inquire into the causes which led to both Lord Hawke and Mr. Priestley receiving invitations to visit the West Indies. It is sufficient to say that both teams had a really splendid time, and were enthusiastically received wherever they went. Moreover they found that cricket had made great strides in the last two years, and it was quickly evident that a carefully chosen West Indian Eleven might at no remote distance of time visit this country with some hope of success. This idea ripened in the next two or three years with the result that in June of 1899, a combined West Indian eleven was invited to visit England. Lord Hawke, who from the first had taken the deepest interest in the cricket of the West Indies. was the author of the invitation, and immediately an acceptance was received, set about to arrange a capital programme of matches. A Selection Committee representative of the whole of the West Indies met in Trinidad in January of this year with the result that the following team was ultimately chosen. The Hon. R. S. Warner (Trinidad), *Captain.* L. Constantine (Trinidad), P. J. Cox (Barbados), W. Bowring (Barbados), L. S. D'Ade (Trinidad), P. A. Goodman (Barbados), F. Hinds (Trinidad), M. W. Kerr (Jamaica), G. C. Learmond

(Demerara), G. L. Livingstone (Jamaica), W. H. Mignon (Grenada), C. A. Ollivierre (St. Vincent), S. W. Sproston (Demerara), Burton (Demerara) and Woods (Trinidad). That the selectors did their work impartially, I have no doubt, but one or two mistakes were necessarily made, as it was impossible to really know the form of many men owing to the distances which separate the various islands from one another, and other difficulties. The Hon. Aucher Warner was chosen Captain, and on May 26th the team left Barbados in R.M.S. "Trent," and after a record voyage arrived at Southampton on June 5th.

After a couple of days practice on the ground of the Hampshire Cricket Club which had been kindly placed at their disposal, the team came up to London, and on Monday, June 11th, the first West Indian Eleven made its appearance in England on the Crystal Palace ground against an eleven collected by the greatest cricketer of all time—W. G. Grace.

And now a few words as to the results of the tour, and the performances of individuals may not be out of place. I will begin "right away," as the Americans say, by stating that the tour was a great success. Considering that the team had never played together before, that they were quite unaccustomed to the strain of three day cricket, and that they lost the toss on no fewer than twelve occasions, out of the seventeen matches that the programme comprised, I think that the judgement I have given will be endorsed on all sides. Of the seventeen matches played five were won, four drawn, and eight lost, and bearing in mind all the circumstances and the opponents they had to meet this was a very creditable performance. At first the tour looked very much like ending in failure, as the first four matches were lost right off the reel, but far from being disheartened by such a bad start, the team improved day after day, and at the end of the tour was quite equal to first-class cricket.

The best performance was undoubtedly the single innings victory over Surrey, who though represented by nothing like their best team had by no means a bad side, as a reference to the match will prove. In this game the West Indians simply outplayed their opponents at every point of the game, Ollivierre and Cox batting splendidly, and Woods and Burton taking all the wickets between them. Other good performances were the single innings defeat of Leicestershire (in which match I had the pleasure of playing for the team), and the victories over Hampshire and Norfolk, while the team shewed capital form in the drawn matches with Derbyshire, and Liverpool and District. Again though beaten by the M.C.C. and Lancashire, in both of these matches the team gained considerable *kudos* by the plucky manner in which they played up. In one respect the team were the equals of any eleven in the world, and that was in the sportsmanlike way in which they played the game.

And now as to individuals. The batting of the team was fairly strong, though at times liable to unaccountable collapses as witness the first innings against Gloucestershire, and the wretched display against Wiltshire. This last was by far the worst performance of the lot. The fielding was at times as good as anyone could wish to see, at others slipshod and lazy. At the beginning of the tour there was a distinct disinclination on the part of one or two members of the side to run after the ball, but as the tour progressed this grievous sin from a cricketer's point of view disappeared, and in the last six or seven matches the fielding was generally good enough, and on occasions brilliant. Woods at shortslip, Sproston at point, Learmond and Ollivierre were perhaps the best fielders on the side.

The bowling practically depended on Woods and Burton, both of whom did well. Woods on occasions was up to his best West Indian form, but at other times he seemed to lose heart very easily, though it must be confessed he was unlucky in the matter of missed catches.

Burton was generally thought in England to be the better bowler of the two. His length was always excellent, and he possessed more finesse and head work than the Trinidad bowler. He sent down a very good yorker, and it was with this ball that he twice had the honour of bowling W. G. Though Woods headed him by the merest fraction in the bowling analysis, it was pretty generally admitted that Burton on the whole accomplished the best work. But both of them did well, and have every reason to be satisfied with their figures, especially when we remember that they had more than their fair share of work.

Next to the two professionals of the team, Mignon was the best bowler, but he was very disappointing, only against Lancashire when he captured ten wickets for 111 runs did he show his true form. At the start of the trip he was by no means fit, and this may have had something to do with his comparative failure. Lord Hawke's team had formed a high opinion of his abilities, and we certainly expected him to do a great deal better. Cox bowled well against Derbyshire, and was more than once useful as a change. He should develop into a fine all-round cricketer in course of time. Ollivierre, Goodman and Hinds occasionally got a wicket, but they were very expensive, and presented little or no terrors to the opposing batsmen. Ollivierre was the best batsman in the eleven. He has strokes all round the wicket, and in many ways reminds one of Ranji.

His 159 against Leicestershire was as good an innings as was played last summer.   He was particularly strong in cutting and playing to leg, and I should be much surprised if he does not develop into one of the best batsmen in Derbyshire.   Considering that his opportunities of playing cricket in St. Vincent must have been very limited, his performance was remarkable.   Constantine hit very finely on many occasions, and was altogether one of the most useful men. His 113 against the M.C.C., was a dashing and faultless display. Cox and Goodman come next in the averages, and both had the satisfaction of scoring centuries during the tour.   Cox especially should develop into a really fine batsman, as he is quite young and the experience he gained on the tour, must in the future be of immense assistance to him.   His style was very pretty, his off driving being particularly good.   Goodman formed a good defence, and when a loose ball came along he hit it very hard.   Stanley Sproston was a little disappointing, and not consistent in his scoring, but when he did get runs he made them beautifully.   His form at Worcester, Southampton and Liverpool was up to his best standard.   Of the other batsman Hinds was often useful in his peculiar style ; was a keen hard working cricketer, but D'Ade did little or nothing until the very end of the tour   He had fallen off considerably from the form he showed in the West Indies in 1897.   The Captain made three or four useful scores, and played particularly well at Nottingham, but just when he seemed to have got into form he was laid low with malarial fever, and took no part in the last seven matches. Bowring except for two good innings did nothing, and Learmond was quite a failure.   He invariably attempted to "hook" every ball that was bowled him, and as often as not missed it.   Moreover he did not profit by experience.   Of the other batsman there is little to be said, except that Burton hit uncommonly well at Lords.

The weakest points of the team were : (1.)—The absence of a reliable wicket-keeper, and (2.)—The bad judgment that was too often displayed in running.   In this respect they improved, but in the early part of the tour they were both individually, and as a team, the worst judges of a run I have ever seen and Ollivierre and D'Ade were the chief offenders.

Stanley Sproston acted as captain in the absence of the Hon : A. Warner and acquitted himself right well.   A curious incident was the fact that the regular "Skipper" of the team never once won the toss.   Finally the team made a very good impression all round, and special praise is due to W. C. Nock for the way in which he acted as manager.   He was indefatigable, and was popular wherever he went.   Englishmen will be right glad to welcome another West Indian eleven within the next three or four years.

P. F. WARNER.

THE WEST INDIAN CRICKET TEAM.

RESULTS OF MATCHES.

Played.	Won.	Drawn.	Lost.
17	5	4	8

Date.	Against Whom.	Where Played.	Result.
June 11	London County C.C.	Crystal Palace.	Lost.
,, 14	Worcester	Worcester.	Lost.
,, 18	Warwickshire	Birmingham.	Lost.
,, 21	M.C.C.	Lords.	Lost.
,, 25	Minor Counties	Northampton.	Won.
,, 28	Gloucester	Bristol.	Lost.
July 2	Leicestershire	Leicester.	Won.
,, 5	*Off days for University Match.*		
,, 9	Notts	Nottingham.	Lost.
,, 13	Wilts	Swindon.	Lost.
,, 16	Lancashire	Manchester.	Lost.
,, 19	Derbyshire	Derby.	Drawn.
,, 24	Staffordshire	Stoke.	Drawn.
,, 26	Hampshire	Southampton.	Won.
,, 30	Surrey	Oval.	Won.
Aug. 2	Liverpool & District	Liverpool.	Drawn.
,, 6	Yorkshire	Bradford.	Drawn.
,, 10	Norfolk	Norwich.	Won.

LONDON COUNTY C.C. *v.* WEST INDIANS.

With little or no previous practice the West Indians came to grief in their first match, although Goodman, Cox, and A. Warner batted well and Burton made a good impression as a bowler. London County were a strong side.

LONDON COUNTY.

W. G. Grace b Burton 71	H. R. Parkes not out 106
J. Gilman b Burton 63	S. M. Tindal l b w b Ollivierre...... 7
Braund b Woods 4	E. H. S. Berridge st Constantine
J. R. Mason c Cox b Ollivierre ...126	b Mignon 50
A. E. Lawton c Constantine b Cox 46	Huish b Sproston 2
Storer b Cox........................... o	Byes 24 l-b 13 w 3 40
W. L. Murdoch c Woods b	
Mignon 23	Total...................538

WEST INDIANS.

1st inn.		2nd inn.	
S. W. Sproston c Storer b Grace...	5	c and b Grace	2
G. C. Learmond b Grace	5	b Mason	7
C. A. Ollivierre run out...............	10	b Mason	20
L. Constantine c Lawton b Grace...	2	c Tindall b Mason	5
P. A. Goodman c Braund b Mason	74	b Grace	7
P. J. Cox c Mason b Storer	53	st Huish b Grace	3
Burton b Mason	10	c Tindall b Mason	18
L. S. D'Ade c Huish b Mason......	4	l b w b Grace	o
A. Warner not out	29	c Huish b Mason	20
W. Mignon b Mason	1	not out	8
Woods c Gilman b Mason	36	b Grace.............................	5
Byes 4 l-b 2 n b 2	8	Byes 2 l-b 5 n b 1	8
Total ....—237		Total ....—103	

BOWLING ANALYSIS.

LONDON COUNTY.—FIRST INNINGS.

	O.	M.	R.	W.		O.	M.	R.	W.
Burton	35	5	127	2	Goodman	13	1	52	o
Woods	26	4	100	1	Ollivierre..........	8	3	24	2
Mignon	19	3	72	2	Constantine......	5	1	24	o
Cox	15	2	84	2	Sproston	3	o	15	1

Cox bowled two wides and Constantine one wide.

WEST INDIANS.—FIRST INNINGS.

	O.	M.	R.	W.		O.	M.	R.	W.
Grace	34	3	102	3	Storer	10	2	42	1
Braund	13	7	21	0	Mason	18.2	5	50	5
Tindall	4	1	14	0					

Mason and Storer each bowled one no ball.

SECOND INNINGS.

	O.	M.	R.	W.		O.	M.	R.	W.
Grace	15.2	2	52	5	Mason	15	4	43	5

Mason bowled one no ball.

WORCESTERSHIRE *v.* WEST INDIANS.

Though beaten severely, the West Indians showed good form, especially Sproston, Cox, and Hinds.

WORCESTERSHIRE.	1st inn.		2nd inn
Bowley b Goodman	63	c Kerr b Cox	29
Pearson b Hinds	12	not out	88
Arnold b Woods	46	b Woods	36
Corden b Woods	0	run out	40
F. W. Romney b Woods	4	b Woods	13
H. K. Foster c Hinds b Cox	79	c Burton b Ollivierre	20
Wheldon run out	32	c and b Ollivierre	0
Hunt l b w b Woods	22	l b w b Ollivierre	4
Wilson c Bowring b Cox	5	c Burton b Ollivierre	0
Gaukrodger not out	14	absent hurt	—
Bannister c Cox b Woods	15	b Cox	7
Byes 13 l-b 1 n b 1	15	Byes 15 l-b 5	20
Total	—307	Total	—257

WEST INDIANS.	1st inn.		2nd inn
C. P. Learmond b Pearson	7	l b w b Foster	20
C. A. Ollivierre c Corden b Pearson	18	b Arnold	1
M. W. Kerr c Gaukrodger b Bannister	3	c Wheldon b Arnold	2
L. Constantine b Pearson	8	l b w b Bannister	12
F. Hinds st Gaukrodger b Bannister	20	st Wheldon b Pearson	40
S. W. Sproston c sub. b Bannister	54	c Arnold b Pearson	46
P. A. Goodman b Pearson	0	l b w b Wilson	4
P. J. Cox b Pearson	48	c and b Pearson	11
W. Bowring c Pearson b Bannister	7	c Corden b Pearson	4
Burton c Bowley b Bannister	14	run out	5
Woods not out	0	not out	5
Bye 1 l-b 3 w 4	8	Byes	13
Total	—187	Total	—162

BOWLING ANALYSIS.
WORCESTERSHIRE.—FIRST INNINGS.

	O.	M.	R.	W.		O.	M.	R.	W.
Burton	16	2	46	0	Ollivierre	3	0	14	0
Woods	26.4	6	77	5	Sproston	2	0	8	0
Hinds	11	0	64	1	Goodman	13	2	36	1
Cox	10	1	47	2					

Burton bowled one no ball.

SECOND INNINGS.

	O.	M.	R.	W.		O.	M.	R.	W.
Burton	13	0	48	0	Goodman	8	2	28	0
Cox	11.4	0	37	2	Constantine	2	0	15	0
Hinds	7	1	27	0	Ollivierre	9	1	37	4
Woods	14	7	45	2					

WEST INDIANS.—FIRST INNINGS.

	O.	M.	R.	W.		O.	M.	R.	W.
Pearson	33	10	73	6	Wilson	6	2	10	0
Foster	4	0	12	0	Corden	3	0	23	0
Bannister	28.4	11	44	4	Arnold	3	0	17	0

Pearson bowled four wides.

SECOND INNINGS

	O.	M.	R.	W.		O.	M.	R.	W.
Bannister	15	4	31	1	Pearson	12.5	5	25	4
Arnold	8	1	41	2	Wilson	11	2	36	1
Foster	5	0	16	1					

WARWICKSHIRE *v.* WEST INDIANS.

Losing the toss for the third time in succession, the West Indians were quite outplayed, heavy rains rendering the wicket very treacherous on the third day.

WARWICKSHIRE.

T. S. Fishwick c Woods b Mignon 16
Quaife (W.G.) c Woods b Olli-
vierre 29
Lilley b Hinds 56
A. Holloway b Woods 4
J. E. Hill c Woods b Ollivierre 145
Whittle c Livingstone b Ollivierre 14
Diver b Hinds 30

H. W. Bainbridge b Woods......... 33
J. H. Cooper c Learmond b Spros-
ton... 13
Moorhouse not out..................... 37
Ward b Woods 39
Byes 35 l-b 14 w 1 50
—
Total 466

WEST INDIANS. 1st inn.

S. W. Sproston b Ward 5
C. A. Ollivierre c Fishwick b Ward 41
P. J. Cox c Moorhouse b Cooper... 79
P. A. Goodman run out............... 27
G. C. Learmond b Whittle 6
F. Hinds c Diver b Quaife 5
W. Bowring b Cooper 33
A. Warner b Ward 5
W. H. Mignon not out 11
Woods b Cooper........................ 9
G. L. Livingstone run out........... 1
Byes 5 l-b 3 w 3 11
Total ....—233

2nd inn.

b Cooper 1
l b w b Ward 18
c Whittle b Ward 10
b Whittle 29
c Whittle b Quaife................. 7
c Whittle 0
b Whittle 28
b Fishwick b Ward................. 9
c Moorhouse b Ward.............. 2
c Ward b Whittle 1
not out 0
Byes 6 l-b 3 w 8 17
Total ....—122

BOWLING ANALYSIS.

WARWICKSHIRE.—FIRST INNINGS.

	O.	M.	R.	W.		O.	M.	R.	W.
Woods	33.2	5	78	3	Hinds	12	1	48	2
Mignon	34	2	110	1	Cox	4	1	13	0
Livingstone	14	2	46	0	Goodman	6	0	23	0
Ollivierre	24	4	81	3	Sproston	5	1	17	0

Woods bowled one wide.

WEST INDIANS.—FIRST INNINGS.

	O.	M.	R.	W.		O.	M.	R.	W.
Ward	24	5	71	3	Quaife (W.G.)	10	2	19	1
Moorhouse	14	4	39	0	Cooper	23	33	49	3
Whittle	17.2	4	44	1					

Quaife bowled two wides, and Ward one wide.

SECOND INNINGS.

	O.	M.	R.	W.		O.	M.	R.	W.
Ward	26.5	8	54	4	Cooper	11	5	16	1
Quaife (W.G.)	7	0	18	1	Whittle	9	4	17	4

Ward bowled eight wides.

M.C.C., *v.* WEST INDIANS.

One of the best performances of the tour, for though beaten in the end, the West Indians played up most pluckily, Constantine and Burton hitting splendidly. The M.C.C. had a good side.

M.C.C. 1st inn.		2nd inn.	
W, G. Grace c Ollivierre b Woods	11	b Burton	3
A. E. Stoddart c Ollivierre b Woods	30	c Cox b Woods	18
J. Gilman b Burton	33	l b w b Woods	6
Lord Harris c Burton b Woods	35	c Sproston b Woods	3
E. C. Mordaunt b Burton	31	not out	51
A. Page b Burton	0	run out	22
A. F. Somerset b Ollivierre	118	not out	0
A. B. Reynolds b Woods	37		
M. M. Barker b Goodman	26		
E. R. de Little b Goodman	0		
A. Montague not out	32		
Byes 17 l-b 9	26	Bye 1 l-b 3	4
Total	—379	Total	—107

WEST INDIANS 1st inn.		2nd inn.	
C. A. Ollivierre l b w b Grace	21	b Stoddart	32
G. C. Learmond b De Little	52	b Stoddart	6
S. W. Sproston b Grace	14	c and b Grace	33
P. J. Cox b Grace	17	b Stoddart	6
P. A. Goodman c and b Grace	0	b Stoddart	6
W. Bowring b Grace	0	b Stoddart	7
A. Warner c Gilman b De Little	22	b Stoddart	3
L. S. D'Ade run out	4	b Stoddart	2
L. Constantine not out	24	st Reynolds b Grace	113
Burton b Stoddart	18	not out	64
Woods st Reynolds b Harris	0	b Montague	0
Byes 17 l-b 1	18	Byes 17 l-b 6	23
Total	—190	Total	—295

BOWLING ANALYSIS.

M.C.C.—FIRST INNINGS.

	O.	M.	R.	W.		O.	M.	R.	W
Burton	37	6	118	3	Cox	3	0	18	0
Woods	41	8	109	4	Goodman	11	0	49	2
Ollivierre	13.5	2	55	1	Sproston	1	0	4	0

SECOND INNINGS.

	O.	M.	R.	W.		O.	M.	R.	W
Woods	19.1	8	47	3	Ollivierre	2	0	17	0
Burton	17	5	39	1					

WEST INDIANS.—FIRST INNINGS.

	O.	M.	R.	W.		O.	M.	R.	W
Stoddart	10	2	32	1	De Little	18	3	46	2
Mordaunt	5	1	30	0	Harris	2.3	0	8	1
Grace	18	3	56	5					

SECOND INNINGS.

	O.	M.	R.	W.		O.	M.	R.	W
Stoddart	32	6	92	7	Harris	7	0	39	0
Grace	21	5	87	2	Montague	4.3	1	15	1
De Little	8	2	39	0					

MINOR COUNTIES *v.* WEST INDIANS.

Victory at last! Right well was it deserved. This was the first occasion on which the West Indians won a toss. Woods and Burton bowled very well.

WEST INDIANS. 1st inn.		2nd inn
C. A. Ollivierre b Thompson	69	b Thompson ... 7
G. C. Learmond c Thompson b Creber	14	b Lowe ... 0
M. W. Kerr b Thompson	0	b East ... 1
P. J. Cox b Thompson	40	c Horton b Williams ... 35
S. W. Sproston l b w b Thompson	2	c Horton b Lowe ... 2
L. Constantine b Creber	27	b Lowe ... 8
Burton st Smith b Creber	19	b Lowe ... 6
W. Bowring b Thompson	18	c Williams b East ... 30
F. Hinds b Thompson	11	c Williams b Lowe ... 68
W. H. Mignon not out	0	c and b Williams ... 4
Woods b Thompson	0	not out ... 1
Byes &c	6	Byes &c. ... 8
Total	—206	Total ... —170

MINOR COUNTIES. 1st inn.		2nd inn.
R. W. Williams (Berkshire) c Hinds b Woods	37	c Constantine b Burton ... 1
Thompson (Northants) c Hinds b Burton	58	l b w b Woods ... 0
E. W. Elliot (Durham) b Burton	26	run out ... 0
L. T. Driffield (Northants) b Burton	3	b Mignon ... 10
East (Northants) c Burton b Mignon	37	b Woods ... 7
Creber (Glamorgan) b Ollivierre	6	c Woods b Burton ... 2
B. C. Smith (Northants) c Learmond b Woods	13	c Constantine b Burton ... 12
C. J. T. Pool (Northants) b Burton	39	b Woods ... 3
T. Horton (Northants) c Constantine b Burton	17	not out ... 9
Lowe (Glamorgan) not out	13	b Mignon ... 1
J. Stops (Northants) c Constantine b Burton	4	b Woods ... 2
Byes &c.	8	Byes &c. ... 7
Total	—261	Total ... —54

BOWLING ANALYSIS.

WEST INDIANS.—FIRST INNINGS

	O.	M.	R.	W.		O.	M.	R.	W.
Thompson	24	4	84	7	Lowe	8	0	44	0
Creber	24	1	68	3	Williams	2	0	4	0

Thompson delivered one no ball.

SECOND INNINGS.

	O.	M.	R.	W.		O.	M.	R.	W.
Creber	6	0	21	0	Lowe	15	2	50	5
Thompson	17	3	37	1	East	15	5	28	2
Williams	10	2	26	2					

MINOR COUNTIES.—FIRST INNINGS

	O.	M.	R.	W.		O.	M.	R.	W.
Woods	17	2	57	2	Mignon	16	8	36	1
Burton	29.3	12	55	6	Cox	8	1	33	0
Ollivierre	13	5	37	1	Hinds	5	0	9	0
Constantine	8	2	26	0					

SECOND INNINGS.

Burton .... 19 ... 14 ... 11 ... 3 | Mignon............ 4 ... 2 ... 5 ... 2
Woods............. 22.4 .. 8 ... 31 ... 4 |

Woods bowled one no ball.

GLOUCESTERSHIRE *v.* WEST INDIANS.

Gloucestershire were too powerful and won easily, but in the second innings several men batted very well, notably Goodman and Ollivierre.

GLOUCESTERSHIRE.

W. S. A. Brown c Mignon b Burton 60
N. O. Tagart c Burton b Mignon 9
Broad c Goodman b Burton........ 3
H. J. Hodgkins b Burton 0
Wrathall c Constantine b Mignon 123
C. L. Townsend b Mignon 140

G. L. Jessop c Hinds b Mignon ...157
O. Wreford-Brown not out 44
Langdon c Sproston b Burton 50
Paish b Burton 0
Roberts b Mignon 11
Byes 15 l-b 6 n b 1.................. 22

Total.............................619

WEST INDIANS.　　1st inn.

S. W. Sproston c Paish b Townsend 1
C. A. Ollivierre c Paish b Roberts 15
G. C. Learmond c Langdon b Townsend 0
P. A. Goodman run out............... 38
F. Hinds l b w b Roberts............ 8
L. Constantine b Roberts............ 21
Burton b Roberts 0
W. Bowring not out 5
A. Warner b Roberts.................. 3
W. H. Mignon b Townsend 1
Woods b Townsend 0
Bye 1 l-b 2 n b 1..................... 4

Total .... —96

2nd inn.

c Townsend b Paish 36
run out 42
c Board b Langdon 17
c Paish b Roberts 34
c Board b Townsend 34
c sub. b Brown 65
c sub. b Townsend.................. 11
c Townsend b Langdon............ 21
l b w b Langdon..................... 24
c Board b Townsend 10
not out 5
Byes 7 n b 1 8

Total ....—307

BOWLING ANALYSIS.

GLOUCESTERSHIRE.—FIRST INNINGS.

	O.	M.	R.	W.		O.	M.	R.	W.
Ollivierre........	23	2	137	0	Mignon	33.3	5	162	5
Burton............	25	4	68	5	Hinds	8	0	72	0
Woods............	33	5	141	0	Goodman.........	7	1	17	0

Woods delivered one no ball.

WEST INDIANS.—FIRST INNINGS

	O.	M.	R.	W.		O.	M.	R.	W.
Townsend	16.5	1	53	4	Roberts	16	8	39	5

Roberts delivered one no ball.

SECOND INNINGS.

	O.	M.	R.	W.		O.	M.	R.	W.
Langdon..........	13	3	57	3	Roberts	18	4	50	1
Brown	27	10	67	1	Townsend	17.1	1	62	3
Paish	15	2	63	1					

Roberts delivered one no ball.

LEICESTERSHIRE *v.* WEST INDIANS.

Ollivierre batted magnificently, and with Woods and Burton bowling well, an innings victory for the West Indians was the result of this match.

WEST INDIANS.

P. F. Warner st Jarvis b Marlow 113
C. A. Ollivierre run out 159
G. C Learmond b Burgess 0
P. J. Cox run out 4
S. W. Sproston b Woodcock 7
P. A. Goodman l b w b Woodcock 26
L. Constantine c Wood b Burgess 41

F. Hinds c Woodcock b Coe 19
Burton c Wood b Coe 9
W. Mignon c Jarvis b Coe 0
Woods not out 0
Byes 3 l-b 5 8
—
Total 386

LEICESTERSHIRE.

	1st inn.	2nd inn.
C. J. B. Wood c Constantine b Woods	3	b Burton 77
C. A. V. Checkland c Woods b Burton	0	b Woods 14
Knight c Hinds b Woods	6	b Cox 0
Coe b Woods	26	b Ollivierre 39
H. Burgess b Woods	0	c Burton b Hinds 25
C. E. de Trafford c Mignon b Burton	0	c Ollivierre b Burton 51
King (J.) c Hinds b Woods	0	b Burton 5
Woodcock b Burton	10	absent hurt —
Haywood not out	19	b Burton 0
Jarvis run out	10	run out 5
Marlow b Burton	4	not out 1
Leg-byes	2	Byes 2
Total	—80	Total —219

BOWLING ANALYSIS.

WEST INDIANS.

	O.	M.	R.	W.		O.	M.	R.	W.
Woodcock	22	2	83	2	Coe	14.3	2	57	3
Marlow	30	9	98	1	Haywood	7	0	38	0
Burgess	22	5	73	2	Wood	3	0	29	0

LEICESTERSHIRE.—FIRST INNINGS.

	O.	M.	R.	W.		O.	M.	R.	W.
Woods	16	4	39	5	Burton	16	4	39	4

SECOND INNINGS.

	O.	M.	R.	W.		O.	M.	R.	W.
Woods	15	1	56	1	Hinds	7	1	25	1
Burton	23	8	63	4	Cox	11	1	35	1
Mignon	4	0	21	0	Ollivierre	4	0	17	1

NOTTS v. WEST INDIANS.

Though batting well in both innings the West Indians were easily beaten by Notts, for whom the famous W. Gunn played a great innings. Burton as usual bowled well.

Shrewsbury c Cox b Burton......... 15	R. H. Howitt b Cox 14
Gunn (W.) c Mignon b Burton 161	Oates not out 15
Pepper b Mignon 14	J. C. Snaith b Burton 18
Iremonger b Hinds......................101	Atkinson c and b Burton 1
Anthony (H.) b Burton 26	Byes 29 l-b 6 w 1 36
H. H. Goodall run out 40	
A. E. Hind c Woods b Mignon ... 60	Total......................501

WEST INDIANS.   1st inn.   2nd inn.

F. W. Sproston b Atkinson 9	b Snaith 72
F. Hinds b Atkinson 7	c and b Atkinson 17
P. J. Cox c Anthony b Snaith 55	c Hind b Gunn 18
C. A. Ollivierre c Howitt b Snaith 13	c Iremonger b Gunn 50
P. A. Goodman b Pepper............ 1	c Howitt b Gunn 16
G. C. Learmond c Shrewsbury b	
Pepper 6	l b w b Hind 15
L. Constantine b Snaith 20	not out 50
A. Warner not out 53	c Hind b Gunn 11
Burton c Shrewsbury b Gunn 31	c Gunn b Anthony.................. 2
W. H. Mignon c Shrewsbury b	
Gunn 0	b Anthony 0
Woods c Hind b Gunn 1	b Atkinson 8
Byes 7 l-b 2 w 2 n b 2 13	Byes 3 l-b 1 w 1 n b 1 6
Total ....—209	Total ....—265

BOWLING ANALYSIS.
NOTTS.—FIRST INNINGS.

	O.	M.	R.	W.		O.	M.	R	W.
Burton	73.2..	23	159	5	Constantine	3	0	14	0
Woods	35	10	82	0	Cox	14	1	49	1
Mignon	37	0	126	2	Ollivierre	2	0	10	0
Hinds	11	4	25	1					

Cox bowled a wide.

WEST INDIANS.—FIRST INNINGS.

	O.	M.	R.	W.		O.	M.	R	W.
Atkinson	19	5	69	2	Pepper	12	2	35	2
Anthony	13	2	25	0	Gunn	2.4	0	12	3
Snaith	15	3	55	3					

Atkinson and Pepper each bowled a no ball, and Snaith and Pepper each a wide.

SECOND INNINGS.

	O.	M.	R.	W.		O.	M.	R	W.
Hind	13	6	15	1	Gunn	22	1	88	4
Pepper	9	2	35	0	Snaith	9	3	24	1
Atkinson	19.5	3	57	2	Anthony	2	0	9	2
Iremonger	6	0	31	0					

Snaith bowled a wide and Anthony a no ball.

WILTSHIRE *v.* WEST INDIANS.

The worst performance of the tour. Constantine and Ollivierre played well, but the others were quite off their game. Woods had a good analysis,

WILTSHIRE.

Newman l b w b Woods 3
H S. Snell c and b Hinds 71
J. E. Stevens b Burton 12
O. G. Radcliffe c Constantine b Woods.................................. 68
W. S. Medlicott c Burton b Ollivierre. 23
A. Miller c Sproston b Burton 62

F. H. Humphrys b Burton 28
H. Taunton b Woods 20
Smart c Constantine b Woods...... 4
Smith not out 1
Overton b Woods 0
    Byes &c. 21
                                            —
    Total.................................313

WEST INDIANS.   1st inn.   2nd inn

S. W. Sproston c Medlicott b Overton 14
L. Constantine run out 43
P. J. Cox st Newman b Smart 0
C. A. Ollivierre not out.............. 26
P. A. Goodman c and b Overton... 10
A. Warner b Smith 1
Burton c Medlicott b Overton 0
F. Hinds l b w b Overton 0
G. L. Livingstone b Overton 9
W. Bowring b Overton............... 4
Woods b Overton 2
    Byes &c. 11
    Total..........................—120

c and b Overton 0
st Newman b Smart 32
l b w b Overton....................... 2
b Smith 21
st Newman b Smart 3
b Humphrys 8
c Smith b Humphrys 5
st Newman b Smart 6
b Humphrys 0
not out.................................. 3
b Humphrys 0
    Byes &c. 13
    Total.......................... —93

BOWLING ANALYSIS.

WILTSHIRE.—FIRST INNINGS.

	O.	R.	M.	W.		O.	M.	R.	W.
Woods	18	5	47	5	Cox	10	1	40	0
Burton	28	4	100	3	Ollivierre	7	2	33	1
Livingstone	4	0	19	0	Sproston	1	0	10	0
Hinds	8	1	32	1	Goodman	4	0	11	0

WEST INDIANS.—FIRST INNINGS.

Smith	15	5	35	1	Overton	13	3	33	7
Smart	9	0	41	1					

SECOND INNINGS.

Overton	15	6	28	2	Smart	4	0	15	3
Smith	10	3	20	1	Humphrys	6	1	17	4

LANCASHIRE *v.* WEST INDIANS.

A very even match, and the West Indians deserve every credit for the good fight they made against a strong side. Ollivierre was again the chief scorer, and Mignon bowled finely on a good wicket.

LANCASHIRE.	1st inn.		2nd inn.
J. Standing b Woods	7	b Woods	46
Hibbert b Burton	10	b Mignon	0
H. Cudworth c Constantine b Woods	102	b Mignon	7
Tyldesley b Mignon	34	c Bowring b Mignon	40
Briggs run out	12	b Burton	64
Hallows c Ollivierre b Mignon	7	b Woods	0
C. R. Hartley b Mignon	0	b Burton	5
A. N. Hornby c sub. b Mignon	4	absent hurt	—
Hallam b Mignon	1	c sub. b Burton	0
Pennington not out	3	c Bowring b Mignon	6
Webb b Mignon	1	not out	6
Byes 4 l-b 1 w 1	6	Byes 5 l-b 2 w 1	8
Total	—187	Total	—182

WEST INDIANS.	1st inn.		2nd inn
S. W. Sproston run out	19	run out	15
C. A. Ollivierre c Pennington b Webb	44	c Pennington b Hallam	60
P. J. Cox b Webb	14	b Briggs	14
J Constantine b Webb	33	b Briggs	2
W. Bowring b Webb	0	b Briggs	3
A. Warner b Hallows	2	b Briggs	0
G. C. Learmond c Tyldesley b Hallows	2	st Pennington b Briggs	5
Burton c Cudworth b Hallam	32	b Briggs	5
F. Hinds st Pennington b Hallam	16	c and b Hallam	12
W. H. Mignon b Webb	0	not out	0
Woods not out	6	l b w b Briggs	12
Byes 4 l-b 2	6	Byes 8 l-b 2	10
Total	—174	Total	—138

BOWLING ANALYSIS.

LANCASHIRE.—FIRST INNINGS.

	O.	M.	R.	W.		O.	M.	R.	W.
Burton	21	3	84	1	Mignon	17.4	3	44	6
Woods	15	1	53	2					

Mignon bowled one wide.

SECOND INNINGS.

	O.	M.	R.	W.		O.	M.	R.	W.
Mignon	27	9	73	4	Woods	11	3	38	2
Burton	25.3	9	49	3	Cox	4	1	14	0

Mignon bowled one wide.

WEST INDIANS.—FIRST INNINGS.

	O.	M.	R.	W.		O.	M.	R.	W.
Hallam	8.5	1	25	2	Hibbert	7	4	8	0
Hallows	20	4	62	2	Hartley	3	0	6	0
Webb	20	1	67	5					

SECOND INNINGS.

	O.	M.	R.	W.		O.	M.	R.	W.
Webb	13	5	27	0	Briggs	24.1	8	43	7
Hallam	21	4	42	2	Hallows	5	0	16	0

DERBYSHIRE v. WEST INDIANS.

A very good show all round. Goodman played very well indeed for his "century", as did Constantine for 62.

DERBYSHIRE.	1st inn.		2nd inn.
L. G. Wright c Constantine b Cox	58		
Dearneley c Woods b Burton	17	l b w b Mignon	26
Bagshaw c Woods b Burton	10	c Constantine b Woods	9
Storer c Goodman b Cox	65	not out	57
A. E. Lawton c Constantine b Cox	0	b Burton	32
Slater b Cox	0	b Mignon	6
F. A. Barrs b Cox	32	run out	0
Cadman c Burton b Mignon	0	b Burton	21
Hulme not out	41	b Woods	0
Humphries b Burton	2	not out	16
Bestwick c Bowring b Burton	0		
Byes 4 l-b 2 w 1 n b 2	9	Byes 8 l-b 4 w 2 n b 1	15
Total	—234	* Total	—182

* Innings declared closed.

WEST INDIANS.

C. A. Ollivierre c Humphries b Hulme	3	W. Bowring c Slater b Hulme	1
P. J. Cox b Hulme	34	Burton c Bagshaw b Hulme	15
L. S. D'Ade c Hulme b Slater	19	Woods b Hulme	15
L. Constantine c Storer b Slater	62	W. H. Mignon c Humphries b Slater	1
S. W. Sproston l b w b Hulme	17	Byes 8 l-b 1 n b 2	11
P. A. Goodman not out	104		
F. Hinds c Cadman b Bagshaw	11	Total	300

In the second innings of West Indians, C. A. Ollivierre scored (not out) 23 ; F. Hinds (not out) 17 ; W. Bowring (b Storer) 2 ; Burton (st Humphries b Storer) 0 ; no balls 3—total 45.

BOWLING ANALYSIS.

DERBYSHIRE.—FIRST INNINGS.

	O.	M.	R.	W.		O.	M.	R.	W.
Burton	29.2	7	78	4	Mignon	20	4	40	1
Woods	15	3	46	0	Cox	20	3	61	5

Woods bowled two no balls and Mignon one wide.

SECOND INNINGS.

	O.	M.	R.	W.		O.	M.	R.	W.
Burton	32	17	63	2	Mignon	20	7	34	2
Woods	14	2	45	2	Hinds	3	0	5	0
Cox	6	1	20	0					

Mignon bowled two wides and Woods one no ball.

WEST INDIANS.—FIRST INNINGS.

	O.	M.	R.	W.		O.	M.	R.	W.
Hulme	41	12	76	6	Slater	16.1	3	50	3
Bestwick	12	2	43	0	Storer	11	0	58	0
Bagshaw	20	8	48	1	Barrs	3	0	14	0

Storer bowled two no balls.

SECOND INNINGS.

	O.	M.	R.	W.		O.	M.	R.	W.
Bagshaw	4	0	12	0	Cadman	2	0	13	0
Storer	5	1	17	2					

Storer bowled three no balls.

STAFFORDSHIRE *v.* WEST INDIANS.

Limited to two days, this match was somewhat uneventful.

STAFFORDSHIRE.	1st inn.		2nd inn
Hollowood c Ollivierre b Cox	...103		
Grimshaw c Sproston b Burton ...	0		
Brown c Hinds b Burton	30	c Bowring b Woods	0
D. Stratton b Burton	0	b Burton	11
C. C. Matt b Burton	13	b Mignon	39
Hassell c Hinds b Burton	34	not out	17
D. H. Brownfield not out	46		
P. Briggs c and b Burton	7	l b w b Goodman	27
G. Price c Woods b Cox	0	not out	1
A. E. Fernie b Burton	0		
J. Poole b Woods	14		
Byes &c.	9	Byes &c.	15
Total	—256	*Total	—110

* Innings declared closed.

WEST INDIANS.

W. Bowring b Grimshaw	27	M. W. Kerr c Hollowood b Fernie	20
L. S. D'Ade b Grimshaw	0	Burton run out	0
F. Hinds c Hassell b Stratton	79	Woods c Grimshaw b Fernie	0
C. A. Ollivierre c Poole b Fernie	15	W. H. Mignon not out	17
P. A. Goodman c and b Hassell ...	30	Byes &c.	16
P. J. Cox run out	14		—
S. W. Sproston c Briggs b Fernie	10	Total	228

In the second innings of West Indians, D'Ade scored (c Grimshaw b Price) 24 ; Ollivierre (c Poole b Fernie) 1 ; Burton (b Brown) 16 ; Woods (not out) 8 ; byes 4—total 53.

BOWLING ANALYSIS.

STAFFORDSHIRE.—FIRST INNINGS.

	O.	M.	R.	W.		O.	M.	R.	W.
Burton	42	10	100	7	Mignon	15	3	40	0
Woods	18.5	5	53	1	Cox	15	2	54	2

Cox bowled one wide.

SECOND INNINGS.

	O.	M.	R.	W.		O.	M.	R.	W.
Goodman	7	2	15	1	Cox	5	0	14	0
Burton	11	1	27	1	Mignon	5	0	16	1
Woods	10	3	23	1					

WEST INDIANS.—FIRST INNINGS.

	O.	M.	R.	W.		O.	M.	R.	W.
Grimshaw	23	5	62	2	Briggs	1	0	9	0
Brown	12	5	17	0	Hassell	6	0	19	1
Price	8	1	18	0	Stratton	2	0	17	1
Fernie	17.3	1	70	4					

Fernie bowled one wide.

SECOND INNINGS.

	O.	M.	R.	W.		O.	M.	R.	W.
Fernie	3	0	15	1	Brown	4	1	8	1
Price	7	2	26	1					

20

HAMPSHIRE *v.* WEST INDIANS.

A victory for the West Indians by 88 runs. Sproston, Cox, Goodman and Bowring all scored well, and were well backed up by Woods, Burton and Mignon.

WEST INDIANS.   1st inn.

	2nd inn.
C. A. Ollivierre c Bird b Llewellyn 28	c Newton b Llewellyn 24
P. J. Cox c Radcliffe b Llewellyn 63	b Baldwin 0
P. A. Goodman b Llewellyn......... 52	c Bird b Baldwin 7
S.W.Sproston c Lamb b Llewellyn 86	st Bird b Llewellyn 4
G. C. Learmond b Webb............ 3	st Bird b Llewellyn 1
F. Hinds c Radcliffe b Llewellyn... 20	b Baldwin 22
L. S. D'Ade b Barton 19	b Webb 26
W. Bowring c Barton b Llewellyn 63	c Radcliffe b Llewellyn............ 12
Burton c Steel b Llewellyn 5	b Llewellyn 0
Woods b Webb 0	c Barton b Llewellyn.............. 4
Mignon not out 12	not out 0
Byes 15 l-b 4 19	Byes 9 l-b 3 12
Total................—370	Total....................—112

HAMPSHIRE.   1st inn.

	2nd inn.
C. Robson run out.................... 14	b Burton 0
Barton c Ollivierre b Woods 59	c Ollivierre b Burton 0
Webb c and b Woods 1	b Burton 15
C. B. Llewellyn c Hinds b Woods 93	c Burton b Woods 6
B. Lamb c Sproston b Woods...... 21	b Burton 10
A. H. Delme Radcliffe c Sproston	
b Mignon 6	c Learmond b Woods 20
E. J. Newton c and b Woods 2	c Woods b Burton 46
P. J. Bird c Ollivierre b Mignon... 32	b Woods 9
D. A. Steele c Ollivierre b Woods 4	l b w b Woods 8
Baldwin c Hinds b Mignon......... 8	run out 18
S. Whiting not out 4	not out 0
Byes 4 l-b 1.......................... 5	Byes 9 l-b 3 w 1 13
Total....................—249	Total....................—145

BOWLING ANALYSIS.
WEST INDIANS.—FIRST INNINGS.

	O.	M.	R.	W.		O.	M.	R.	W.
Barton	19	8	42	1	Robson	9	0	35	0
Llewellyn	54	10	153	7	Whiting	6	1	16	0
Steele	2	0	4	0	Webb	19	6	42	2
Baldwin	23	8	59	0					

SECOND INNINGS.

Llewellyn	24.2	7	34	6	Baldwin	16	8	23	3
Steele	3	0	22	0	Webb	6	1	21	1

HAMPSHIRE.—FIRST INNINGS.

Woods	30	6	93	6	Mignon	9.4	1	45	3
Burton	23	3	87	0	Cox	3	0	19	0

SECOND INNINGS.

Woods	16	9	55	4	Mignon	3	1	11	0
Burton	28.2	13	50	5	Cox	4	1	16	0

Mignon bowled one wide.

SURREY v. WEST INDIANS.

A grand performance all round, for Surrey had by no means a bad team. Ollivierre and Cox batted magnificently and hit up a hundred for the first wicket. Woods and Burton were in their best form throughout the match.

WEST INDIANS.

C. A. Ollivierre c Barker b Walker 94	W. Bowring b Walker 1
P. J Cox b Walker 142	Burton b Walker 0
F. Hinds c Dowson b Walker 7	W. H. Mignon b Knox.............. 0
L. Constantine b Walker 4	Woods st Strudwick b Knox ... 13
S. W. Sproston c and b Walker ... 0	Byes 10 l-b 8 18
P. A. Goodman not out.............. 34	—
L. S. D'Ade b Walker 15	Total....................328

SURREY.	1st inn.		2nd inn.
Brockwell c D'Ade b Woods	6	c Hinds b Burton	28
D. H. Butcher b Woods	9	not out	24
F. P. Knox b Woods..................	4	b Woods	0
H. L. Dawson b Woods	1	b Burton	4
K. F. M. Barker b Woods	0	l b w b Woods	8
E. M. Dowson run out	1	run out	26
J. Shuter c Sproston b Burton......	19	b Burton	7
J. W. Crawfurd c Constantine b Burton	13	b Woods	21
L. Walker not out	34	c Bowring b Woods	38
Richardson b Woods..................	20	b Woods	0
Strudwick b Woods	0	b Burton	1
Byes	10	Byes 19 l-b 1	20
Total....................—117		Total....................—177	

BOWLING ANALYSIS.

WEST INDIANS.—FIRST INNINGS.

	O.	M.	R.	W.		O.	M.	R.	W
Knox..............	13	3	50	2	Barker	7	1	39	0
Richardson	18	2	54	0	Crawfurd	3	0	14	0
Dowson...........	13	4	41	0	Walker.............	15	3	72	8
Brockwell.........	17	3	40	0					

SURREY.—FIRST INNINGS.

	O.	M.	R.	W.		O.	M.	R.	W
Burton	19	5	53	2	Mignon	2	0	6	0
Woods	19	5	48	7					

SECOND INNINGS

	O.	M.	R.	W.		O.	M.	R.	W
Burton	26.1	9	67	4	Mignon	6	2	16	0
Woods............	29	3	68	5	Hinds	2	0	6	0

LIVERPOOL AND DISTRICT *v.* WEST INDIANS.

Another good display. Sproston's 118 was beautifully made and Cox and Constantine also did well. A drawn game.

WEST INDIANS. 1st inn.   2nd inn.

C. A. Ollivierre c Burrough b
  Gregory 22   b Burrough 6
P. J. Cox c Holden b Gregory 76   b Burrough 7
L. S. D'Ade b Gregory 0   not out 12
P.A.Goodman c Kemble b Burrough 15   not out 42
L. Constantine c Barnes b Gregory 1   l b w b Burrough 28
W. Bowring c aud b Burrough ... 16   b Burrough 11
S. W. Sproston c Stott b Garnett 118   b Stott 11
F. Hinds c Stott b Gregory 0
Burton c Gregory b Burrough 5
Woods b Burrough 0
W. H. Mignon not out 1
Byes 8 l-b 2 n b 1 11   Byes 6 n b 1........................ 7

    Total....................—265   *Total ....—124
       * Innings declared closed.

LIVERPOOL AND DISTRICT.

H. C. Pilkington c Woods b Bur-   G. Bardswell c Bowring b Cox ... 8
  ton 12   A Stott c Woods b Cox 11
C. Holden c Hinds b Burton 86   A. T. Kemble b Burton 4
T. Ainscough c Cox b Burton 25   Gregory b Cox 3
H. G. Garnett c Sproston b Cox... 1   Ringrose not out.................... 1
R. J. Burrough c Hinds b Burton 13   Byes &c. 19
W. P. Barnes b Cox 45
                     Total............................218

In the second innings of Liverpool and District Holden scored (not out) 23 ; Pilkington (not out) 68 ; byes &c. 9—total 100.

BOWLING ANALYSIS.

WEST INDIANS.—FIRST INNINGS.

	O.	M.	R.	W.		O.	M.	R.	W
Gregory	36	13	111	5	Stott	6	0	36	0
Ringrose	19	4	43	0	Garnett	1	0	4	1
Burrough	15	4	60	4					

Ringrose bowled one no ball.

SECOND INNINGS.

Gregory	16	3	39	0	Ringrose	4	0	10	0
Burrough	24	11	42	4	Barnes	1	0	6	0
Stott	4	0	20	1					

Burrough bowled one no ball.

LIVERPOOL AND DISTRICT.—FIRST INNINGS.

Woods	19	4	43	0	Cox	23.2	5	64	5
Burton	40	11	98	5	Mignon	7	4	4	0

Mignon bowled two wides.

SECOND INNINGS.

Burton	5	0	15	0	Goodman	9	3	27	0
Hinds	2	0	12	0	Mignon	6	3	22	0
Woods	5	3	4	0	Cox	3	0	11	0

Mignon bowled one wide.

YORKSHIRE *v.* WEST INDIANS.

Bad weather : no play after the first day, when only twenty minutes play was possible.

YORKSHIRE.

T. L. Taylor, not out.................. 18 | Wainwright, not out 5

Total.............................. 23

Denton, T. H. Fearnley, Washington, R. W. Frank, Lord Hawke, Riley, Wilson (H.), Oyston, and Bairstow did not bat.

WEST INDIANS.—L. Constantine, P. A. Goodman, S. W. Sproston, G. C. Learmond, L. S. D'Ade, W. Bowring, F. Hinds, Burton, Woods, C. A. Ollivierre, and P. J. Cox.

BOWLING ANALYSIS.

YORKSHIRE.—FIRST INNINGS.

	O.	M.	R.	W.		O.	M.	R.	W.
Burton	5	1	9	0	Goodman	1	0	1	0
Woods	4	0	13	0					

NORFOLK *v.* WEST INDIANS.

A fitting wind up. Burton bowled superbly, and his analysis is worth noting. D'Ade at last showed in his true form.

NORFOLK.	1st inn.		2nd inn.
P. A. Fryer b Cox	29	c Goodman b Burton	0
F. Davies b Woods	7	c Hinds b Burton	1
W. L. B. Hayter c Constantine b Woods	6	c Hinds b Burton	0
G. G. Heslop c Ollivierre b Cox...	0	b Burton	0
P. W. Partridge c Woods b Cox...	2	c Hinds b Burton	5
C. F. Garnett c and b Woods	0	c Hinds b Burton	8
L. Barratt c D'Ade b Cox	14	b Woods	0
B. K. Wilson c Goodman b Woods	10	b Burton	13
S. D. Page b Woods	18	not out	3
G. F. Blake c D'Ade b Goodman	26	b Woods	0
Shore not out	0	c Hinds b Burton	1
Byes 2 l-b 3	5	Leg-bye	1
Total	—117	Total	—32

WEST INDIANS.

C. A. Ollivierre c and b Shore	0	F. Hinds c Barratt b Heslop	24
P. J. Cox b Shore	10	M. W. Kerr c Shore b Barratt ...	3
W. Bowring c Page b Barratt	6	Burton c Davies b Shore	2
L. S. D'Ade not out	68	Woods b Shore	14
S. W. Sproston c Blake b Shore...	17	Byes 7 w 1	8
P.A. Goodman c Wilson b Garnett	4		—
L. Constantine c Wilson b Garnett	9	Total	165

BOWLING ANALYSIS.

NORFOLK.—FIRST INNINGS.

	O.	M.	R.	W.		O.	M.	R.	W.
Woods	20	5	38	5	Cox	15	1	44	4
Burton	11	5	19	0	Goodman	3.2.	0	11	1

SECOND INNINGS.

	O.	M.	R.	W.		O.	M.	R.	W.
Burton	10.4	7	9	8	Woods	10	3	22	2

WEST INDIANS.—FIRST INNINGS.

	O.	M.	R.	W.		O.	M.	R.	W.
Shore	31.5	0	64	5	Garnett	9	3	30	2
Barratt	24	6	56	2	Heslop	2	0	7	1

Garnett bowled one wide.

BATTING AVERAGES.

	No. of Inns.	Times not out	Total Runs.	Most in an Inns.	Average
C. A. Ollivierre	29	2	883	159	32·70
L. Constantine	22	2	610	113	30·50
P. J. Cox	25	0	755	142	30.20
P. A. Goodman	23	3	563	104*	28·15
S. W. Sproston	27	0	600	118	22·22
F. Hinds	23	1	443	79	20·13
L. S. D'Ade...	13	2	193	68*	17·54
A. Warner	14	2	190	53*	15·83
W. Bowring	23	2	309	63	14·71
Burton	26	1	291	64*	11·64
G. C. Learmond	19	0	173	52	9·10
Woods	27	7	145	36	7·25
W. H. Mignon	19	8	68	17*	6·18
M. W. Kerr...	6	0	29	20	4·83
G. L. Livingstone	4	1	10	9	3·33

P. F. Warner batted once and scored 113.

* Signifies not out.

BOWLING AVERAGES.

	Overs.	Mdns.	Runs.	Wkts.	Average.
Woods	547·4	128	1551	72	21·54
Burton... ...	660·5	188	1681	78	21·55
S. W. Sproston ...	12	1	54	2	27·00
P. J. Cox	185	22	673	24	28·04
W. H. Mignon ...	285·5	65	883	30	29·43
C. A. Ollivierre ...	108.5	19	462	13	35·53
P. A. Goodman ...	82·2	11	270	5	54·00
F. Hinds	76	8	325	6	54·16
G. L. Livingstone ...	18	2	65	0	—
L. Constantine ...	18	3	79	0	—

Woods delivered five no-balls and one wide, Cox one no-ball and one wide Mignon seven wides, Constantine one wide, and Burton one no-ball.

HUNDREDS FOR.

L. Constantine, v. M.C.C., June 22	113
P. J. Cox, v. Surrey, July 30	142
P. A. Goodman, v. Derbyshire, July 19	104*
C. A. Ollivierre, v. Leicestershire, July 2	159
S. W. Sproston, v. Liverpool and District, August 2	118
P. F. Warner, v. Leicestershire, July 2	113

* Signifies not out.

HUNDREDS AGAINST.

H. Cudworth, for Lancashire, July 16	102
Gunn (W.), for Notts, July 9	161
J. E. Hill, for Warwickshire, June 18	145
Hollowood, for Staffordshire, July 23...	103
Iremonger, for Notts, July 9	101
G. L. Jessop, for Gloucestershire, June 28	157
J. R. Mason, for London County, June 11	126
H. R. Parkes, for London County, June 11	106*
A. F. Somerset, for M.C.C., June 22	118
C. L. Townsend, for Gloucestershire, June 28	140
Wrathall, for Gloucestershire, June 28	123

* Signifies not out.

" THE FIELD,"—On the West Indians.

It is to be regretted that the public has shown so little interest in the now finished campaign of the West Indian cricket ers ; although Englishmen in general have doubtless been glad to receive them, there has been no adequate demonstration of welcome. While modestly announcing that they came to England to learn the game, they have afforded a very gratifying and convincing proof that in their tropical homes cricket is played in much the same fashion as in the motherland and with no less skill. The programme arranged for them was so difficult that they could hardly have hoped to win more than one or two of the matches, and it was somewhat unfortunate that they were heralded as the equals of all but a few of the strongest of the county elevens. There was also a mistake in the preliminary estimate of the efficiency of their bowling ; but, on the other hand, they have shown much better batting than could reasonably be expected. An unbroken series of three day matches demands a different style of play from that which is encouraged by occasional club games, and puts a premium on patience and endurance. Our visitors must have been astonished at the high pitch to which these qualities have been cultivated by some of their professional opponents ; but, though they have evidently learned the value of discretion in batting, they played lively cricket to the end of their tour, and are not likely to take back with them enough of the " stone wall " style to bedim the gaiety of West Indian cricket. That they stood the strain of playing six days a week and actually improved in their last matches is very much to their credit ; that they were in no way discouraged by early reverses redounds not only to their own glory but that of the national game. If they could not attract attention and make history by introducing us to a Spofforth, a Boyle, a Murdoch, or a Blackham, they have at least gained the respect of English cricketers by better sportsmanship than has been observed in greater players. A curious part of their experience was the discomfort occasioned by the great heat of July, which might have been thought congenial to dwellers between the tropics. The illness of Mr. Warner, which has saddened the last weeks of the tour, is attributed in some part to sunstroke.—*August 18th 1900.*

————:o:————

A FURTHER APPRECIATION

On Wednesday the members of the West Indian team, with the exception of Messrs. Sproston, Mignon, and Warner, who are, for various reasons, staying some weeks longer in this country, and Mr. Ollivierre, who is credited with the intention of qualifying for Derbyshire by residence, left Waterloo on their homeward journey, and subsequently embarked on the Royal Mail steamer Don at Southampton.

With their brilliant victory over an eleven of Norfolk the team brought their programme to a close on the 18th inst. After losing four matches in succession they defeated the Minor Counties handsomely at the end of June, and subsequently gained a single innings triumph over Leicestershire. They were next beaten by Notts, Wiltshire, and Lancashire, but in their last seven engagements were undefeated; while they were seen at their best in disposing of Surrey and Hampshire. Of seventeen matches they were successful in five and lost eight, the remaining four being indecisive. Towards the close of their tour they had so much improved as to be almost a match for most of the first-class counties. Such success as fell to their lot is mainly attributable to their consistent batting. It will be seen that Ollivierre has the best average, and in point of style he certainly justified his right to his position at the head of the list. He is a graceful batsman, very quick in his movements, and well able to make the most of short-pitched balls. Constantine, the second on the list, is a daring hitter with a good eye, and quick on his feet. Cox, Goodman, and Sproston are all batsmen of ability, and the team as a whole could usually be counted upon for a respectable score. The bowling was not quite up to the standard of the batting, but Burton, a medium pace bowler of considerable accuracy, was always formidable, and Woods was very fast and straight. This pair would undoubtedly have had much better figures if they had been more frequently relieved, but the limited resources of the team imposed upon them a great deal more than their proportionate share of work. The players have good reason to congratulate themselves on the results of their enterprise.—*The " Field," August 25th, 1900.*

BANQUET TO THE VISITORS

BY

THE WEST INDIAN CLUB.

Y invitation of the West Indian Club a dinner was held on the evening of Monday, August 13th, 1900, at the Grand Hotel, Charing Cross, to meet the members of the West Indian Cricket Team, The Right Honourable Lord Harris, G.C.S.I., G.C.I.E., occupied the Chair, and there were also present :—The Earl of Selborne, Under Secretary of State for the Colonies, The Earl of Stamford. Sir W. Robinson, G.C.M.G., Sir Henry Thompson, K.C.M.G., Sir Cuthbert Quilter, Bart., M.P., Sir Nevile Lubbock, K.C.M.G., Sir Charles Walpole, Mr. S. W. Sproston, Mr. C. P. Lucas, Mr. W. C. Nock, Mr. J. B. Wastinholm, Hon. H. A. Bovell, Q.C., Mr. Horace G. Bowen, Mr. H. Courthope Bowen, Mr. Arthur J. Bowen, Mr. Arthur Johnson, Mr. W. C. Branday, Mr. J. W. Branday, Mr. J. J. Macfayden, Mr. C. H. Ward, Mr. L. de Mercado, Colonel J. Roper Parkington, J.P., D.L., Mr, Alfred L. Jones, Mr. J. B. Austin, Mr. R. Berens, Mr. A. N. Lubbock, Mr. G. Hudson Pile, Dr. G. B. Mason, Mr. L. Portman, Mr. G. E. D. Astwood, Mr. W. Mignon, Mr. W. Bowring, Mr. R. Wilson, Mr. A. F. Turnbull, Mr. P. A. Goodman, Mr. P. J. Cox, Mr. R. Innes Taylor, Mr. H. Smith-Turberville, Mr. Percy Quilter, Mr. G. L. Bannerman, Mr. J. E. Sprott, of the St. Vincent " Sentry," Mr. C. A. Ollivierre, Mr. L. S. D'Ade, Mr. F. Hinds, Mr. G. C. Learmond, Mr. Paul Cressall, Mr. H. Astley Berkeley, Mr. H. Edmund G. Boyle, Dr. E. R. Corbin, Mr. John H. Wilkinson, Mr. T. J. Wilkinson, The Hon. A. C. Ponsonby, and Mr. Algernon E. Aspinall, Hon. Sec. of The West Indian Club. The Toast List was as follows :—

" THE QUEEN."
" The Prince of Wales and rest of the Royal Family."
" The West Indian Cricket Team."
Proposed by Hon LORD HARRIS, G.C.S.I., G.C.I.E.
Responded to by Mr. STANLEY W. SPROSTON and Mr. W. C. NOCK.
" The Colonial Office."
Proposed by Sir CUTHBERT QUILTER, Bart., M.P.
Responded to by the EARL OF SELBORNE.
" The West Indian Club."
Proposed by Sir WILLIAM ROBINSON, G.C.M.G.
Responded to by the Earl OF STAMFORD.
" The Chairman."
Proposed by Sir NEVILE LUBBOCK, K.C.M.G.

THE CHAIRMAN.—My Lords and Gentlemen, I rise to propose the health of Her Majesty the Queen, and I suppose that in all the wide expanse of Her Majesty's dominions there is no wish more heartily prayed for than that her Majesty's health may be maintained. (Hear, hear.) Recently there has happened one of those mysterious occurences which draw us in the British Empire closer to the Queen. She has had a great loss in her family, and the Queen has so endeared herself to her people by her motherly love for them in all parts of Her Majesty's Empire that when she suffers we suffer with her. (Hear, hear.) I remember a very distinguished Hindoo saying once on a similar occasion, when Prince Eddy died, " In Hindoo religion the Queen is our mother, she is the mother of us all, and when she suffers here like this we grieve for her like our mother." That seemed to me a most beautiful idea, and one which does Her Majesty the Queen most infinite credit. By her marvellous sympathy with all parts of the Empire, she has endeared herself to all alike; she has shown absolute im—partiality to all parts of the Empire, and I am sure you will join with me in drinking most heartily the health of Her Majesty the Queen.

The toast was enthusiastically received and drunk with the utmost loyalty, every one present rising to his feet and joining in singing a verse of the National Anthem.

THE CHAIRMAN.—My Lords and Gentlemen, I rise to propose the toast of the evening, that of the West Indian Cricket Team. (Cheers.) And I regard it as a very great honour that I should have had this opportunity of proposing this toast, both from the point of view of cricket and from the point of view of the Empire. Taking the least important first, I think it was very courageous of the West Indian Cricket Team, so to speak, to beard the lion in his den—(laughter)—or on his native sward. Cheers.). But I have had myself—except in the one match I had the pleasure of playing with them—no experience of West Indian cricket, at least I do not think I played cricket when I was last in the West Indies—I do not remember it at any rate. (Laughter.). But there are others amongst English cricketers who are better judges far than myself, and who have been proved to be right by results. I hold in my hand a telegram from Lord Hawke—(cheers)—who I suppose knows better than anyone in the British Isles what are the capacities of cricketers throughout the Empire. (Hear, hear.) Lord Hawke by unremitting zeal for the game, and by that genial presence—(hear, hear)—and that knowledge of the game he possesses has become acquainted with cricketers in every part of the British Empire, and there is no better judge of what cricketers of any part of the Empire can do, and it was largely due to him and

Mr. P. F. Warner, I fancy that the West Indian Cricket Team were induced to come to this country. (Hear, hear.) Well, I hold in my hand a telegram from Lord Hawke, who, of course, is engaged elsewhere or he would have been here, and he telegraphs this :—.

" Best wishes for a pleasant evening. So sorry I cannot be with you Many congratulations to the Team on their successful tour. (Hear, hear.) I am glad to think that they have fully justified my high opinion of their ability to play a grand sportsmanlike game. (Hear, hear.) I heartily wish them *bon voyage*, and hope to see them return ere long fully qualified to try the full strength of our leading counties." (Cheers.)

Well, now there is a good deal in that from the cricketer's point of view. In the first place it shows that Lord Hawke from his visits to the West Indies had formed a very high opinion of the class of cricket that is played there. And he goes on to say that he considers that the results of their tour here have fully justified those anticipations of his. And I think that all those who have watched the performances of the West Indian Cricket Eleven here will bear him out. (Hear, hear.) It is a very responsible undertaking from such a small community to attempt to play the very high class cricket which the West Indian Team has done. (Hear, hear.) They have attempted it and I will speak about the result presently. But whatever the result was, there is but one opinion in cricket circles which bears out what Lord Hawke has stated in his telegram, that they have played the game in a thorough sportsmanlike spirit—(hear, hear)—in a way which we in England who hold the game in very great respect want to see it played. Well, as regards results, the press has supplied us with them this morning, and it is very much better to judge of a team's performances by the results drawn altogether, as the Press does in an easily acquired form. We see by the results that they played seventeen matches out of which they have won five, lost eight, and drawn four, and when you look at the class of cricket they have played, cricketers I think will not be surprised that they should have lost eight matches. They played a very strong team at the Crystal Palace, and then they played Worcestershire, Warwickshire, Gentlemen of M.C.C., the Minor Counties, Gloucestershire, Leicestershire, Nottinghamshire, Wiltshire, Derbyshire, Surrey, Liverpool and District, Yorkshire and Norfolk. Well, that is as about as high a trial for a young team as I can imagine, and the encouraging thing about it is this, that the longer they stayed the better they got. (Hear, hear.) And the happiest part of it all was their concluding match, because if ever a match was pulled out of the fire and won in magnificent form it was their match against Norfolk, where they had all the worst of it up to the middle of their first innings, and eventually won quite easily, their bowler doing, I fancy, almost a record—five overs, five maidens, five wickets. (Cheers.) Well now, from the cricketer's point of view, all that, I submit, is highly satisfactory to them, and highly satisfactory to us who were anxious that they should have a successful tour as well as a pleasant one. (Cheers.) I hope it has been a pleasant one. I hope that wherever they have been they have been received with courtesy, and with an anxiety to make the game pleasant to them as well as their visit to England pleasant. What pleases us, is, as I have already said, that they have played the game in the very best style, in the very best form and with an anxiety—an evident anxiety to learn, and I am sure that they came here knowing that they had got to learn. (Hear, hear.) It is no boast—no unnecessary boast to say that if you have got to learn first class cricket you have got to come to England. To see it in the quantity that you can in England, you cannot see it anywhere else but in England. (Hear, hear.) And I think that they were perfectly right, or I imagine that their advisers were perfectly right, in pitting them against the best class of cricket they could play, because the way to learn is to play against somebody better than yourself. It is no good playing against weak elevens, it only degenerates into contempt. They have played against better elevens than themselves, and whilst they have been playing so many matches and losing so many matches they have learned a good deal. They will go back and what they learned will certainly spread throughout the Islands. It is perfectly certain to improve cricket. I hope what they will say of us will encourage cricket, and will encourage a number of young men to take to the game, and I do not think that that is an unreasonable aspiration, although perhaps I am regarded as rather a monomaniac on the subject. But I hold and I believe I shall continue to hold to the last day of my life that cricket is a magnificent educational medium—(hear, hear)—that you can learn in it very many of the best lessons you can learn in any profession in this world—(hear, hear)—and I should hope that the West Indian Eleven have added to the lessons that they have learned in the game, and that they will be able to disseminate those lessons amongst their friends out there, and I sincerely trust that the West Indian Eleven will come here again at no very distant date. (Cheers.) If they can manage it they may be perfectly certain that they will be perfectly welcome here. (Renewed cheers.) I should like myself to see the thing go further. I should like to see matches between representative elevens of different parts of the Empire playing against each other in England, because I have a very high opinion of the advantage to the Empire of those visits, from various parts of the Empire to England and from England to various parts of the Empire in connection with the game. I think

it is a good education for us and a good education for them. I
remember when the first Australian Eleven came, the first white
Australian Eleven, that some of them and some of the people who
were interested in them were very indignant because the people at
Nottingham where they played first said, "Oh, but they ain't
black." Many people were very indignant; the Australians were
very indignant at such a thing being said. There was some reason
for it because the first Australian Team that came to this country
and the last that had come to this country before that team was a
Black Australian Team. People forget that the first Australian
Team that came to England from Australia was a black team—the
Aborigines—and very good players they were, and the next that
came was the first white eleven that came from Australia. That
taught the people in England something. There was an old story
which is constantly repeated in Australia of the gentlemen who was
so ignorant that he addressed a letter to Melbourne, New South
Wales. But I daresay there are lots of people in England—in fact
I know there are some people in England who are extremely
ignorant as to who the West Indians were. I was asked, "Now who
are these gentlemen who are playing here?" "Well," I said, "I
do not know, they come from the West Indies." "Yes, I know
but what race are they," I said, "They are Englishmen, I do not
know what other race they are, they happen to be Englishmen who
happen to reside in the West Indies." "But," they said, "We
did not understand that." That is an education for these particularly ignorant people who asked that question. (Cheers.) And
you may depend upon it that there are lots of other people whose
attention has been attracted to the West Indies by the fact that
there is a West Indian Eleven playing here, not so much for the
game, though the game is doing great things. The game is rubbing
off the rough edges. The interchange of matches between Englishmen and Australians has done a great deal to rub off rough edges
so far as cricket is concerned. (Hear, hear.) The thing is conducted on far more generous and friendly lines than it was when I
first remember it twenty years ago. And this has done good you
may depend upon it, and who can say how much good, who can say
how much it has contributed to the help that the Colonies have
extended to us in the last Transvaal war. I had the temerity to
boast once that cricket had done as much to bring the Australian
Colonies and England together as all the Treaties, Agreements and
Acts of Parliament that had been passed. (Hear, hear.) That of
course was rather playing to the gallery. (Laughter.) I do not
think that anybody can deny but what it has done good. It has
brought us more closely together; it has shown us that we have
got affinities which are attractive, and has helped each other to
understand each other better. Well, that can be extended to other
parts of the Empire, and I am perfectly certain that the fact of the

West Indian Eleven being in this country has done something to
attract attention to the West Indies—I should hope has induced
some sympathy for the trials that the West Indies have gone
through—possibly, I do not know, I should not like to say that
with Sir Nevile Lubbock here—I was almost going to say has
attracted as much attention as the Report of the Commission.
(Laughter.) I will not say that because the Report was
admirable, whereas I am sure that some of the English cricket at
any rate has not been admirable. Well now, I said that I should
very much like to see these visits extended, and I tried once to help
that idea myself at the time of the great American Exhibition at
Chicago, I suppose about 1892 or 1893—something of that sort. I
did my very best to get a Parsee Eleven—I could have got a Parsee
Eleven, there was no difficulty about that—to play against the
Philadelphians there. I thought that would have been a tremendous triumph for England to get a team from India to play against a
team from Philadelphia. It was not the fault of our side in India
that it did not come off, but that is the kind of thing that I am
thinking of, and I do hope to see matches played in England between representative teams from other parts of the Empire, as well
as against England itself before I am bowled out. Well now,
gentlemen one can go on rambling about cricket you know for any
amount of time, but it is rather exhausting running on ; there are
other toasts to follow, and so I must not detain you long. (Cries of
" Go on.") The grounds on which I propose to you the health of
our friends are these, that in the first place it was a very courageous
thing to come here and attempt the class of cricket that they did.
I remember very well the first visit I ever made out of this country.
I went with the Gentlemen of England to Canada and the United
States in 1872, and I thought that was rather a serious undertaking although we had—putting myself on one side altogether,
really a very fine team. And if one thought that was a
serious undertaking what must it be for an eleven such
as the West Indies could turn out, having had no previous experience of that class of cricket except from the
visits of an English Team over there, which under the effects of
climate and hospitality, a long sea voyage and so on—(Laughter)—
did not play quite so well as it does in England, with that only experience what a very gallant thing it was for them, to undertake to
come here and play the first class counties. (Hear, hear.) Then
I submit to you that they played the game in the very best spirit—
(Hear, hear),—and lastly I submit to you, that they have been
as successful as it was possible for them to hope themselves, or for
their friends to expect. And in conclusion I submit to you that in
doing, as they have done, they have done something to add another
thread to that web, which is connecting together every part of the
British Empire. (Cheers.) I propose to you, the toast of the

West Indian Eleven, coupled with the name of Mr. Nock. I am extremely sorry, and I know he is, that I cannot connect with this toast the name of the gentleman who has been captain through nearly all the matches—Mr. Warner. I believe I might have connected the name of Mr. Sproston, but he is anxious that Mr. Nock should appear as the speech-maker, rather if not as the Captain of the Team. I propose to you the toast of the West Indian Eleven, coupled with the name of Mr. Nock.

MR. NOCK.—In the absence of our captain Mr. Warner and the modesty of Mr. Sproston I have been called upon. It is my pleasure this evening to respond on behalf of the West Indian Cricket Team to your very kind entertainment here this evening. We have just had a most pleasant tour, it has done us an immense amount of good, it will do good I think, as Lord Harris has said, in developing cricket among the younger men of our colonies but it will also be a very great factor in bringing us more closely together as sons of the mother country. (Hear, hear). I think I can safely say that this is one of the great objects of those who promoted this tour. (Hear, hear). I thank you Gentlemen on behalf of the Team for this very enjoyable evening which you have afforded us. We are not quite suprised at it because we fully expected it. It is only a sort of instance, if I may call it such, of the many enjoyable days we have spent in the mother country. We have toured almost throughout the Kingdom, barring a few counties, and we have met with nothing else but the most absolute kindness and attention wherever we have been. (Hear, hear). I thank you Gentlemen very much indeed for the very kindly way in which you have received the toast which has been proposed to you. (Cheers.)

SIR CUTHBERT QUILTER, Bart., M.P.—Lord Harris and Gentlemen, I do not know why I have been selected for the honour of proposing a toast of this importance except it may be perhaps because I have not long since had the great pleasure of visiting and receiving the hospitality of many of the Islands which are so well represented here this evening. (Hear, hear). With regard to the West Indian Team, I am very glad to be able to-night to bid them welcome and to express my great regret that other more important engagements, well and adequately arranged for as they have been, prevented their paying us a visit in the county of Suffolk. (Hear, hear). I am sure they would have received a hospitable welcome. Alas! the county of Suffolk from various reasons (perhaps from its division or from other causes into which I cannot go here) is not even in the list of the Minor Counties and therefore it has added another to its many grievances from a cricket point of view in that it has not been enabled to entertain and to play a match with the West Indian Team. The only consolation we have is that they managed to beat handsomely the neighbouring County of Norfolk. (Hear, hear and Laughter). Therefore we can only imagine what would have happened to us if they had met a team from our county. (Cries of No, no). I must confess that when I first heard of this visit, fond as I am of cricket, I looked upon it as possessing a deeper significance. I thought possibly it might, as Lord Harris has so well said, forge another link in the chain which binds the Colonies to the mother country. (Hear, hear). A chain which, I am sorry to say even in the presence of Lord Selborne and other distinguished representatives of the Colonial Office, has not always in times past been held up at our end with that vigour and with that strength which we should like. But things have altered now, and under Mr. Chamberlain and Lord Selborne we have learned a more excellent way. (Cheers). Gentlemen, the Colonial Office is the toast that I have to propose now. (Hear, hear). The Colonial Office may be said to have occupied the most important position in the thoughts of our countrymen of any Office during this eventful year, and it is fortunate indeed that we have at the head of that Office a Statesmen so patient, so brave, so far-seeing as Mr. Chamberlain.—(Cheers),—so well seconded in the House of Lords by the Noble Lord whom I shall ask to respond to this toast. (Renewed cheers). Gentlemen the treatment that has been meted out to our Colonies in years past has not added lustre to our annals. (Hear, hear). But I think we need not fear a repetition of that want of policy—I will not call it a policy— that want of policy we need fear no longer. The sympathy of the Colonies in the terrible war in which we have been engaged has been the great factor that has sustained the honour and kept up the courage to renewed efforts of the United Kingdom. It must not altogether be forgotten that in England's difficulty the first note of Colonial sympathy came across the water in that celebrated message to Mr. Pitt in which he was told, when the stress of circumstances pressed old England hard, not to be afraid, that Barbados was with him! (Laughter and cheers, and a voice, "good old Barbados"). And not only was Barbados with him, but with us. I am glad to say and I know Lord Selborne will corroborate me, that assistance in men and in sympathy have been forthcoming in recent times from the West Indian Islands—(Hear, hear)—not- ably from the Island of Trinidad, who offered us men in the time of our greatest need in the dark days of last winter. And not only so, but since then I think the Colonial Office have been glad to avail themselves, or would have availed themselves, had necess- ity required it, of the service of the Volunteers from Jamacia and elsewhere had not the Ashanti War been so successfully dealt with by the forces on the spot. Gentlemen, no matter where the Colony is, the bond to the mother country seems to grow stronger and stronger, and I heartily re-echo the words of your Noble Chairman when he said that of all the things which bind the Colonies to the mother country, I think we may put sport and such sport as cricket in the forefront. It teaches us that we have to exercise the same bravery, the same forbearance, the same patience and while these qualities which have recently been exhibited so conspicuously in the Transvaal by the representatives from every part of the Empire is maintained, I do not think we need have any fear about foreign alliances or about foreign complications. (Cheers). Gentlemen, we must not forget that our toast is the Colonial Office, and I think we must admit that the Colonial Office has had on its hands this year, affairs of so pressing a nature, that we could not expect very much attention to be paid even to West Indian affairs. But the year has not passed without one notable instance. I am glad to find that the Colonial Secretary and those who assist him have found time to conclude an arrangement with that celebrated firm which seems to succeed in all its undertakings—the firm of Elder Dempster, which has now become the household word amongst us—for a fast service to Jamaica—it is not only Jamaica that requires a fast service—and a service between the Islands. But these questions I must not go into now. I only desire in proposing the toast of the Colonial Office to express on your behalf, and I believe on behalf of almost every inhabitant of this great Empire our hearty approbation of the policy which has been of late years pursued at the Colonial Office, by its distinguished head, by the Noble Lord who I am so glad to see amongst us to-night, and who has to answer this toast, and also Mr. Lucas, whom I am glad—we are all glad to see here—who especially has West Indian affairs in his charge, and, who brings to bear on those affairs a mind thoroughly well trained, and a sympathy as large and wide as you can expect from any English Official. (Cheers and laughter). Gentlemen, without any more to do I give you the toast to which we are all now proud to do honour,—the Colonial Office, coupled with the name of Lord Selborne. (Cheers).

THE EARL OF SELBORNE.—My Lords and Gentlemen, Sir Cuthbert Quilter, my old colleague in the House of Commons, has proposed this toast with his accustomed geniality but I cannot help feeling that this toast has been brought into your proceedings under more or less of a false pretence. (Cries of No. no). Well, we do a good many things in the Colonial Office and we are accustomed to Office Fixtures for the Crown Colonies of almost any type from a girder bridge to a door scraper, but cricket fixtures have not yet been part of the commodities which are we willing to retail. I think that we should be quite capable

of adding that department if it were not for the fact that we have
parted with our principal cricket authority, Sir Augustus Hemming,
to the West Indies, and therefore till another cricketer as renowned
has arisen in the Colonial Office I am afraid we must defer the
opening of that fresh department. Sir Cuthbert Quilter could
not restain himself from a little backward glance at the Colonial
Office of past years. Now, I tell you frankly Gentlemen, I did not
come here to answer for the Colonial Office of the past ; I have
quite enough to do to answer for the Colonial Office of the present,
But that is an answer that I am very proud to give. (Hear, hear.)
Now, public conception of the Colonial Office is a very odd mixture.
I often see in the Press—in a certain kind of Press, an allusion to
the Colonial Office, as if it were a conglomeration of individuals of
the most astonishing ignorance and the most persistent perversity,
who were always delighted in flying in the light of common sense,
and of doing all they could and can possibly do, to do the wrong
thing. Now I am sure that is not really the Colonial Office.
What is the Colonial Office ? It is a collection of permanent civil
servants, presided over by two birds of passage, who are Parliamentary. Those Parliamentary heads, no doubt, have a great influence on the policy of the Colonial Office of their day, but the
civil servants through whom alone they can work, are the most loyal
and devoted set of public servants that this world has ever seen.
(Hear, hear.) They do not differ in that from the civil servants of
other departments—of course they make mistakes. Why it is perfectly ridiculous to set up the thesis that any public office does not
make mistakes. I certainly am not going to defend any public
office, with which I am connected, by setting up any preposterous
theory that they cannot make mistakes. The fact is simply as I
have said that you have in the Colonial Office, a set of civil servants, whose whole heart and soul are with the Colonies and in
the Colonies with which they have to deal, who devote their whole
lives to the service of those Colonies, and who gradually accumulate
in themselves a most astonishing mass of experience and information. Their centralized opinions are probably and necessarily
checked by local opinion, and that local check is necessary to them,
as the check of their experience is to the local Government. (Hear,
hear.) Now Gentlemen, I have rather deviated from the convivial
topics of the evening, but Sir Cuthbert Quilter led me on to serious
ground. I think our Chairman has trodden with extraordinary
skill on the debatable line, which runs between the serious and the
convivial. He has sketched out to you very lightly the influence
which cricket and cricket tours such as that of the West Indian
Team may have on the great issues such as the relation of the
mother country with her Colonies, and of the different parts of the
British Empire with each other. Of course it would be possible

to exaggerate the importance in our Imperial unity, which our Imperial sports may play, but I am quite sure he would be a very foolish man who would deny that cricket and our tastes as a race for sport, have had a real influence in harmonising and consolidating the different parts of the Empire. (Hear, hear.) Lord Harris touched very lightly on the example from Australia. (Hear, hear.) There are some people who say that the West Indies have suffered from a want of common interest, that they have been too much like the unbound sticks (a voice " Quite right ") that might have been a bundle of faggots, but which were not. Now that is a big subject on which I do not mean to trench to-night, I only indicate that that has been suggested, Look what your Australian fellow-countrymen have done. They also were a disunited bundle of sticks ; they now have united into the great Commonwealth of Australia. And who shall say Gentlemen, that it has not been a really important factor in that consolidation, the difficulty that there was beforehand of selecting a united Australian team. Look at the divergences that had to be reconciled, if there was not an equal number. You cannot divide six into eleven so that all may get the same number. But with one united Australia, the selection of the team is simple. Again the separate Colonies in the West Indies have complained very much at different times, of the scanty nature of their telegraphic service. Well, that again is a large question that I do not mean to attempt to deal with at length to-night, but look at the example of Australia. They found that the telegraphic service was so inadequate to supply the people of this country with a proper report of the cricket matches that they insisted on having a Pacific cable. (Laughter.) And again, to touch upon another great subject, the military authorities in this country have more than once thought that it would be advisable if some of the gallant Australian troops came over to this country, to perfect their drill and their discipline. Well, difficulties always supervened, and it may have been merely a coincidence, but when the last Australian Team came over, a squadron of New South Wales Lancers came over too and I have always held privately the theory that what really overcame all difficulties was the determination on the part of the promoters of the cricket tour to have a sufficent number of substitutes in England at that time, in case any failure in health should occur amongst the Australian Team, With reference to your force also in the West Indies, all that we feel towards our Australian fellow-countrymen who came forward in the hour of the anxiety of the mother country, we feel to the West Indies. All that they could offer, they offered to us ; all that it has been in their power to do to help in this great national struggle they have done—(Hear hear,)—and just as we shall never forget and never can forget what Australia and Canada have done, do not believe because what the

West Indies have been able to do, has been less in quantity that we regard it the least bit as less in quality. (Cheers.) We only hope that you will in all seriousness endeavour to copy the example of Australia according to your comparative means. If you can find measures by which your soldiers can be sent over here, to be trained in fraternity with the Imperial troops, they would indeed be welcome. If the means that can be brought to bear, can go on increasing the means of communication as they are being increased, as Sir Cuthbert Quilter has just reminded you, owing to the enterprise of our friend Mr. Jones whom we are glad to see with us to-night, I can only assure you that nothing the Colonial Office can do to accelerate and facilitate those communications will be wanting. Long may the connection between sport and Imperial unity continue, and the spirit I see to-night is the best augury for the future. (Cheers.)

SIR WILLIAM ROBINSON.—My Lords and Gentlemen, suffering as I am, from bronchial catarrh, a fact which I notified to the Secretary of this Club, I had hoped that I would have been spared the exertion this evening of making a speech. But it would appear that Mr. Aspinall's dictum is like the law of the Medes and Persians which changeth not, and he courteously informed me by telegram, that what he had written, he had written, therefore, I bow respectfully to his mandate. I can assure you that it gives me a very great deal of pleasure to propose the toast of the West Indian Club, which is second in importance only to the toast of the Cricket Team, which has been so ably proposed by Lord Harris. Why I should have been selected for this toast, like Sir Cuthbert Quilter I cannot possibly say, excepting that it may be from the fact that I am not even a member and certainly not a vice-president of this Club, and that I did not know of its existence, even more than a year ago, but I do hope that Lord Stamford, one of the vice-presidents, will be able to enlighten you much more than I can upon those points. You will all have had a report of the Club, and you will have noticed, as I have noticed, that it is a very young Club, only three years old, in its infancy, yet we hope to carry it to its maturity. One feature you will all have noticed, and that is that there is a balance in hand to the credit of the Club of the large sum of £1 14 2. (Laughter.) Gentlemen, you need not laugh at that I can assure you, because that is £1 9 10 more than was found in the Treasury Chest in Queensland, when the late Sir George Brown and Sir Robert Herbert respectively assumed the appointments, of Governor and Colonial Secretary. (Laughter.) My Lord Harris has spoken in a most interesting and able manner, on the question of cricket, but he has not referred to the prophecies of Lord Hawke. There has been a good deal of talk lately, about Moore's Almanack, and Zadkiel's Almanack, but there are two prophecies in Lord Hawke's letter to this Club, which certainly deserve attention. He said in his letter to the Club, " doubtless many of them on their first appearance will have much to learn, and suffer many defeats." That was a very safe prophecy, but he quite omitted to state that five of these gentlemen would make centuries, which they have done. The objects of the Club, of course are most praiseworthy, and I quite agree with Sir Cuthbert Quilter, in what he said, that so long as Mr. Chamberlain and Lord Selborne are at the head of the Colonial Office, to which I had the honour to belong, in that bad time to which you have referred, some twenty-five years ago—so long as these able men are at the head of the Office, the interests of all the Colonies will certainly not suffer. In the last prophecy Lord Hawke, whose absence is very much to be regretted to-night, and also the absence of Mr. Warner, said " the result of such a visit will be far-reaching, not only from the sporting point of view, but also from the Imperial standpoint, helping as it would do, to draw closer the ties that bind us to the mother country." That is perfectly true, and Lord Harris has referred to that very happily in his speech, and I am quite sure if you had listened to the cheers which I heard at the Oval a fortnight ago, you would believe that this result had been accomplished. And I am sure of this, Gentlemen, that the man in the street no longer thinks that Trinidad is on the mainland of South Africa, and that British Guiana as was held many years ago, by the highest possible authorities, was a West Indian Island. (Cheers and laughter.) I have very great pleasure in proposing the toast of success to the West Indian Club, and I may say, that if I am offered the proverbial shilling I shall possibly accept it. I have pleasure in calling upon Lord Stamford to succeed me and I am quite sure he will tell you a great deal more about the Club and its future prospects, which I hope will be successful, than I have been able to do. (Cheers.)

THE EARL OF STAMFORD.—Lord Harris and Gentlemen, I am afraid I shall hardly be able to fulfil the expectations which Sir William Robinson has raised in your minds, of being able to tell you from very intimate knowledge, of the details of the work which the West Indian Club proposes to do, but I know something of the indefatigable labour which others have devoted to making the Club a success, and I rejoice with them in the substantial success which the Club has already attained. For myself, I felt that an institution of this kind had great claims upon me. I have always looked back—I look back still with most affectionate interest to the West Indies, in which I spent six very happy years, and in which I made many most valuable friends, and learned a great deal of the most valuable discipline of my life. (Hear, hear.) And I was of course most eager to associate myself with a move- ment of this kind, which should draw together West Indians in England, and link them with West Indians across the water. I suppose I happen to know rather better than most people, the ins and outs of the West Indies. I think I have visited nearly every British Island in the West Indian Colonies, not to speak of num- erous French and Dutch and Spanish Islands as well, and I have always felt the great charm which the West Indies must necess- arily excerise over those who have once seen them ; and I feel how much people in England miss, from not being acquainted with those ancient and most beautiful colonies. What a charming resort the West Indies are for the winter season ; if only they were better known, one thinks how people would flock out there, to take advantage of that lovely climate and those beautiful surroundings, and all that most generous open-handed hospitality which is dis- pensed there. (Hear, hear.) And one has that sort of feeling, how far the West Indies have been kept in the back-ground hitherto, how little comparatively has been known of them, and how much better they deserve to have been known ; there seems to have been from earliest days, a certain amount of grievance associated with them, a grievance which we in England should do our best to remedy. And after all it is in the West Indies that some of the most interesting problems of Government are being solved and have been solved in the past ; the gradual amalgamation of diff- erent races, a problem which the United States of America have solved far less satisfactorily than we in the West Indies have done hitherto. I went from the West Indies and spent a year in the United States, and I felt how far backward in many respects the United States of America, with all their advancement, were in the way of dealing with other races which were included in their do- minion. (Cheers.) When I narrated in the United States some of our experiences in the West Indies, how I valued my association with many of the African races, it was received with great coldness, in the United States of America. I will not say more than that, but one recognised how many years behindhand, in some import- ant respects, that progressive country is as compared with England (Cheers.) Well, what I feel, with regard to a Club like this, is how much more may be done, simply in the way of enjoyment, than by business, than by hard work. After all it is in the moments of relaxation, that one gets ahead : first of all in many cases, I dare- say, those moments would be of very little use unless the way had been prepared by hard business work before them and yet some- how, one seems to get on in these moments of enjoyment, these opportunities of dining together, of speaking face to face with the people, who have come from over the water, more is done than is done, by reams of correspondence, emanating from the Colonial Office, or from other sources in England, and addressed to the Colonies. (Cheers.) And what those who are interested, who have this affectionate interest in the West Indies, have most at heart, is in the first place the drawing together of the West Indian Colonies themselves, and then the drawing together with the bonds of Empire, for if one wishes to draw a body together, you must have your body to deal with, in the first instance. That, as Lord Selborne so thoughtfully and wisely pointed out, has been the great trouble hitherto. The West Indies have been proud of being independent units, and I suppose each of us has felt that in our individual life, that at one time or another in our lives, we have been proud of standing by ourselves and fighting for our own hand ; and I venture to think that that has been the feeling and is so still, of many of the West Indian Islands, " We are proud of our own little Colony, we want to stand by ourselves, we do not want to be mixed up with other people," and yet we find after all, that personally and socially, that is not the way to get through life. We must work in—we must follow in—the same tracks, we must give and take, we must make allowances for others, and we must unite with each other, in order to make any real way in the world. And in that connection, I regard cricket, as one of the most valuable of disciplines. Cricket is one of those games, where you do not play for your own hand, where you all have to work together ; you cannot consider yourself, you must consider the interests of the whole eleven ; and there is that wholesome lesson to be drawn from cricket, that we must play into each others hands if we are going to win the game. So the West Indies will find, that they must play into each others hand also, and win the game. (Cheers.) Each part of the great dependencies, the great states which are joined together in the British Empire, have their own special gift to contribute to the welfare of the whole Empire, and the West Indies, as I well know, have brilliant gifts of their own. They have, as I said, that of generous hospitality, they have a certain Southern fervour which they may bring and waken up our own somewhat stolid attitude in England. The gifts which they have to contribute are welcome indeed to us in England, and they give them, contribute to make up some part of that great united whole, a whole which is becoming year by year more and more united—the total City of the British Empire. I have been rambling on in this way—(Cries of " go on ")—but I do feel the necessity for unity. (Hear, hear.) I feel the necessity for the working together of all those valuable elements, which make up our world wide Empire, and I feel very strongly indeed, how by working together on simple straightforward business-like principles that I recognise, more and more as I live, how much good solid business has to do with the drawing together of the various parts of the Empire; and I need not say, how much I welcome those words which fell a little before I spoke, about this great business enterprise which is beginning now with the Island of Jamaica, and which I believe will extend further—(Cheers)—how much work of that kind will tend to draw together those bonds which we all desire to see more closely drawn. I respond then, I thank you very much for the way in which the toast of the West Indian Club has been proposed and received, because I believe that the West Indian Club is one factor in that union, in that drawing together of the West Indies themselves, and of the West Indies with the British Empire at large, and I thank you with the utmost cordiality, for the way in which you have received the toast. (Cheers.)

THE HON. A. C. PONSONBY.—My Lords and Gentlemen, it has been very strongly impressed upon me from this end of the table, and from the other, that before we separate to-night, and before we propose the toast of our Noble Chairman, one toast should not be overlooked, which is the toast of Mr. A. N. Lubbock. (Cheers.) The reason why Mr. Lubbock has been selected for the honour of having his health proposed and drunk by this assembly, is that upon him has fallen the whole responsibility for the bringing over from the West Indies of this Team. (Cheers.) All the arrangements have been made by him, also the whole of the finances have been put in order by him alone. Sir William Robinson a few minutes ago, in his notable speech, referred to the question of the size of the balance of the West Indian Club. It is certainly very small, but it is one of those balances which can be easily rectified, if those gentlemen will assist the Club to put them in order. It is very simple how that can be done. Mr. Lubbock, is the Treasurer of our Club; he is always at the seat of custom, and is always prepared to receive any donation which any gentleman may be pleased to give. (Cheers and laughter.) My Lord Harris, I believe it is generally conceded, that in the House of Legislature which you adorn, the work is done by the few, rather than by the many. And that is exactly the same in the Committee of our Club; the work is done by a few. I am not going to mention the name of Mr. Aspinall, because the honours are thick upon him, therefore it remains to point out the services which Mr. A. N. Lubbock has rendered and to ask you to drink his health. I give you the toast of Mr. A. N. Lubbock.

MR. A. N. LUBBOCK.—My Lords and Gentlemen, I beg to thank you very heartily for the very kind way in which you have drunk my health. There were one or two gentlemen here to-night, who thought it rather a peculiar thing that they were asked to propose a toast, and if they were in any trouble you can imagine what trouble I am in, when my name is not even down on the toast list. There is only one remark which I would like to make, which I think would interest everyone here to-night, and that is with reference to the part of the speech which was made by our Chairman at the beginning of the evening, in connection with the subject of cricket teams from the Colonies playing together. When it was decided to bring a West Indian Eleven over here by the Committee of the West Indian Club, almost at exactly the same time it was decided to bring over a team of cricketers from South Africa—(Cheers),—and so far did this go, that our printed list of matches for the West Indian cricketers actually included one match which was to be " The West Indies v. South Africa," at Lords. (Cheers.) The dates had actually been fixed. Although Lord Hawke thought at the time that it would be exceedingly difficult to get a team over from South Africa, the South Africans so fervently believed that there would be no bother, that the war would be over by that time, that they telegraphed so late as March, to say that they were coming. The date was arranged, and when the telegram came to say they would not be able to come, I received a letter from Lord Hawke, in which he said that one of the dreams of his life had passed away. I shall never forget the letter. It reminded me at the time, as our worthy Chairman has said, of what a grand thing it would be to have a match between the different Colonies at Lords. It has been a very great pleasure to me to do all that I could, not only to further this scheme, but all the work I have been doing, has been done under the supervision of the worthy Chairman of our Sports Committee—Lord Hawke. The first time I ever had to do any work for Lord Hawke, was at my first private school, when I was cricket fag to him, and I may say that I have had great pleasure in renewing my work under Lord Hawke, and I hope I may do so many times again. I beg to thank you very much for the kind way in which you have received the toast of my health. (Cheers.)

Sir NEVILE LUBBOCK.—My Lords and Gentlemen, I have been asked to propose the next toast, and I can assure you that it gives me the greatest satisfaction to propose the health of an old Etonian, and also to propose the health of an old cricketer with myself many years ago. (Hear, hear.) I am afraid that since Lord Harris and myself played for the County of Kent a great many years have elapsed. We also played very frequently together in a club that was called the Ramblers Club, an old Etonian Club, and I am sure that he as well as myself look back upon those matches with the greatest pleasure, and they are always a sort of sign of association between us and between all Ramblers. But I am sure that since the days when we played for Kent and when we played together for the Ramblers a great many years have elapsed, and I am sorry to say that a greater number of years have elapsed since I played, than since Lord Harris played. In those days I may say cricket was unknown in the West Indies. When I first went to the West Indies in 1870, I do not think I saw a cricket bat at all. About three years ago I was in the West Indies and I then saw that a very great change had come over the scene. I was on one of our estates in British Guiana—those of you who come from British Guiana will know the estate, I mean the estate called Hampton Court—and it so happened that when I got up in the morning there had been six inches of rain the day before; in front of me there was a large ridge and furrow field. The furrows of this field were under water, and in it little boys were fishing with cast nets. On the top of the furrows other little boys were playing cricket. I think this shows a great advance. It occurred to me then, here is a little bond of feeling between us all in England and between the little dark boys, as they were some of them little coolie boys from India, some of them little black boys of African descent, and I could not help thinking myself that here we in England are holding out the hand of fellowship to the coloured races all over the world, to the descendants of Africans in the West Indies, and the descendants of Indians in India, and I cannot but feel the hope that that hand of fellowship which is held out by the whites of England will be cordially grasped by those descendants of the Africans who are in the West Indies and by those descendants of the coloured races in India. I believe that in India that bond of relationship is pretty fast at the present moment. I cannot but hope as years go on that that bond will become faster and faster between the African descendants in the West Indies and the whites. I throw that out as a suggestion only, because I think nothing could be more injurious to the West Indies than that there should be anything of a colour feeling there. I do not think there is any colour feeling there worth speaking of in the white members of the population, and I think there would be no greater disadvantage to the West Indies than that there should be any such feeling at all fostered by the descendants of the races from Africa. That is the only serious remark I wish to make to night. With regard to our chairman those of you who have been in Trinidad know the feeling of esteem and veneration in which his father's name is still held. (Cheers.) Lord Harris's father was Governor of Trinidad in a period of the greatest depression in the West Indies, and the manner in which he struggled against that depression, the sympathy which he showed with the West Indies during that time, has left a name in Trinidad which, I believe, will never be forgotten. I think, therefore, it is especially appropriate, for that reason, that Lord Harris should have taken the chair to-night. (Cheers.) And that is apart from his sympathy of course as a cricketer. We all know he has been a most ardent cricketer. He has probably done as much as anybody in England to promote the game, and when I say to promote the game I mean the game played in a gentlemanly spirit. I am a little bit afraid myself, as an old stager, that some of our old games and sports are degenerating into the professional element. I am very glad to hear about the West Indian Team that they played their matches as gentlemen. I am very glad to think, being connected with the West Indies, that those coming from the West Indies have played their game as gentlemen. There is such a thing as being able to lose a match as gentlemen. For my part I would much rather lose a match as a gentleman than pull it out of the fire by any means that will not bear the closest inspection. I am very glad to think that the West Indian Team have done themselves credit in that respect, that there has not been a breath of suspicion against them in any of the matches they have played, that they have played as thorough gentlemen throughout, and I venture to think that it will be a good thing for cricket if it is always played in that spirit. I venture to think that the good sense of this country will see that it is so. As a cricketer and as a friend of the West Indies I ask you to join me in drinking to Lord Harris, and I am sure on your behalf I must thank him most cordially for coming here to preside over us. (Cheers.)

The toast was enthusiastically responded to with musical honours, and "one cheer more for Lady Harris."

THE CHAIRMAN.—Sir Nevile and Gentlemen, it is very pleasant to have one's health proposed by an old friend, an old comrade like Sir Nevile, and I am very grateful to you for having received the toast in the way in which you have done. I am very happy, I am sure Sir Nevile will be equally glad, that I can corroborate him as regards one part of his speech. I have some advantage or disadvantage, at any rate I have some twenty years older experience of the West Indies than he has, and I can say that I never saw a cricket bat when I was there. (Laughter.) But gentlemen I can assure you that although the time that has separated me from Trinidad is very very long, and although the connection has been very slight, consisting as it does of the kind recollection in which my father's name is held there, and of relatives still residing in Trinidad, slight as that connection is it is impossible for me to have dis-regarded the fact of its being my birth place, and of the interest of which I ought and I am glad to think I naturally take in it. And I think one of the greatest compliments ever paid to me, not for anything I have done but for my father's sake, that has ever been paid to me was in 1897. I was invited, as I read it by them—it came from the Governor of Trinidad—I was invited to attend the centenary festivity as guest of the island. I regarded it as a compliment to what my father had done for the island, and I appreciated it profoundly. I regret even more than I can say that engagements in this country—I discussed it very carefully with Lady Harris—engagements in this country prevented me accepting this invitation. Now it is a curious thing, Sir Nevile has referred to my father's time of anxiety in Trinidad when he was there, and to what he did for the introduction of coolie labour there—now it is a curious thing that only within this last month we have been seeing considerable differences as regards the importation of foreign labour, coloured labour into the Transvaal and having business connections with the Transvaal, and knowing that, within the last six months I have had extracted from blue books, letters which passed between my father and the then Secretary of State for the Colonies as regards the importation of native labour from outside, believing that those letters would show the attitude that the Colonial Office is bound to take up having regard for the inherent anxiety which exists in England that labour in all our Colonies should be free. Having regard to that anxiety, I believe that those extracts will be of use some day or other in the Transvaal. Well, it is a curious coincidence, that fifty years ago, this introduction to this subject should have taken place in the West Indies, and that fifty years afterwards in connection with the game of which my father was a devoted admirer, and I believe a very excellent practical exponent, that fifty years afterwards, Sir Nevile Lubbock should refer to the subject, and that I myself, then a baby in Trinidad should have the opportunity of referring to it here in connection with another part of the Empire. (Cheers.) I do not think that amongst the many public dinners that I have, and that we all have to attend in this country, that I have attended any more interesting than this. The speeches seem to have been admirably condensed and at the same time highly interesting. I should have ventured to have advanced my own opinion if that had not been more admirably expressed by Lord Stamford in a speech, which I think, if I may venture to say so it would be impossible to improve upon as regards its imperial tone, and at the same time its sympathetic tone for the Colonies themselves, a speech which I wish he had had the opportunity of delivering in the other assembly which he graces as well as here. And if I may venture to suggest that is one of the very great advantages that we possess in our Upper Chamber, that we have there very many gentlemen who have, and who take the opportunity afforded them by their position and their leisure, of making themselves thoroughly acquainted with all parts of the British Empire, and that there is condensed there a mass of information, and influenced by the independent spirit of the Upper Chamber, on occasions makes itself felt and permeates through the whole mass and the heart of the Empire—the Parliament of Great Britain—most effectively; and therefore it having been well said there is no need for me to dilate upon those more important subjects. I would like before I sit down to touch upon one subject which is important to cricket if to nothing else, which was referred to by Sir Nevile—the subject of professionalism in cricket. As regards other parts of the Empire it is impossible for me to say anything, because I do not understand what the circumstances might be, but as regards England I think I know something about it, and I say as regards cricket in England that it would have been impossible for cricket to have attained the very high status that it has in the appreciation of the public if it had not been for professional cricket. (Hear, hear.) Some weeks ago, I think it was about the middle of July, in a newspaper, I think it was the St. James's Gazette, in a sub-editorial article, I saw an expression which gave me the greatest surprise and the greatest pain. It used this phrase: "The taint of professionalism in cricket." Well as a very old cricketer and as a lover of the game, and with a very close acquaintance with professionalism and with professionals in cricket, I do not hesitate to say that such an expression is absolutely unjustified and unworthy of the class to whom it referred. (Cheers.) I have spent a great deal of my time, when I had the opportunity of playing cricket, with professional cricketers, and I say that as a class they are as respectable as the professionals of any class in this country. (Cheers.) And that they have done a great deal to raise the tone of cricket in this country, and that they go on improving from year to year. (Hear, hear.) I do not as a cricketer or as a man regard it as any discredit to them that they have to take money to recompense them for the time they give to the game. It would be a very evil day for England, because I think that cricket has a very great beneficial influence in the country, it will be a very evil day for England if professionalism were shut out of the game of cricket. I have no doubt it has got to be controlled and wisely controlled, and I think it is wisely controlled at this moment. There have been times when the professionals have made their voices heard, but by the fortunate circumstance that the gentlemen who play are friends with professionals and are comrades with them, any difficulty that could have arisen from that circumstance has been avoided, and the old pleasant relations have never been broken whilst the position of the professionals has been improved. I am glad to have this opportunity of repudiating in the strongest terms—and I think I shall be supported by all amateurs in this country—the expression I have referred to. (Cheers.)

Sir NEVILE LUBBOCK.—Might I say Lord Harris you misunderstood.

THE CHAIRMAN.—I mean this, not other parts of the Empire.

Sir NEVILE LUBBOCK.—It was rather the gambling.

THE CHAIRMAN.—Quite so ; yours was a general expression which gave me the opportunity. Gentlemen, once more referring to myself I cannot say how grateful I am to you for having paid me the compliment of asking me to take the chair to-night. I felt when the West Indian Eleven came here that in my small way I ought to, and I was anxious to, do something to welcome them to this country, and I thought that possibly the easiest way I could do that would be to weaken the M.C.C. Team by insisting on their including me as a member of it. (Laughter.) And I am sure that the West Indian Eleven must acknowledge that I did not hurt them very much. (Renewed laughter.) I was very delighted to have the opportunity. My appearances at Lords have passed away, but this was an occasion when I thought that I must make an appearance at headquarters and welcome as far as I could the West Indian Team by appearing against them. And now to that has been added this opportunity of presiding at this dinner which the Club has given them. I can assure them that what I said in my first speech was no mere form of words. I do think it was a most gallant effort of them to come to this country, and I am very pleased that the result has been so satisfactory to them, and that they now go back to the West Indies, thinking, I hope, a great deal better of themselves, very much more confident as to their capacity to meet the best bowlers in England, and with the resolution to encourage all whom they may meet in the West Indies to take up the game, but also with the determination to come back here again some day and try once more which of us is best—they or our counties here. (Cheers.)

Sir NEVILE LUBBOCK.—May I be allowed to say I did not wish to say a word against professional cricket. I have played with professional cricketers and many of them are most honourable men—most of them : I rather meant the gambling spirit which is rather overcoming some of our games and which I think is a detrimental one.

The proceedings which throughout were of a most enjoyable character were then brought to a close.

During the evening the following programme of music was performed by the " Bijou " Orchestra.

1. MARCH ... " Le Regiment Favori," ... ... *Ert'l.*

2. VALSE... ... " Arc en Ciel," ... ... *Waldteufel.*

3. SELECTION ... " San Toy," ... ... *S. Jones.*

4. SONG & DANCE " Come my lubly Darling,"... ... *Schartan.*

5. VALSE... ... " The Messenger Boy," ... ... *Caryll.*

6. MARCIA ... ... " A Frangesa," ... *P. M. Costa.*

7. SELECTION ..." The Belle of New York," ... ... *Kerker.*

8. VALSE ... ... " Florodora," ... ... *L. Stuart.*

9. COCOANUT DANCE... ... ... *Bray.*

10. SELECTION ... " The Geisha," ... ... *S. Jones.*

11. VALSE ... ... " Modestie," ... ... *Waldteufel.*

" God save the Queen."

Conductor ... ... Mr. J. POUGHER.

Notes

Chapter One

1. See, with special reference to the construction of 'coloured' in Jamaica, Rex Nettleford, 'Freedom of Thought and Expression: Nineteenth Century West Indian Creole Experience', *Caribbean Quarterly* 36, nos. 1&2, (June 1990).

2. Elsa Goveia, *Slave Society in the British Leeward Islands at the End of the Eighteenth Century* (New Haven: Yale University Press, 1965), 258–60.

3. Gordon Rohlehr, *Calypso and Society in Pre-Independence Trinidad* (Port of Spain: The Author, 1990), 3.

4. Anon., 'Proud of Our Cricket', in *Guyana Sports Annual, 1962–3* (Georgetown: Guiana [sic] Graphic Ltd., 1963), 45–6.

5. See Maureen Warner-Lewis, *Central Africa in the Caribbean: Transcending Time, Transforming Cultures* (Kingston, Jamaica: University of the West Indies Press, 2003), Chapter 8.

6. See Hilary Beckles, 'The Origins and Development of West Indies Cricket Culture in the Nineteenth Century: Jamaica and Barbados', in *Liberation Cricket: West Indies Cricket Culture*, eds. Beckles and Stoddart (Kingston, Jamaica: Ian Randle Publishers, 1995) 33–43.

7. Michael Manley, *A History of West Indies Cricket* (London: Andre Deutsch, 1995 [1988]), 19–20.

8. Ibid., 18, 20.

9. Richard D.E. Burton, *Afro-Creole: Power, Opposition and Play in the Caribbean* (Ithaca, NY: Cornell University Press, 1997), 30.

10. Ibid. See Marcus Williams, 'Mystery of a Mud-Covered Buckle', *The Times*, November 5, 1986.

11. Ibid. [Williams].

12. Burton, op. cit. [1997], p. 177.

13. Ibid., 177–8.

14. See note 5 [pp.207–8].

1 5 . Ibid. [p. 208].

1 6 . Hilary Beckles, *The Development of West Indies Cricket: Vol.1 The Age of Nationalism* (Kingston, Jamaica: The University of the West Indies Press, 1998), 7–8.

1 7 . Ibid., Chapter 1: 'West Indian Embrace of Englishness'.

1 8 . Jack Williams, *Cricket and Race* (Oxford: Berg, 2001), 15–6.

1 9 . John Hearne, 'What the Barbadian Means to Me', *New World Quarterly* III, nos. 1&2 (1966–67), [Reproduced in *On the Canvas of the World*, ed. George Lamming, (1999), 165].

2 0 . Hilary Beckles, ed., 'Introduction', in *An Area of Conquest: Popular Democracy and West Indies Cricket Supremacy* (Kingston, Jamaica: Ian Randle Publishers, 1994), xiv–xv.

2 1 . Christopher Nicole, *West Indian Cricket* (London: Phoenix House, 1957), 11–12.

2 2 . Brian L. Moore, 'Colonialism, Cricket Culture and Afro-Creole Identity in the Caribbean after Emancipation: The Case of Guyana', *The Journal of Caribbean History* 33, nos. 1&2, (1999): 60–1.

2 3 . Brian L. Moore, *Cultural Power, Resistance and Pluralism: Colonial Guyana, 1838-1900* (Montreal: McGill-Queen's University Press, 1995), 132–3.

2 4 . Marcus Williams and Gordon Phillips, *The Wisden Book of Cricket Memorabilia* (Oxford: Lennard Publishing, 1990), 246.

Chapter Two

1 . C.L.R. James, *Beyond a Boundary* (London: Serpent's Tail, 1983 [1963]), 3 .

2 . Edgar Mittelholzer, *A Swarthy Boy* (London: Putnam, 1963)[, 155.]

3 . Brian L. Moore, 'Colonialism, Cricket Culture and Afro-Creole Identity in the Caribbean after Emancipation: The Case of Guyana', *The Journal of Caribbean History* 33, nos. 1&2 (1999): 58–9.

4 . *Jamaica Daily Telegraph*, May 1, 1900.

5 . Hilary Beckles, *A History of Barbados: From Amerindian Settlement to Nation-State* (Cambridge: Cambridge University Press, 1990), 89–90.

6 . F.A. Hoyos, *Grantley Adams and the Social Revolution* (London: Macmillan, 1974), 4.

7 . Bridget Brereton and Kevin A. Yelvington, 'Introduction: The Promise of Emancipation', in *The Colonial Caribbean in Transition: Essays on Post-Emancipation Social History,* eds. Brereton and Yelvington (Kingston, Jamaica: The University of the West Indies Press, 1999), 8–9.

8 . Keith A.P. Sandiford, *Cricket Nurseries of Colonial Barbados: The Elite Schools, 1865-1966* (Kingston, Jamaica: The University of the West Indies

Press, 1998), 3.

9. Ibid., 2.

10. Sir Pelham Warner, *Long Innings: The Autobiography of Sir Pelham Warner* (London: George G. Harrap, 1951), 15.

11. Ibid., 16.

12. See note 8 [p. 45]; See also Keith A.P. Sandiford and Brian Stoddart, 'The Elite Schools and Cricket in Barbados: A Study in Colonial Continuity', in *Liberation Cricket: West Indies Cricket Culture*, eds. Hilary Beckles and Brian Stoddart (Kingston, Jamaica: Ian Randle Publishers, 1995), 46–7.

13. See note 8 [p. 5].

14. *Argosy*, January 27, 1900.

15. See note 8 [Sandiford and Stoddard (1995)], pp. 47–8.

16. Ibid., 48.

17. Keith A.P. Sandiford and Earle H. Newton, *Combermere School and the Barbadian Society* (Kingston, Jamaica: The University of the West Indies Press, 1995), 20, 22.

18. J.A. Mangan, *Athleticism in the Victorian and Edwardian Public School: The Emergence and Consolidation of an Educational Ideology* (Cambridge: Cambridge University Press, 1981), 136–37.

19. A.J. Jukes Browne, 'Barbadians at Home (Part I): The English in Barbados', *The Argosy*, January 7, 1893.

20. Richard Holt, *Sport and the British: A Modern History* (Oxford: Clarendon Press, 1989), 205.

21. See note 1 [pp. 24-5], for James's reaction to Aneurin Bevan's sneering at the public school code.

22. Ibid., 112.

23. Ibid., 24-5.

24. Ibid., 25-6.

25. *Times* (London), November 13, 1865.

26. Aviston A. Downes, 'The Contestation for Recreational Space in Barbados, 1880–1910', in *In the Shadow of the Plantation: Caribbean History and Legacy*, ed. Alvin O. Thompson (Kingston, Jamaica: Ian Randle Publishers, 2002), 382, 376–7.

27. See note 8 [p. 147].

28. A.J. Jukes Browne, 'Barbadians at Home (Part II): The English in Barbados', *Argosy*, January 14, 1893.

29. John Hearne, 'What the Barbadian Means to Me', *New World Quarterly* III, nos. 1&2 (Barbados Independence Issue, 1966–67), [Reproduced in *On the Canvas of the World*, ed. George Lamming, 1999), 164–65].

30. See note 6 [p. 9].

31. Ibid., 15.

3 2. C.L.R. James, 'Discovering Literature in Trinidad: The Nineteen Thirties', *Savacou*, no. 2, (September 1970): 55.

3 3. Clem Seecharan, *'Tiger in the Stars': The Anatomy of Indian Achievement in British Guiana, 1919–29* (London: Macmillan, 1997), 310. The quote from Scoles is taken from his *Sketches of African and Indian Life in British Guiana* ([Georgetown], British Guiana: The Argosy Press, 1885), 33–4.

3 4. Ibid. [Seecharan, pp. 310–11].

3 5. See Brain Stoddart, 'Cricket, Cultural Formation and Cultural Continuity in Barbados', in *Liberation Cricket: West Indies Cricket Culture*, eds. Beckles and Stoddart (Kingston, Jamaica: Ian Randle Publishers, 1995); and Bruce Hamilton, *Cricket in Barbados* ([Bridgetown], Barbados: The Advocate Press, 1947).

3 6. Hilary Beckles, 'The Political Ideology of West Indies Cricket Culture', in *Liberation Cricket*, eds. Beckles and Stoddart [p.149].

Chapter Three

1 . Clem Seecharan, *Joseph Ruhomon's India: The Progress of her People at Home and Abroad and How those in British Guiana may Improve Themselves* (Kingston, Jamaica: The University of the West Indies Press, 2001), 28–30.

2 . Quoted in Patrick Bryan, *The Jamaican People, 1880-1902: Race, Class and Social Control* (London: Macmillan, 1991), 221.

3 . Quoted in Ibid., 223–4.

4 . Peter Roberts, *From Oral to Literate Culture: Colonial Experience in the English West Indies* (Kingston, Jamaica: The University of the West Indies Press, 1997), 153.

5 . Bridget Brereton, 'Social Organisation and Class, Racial and Cultural Conflict in 19th Century Trinidad', in *Trinidad Ethnicity*, ed. Kevin Yelvington (London: Macmillan, 1993), 47–8.

6 . Quoted in Joy Lumsden, 'Dr. Robert Love and Jamaican Politics, 1889–1914', (PhD thesis, University of the West Indies, Mona, 1988), 194.

7 . Ibid., 196.

8 . Ibid., 199.

9 . Ibid., 210.

1 0. Ibid., 207, 209.

1 1. Ibid., 200.

1 2. See note 2 (Chapter 2, pp. 11–21).

1 3. Ibid., 14.

1 4. Ibid., 262.

1 5. *Daily Gleaner*, October 9, 1899.

16. *Daily Gleaner*, October 10, 1899.
17. *Daily Gleaner*, October 11, 1899.
18. *Daily Gleaner*, October 12, 1899.
19. *Daily Gleaner*, October 13, 1899.
20. Ibid.
21. *Daily Gleaner*, October 21, 1899.
22. The Archbishop of the West Indies, 'The Present and the Future of Jamaica', *Daily Gleaner*, October 25, 1899.
23. Leader, *Daily Gleaner*, October 26, 1899.
24. *Daily Gleaner*, October 7, 1899.
25. Leader, *Daily Gleaner*, October 9, 1899.
26. *Daily Gleaner*, October 13, 1899.
27. *Daily Gleaner*, October 4, 1899.
28. Lord Olivier, *Jamaica: The Blessed Island* (London: Faber and Faber, 1936), 191.
29. Quoted in Patrick Bryan, op. cit., [1991], 233.
30. John Edward Bruce, 'Dr. Theophilus E.S. Scholes, M.D.', *The Voice* [New York], (January 1907), 114–15.
31. Patrick Bryan, op. cit. [1991], 251.
32. T.E.S. Scholes, *Glimpses of the Ages or the 'Superior' and 'Inferior' Races so-called, Discussed in the Light of Science and History, Vol. 1* (London: John Long, 1905), 235, 220.
33. Quoted in Peter A. Roberts, op. cit., [1997], 124.
34. See note 32 [pp. 236, 249–50].
35. Ibid., 266–7.
36. Ibid., 64.
37. Ibid., 281.
38. Ibid., 267–8.
39. Leader, *Daily Gleaner*, December 8, 1899.
40. *Daily Gleaner*, December 23, 1899.
41. Ibid.
42. See note 32 [pp. 281–2].
43. Patrick Bryan, op. cit., [1971], 259.
44. Quoted in Ibid., 258.
45. *Daily Gleaner*, October 30, 1899.
46. Ibid.
47. Leader, *Daily Gleaner*, November 4, 1899.
48. *Daily Gleaner*, December 6, 1899.
49. *Daily Gleaner*, December 7, 1899.

50. *Daily Gleaner*, December 16, 1899.

51. *Daily Gleaner*, June 20, 1899.

52. Quoted in Rupert Lewis, 'Garvey's Forerunners: Love and Bedward', *Race and Class*, Vol. XXXVIII, no. 3, (1987): 34–5.

53. Ibid., 35.

54. See note 1 [Chapter Two: 'H.V.P. Bronkhurst and Joseph Ruhomon: The Shaping of an Intellect', pp. 11–18.]

55. Ibid., 53, 52, 65.

56. Ibid., 57–8.

57. Ibid., 63, 60.

58. Ibid., 70, 69.

59. Ibid., 29–30.

60. Quoted in Ibid., 28–9.

61. Quoted in Ibid., 29.

62. See note 59.

63. *Barbados Globe*, July 13, 1893.

64. *Argosy*, August 11, 1894.

65. Keith A.P. Sandiford, 'Guyana's Contribution to West Indies Cricket', *Journal of the Cricket Society* 20, no. 1 (Autumn 2000): 14.

66. *Barbados Globe*, February 20, 1893.

67. *Daily Chronicle*, October 7, 1892.

68. *Port of Spain Gazette*, June 27, 1900.

69. See note 1 [p. 63].

70. Ibid., 39–40.

71. Ibid., 43.

72. Michael Manley, *A History of West Indies Cricket* (London: Andre Deutsch, 1995), 132.

73. A.A. Thomson, *Cricket: The Golden Ages* (London: The Sportsman Book Club, 1962 [1961]), 87–8.

74. Ibid., p. 88.

75. Trevor Bailey, 'Rohan Kanhai: The Magician from Guyana', in his *The Greatest of My Time* (London: The Sportsman Book Club, 1970 [1968]), 107, 109.

Chapter Four

1. Bridget Brereton, 'Social Organisation and Class, Racial and Cultural Conflict in 19th Century Trinidad', in *Trinidad Ethnicity*, ed. Kevin Yelvington (London: Macmillan, 1993), 40.

2. Ibid., 40–1.

3. Hilary Beckles, '"The Unkindest Cut": West Indies Cricket and Anti-Apartheid Struggles at Home and Abroad, 1893–1993', in *A Spirit of Dominance: Cricket and Nationalism in the West Indies*, ed. Beckles (Kingston, Jamaica: Canoe Press, University of the West Indies, 1998), 101.

4. Ibid., 100–1.

5. *Cricket*, December 28, 1894.

6. *Cricket*, January 31, 1895.

7. C.P. Bowen, *English Cricketers in the West Indies: An Account of the Cricket Matches Played between Mr. R. Slade Lucas's English Team and the West Indian Cricket Teams during the Season of 1895* (Bridgetown, Barbados: Herald Office, 1895), 12.

8. *Cricket*, April 25, 1895.

9. *Cricket*, April 11, 1895.

10. Ibid.

11. Hilary Beckles, *The Development of West Indies Cricket, Vol. 1: The Age of Nationalism* (Kingston, Jamaica: The University of the West Indies Press, 1998), 23–4.

12. *Cricket*, February 28, 1895.

13. Ibid.

14. Ibid.

15. Leader, *Barbados Globe*, January 31, 1895.

16. See note 12.

17. *Cricket*, March 28, 1895.

18. Bridget Brereton, *Race Relations in Colonial Trinidad* (Cambridge: Cambridge University Press, 1979), 219.

19. Ibid., 57.

20. Ibid., 42.

21. See Clem Seecharan, 'The Shaping of the Indo-Caribbean People: Guyana and Trinidad to the 1940s', *Journal of Caribbean Studies* 14, nos. 1&2, (Fall 1999–Spring 2000): 61–92.

22. See Brereton, op. cit. [1979], Chapter 5: 'The Rise of a Coloured and Black Middle Class'.

23. See Donald Wood, *Trinidad in Transition: The Years after Slavery* (London: Oxford University Press, 1968), for the massive contribution of Charles Warner to the shaping of Trinidad after Emancipation.

24. See note 17.

25. Ibid.

26. *Port of Spain Gazette*, February 28, 1895.

27. Quoted in Hilary Beckles, 'The Origins and Development of West Indies

Cricket Culture in the Nineteenth Century: Jamaica and Barbados', in *Liberation Cricket*, eds. Beckles and Stoddart, 39–40.

28. Anna Grimshaw ed., *Cricket: C.L.R. James* (London: Allison and Busby, 1986), 16.

29. Ibid., 249.

30. Keith A.P. Sandiford, *Cricket Nurseries of Colonial Barbados: The Elite Schools, 1865–1966* (Kingston, Jamaica: The University of the West Indies Press, 1998), 77.

31. Learie Constantine, *Cricket in the Sun* (London: Stanley Paul, n.d. [1947]), 63.

32. C.P. Bowen, op. cit., [1895], p.14.

33. Quoted in Ibid., 13, 15.

34. *The English Cricketers in Barbados, January–February, 1895* ([Bridgetown], Barbados: The Agricultural Reporter, 1895), 19.

35. Brian Stoddart, 'Cricket, Social Formation and Cultural Continuity in Barbados', in *Liberation Cricket*, eds. Beckles and Stoddart, 66.

36. See Richard D.E. Burton, 'Cricket, Carnival and Street Culture in the Caribbean', in *Liberation Cricket*, eds. Beckles and Stoddart, 89–106.

37. C.P. Bowen, op. cit., [1895], pp. 18–9.

38. Ibid., 19.

39. Ibid., 24.

40. Ibid., 1–2.

41. Ibid., 20–1.

42. Ibid., 21.

43. Ibid., 3.

44. Bruce Hamilton, *Cricket in Barbados* ([Bridgetown], Barbados: The Advocate Press, 1947), 62.

45. Ibid., 50.

Chapter Five

1. *Daily Chronicle*, January 1, 1897.

2. See Walter Rodney, *A History of the Guyanese Working People, 1881–1905* (Baltimore: The Johns Hopkins University Press, 1981), Chapter 5: 'The Politics of the Middle Class and the Masses, 1880–92'.

3. CO 111/500, (Individuals: H.K. Davson), Henry K. Davson to Edward Wingfield (CO), November 11, 1897.

4. Leader, *Argosy*, January 9, 1897.

5. See note 1.

6. Leader, *Daily Chronicle*, January 6, 1897.

7. Leader, *Daily Chronicle*, January 8, 1897.

8. *Argosy*, February 6, 1897.

9. Leader, *Argosy*, January 9, 1897.

10. *Argosy*, January 23, 1897.

11. *Argosy*, January 30, 1897.

12. See note 10.

13. See note 8.

14. *Argosy*, January 16, 1897.

15. *Argosy*, March 27, 1897.

16. Leader, *Daily Chronicle*, March 28, 1897.

17. P.F. [Plum] Warner, 'Cricket in the West Indies and America', *Wisden*, 1898.

18. *Cricket*, February 25, 1897.

19. Ibid.; *Wisden*, 1898.

20. Ibid.

21. *Sportsman*, February 20, 1897.

22. See note 18.

23. *Barbados Globe*, January 8, 1897.

24. *Barbados Globe*, February 22, 1897.

25. *Sportsman*, March 20, 1897.

26. *Port of Spain Gazette*, February 4, 1897.

27. Ibid.

28. *Port of Spain Gazette*, February 16, 1897.

29. Ibid.

30. See note 26.

31. Ibid.

32. P.F. [Plum], *Cricket in Many Climes* (London: Heinemann, 1900), 13–4.

33. *Trinidad Guardian*, January 6, 1942.

34. Neville Cardus, 'Preface', in Learie Constantine, *Cricket and I* (London: Philip Allan, 1933).

35. Hilary Beckles, *The Development of West Indies Cricket, Vol. 1: The Age of Nationalism* (Kingston, Jamaica: The University of the West Indies Press, 1998), 39.

36. Sir Pelham [Plum] Warner, *Long Innings: The Autobiography* (London: George G. Harrap, 1951), 43.

37. See note 18.

38. Lord Hawke, *Recollections and Reminiscences* (London: Williams and Norgate, 1924), 168–70.

39. Warner, op. cit., [1900], p. 7.

40. Ibid., 8–9.

41. Ibid., 9.

42. Ibid.

43. See note 40.

44. A.A. Thomson, 'P.F. Warner', in *Great Cricketers*, ed. Denzil Batchelor (London: Eyre and Spottiswoode, 1970), 56–7.

45. *Argosy*, April 17, 1897.

46. Ibid.

47. Ibid.

48. Gerald Howat, *Plum Warner* (London: Unwin Hyman, 1987), 19.

49. Leader, *Daily Chronicle*, January 8, 1897.

50. Ibid.

51. Quoted in Harold A. Lutchman, 'The British Guiana Constitutional Change of 1891', *History Gazette*, No. 40, (January 1992): 4.

52. Ibid., 7.

53. Hilary Beckles, *A History of Barbados: From Amerindian Settlement to Nation-State* (Cambridge: Cambridge University Press, 1990), 116.

54. Ibid., 118.

55. Ibid., 118–120.

56. Ibid., 120.

57. Ibid., 126.

58. Theophilus E.S. Scholes, MD, *Sugar and the West Indies* (London: Elliot Stock, 1897), 3–4.

59. Ibid., 6.

60. Ibid., 5.

61. Ibid., 15–6, 19.

62. Ibid., 19.

63. *Report of the West India Royal Commission* [H.W. Norman, Chairman], (London: HMSO, 1897), paragraphs 111–8.

64. Quoted in Francis Lee, *Fabianism and Colonialism: The Life and Political Thought of Lord Sydney Olivier* (London: Defiant Books, 1988), 102–3.

65. Ibid., 102–3, 127.

66. *Daily Gleaner*, September 29, 1900.

67. Holbrook Jackson, *The Eighteen Nineties: A Review of Arts and Ideas at the Close of the Nineteenth Century* (Harmondsworth: Penguin, 1939 [1913]), 26.

68. Clem Seecharan, *Joseph Ruhomon's India: The Progress of her People at Home and Abroad and How those in British Guiana may Improve Themselves* (Kingston, Jamaica: The University of the West Indies Press, 2001), 65.

Chapter Six

1. Keith A.P. Sandiford, 'The Spartan Cricket Club, 1893–1993', *The Journal of the Cricket Society* 16, no. 3 (1993): 43.
2. Keith A.P. Sandiford, *Cricket Nurseries of Colonial Barbados: The Elite Schools, 1865–1966* (Kingston, Jamaica: The University of the West Indies Press, 1998), 12.
3. Ibid.
4. *Argosy*, April 21, 1900.
5. Reproduced in the *Port of Spain Gazette*, December 25, 1899.
6. *Port of Spain Gazette*, January 17, 1900.
7. See note 4.
8. Leader ('The West Indian Team for England'), *Barbados Globe*, December 12, 1900.
9. Leader ('A Stab in the Dark'), *Barbados Globe*, December 12, 1900.
10. Hilary Beckles, *A History of Barbados: From Amerindian Settlement to Nation-State* (London: Macmillan, 1990), 132–3.
11. Bruce Hamilton, *Cricket in Barbados* ([Bridgetown], Barbados: The Advocate Press, 1947), 60.
12. Keith A.P. Sandiford, op. cit., [1998], p. 13.
13. Ibid., 61, 64.
14. Ibid., 67–8.
15. Ibid., 110.
16. *Argosy*, July 14, 1900.
17. Ibid.
18. *Wisden*, 1901.
19. *London Times*, August 13, 1900.
20. *Cricket*, June 28, 1900.
21. *Argosy*, July 28, 1900.
22. See notes 19 and 18 respectively.
23. *Cricket*, June 14, 1900.
24. Leader, *Cricket*, August 16, 1900.
25. Ibid.
26. Ibid.
27. W.A. Bettesworth, 'Chats on the Cricket Field: Mr. S.W. Sproston', *Cricket*, August 30, 1900.
28. W.A. Bettesworth, 'Chats on the Cricket Field: Mr. W.C. Nock', *Cricket*, August 23, 1900.
29. *Cricket*, July 5, 1900; C.L.R. James, *Beyond a Boundary* (London: Serpent's Tail, 1983 [1963]), 72.

30. Ibid., [James], 72–3.
31. Ibid., 72.
32. *Star*, June 11, 1900.
33. *Cricket*, June 14, 1900.
34. *Port of Spain Gazette*, August 19, 1900.
35. W.A. Bettesworth, 'Chats on the Cricket Field: J. Woods', *Cricket*, September 13, 1900.
36. Reproduced in the *Argosy*, August 25, 1900.
37. Reproduced in the *Port of Spain Gazette*, August 26, 1900.
38. C.L.R. James, op. cit., [1983], p. 73.
39. Sir Pelham [Plum] Warner, *Lord's 1787–1945* (London: The Sportsman's Book Club, 1951 [1946]), 125.
40. *Argosy*, July 14, 1900.
41. Ibid.
42. *Argosy*, September 1, 1900.
43. *Wisden*, 1901.
44. Clayton Goodwin, *West Indies at the Wicket* (London: Macmillan, 1986), 154.
45. H.A. Altham, *A History of Cricket: From the Beginning to the First World War, Vol. 1* (London: George Allen and Unwin, 1962 [1926]), 276.
46. Jack Williams, *Cricket and Race* (Oxford: Berg, 2001), 22.
47. *London Times*, August 14, 1900.
48. Ibid.
49. *Argosy*, October 17, 1900.
50. P.F. [Plum] Warner, 'The West Indian Cricket Team', *Wisden*, 1901.
51. See note 49.
52. *Port of Spain Gazette*, September 6, 1900.
53. Reproduced in the *Argosy*, September 1, 1900.
54. *Wisden*, 1901.
55. *Cricket*, August 30, 1900.
56. *Cricket*, August 23, 1900.
57. See note 39 [pp.125, 188].
58. Learie Constantine, *Cricket and I* (London: Philip Allan, 1933), 4.
59. Ibid., 4–5.
60. Ibid., 5.
61. C.L.R. James, op. cit., [1983], pp. 54–5.
62. Ibid., 102

6 3. Learie Constantine, 'Cricket in the Sun', in *The Changing Face of Cricket*, Learie Constantine and Denzil Batchelor (London: Eyre and Spottiswoode, 1966), 86–7.

6 4. Eric Williams, *Inward Hunger: The Education of a Prime Minister* (London: Andre Deutsch, 1969), 30–3.

6 5. Reproduced from *Barbados Bulletin*, August 18, 1900.

6 6. Ibid.

6 7. *Port of Spain Gazette*, September 6, 1900.

6 8. *Barbados Globe*, September 30, 1901.

6 9. *Port of Spain Gazette*, September 5, 1900.

7 0. J. Wood Davis to the Editor, the *Argosy*, September 22, 1900.

7 1. Ibid.

7 2. *Daily Gleaner*, July 24, 1900.

7 3. *Daily Gleaner*, August 10, 1900.

7 4. *Port of Spain Gazette*, August 24, 1900.

7 5. *Daily Gleaner*, August 11, 1900.

7 6. See note 73.

7 7. Ibid.

7 8. James R. Hooker, *Henry Sylvester Williams: Imperial Pan-Africanist* (London: Rex Collins, 1975), Chapter 4.

7 9. See note 65.

8 0. Ibid.

8 1. Reproduced in the *Daily Gleaner*, September 22, 1900.

8 2. Quoted in Undine Giuseppi, *A Look at Learie Constantine* (London: Nelson, 1974), 114–5.

8 3. Ibid., 115–6.

8 4. A.G. Moyes, 'L.N. Constantine', in his *A Century of Cricketers* (London: The Sportsmans Book Club, 1954 [1950]), 148–9.

8 5. Ivar Oxaal, *Black Intellectuals Come to Power: The Rise of Creole Nationalism in Trinidad and Tobago* (Cambridge, Mass: Schenkman, 1968), 63.

Chapter Seven

1. *Port of Spain Gazette*, February 22, 1900.

2. *Wisden*, 1901.

3. *Port of Spain Gazette*, September 6, 1900.

4. *Argosy*, August 4, 1900.

5. Reproduced in the *Daily Chronicle*, August 25, 1900.

6. *Port of Spain Gazette*, July 6, 1899.

7. See Bruce Hamilton, *Cricket in Barbados* ([Bridgetown], Barbados: The

Advocate Press, 1947), Chapters 2 and 5; *Port of Spain Gazette*, September 8, 1899.

8. Ibid.

9. *Argosy*, September 7, 1895.

10. *Port of Spain Gazette*, August 10, 1899.

11. *Port of Spain Gazette*, September 21, 1899.

12. Ibid; *Port of Spain Gazette*, September 23, 1899.

13. *Port of Spain Gazette*, September 22, 1899.

14. *Port of Spain Gazette*, October 10, 1899.

15. *Port of Spain Gazette*, December 15, 1899.

16. *Port of Spain Gazette*, January 17, 1900.

17. *Daily Gleaner*, October 3, 1899.

18. *Daily Gleaner*, October 7, 1899.

19. Ibid.

20. *Daily Gleaner*, October 9, 1899.

21. Ibid.

22. *Daily Gleaner*, October 20, 1899.

23. *Daily Gleaner*, October 23, 1899.

24. *Daily Gleaner*, October 24, 1899.

25. Ibid.

26. Ibid.

27. Ibid.

28. *Daily Gleaner*, November 14, 1899.

29. *Daily Gleaner*, January 9, 12, 1900.

30. See note 24.

31. Ibid.

32. *Daily Gleaner*, December 6, 1899.

33. Ibid.

34. *Daily Gleaner*, January 20, 1900.

35. *Daily Gleaner*, January 27, 1900; *Argosy*, February 3, 1900.

36. Quoted in *Daily Gleaner*, February 10, 1900.

37. *Argosy*, February 3, 1900.

38. See note 32.

39. *Port of Spain Gazette*, March 8, 1900.

40. *Daily Gleaner*, March 10, 1900.

41. *Daily Gleaner*, March 16, 1900.

42. Ibid.

43. *Daily Gleaner*, April 10, 23, 1900.

44. *Argosy*, April 28, 1900.

45. Reproduced in *Port of Spain Gazette*, February 8, 1900.

46. *Daily Gleaner*, April 10, 1900.

47. Reproduced in the *Daily Gleaner*, April 23, 1900.

48. Hilary Beckles, 'The Origins and Development of West Indies Cricket Culture in the Nineteenth Century: Jamaica and Barbados', in *Liberation Cricket: West Indies Cricket Culture*, eds. Beckles and Stoddart (Kingston, Jamaica: Ian Randle Publishers, 1995), 41.

49. *Port of Spain Gazette*, May 18, 1900.

50. *Daily Gleaner*, May 18, 1900.

51. Ibid.

52. *Jamaica Daily Telegraph*, May 14, 1900.

53. *Daily Chronicle*, May 19, 1900.

54. *Daily Gleaner*, September 22, 1900.

55. *Daily Gleaner*, September 8, 1900.

56. Ibid.

57. Brian L. Moore and Michele A. Johnson, 'Challenging the "Civilising Mission": Cricket as a Field of Socio-cultural Contestation in Jamaica, 1865-1920', in *In the Shadow of the Plantation: Caribbean History and Legacy*, ed. Alvin O. Thompson (Kingston, Jamaica: Ian Randle Publishers, 2003), 363.

58. Ibid., 374–5.

59. Ibid., 364–5

60. Ibid., 365–6.

61. Leader, *Daily Chronicle*, March 28, 1897.

Chapter Eight

1. C.L.R. James, *Beyond a Boundary* (London: Serpent's Tail, 1983 [1963]), 3.

2. C.L.R. James, 'Garfield Sobers', in *Cricket: The Great All-Rounders: Studies of Ten of the Finest All-Rounders of Cricket History*, ed. John Arlott (London: The Sportsmans Book Club, 1971 [1969]), 162.

3. Ibid., 162–3.

4. Philip Lindsay quoted in C.L.R. James, op. cit., [1983], p. 93.

5. Ibid.

6. Anna Grimshaw, ed., *Cricket: C.L.R. James* (London: Allison and Busby, 1986), 116–17.

7. C.L.R. James, op. cit., [1983], p. 121.

8. Ibid., 121–2.

9. Gordon K. Lewis, *The Growth of the Modern West Indies* (New York: Monthly

Review Press, 1968), 114–15.

10. Quoted in personal correspondence from Ian McDonald (great-great-great grandson of Baynes), Georgetown, Guyana, March 11, 2003, encl.

11. Quoted in Leader, the *Daily Chronicle*, June 16, 1900.

12. Ibid.

13. Leader, *Jamaica Daily Telegraph*, May 9, 1900.

14 Paul Rich, 'Sydney Olivier, Jamaica and the Debate on British Colonial Policy in the West Indies', in *Labour in the Caribbean: From Emancipation to Independence*, eds. Malcolm Cross and Gad Heuman (London: Macmillan, 1987), 208, 228–9.

15. Leader, *Jamaica Daily Telegraph*, May 1, 1900.

16. Clem Seecharan, *Joseph Ruhomon's India: The Progress of her People at Home and Abroad and how those in British Guiana may Improve Themselves* (Kingston, Jamaica: The University of the West Indies Press, 2001), 68, 70.

17. Richie Benaud, 'Postscript', in *Frank Worrell: A Biography*, Ivo Tennant , 107–8 (Cambridge: Lutterworth Press, 1987), 107–8.

18. C.L.R. James, op. cit., [1983], pp. 259–61.

19. John Hearne, 'What the Barbadian Means to Me', *New World Quarterly* III, nos. 1&2 (Barbados Independence Issue, 1966–67) [Reproduced in *On the Canvas of the World*, ed. George Lamming (1999), 165–6].

20. Alan Metcalfe, 'C.L.R. James's Contribution to the History of Sport', *Canadian Journal of the History of Sport* 2, (1987): 52,57.

21. V.S. Naipaul, 'Cricket', *Encounter*, (September 1963), reproduced in his *The Overcrowded Barracoon* (London: Andre Deutsch, 1972), 17–22. The quote is on p.22.

22. Elsa Goveia, *The West Indian Slave Laws of the 18th Century* (Aylesbury, Bucks: Ginn, 1970), 34.

23. See *Weekly Recorder*, February 3, 24, March 24, 1900.

24. *Weekly Recorder*, March 17, 1900.

25. *Weekly Recorder*, June 23, 1900.

26. *Weekly Recorder*, July 21, 1900.

27. *Weekly Recorder*, September 1, 1900.

28. *Weekly Recorder*, September 8, 1900.

29. *Weekly Recorder*, September 22, 1900.

30. *Weekly Recorder*, October 6, 1900.

31. *Weekly Recorder*, December 8, 1900.

32. *Weekly Recorder*, December 22, 1900.

33. C.L.R. James, 'Discovering Literature in Trinidad: The Nineteenth Thirties', *Savacou*, no. 2, (September 1970): 54.

34. Ibid., 56.

Bibliography

Primary Sources

Newspapers

The *Argosy* [British Guiana]
The *Barbados Advocate*
Barbados Bulletin
Barbados Globe
Cricket [London]
The *Daily Chronicle* [British Guiana]
The *Daily Gleaner* [Jamaica]
The *Daily Telegraph* [Jamaica]
The *Port of Spain Gazette* [Trinidad]
The *Sportsman* [London]
The *Times* [London]
The *Weekly Recorder* [Barbados]

Reports

Comins, D.W.D, *Note on Emigration from India to British Guiana* (Diary). Calcutta: Bengal Secretariat Press, 1893.
Report of the West India Royal Commission, 1897 (H.W. Norman, chairman). London: HMSO, 1897.

Secondary Sources

Articles, Books and Pamphlets

Altham, H.S. *A History of Cricket: From the Beginnings to the First World War.* London: George Allen and Unwin, 1962 [1926].
Bailey, Trevor. 'Rohan Kanhai: The Magician from Guyana'. In his *The Greatest of my Time.* London: The Sportsman Book Club, 1970 [1968].
Beckles, Hilary. *A History of Barbados: From Amerindian Settlement to Nation-State.* Cambridge: Cambridge University Press, 1990.

———. 'Barbados Cricket and the Crisis of Social Culture'. In *100 Years of Organised Cricket in Barbados, 1892–1992*. Bridgetown: Barbados Cricket Association, 1992.

———, ed. *An Area of Conquest: Popular Democracy and West Indies Cricket Supremacy*. Kingston, Jamaica: Ian Randle Publishers, 1994.

———, ed. *A Spirit of Dominance: Cricket and Nationalism in the West Indies*. Mona, Jamaica: Canoe Press, University of the West Indies, 1998.

———. *The Development of West Indies Cricket, Vol. 1: The Age of Nationalism*. Mona, Jamaica: The University of the West Indies Press, 1998.

———. 'The Origins and Development of West Indies Cricket Culture in the Nineteenth Century: Jamaica and Barbados'. In *Liberation Cricket*, eds. Beckles and Stoddart, 33–43. Kingston, Jamaica: Ian Randle Publishers, 1995.

———. 'The Making of the First "West Indian" Teams, 1886-1906'. In *Liberation Cricket*, eds. Beckles and Stoddart, 192–204. Kingston, Jamaica: Ian Randle Publishers, 1995.

———, ed. 'The Radical Tradition in the Culture of West Indies Cricket'. In *An Area of Conquest: Popular Democracy and West Indies Cricket Supremacy*, 42–54. Kingston, Jamaica: Ian Randle Publishers, 1994.

Beckles, Hilary and Brian Stoddart, eds. *Liberation Cricket: West Indies Cricket Culture*. Kingston, Jamaica: Ian Randle Publishers, 1995.

Birbalsingh, Frank. *The Rise of West Indian Cricket: From Colony to Nation*. London: Hansib, 1996.

Birbalsingh, Frank and Clem Seecharan. *Indo-West Indian Cricket*. London: Hansib, 1988.

Birley, Derek, *Sport and the Making of Britain*. Manchester: Manchester University Press, 1993.

———. *Land of Sport and Glory: Sport and British Society*. Manchester: Manchester University Press, 1995.

Bolt, Christine. *Victorian Attitudes to Race*. London: Routledge and Kegan Paul, 1971.

Bowen, C.P. *English Cricketers in the West Indies: An Account of the Cricket Matches Played Between Mr. R. Slade Lucas's English Cricket Team and the West Indian Cricket Teams During the Season of 1895*. Bridgetown, Barbados: Herald Office, 1895.

Bowen, Roland. *Cricket: A History of its Growth and Development Throughout the World*. London: Eyre and Spottiswoode, 1970.

Brereton, Bridget. *Race Relations in Colonial Trinidad, 1870-1900*. Cambridge: Cambridge University Press, 1979.

———. 'Social Organisation and Class, Racial and Cultural Conflict in 19th Century Trinidad'. In *Trinidad Ethnicity*, ed. Kevin Yelvington. London; Macmillan, 1993.

———. 'The White Elite of Trinidad'. In *The White Minority in the Caribbean*, eds. Howard Johnson and Karl Watson. Kingston, Jamaica: Ian Randle Publishers, 1998.

Brereton, Bridget and Kevin A. Yelvington, eds. *The Colonial Caribbean in Transition: Essays on Postemancipation Social and Cultural History.* Kingston, Jamaica: The University of the West Indies Press, 1999.

Bruce, John Edward. 'Theophilus E.S. Scholes, M.D.'. *The New York Voice.* January 1907.

Bryan, Patrick. *The Jamaican People, 1880–1902: Race, Class and Social Control.* London: Macmillan, 1991.

————. 'Black Perspectives in Late Nineteenth Century Jamaica: The Case of Dr. Theophilus E.S. Scholes'. In *Garvey: His Work and Impact*, eds. Rupert Lewis and Patrick Bryan. Trenton, NJ: Africa World Press, 1991.

————. 'The White Minority in Jamaica at the End of the Nineteenth Century'. In *The White Minority in the Caribbean*, eds. Howard Johnson and Karl Watson. Kingston, Jamaica: The University of the West Indies Press, 1998.

Burton, Richard D.E. *Afro-Creole: Power, Opposition, and Play in the Caribbean.* Ithaca, NY: Cornell University Press, 1997.

Cardus, Neville. 'Learie Constantine: Life, Sunshine and Lustre'. In *The Playfair Cardus: Essays by Neville Cardus.* London: The Dickens Press, 1963.

Cashman, Richard. 'Cricket and Colonialism: Colonial Hegemony and Indigenous Subversion?' In *Pleasure, Profit and Proselytism: British Culture and Sport at Home and Abroad, 1700–1914*, ed. J.A. Mangan. London: Frank Cass, 1988.

Coleman, W.L.A. 'The First West Indians'. *The Cricketer*, May 1988.

Constantine, Learie. *Cricket and I.* London: Philip Allan, 1933.

————. *Cricket in the Sun.* London: Stanley Paul, n.d. [1947].

————. and Denzil Batchelor. *The Changing Face of Cricket.* London: Eyre and Spottiswoode, 1966.

————. 'L.S. Constantine'. In *Great Cricketers*, ed. Denzil Batchelor. London: Eyre and Spottiswoode, 1970.

Downes, Aviston D. 'Boys of the Empire: Elite Education and the Socio-Cultural Construction of Hegemonic Masculinity in Barbados, 1875–1920', mimeo., n.d.

————, 'The Contestation of Recreational Space in Barbados, 1880–1910'. In *In the Shadow of the Plantation: Caribbean History and Legacy*, ed. Alvin O. Thompson. Kingston, Jamaica: Ian Randle Publishers, 2003.

The English Cricketers at Barbados, January and February 1895. Bridgetown, Barbados: 'The Agricultural Reporter', 1895.

Fergus, Claudius. 'Another Kind of Ball Game: The Assertion of Afrocentric Masculinity on Colonial Cricket Culture at the Turn of the 20th Century'. Paper presented at the 'Henry Sylvester Williams and Pan-Africanism Conference', University of the West Indies, St. Augustine, Trinidad, January 2001.

Giuseppi, Undine. *A Look at Learie Constantine.* London: Nelson, 1974.

Grimshaw, Anna, ed. *Cricket: C.L.R. James.* London: Allison and Busby, 1986.

Goveia, Elsa. *Slave Society in the British Leeward Islands at the End of the Eighteenth Century*. New Haven: Yale University Press, 1965.

———. *The West Indian Slave Laws of the 18th Century*. Aylesbury, Bucks: Ginn, 1970.

Guyana Sports Annual, 1962–3. 'Proud of Our Cricket'. Georgetown: Guyana Graphic Ltd, 1963.

Hamilton, Bruce. *Cricket in Barbados*. [Bridgetown], Barbados: The Advocate Press, 1947.

Harris, Lord. *A Few Short Runs*. London: John Murray, 1921.

Hawke, Lord. *Recollections and Reminiscences*. London: Williams and Norgate, 1924.

Hearne, John. 'What the Barbadian Means to Me'. *New World Quarterly* III, nos. 1&2 (Barbados Independence Issue, 1966–67) [Reproduced in *On the Canvas of the World*, ed. George Lamming, 1999].

Holt, Richard. *Sports and the British: A Modern History*. Oxford: Clarendon Press, 1989.

Hooker, J.R. *Henry Sylvester Williams: Imperial Pan-Africanist*. London: Rex Collings, 1975.

Howat, Gerald. *Learie Constantine*. Newton Abbott: Readers Union, 1976 [1975].

Hoyos, F.A. *Grantley Adams and the Social Revolution: The Story of the Movement that Changed the Pattern of West Indian Society*. London: Macmillan, 1974.

Hutchinson, Lionel. 'Conrad Reeves: A Kind of Perfection'. *New World Quarterly* III, nos. 1&2 (Barbados Independence Issue, 1966–67).

Hutton, Len. 'Learie Constantine [Obituary, April 4, 1971)'. In *The Observer on Cricket: An Anthology of the Best Cricket Writing*, ed. Scyld Berry. London: Unwin, 1987.

Jackson, Holbrook. *The Eighteen Nineties: A Review of Art and Ideas at the Close of the Nineteenth Century*. Harmondsworth: Penguin, 1939 [1913].

James, C.L.R. *The Life of Captain Cipriani: An Account of British Government in the West Indies*. Nelson, Lancs: Coulton, 1932.

———. *Beyond a Boundary*. London: Serpent's Tail, 1994 [1963].

———. 'Discovering Literature in Trinidad: The Nineteen Thirties'. *Savacou*, no. 2 (1970).

———. 'Sir Learie Constantine'. in *Cricket: The Great All-Rounders*, ed. John Arlott. London: The Sportsmans Book Club, 1971 [1969].

———. 'Garfield Sobers'. In *Cricket: The Great All-Rounders*, ed. John Arlott. London: The Sportsmans Book Club, 1971 [1969].

———. 'Sir Frank Worrell'. In *Cricket: The Great Captains*, ed. John Arlott. Newton Abbot, Devon: Sportsmans Book Club, 1972 [1971].

Jukes Browne, A.J. 'Barbadians at Home (Part 1): The English in Barbados'. The *Argosy*, January 7, 1893.

———. 'Barbadians at Home (Part II): The English in Barbados'. The *Argosy*, January 14, 1893.

Kanhai, Rohan. *Blasting for Runs*. London: Souvenir Press, 1966.

Lamming, George, ed. *On the Canvas of the World*. Port of Spain: The Trinidad and Tobago Institute of the West Indies, 1999.

Lee, Francis. *Fabianism and Colonialism: The Life and Political Thought of Lord Sydney Olivier*. London: Defiant Books, 1988.

Lewis, Gordon K. *The Growth of the Modern West Indies*. New York: Monthly Review Press, 1968.

Lewis, Rupert. 'Garvey's Forerunners: Love and Bedward'. *Race and Class* XXVIII, no. 3 (1987).

Lindsay, Philip. *Don Bradman*. London: Phoenix House, 1951.

Lumsden, Joy, 'Robert Love and Jamaican Politics, 1889–1914'. PhD thesis, University of the West Indies, Mona, Jamaica, 1987.

Lutchman, Harold A. 'The British Guiana Constitutional Change of 1891'. *History Gazette*, no. 40 (January 1992).

Mandle, W.F. 'Cricket and Australian Nationalism in the Nineteenth Century'. *Journal of the Royal Australian Historical Society* 59, Part 4 (December 1973).

Manley, Michael. *A History of West Indies Cricket* [revised ed.]. London: André Deutsch, 1995 [1988].

Mangan, J.A. *Athleticism and the Victorian and Edwardian Public School: The Emergence and Consolidation of an Educational Ideology*. Cambridge: Cambridge University Press, 1981.

————, ed. *Pleasure, Profit, Proselytism: British Culture and Sport at Home and Abroad, 1700–1914*. London: Frank Cass, 1988.

————, ed. *'Benefits Bestowed'?: Education and British Imperialism*. Manchester: Manchester University Press, 1988.

Metcalfe, Alan. 'C.L.R. James's Contribution to the History of Sport'. *Canadian Journal of the History of Sport*, vol. 2 (1987).

Moore, Brian L. *Cultural Power, Resistance and Pluralism: Colonial Guyana, 1838–1900*. Montreal: McGill-Queen's University Press, 1995.

————. 'The Culture of the Colonial Elites of Nineteenth Century Guyana'. In *The White Minority in the Caribbean*, eds. Howard Johnson and Karl Watson. Kingston, Jamaica: Ian Randle Publishers, 1998.

————. 'Colonialism, Cricket Culture, and Afro-Creole Identity in the Caribbean after Emancipation: The Case of Guyana'. *The Journal of Caribbean History* 33, nos. 1&2 (1999).

Moore, Brian and Michele A. Johnson. 'Challenging the "Civilising Mission": Cricket as a Field of Socio-Cultural Contestation in Jamaica, 1865–1920'. In *In the Shadow of the Plantation: Caribbean History and Legacy*, ed. Alvin O. Thompson. Kingston, Jamaica: Ian Randle Publishers, 2002.

Moyes, A.G. 'L.N. Constantine'. In his *A Century of Cricketers*. London: The Sportsmans Book Club, 1954 [1950].

Nettleford, Rex. 'Freedom of Thought and Expression: Nineteenth Century West Indian Creole Experience'. *Caribbean Quarterly* 36, nos.1–2 (June 1990).

Nicole, Christopher. *West Indian Cricket: The Story of Cricket in the West Indies with Complete Records*. London: Phoenix House, 1957.

Olivier, Lord. *Jamaica: The Blessed Island*. London: Faber and Faber, 1936.

Oxaal, Ivar. *Black Intellectuals Come to Power: The Rise of Creole Nationalism in Trinidad and Tobago*. Cambridge, Mass: Schenkman, 1968.

Pentelow, J.N. *Cricket in the West Indies: A Brief Historical Sketch*. Reproduced from *The Sportsman* (London), January–February, 1911.

Roberts, Peter A. *From Oral to Literate Culture: Colonial Experience in the English West Indies*. Mona, Jamaica: The University of the West Indies Press, 1997.

Rodney, Walter. *A History of the Guyanese Working People, 1881–1905*. Baltimore: The Johns Hopkins University Press, 1981.

Rohlehr, Gordon. *Calypso and Society in Pre-Independence Trinidad*. Port of Spain, Trinidad: self-published, 1990.

———. 'C.L.R. James and the Legacy of *Beyond a Boundary*'. In *A Spirit of Dominance: Cricket and Nationalism in the West Indies*, ed. Hilary Beckles. Kingston, Jamaica: Canoe Press, University of the West Indies, 1998.

Sandiford, Keith A.P. 'Cricket and the Barbadian Society'. *Canadian Journal of History*, vol. 21 (1986).

———. 'The Role of Barbados in the Development of West Indies Cricket'. *The Journal of the Cricket Society* 18, no. 4 (Spring 1988).

———. '100 Years of Organised Cricket in Barbados, 1892–1992'. In *100 Years of Organised Cricket in Barbados*. Bridgetown, Barbados Cricket Association, 1992.

———. 'The Spartan Cricket Club, 1893–1993'. *The Journal of the Cricket Society* XVI, no. 3 (Autumn, 1993).

———. 'Imperialism, Colonial Education and the Origins of West Indies Cricket'. In *An Area of Conquest: Popular Democracy and West Indies Cricket Supremacy*, ed. Hilary Beckles. Kingston, Jamaica: Ian Randle Publishers, 1994.

———. *Cricket and the Victorians*. Aldershot, Hants: Scolar Press, 1994.

———. *Cricket Nurseries of Colonial Barbados: The Elite Schools, 1865–1966*. Mona, Jamaica: The University of the West Indies Press, 1998.

———. 'Guyana's Contribution to West Indies Cricket'. *Journal of the Cricket Society* 20, no. 1 (Autumn 2000).

Sandiford, Keith A.P., and Earle H. Newton. *Combermere School and the Barbadian Society*. Mona, Jamaica: The University of the West Indies Press, 1995.

Sandiford, Keith A.P., and Brian Stoddart. 'The Elite Schools and Cricket in Barbados: A Study in Colonial Continuity'. *The International Journal of the History of Sport* 4, no. 3 (1987).

Scholes, Theophilus E. Samuel. *Sugar and the West Indies*. London: Elliot Stock, 1897.

———. *Glimpses of the Ages or the "Superior" and "Inferior" Races, so-called, Discussed in the Light of Science and History, 2 Vols*. London: John Long, 1905, 1907.

Scoles, Ignatius. *Sketches of African and Indian Life in British Guiana*. [Georgetown], Demerara: The Argosy Press, 1885.

Seecharan, Clem. *India and the Shaping of the Indo-Guyanese Imagination, 1890s–1920s*. Leeds: Peepal Tree Press, 1993.

———. *'Tiger in the Stars': The Anatomy of Indian Achievement in British Guiana, 1919–29*. London: Macmillan, 1997.

———. 'The Shaping of the Indo-Caribbean People: Guyana and Trinidad to the 1940s'. *Journal of Caribbean Studies* 14, nos. 1&2 (Fall 1999–Spring 2000).

———. *Joseph Ruhomon's India: The Progress of her People at Home and Abroad, and how those in British Guiana may Improve Themselves*. Kingston, Jamaica: The University of the West Indies Press, 2001.

Smith, Raymond T. 'Religion in the Formation of West Indian Society: Guyana and Jamaica'. In *The African Diaspora: Interpretive Essays*, eds. Martin L. Kilson and Robert I. Rotberg. Cambridge, Mass: Harvard University Press, 1976.

———. 'Race and Class in the Post-Emancipation Caribbean'. In *Racism and Colonialism*, ed. Robert Ross. The Hague: Martinus Nijhoff, 1982.

Soares, David. 'Cricket in Jamaica: A Brief Sketch of its Development in the Nineteenth Century'. *Jamaica Journal* 22, no. 2 (1989).

Stoddart, Brian. 'Sport, Cultural Imperialism, and Colonial Response in the British Empire'. *Comparative Studies in Society and History*, vol. 30 (1988).

———. 'Cricket and Colonialism in the English-speaking Caribbean to 1914'. In *Liberation Cricket*, eds. Beckles and Stoddart, 9–32. Kingston, Jamaica: Ian Randle Publishers, 1995.

———. 'Cricket, Social Formation and Cultural Continuity in Barbados'. In *Liberation Cricket*, 44–60. Kingston, Jamaica: Ian Randle Publishers, 1995.

———. 'Caribbean Cricket: The Role of Sport in Emerging Small-nation Politics'. In *Liberation Cricket*, 239–55. Kingston, Jamaica: Ian Randle Publishers, 1995.

Stoddart, Brain, and Keith A.P. Sandiford, eds. *The Imperial Game: Cricket, Culture and Society*. Manchester: Manchester University Press, 1998.

Stollmeyer, Victor. '"Learie"'. In *Queen's Park Cricket Club, 75th Anniversary, 1896–1971*. Port of Spain: QPCC, 1971.

Tennant, Ivo. *Frank Worrell: A Biography*. Cambridge: Lutterworth Press, 1987.

Thomson, A.A. *Cricket: My Happiness*. London: The Sportsman Book Club, 1956.

———. *Cricket: The Golden Ages*. London: The Sportsman Book Club, 1962 [1961].

———. 'P.F. Warner'. In *Great Cricketers*, ed. Denzil Batchelor. London: Eyre and Spottiswoode, 1970.

Thorn, Philip. *Barbados Cricketers, 1865–1990*. Nottingham: The Association of Cricket Statisticians, n.d. [1991].

Tikasingh, Gerad I.M. 'The Establishment of the Indians in Trinidad, 1870–1900'. PhD thesis, University of the West Indies, St. Augustine, Trinidad, 1976.

Underdown, David. *Start of Play: Cricket and Culture in Eighteenth Century England.* London: Penguin Books, 2000.

Vaughan, H.A. 'Samuel Prescod: The Birth of a Hero'. *New World Quarterly* III, nos. 1&2 (Barbados Independence Issue, 1966–67) [Reproduced in *On the Canvas of the World*, ed. George Lamming, 1999].

Warner, Sir Pelham [P.F.]. 'Cricket in the West Indies and America'. *Wisden*, 1898.

———. *Cricket in Many Climes.* London: Heinemann, 1900.

———. 'The West Indian Cricket Team'. *Wisden*, 1901.

———. *Cricket Between Two Wars.* London: Chatto and Windus, 1942.

———. *Lord's, 1787–1945.* London: The Sportsman Book Club, 1951 [1946].

———. *Long Innings.* London: George G. Harrap, 1951.

Warner-Lewis, Maureen. *Central Africa in the Caribbean: Transcending Time, Transforming Culture.* Kingston, Jamaica: The University of the West Indies Press, 2003.

Williams, Eric. *Inward Hunger: The Education of a Prime Minister.* London: André Deutsch, 1969.

Williams, Jack. *Cricket and Race.* Oxford: Berg, 2001.

Williams, Marcus. 'Mystery of a Mud-covered Buckle'. The *Times*, November 5, 1986.

Wilson, C.A. *Men of Vision: A Series of Biographical Sketches of Men who have Made their Mark upon our Time.* Kingston, Jamaica: The Gleaner Co Ltd, 1929.

Wolstenholme, Gerry. *The West Indian Tour of England, 1906.* Blackpool: self-published, 1992.

Wood, Donald. *Trinidad in Transition: The Years after Slavery.* Oxford: Oxford University Press, 1968.

Index

Adams, Fitzherbert, 26

Adams, Grantley, 26; and muscular learning, 41–43

Africa: West Indians in, in the late nineteenth century, 74

African Colonization Enterprise: of Dr J. Albert Thorne, 70–73

African cultures: in slave societies, 1

Afro-Saxons, 37

All Trinidad XI: blacks and coloureds in, 105; against Lord Hawke's team, 139–147; against Lucas's team, 104–105, 111–113; against Priestley's team, 147; opening batsmen of, 112; significance of, for non-white West Indians, 139, 144

Amateurs: and professionals, in West Indies cricket, 181

Anderson, Dr R.B.: and Lucas's tour of the West Indies, 99; on cricket in the West Indies, 100–103

Asiatic Cricket Club (Guyana): formation of, 80

Attale, C., 112

Austin, Sir Harold, 113; as father of West Indies cricket, 28, 114; on Lucas's, Hawke's and Priestley's tours, 123

Barbadians: black, and perception of cricket, 122; in West Indian education, 46

Barbados: class discrimination in cricket in, 44–45, 179–180; cricket in, 9–10; cricket and the classics in school curriculum of, 27; cricket among non–whites at the end of the 19th century, 186–187; development of education in, 25–34; internal dynamics of whites in, at the end of the nineteenth century, 183–188; leading schools in, 27–28; Lucas's tour in, 105–107; muscular learning in, 10; race in cricket in early, 119; self-perception of whites in, 35

Barbados Challenge Cricket Cup, 45

Bat: symbolism of, 11

Batsmanship, West Indian: pedigree of, 11

Batsmen: on West Indies team to England, 1900, 191

Batting: and stick-fighting, compared, 11

Baynes, Edward Dacre, 272

Beckles, Hilary: on Colin Jackman Prescod, 164–165; on Plum Warner, 152–153; on Sir Conrad Reeves, 166

Belt buckle: depicting slave playing cricket, 8–10, 19

Beyond a Boundary, C.L.R. James, 268–269, 278–279

Black affirmation: Robert Love and, 51

Black cricketers: perception of, as liberators among African people, 97

Black men, enslaved: and perception of potential of cricket, 16

Blacks: in the colonial civil service, 1850s–1860s, 21

Blacks, free: mobility of, before Emancipation, 3

Blyden, Edward Wilmot, 27, 65, 69–70, 74

Bowring, William, 184–185; selection of, to 1900 West Indies team, 254–255

Bradley, R.W.: and selection of the 1900 West Indies team, 250–254

'Breaking': in stick-fighting, 11

British culture: cricket and education in transmission of, 17–19

British Empire and Alliances, The, Dr T.E.S. Scholes, 62–63, 67–68

British Guiana: cricket cult among Indians in, 82; exclusion of blacks from representative teams in, 158; as Indian cultural site in the 1890s, 84; plantocracy in, 131; socio–political situation, in the 1890s, 127–134

British West Indies: composition of, 1; cricket and identity in, 16–17

Brown, Arthur Barrington: and election to Court of Policy (British Guiana), 128–129; on George William Gordon, 189–190

Bryan, Patrick: on Dr T.E.S. Scholes, 63

Burslem, William, 30, 37

Burton, G.B.R., 33

Burton, W.J. 'Tom': on first West Indies tour of England, 177, 225; Plum Warner on, 206–207

Camacho, Stephen, 187

Captains: selection of, for early West Indies teams, 114

Challenor, George, 28, 209

Chamberlain, Joseph: criticism of, by Dr Love, 56–57; thesis of, on self-government in the West Indies, 51, 55

Christianity: and civilization, 3; muscular, 17

Civil service: blacks in the colonial, in the 1850s–1860s, 21

Civilization: colour and, in the British West Indies, 2; and constructions of Englishness, 1, 35–36, 278; cricket and, 120; indices of, 3; notion of cycles of, 69

Class discrimination: in Barbados cricket, 44–45

Classics: and cricket in Barbados school curriculum, 27

Cole, H.A., 219; withdrawal of, from 1900 West Indies team to England, 180–181

Colonial space: access to, after Emancipation, 2

Colour: and civilization, in the British West Indies, 2

Coloureds: in St. Kitts, 2; significance of, in British West Indies, 1–2

Combermere School: curricular development at, 32–33

Constantine, Learie, 211, 216–217, 225–226, 228; *Cricket and I*, 151; on Lebrun Constantine, 211–212; Neville Cardus on, 151, 152; on race in West Indies captain selection, 114

Constantine, Lebrun, 112, 124, 145, 151; and Shannonism, 212–215; on first West Indies tour of England, 177, 191, 213–214; Learie Constantine on, 211–212; second tour of England, 214–215

Constitutional reform: campaign for, in British Guiana, 161–163

Cox, G.B.Y. 'Gussie', 30–31

Cox, Percy, 185

Creoles: rivalry between French and English, in Trinidad, 109–110

Creolization: of cricket, in the West Indies, 18–19

Cricket: and advancement of black people's rights, 97–98; in Barbados, 9–10; and British West Indian identity, 16–17, 276; and civilization, 3, 120; and the classics in Barbados's school curriculum, 27; and confidence–building in the West Indies, 95; creolization of, in the West Indies, 18–19; in Demerara, 5; and divisions in West Indian society, 45–46; Dr R.B. Anderson on, in the West Indies, 100–103; and education, for blacks, 16–17, 23; and education, for Indians, 75; and Englishness, 5; and freedom, in the West Indies, 6; and Indians in the West Indies, 79–80; and liberation, 46; as mirror of West Indian society, 43; among non-whites in Barbados, at end of the 19th century, 186–187; as political instrument in the British West Indies, 19, 177; reshaping of, in the West Indies, 44; and resistance in the West Indies, 7–8, 13–14; role of, in the Imperial mission, 17–18; and shaping of West Indian consciousness, 43–44; slaves and, 5–6, 8–10; symbolism of, 8; views of English elite on, in the Empire, 205–206; in the West Indies in the eighteenth century, 4–15

Cricket, West Indies: English cricketers in the making of, 138; in identity construction, 230, 265; race in, 114, 119, 182

Cricket clubs: Asiatic (Guyana), 80; composition of first division, in Jamaica, 255–256; Empire (Barbados), 45; Fenwick (Barbados), 280; Georgetown (Guyana), 83, 133, 158; Kensington (Jamaica), 233; Kingston (Jamaica), 255; Lucas (Jamaica), 257; Lusitana (Guyana), 80; Maple (Trinidad), 212; Melbourne (Jamaica), 261; Pickwick (Barbados), 45; Queen's Park (Trinidad), 108; Shannon (Trinidad), 212; Spartan (Barbados), 45, 280; Stingo (Trinidad), 212; in Trinidad, 212; Wanderers (Barbados), 44

Cricket and I, Learie Constantine, 151

Cricket in Many Climes, Pelham Warner, 149–150

Cumberbatch, Archie, 124, 249–250; bowling analysis of, against Lord Hawke's team, 144; in West Indies fast bowling tradition, 147

Dance: among the enslaved, 3; planters' perception of, 4

Dargan, Patrick, 129, 161; and campaign for constitutional reform in British Guiana, 161

Davson, Edward, 162–163

Davson, Henry K.: on economic and political situation in British Guiana, 1897, 127–128

Day, Charles, 49

Deighton, Horace: and muscular learning in the West Indies, 28; 'Plum' Warner on, 29

deLisser, H.G., 273

Dingwall, Rev Robert, 70, 75

Dress: and civilization, 3

East Indian Institute: founding of, 84

Economic depression: in British Guiana, 126–127; in the West Indies in the late 19th century, 126, 183

Education: Barbadians in West Indian, 46; and British West Indian identity, 276; and civilization, 3; and cricket, for blacks, 16–17, 23; and cricket, for Indians, 75; development of, in Barbados, 25–34; and political mobility, 56

Education, compulsory: call for, in Jamaica in 1884, 48; and social mobility of blacks, 23–26

Education, elementary: impact of, on rural West Indian societies, 48

Empire Cricket Club (Barbados): founding of, 45

Emtage, Oliver DeCourcey, 31–32

English culture: freedom and mobility and, 1

English tour, 1895: All Trinidad XI performance in, 104–105, 111–113; Queen's Park against, 108–109; significance of, 101–103, 104–105. *See also* Lucas, R. Slade; Lucas tour

Englishness: constructions of, and civilization, 1, 35–36, 278; cricket and, 5

Fabian Colonial Bureau, 271

Falconer, Charles, 49

Fast bowling: by blacks in All Trinidad team, 155; by Cumberbatch, 155; significance of, 7–8; tradition of, in the West Indies, 126, 147, 201; by Woods, 155

Fenwick Cricket Club (Barbados), 280; in Barbados Challenge Cup, 281–283

'Fitz Lily' Affair, 179–186; and prejudice in Barbados, 179–180; response of Goodman family to, 185–187

Freedom: cricket and, in the West Indies, 6

Games: purpose of, in schools, 27–28

Garvey, Marcus, 73

Georgetown Cricket Club (Guyana), 83, 133; Hawke's team against, 158

Girls: education of, in late 19th century West Indies, 24–25; public school code and, 264

Glimpses of the Ages..., Dr T.E.S. Scholes, 63

Goodman, Clifford, 113, 114, 145, 150; match analysis of, against Lord Hawke's team, 145

Goodman, Percy, 184

Goodman family, 45, 113–114, 184, 280; response of, to the 'Fitz Lily' affair, 185–187

Gradualism, 58, 137, 152; among non-whites in the British West Indies, 97

Groundsmen, black: as professionals, 150–151

Guyana. *See* British Guiana

Harrison College: products of, under Horace Deighton, 28–30

Hawke, Lord: on composition of the 1900 West Indies team to England, 236–237; and early West Indies cricket, 121; tour of English team under, 1897, 124

Hawke's team: against Georgetown Cricket Club, 158; assessment of, 126; members of, 138; reception of, in British Guiana, 135, 137; results of matches played, 135

Hinds, Fitz: discrimination against, by Spartan, 179; on West Indies tour of England, 1900, 177, 191; 'Fitz Lily' Affair, 179–186

Hotham family, 10

Hutson, D.M., 129

Identity construction: among Africans and coloureds in the West Indies, 26–27; cricket and education in, 276; Indo-West Indian, 87–94; West Indies cricket in, 230

Indians: and cricket, in the West Indies, 79–80

Indo-West Indian identity: construction of, 87–94

Insularity: in the West Indies, 231

Inter-colonial Challenge Cup, 238

Jamaica: loss to Lucas, 231; loss to Priestley's team, 231; marginalization of, in emergence of West Indies cricket, 231, 237; selection of players for West Indies team, 1900, 235–236, 238–239; in West Indies team to England, 1900, 232–233

Jamaica Advocate: in advocacy of self-government, 51; on Africa and colonialism, 74

James, C.L.R.: *Beyond a Boundary*, 268–269, 278–279; and muscular learning, 37; on public school code, 37–38, 269–270; on the rise of the black cricketer, 266; on Shannonism, 212, 213

Journalism, radical: in the British West Indies in the mid-nineteenth century, 48–51

Kalenda: in Trinidad, 11, 12

Kalinda. *See* Kalenda

Kanhai, Rohan, 93–94

Kensington Cricket Club (Jamaica), 233

Kerr, M.M., 257; interviewed, 259–260; in West Indies tour of England, 1900, 232, 258–260

Kingston Cricket Club, 255

Learmond, G.C., 187–188

Legitimus, Hegesippe, 27

Leisure time: value of, to the enslaved, 4

Liberal democracy: in political culture of former British colonies, 167

Livingston, G.V.: in West Indies tour to England, 1900, 232–233, 243, 255

Lodge School, the: muscular learning at, 31–32

Love, Robert, 27; and black affirmation, 51; criticism of Chamberlain by, 56–57; on the education of black women, 61–62; and founding of the *Jamaica Advocate*, 51; and support for self-government, 51–62

Lucas, R. Slade: on response of Barbadians to the tour, 114–116

Lucas Cricket Club (Jamaica), 257; rise of, 261–262

Lucas tour: of the West Indies, 1895, 99, 104; in Barbados, 105–107; impact of, on West Indians, 117–119; visit to St Kitts, 107–108

Lusitana Cricket Club (Guyana), 80

Mangan, J.A.: on the Victorian public school, 34

Manley, Michael: on the effect of cricket on slaves, 6 –7

'Marrying light', 26, 43

Melbourne Cricket Club (Jamaica), 261

Middle class, black: belief of, in representative institutions, 163; in Bridgetown, in the early 1890s, 40; emergence of, in the 1890s in the West Indies, 20–25, 62; in late nineteenth-century Trinidad, 95–96; shaping of intelligentsia, in the late nineteenth century, 49–50

Middle class, Indian: emergence of, in the 1890s, 75

Mobility: education and cricket in Indian, 75–76; education and political, 56; of emerging black middle class, 23; English culture and, 1; in slave society, 2, 3; and the education of women, 78

Morant Bay Rebellion: letters of E.C. Luard on, 189

Muscular learning: in Barbados, 10; cricket and, 17–18; impact of, in Barbados, 30–34; as instrument of mobility for blacks, 32–33; merits of, 263

Music: among the enslaved, 3

Naoroji, Dadabhai, 84–86

Newspapers: of blacks and coloureds, in the British West Indies, 49–51; in shaping of democratic practices in the British West Indies, 50

Nock, W.C., 248

Norman Commission, 39; report of, 172; Sydney Olivier and, 171–173; visit of, to British Guiana, 134–135

Olivier, Sydney: and Norman Commission, 171–173; vision of, in Jamaica, 174–175

Ollivierre, C.A., 112, 208–209; batting of, on 1900 tour, 201–205; in county cricket, 204–205; on first West Indies tour of England, 177, 191, 201

Ouckama, D., 131–132

Pan-African Conference: in London, 221–226, 273

People's Association (British Guiana), 127

Pickwick Cricket Club (Barbados): founding of, 45

Plantation Port Mourant (Berbice): and foundation of cricket in Guyana, 79–80

Play: and African peoples in slave society, 3; and resistance, 4

Plum Warner Project, 152–154, 155–158

Port of Spain Gazette: on Crown Colony system, 219

Prescod, Colin Jackman, 163–165

Prescod, Samuel, 27

Prescott, Samuel, 49

Priestley, Arthur: tour of the West Indies, 1897, 124

Priestley's team: members of, 138; defeat of, by All Trinidad, 147

Professionals: and amateurs, in West Indies cricket, 181, 217–219, 238, 245; black groundsmen as, 150–151

Progressive Association (British Guiana): founding of, 129–130

Public school: C.L.R. James on code of, 37–38; ethos of the Victorian, 34; impact of code of, 36; imperialism and, 34

Queen's Park Cricket Club (Trinidad): against Lord Hawke's team, 1897, 139; selection policy of, 108

Queen's Royal College, Trinidad: muscular learning at, 37

Race: in early Barbados cricket, 119; and selection of captains of the West Indies teams, 114; in West Indies cricket, 182

Ranjitsinhji, Prince Kumar Shri, 81–82, 88–93

Reeves, Sir Conrad, 163, 166; and founding of Spartan Cricket Club, 45

Resistance: cricket and, 7–8, 13–14

Rohlehr, Dr John, 161

Rudder, S.A., 219

Ruhomon, Joseph, 62, 75–79; on education among Indians, 47

Scholes, Dr Theophilus E.S., 62–69, 161; *The British Empire and Alliances*, 62–63, 67–68; *Glimpses of the Ages...*, 63; and notion of 'cycles of civilisation', 69; Patrick Bryan on, 63; radical democratic orientation of, 167; on social conditions of blacks in Jamaica, 167–171; views of, 63–69

Schools: for girls, in late nineteenth-century Kingston, 24–25

Schools, elite: in Barbados, 27–28; Victorian values in, in the West Indies, 20

Selection: basis of, in early West Indies cricket, 105, 133, 146; of captains, for early West Indies teams, 114; of West Indies team for 1900 tour of England, 190, 234, 239–255

Shannonism, 283; Eric Williams and, 215–217; Lebrun Constantine and, 212–215

Slave societies: African culture in, 1; play in, 3

Slaves: and cricket, 5–6, 8–10; depiction of, on belt buckle, playing cricket, 8–10; stick-fighting among, 10–11

Smith, R.T.: on impact of elementary education in rural West Indian societies, 48

Sobers, Sir Garfield, 265; C.L.R. James on, 265–266

Somers-Cocks, Arthur: and muscular learning in the West Indies, 28, 30

Spartan Cricket Club (Barbados), 280; discrimination against Fitz Hinds by, 179; founding of, 45

Speed, Rev T. Lyall: legacy of, 33–34

Sproston, Stanley, 209

St Hill, Edwin: batting of, 267

St Kitts: coloureds in: 2

Stick-fighting: and batting, compared, 11; among slaves, 10–11

Thomas, J.J., 27, 49

Thorne, Dr J. Albert: African Colonization Enterprise scheme of, 70–73; interviewed, by the *Gleaner*, 71; and Marcus Garvey, 73

Trinidad: cricket and education in, 228; middle class in, in post-Emancipation period, 95–96; racial attitudes in, 110–111, 238; selection policies in, 105, 237; urban orientation of black and coloured middle class, 111

Turney, Rosa Frances, 26

Victorian values: in elite schools in the West Indies, 20

Wanderers Cricket Club (Barbados): founding of, 44

Warner, Aucher, 109, 112, 121; selection policy of, 146

Warner, Pelham 'Plum', 28–30, 121, 124; and challenge of white authorities in West Indies cricket, 155–156; *Cricket in Many Climes*, 149–150; on foundation of West Indies cricket, 209, 211; on Horace Deighton, 29; on performance of All Trinidad team against Hawke's team, 143–144; tribute to, 157–158; on visit of Priestley's team, 149–150

Warner family, 109, 111–112

West Indies: intellectual uniqueness of, 275

West Indies Challenge Cup, 236

West Indies cricket team: initiative for composite, 83; in the making of the British West Indies, 231

West Indies tour of England, 1900, 123, 157; blacks on, 177; conclusion of, 205–206; Jamaicans in, 232–233; legacy of, 210–211, 217–219; performance of team, 192–193; selection of members of, 190, 239–255; significance of, 189

Wharton, William Hewley, 84, 87

White men: significance of cricket for, 14–15

Whites: in Barbados, and representations of Englishness, 35; in Barbados, at the end of the 19th century, 183–188

Williams, Eric: and Shannonism, 215–217

Williams, Henry Sylvester: and Pan-African Conference, 221–226

Wilson, G., 112

Women: Dr Love on the education of black, 61–62

Woods, J. 'Float', 112, 124; bowling analysis of, against Lord Hawke's team, 144; on first West Indies tour of England, 177, 193–201; interviewed, 197–200; in West Indies fast bowling tradition, 147, 201

Worrell, Frank, 276–277

Yard: significance of, in the Caribbean, 3–4